BLACK PATRIOTS

BLACK PATRIOTS

RECOVERING A LOST HISTORY OF THE AMERICAN REVOLUTION

PATRICK S. POOLE

Book Design & Production:
Columbus Publishing Lab
www.ColumbusPublishingLab.com

LCCN: 2024922315

Hardcover ISBN: 978-1-63337-863-6
Paperback ISBN: 978-1-63337-851-3
E-Book ISBN: 978-1-63337-852-0

Printed in the United States of America
1 3 5 7 9 10 8 6 4 2

CONTENTS

AUTHOR'S PREFACE

THIS WAS A BOOK I never planned to write, but eventually felt compelled to write. Almost four years later, I'm sad that there was so much that had to be left out. The stories of bravery and sacrifice of Black Patriots in our first fight for freedom could fill many more volumes, and they are important to better understand the complexity and shortcomings of the American founding.

My goal in writing about the Black Patriots was to take their stories from scattered histories and pension statements to put them in context of the war itself. Anywhere you want to look at the War for Independence, *they are there*. From the first shots at Lexington Green to the British evacuation of New York eight long years later, Black Patriots are present and have their stories to tell. There may have been better, easier ways to present their stories, but looking at their experiences in the context of the war itself seemed the most clear to me. There is not a single moment of the war that is free from the participation and influence of the thousands of Black Patriots who served in many ways during the Revolutionary War. There are many more of their stories to tell, and I hope this effort here will encourage others to take up the task of recovering this lost history.

One thing I wanted to avoid is having this read like an academic dissertation. If I'm citing information from a specific source, I tried to identify it in the text, and all of my sources are cited in the bibliography. But adding another hundred-plus pages of endnotes would have unnecessarily cluttered an already busy and dense text, so I've only noted direct citations. I have largely left the spelling of original documents intact, unless a change was needed to add clarity.

As I was writing this book, there were several works and sources that were constantly within an arm's reach. My well-worn copies of Jack Darrell Crowder's *African Americans and American Indians in the Revolutionary War*, *African-American Patriots in the Southern Campaign of the American Revolution* by Bobby G. Moss and Michael C. Scroggins, and John Rees's *'They were Good Soldiers': African-Americans Serving in the Continental Army, 1775–1783*, proved indispensable. George Quintal's National Park Service report "Patriots of Color: African Americans and Native Americans at Battle Road and Bunker Hill" was invaluable to understand the role of Black Patriots in the opening months of the war. Glenn Knoblock's *'Strong and Brave Fellows': New Hampshire's Black Soldiers and Sailors of the American Revolution, 1775–1784* and Daniel Popek's exhaustive study, *They "...fought bravely, but were unfortunate": The True Story of Rhode Island's "Black Regiment" and the Failure of Segregation in Rhode Island's Continental Line, 1777–1783* are models of how state-specific research in this area of study should be conducted. Two websites, Paul Heinegg's Free African Americans in the Revolution (freeafricanamericans.com) and Henry Schenawolf's articles recounting individual Black Patriot stories at Revolutionary War Journal (revolutionarywarjournal.com), were both rich resources.

Early on in the research process I settled on the term "Black Patriots" for this book. I am aware there is considerable debate about the use of terms in this field, but I believed (and still do) that this respectfully and adequately describes the subject that also took no position on those various debates. There are terms used throughout this work that seem out of place in our time. Describing someone as an "owner" of another human being is thankfully completely foreign to our experience today, but in their own time it was a tragic reality. One term I intentionally avoided was describing someone escaping slavery as a "runaway" (the common parlance of the time), as it seems to me to carry with it negative connotations. Fleeing slavery was a natural and profoundly moral endeavor.

I feel compelled to make clear that I reject any attempts to cast slavery as benign or pastoral in any way. Stealing someone from their family and their homes, forcing them into labor under threats of violence, subjecting them to unrestricted punishments and sexual violence, and living under a constant specter of additional separations and mutilations are among the most cruel and inhuman activities devised by man. Its continuation is the greatest stain on the legacy of the American founding, and it is impossible to overstate how evil it was.

There are many people to thank, and I'm unable to do it justice here. I want to mention my late parents and grandparents, who from an early age took my brother and I to battlefields and many other historic places, which inspired in me a lifelong interest in history and government. The friends and family that have helped and encouraged me over the years are innumerable, and I owe them all more than I can ever recount or repay. And I'm grateful to Emily Hitchcock for helping take this rough manuscript and making it a readable reality.

Finally, I could never have undertaken this effort, let alone finished it, without the constant encouragement and support of my love and partner, Kara. In so many ways, this is as much her work as mine. She was always the first to read through the chapters of this book as they were finished, providing excellent suggestions and corrections. Her forbearance with the many surprise side trips to out-of-the-way cemeteries to track down a grave, or stopping at battlefields or monuments, enduring a wide range of weather and terrain, was admirable. Two crazy kids, indeed.

Patrick S. Poole
June 19, 2024
Juneteenth

CHAPTER 1
SONS OF LIBERTY

BLACK PATRIOTS SERVING in and supporting the Continental army played an outsized role in securing American independence. From the first shots of the war at Lexington Green to the siege at Yorktown; from the depths of the frontier to the high seas; many times fighting not only the British Empire but more pervasive social, economic, and legal obstacles; slaves and free men fought on battlefields from Canada to Georgia, many losing their lives to combat and disease. Others served as wagoners, cooks, bakers, and even spies in a cause whose benefits would be slow to trickle down to them and their descendants for the next two centuries. Serving by the dozens in the early weeks of the war at the Battle of Bunker Hill, by the time of the great Patriot victory at Saratoga just over two years later, having endured the wintertime sufferings at Valley Forge and having fought the British to a stalemate in the northern states at Monmouth, they enlisted in the Continental army by the hundreds. When British might turned south, hoping to split the nascent country in two by capturing Charleston, Savannah, and Augusta and pushing into the Carolina backcountry, Black Patriots marched with Daniel Morgan and Nathanael Greene and rode with partisan leaders including Francis Marion and Thomas Sumter. The southern campaign eventually forced Lord Cornwallis to retreat to Yorktown, hoping for reinforcements and resupply. There he was met by more Black Patriots during the siege that marked the beginning of the end of the war. Having helped secure victory and peace, the Black Patriots had to continue their own fight for freedom and equality as American citizens.

The pervasive presence of these Black Patriots throughout the entire American Revolution came as a shocking revelation to me, not because it was unbelievable but because it was entirely unknown. Considering myself fairly well-read in the War of Independence and early American history, the accidental discovery of the role they played in the founding of our country led me to several years of investigative research and travel to discover whether I could exhaust what could be learned about this lost history. I'm still working.

What I discovered is that over the eight years of the American Revolution, thousands of Black Patriots swelled the rolls of the Continental army. Some had entered of their own volition as freemen. In 1775, there were an estimated one thousand freemen in Virginia; about half of them enlisted in the American cause during the war. In 1778, the Rhode Island legislature purchased the freedom of nearly one hundred slaves willing to enlist. Others, freemen and slaves alike, served as substitutes for Whites drafted into the militias. Others were slaves freed on the condition of completing their term of service. Tragically, some of those who served for the cause of liberty were returned to slavery after the war.

With only a few exceptions, Black Patriots served in integrated units, receiving the same pay, eating the same rations, suffering the same hardships, and marching into harm's way at the risk of death, shoulder to shoulder with White soldiers. They fought in every major military engagement and skirmish, experiencing both victory and defeat. In some of the darkest hours of the revolution, Black Patriots answered the call for recruits to restore life to the Continental army. They accounted for at least 7 percent of American forces at the largest engagement of the war, the Battle of Monmouth in June 1778, where the British fought to a stalemate and abandoned the field in the dark of night. Serving not just on land, Black Patriots took to sea on Continental ships, state navies, and privateers. Eventually, they accounted for one quarter of the crews on American ships during the war, even serving with early American naval hero John

Paul Jones on the *Ranger* and *Bon Homme Richard*. As noted in the next chapter, the first ships of the Continental navy, which delayed British reinforcements from Canada in the crucial first year of the war, were built by slaves and indentured servants.

Some only saw freedom in death on battlefields from Vermont to Georgia or on British prison hulks. They shared mass graves with their White comrades and officers across the colonies. They died by the scores in the winter encampments of Valley Forge and Morristown. Horrific injuries, including the loss of limbs, were a lifelong testament to their role in securing American independence. The service of Black Patriots during the entirety of the Revolutionary War showed their equality as men and women in every way. From Lexington Green to the redoubts of Yorktown, the bravery and heroics they displayed are as honorable as any in the annals of American military history.

With the war over, many enjoyed freedom for the first time. While the Revolutionary War had ostensibly been fought over political freedoms, Black Patriots were fighting for freedom itself. Historian Gary Nash explained the difference, noting, "White Americans were fighting to protect their liberty; enslaved Americans fought to attain it." Sadly, after serving in the war, some would return to slavery. Jack Arabus, discharged in 1783 after six years of service, had been promised freedom by his owner in Connecticut in exchange for his military service as a substitute for the owner's son. It took a lawsuit to free him and others who had honorably served but been denied their promised freedom. In Virginia, heroes of the revolution, including James Lafayette and Ned Streater, were freed by order of the legislature, who condemned their continued enslavement as "contrary to principles of justice." Even after the war, freedom for Black Patriots was a random and precarious matter bound up with the status of and disputes over slavery in their respective states, staining the legacy of the American founding.

Much of this story has been neglected and forgotten. However, there have been important efforts to revive this lost history. When introducing one of the first histories to chronicle the stories of the Black Patriots, *The Colored Patriots of the American Revolution* by William Cooper Nell, Harriet Beecher Stowe, the famous author of *Uncle Tom's Cabin*, remarked how Black Patriots' military service stood in stark contrast to the status they held in the country they fought for:

> [W]e are to reflect upon them as far more magnanimous, because rendered to a nation which did not acknowledge them as citizens and equals, and in whose interests and prosperity they had less at stake. It was not for their own land they fought, not even for a land which had adopted them, but for a land which had enslaved them, and whose laws, even in freedom, oftener oppressed than protected. Bravery, under such circumstances, has a peculiar beauty and merit.[1]

This "peculiar beauty and merit" of Black Patriots in our country's founding is why this lost history needs to be recovered. This begins with the understanding that the history of Black Patriots reaches even further back than the American Revolution.

BLACK PATRIOTS IN THE COLONIAL WARS

Even without personal freedoms or political liberties, for more than a century before the War of Independence Black Patriots had been contributing to the defense of the American colonies. While most colonies had laws against arming slaves for fear of slave insurrections, when danger presented itself those prohibitions usually gave way to reality. This double-sided policy extended into the early years of the Revolutionary War. Some colonies required slaves to assist in military emergencies, such as Virginia, which adopted that policy in 1639. Other colonies counted slaves in their assessment of military strength. Absalom Pearse was listed on militia rolls for the Plymouth Colony in 1643 despite a standing militia regulation that only "such as are of honest and good report, and freemen"[2] should be enlisted. Massachusetts' policy vacillated over the years, allowing the enlistment of slaves and prohibiting the practice, fluctuating with the various conflicts of the European powers.

The New World was an ongoing front for the raging wars of Europe throughout the seventeenth and eighteenth centuries. Indian raids on the colonies, frequently aided by competing European powers, added to the threat. These colonial wars were the training ground for Black Patriots, both slaves and freemen. During Queen Anne's War (1702–1713), Virginia authorized the arming of slaves in 1703. Massachusetts ordered all "free negroes, mulattoes, and Indians" to enter militia service in 1707 or face fines. North Carolina made no distinction between Black or White for militia service, declaring that all able-bodied men between fifteen and fifty were expected to serve.

The Indian and colonial wars also saw the first Black Patriot casualties in the New World in service to their country and communities. In 1690, a slave was killed serving aboard a British ship; his owner was later reimbursed for his loss. Isaiah Diggers died in action aboard the HMS *Princess Caroline* on June 9, 1741. Rebecca Jones appealed to the Virginia House of Burgesses for compensation after the death of her husband, James Jones, on a British expedition to Jamaica. Her appeal for a widow's pension was granted in the amount of five pounds.

Service in these early conflicts also set a generational precedent that extended into the American Revolution. Nero Benson, who was born in Africa and became the slave of Reverend James Swift, served as a trumpeter in Captain Isaac Clark's company of the Framingham, Massachusetts, militia, fighting the Abenaki in Dummer's War (1722–1725). Benson married another slave, Dido Dingo, in 1721. After Swift's death, his will divided ownership of the family, and Benson was sent to the home of Swift's son-in-law. Despite his status as a slave, Benson was received into the church in 1746. Just a year later, he was granted his freedom from yet another owner. He died on July 4, 1757. Nero and Dido's grandson, Abel Benson, later played an important role in the first hours of the American Revolution at Lexington and Concord and enlisted in the Continental army. Abel's sister Katy married Peter Salem, a Black Patriot widely acknowledged as one of the heroes of the Battle of Bunker Hill.

Lucy Terry Prince was a rare example of pre-Revolutionary War literature of the African-American community, documenting her experiences as part of the early American historical record, and she is acknowledged as the earliest known poet from that tradition. Born in Africa in 1733, she was abducted at a very early age and brought to Rhode Island, the New England slave-trade hub. At age five she was purchased and taken to Deerfield, Massachusetts. When her town was attacked by Indians in 1746, killing several families, as a still-enslaved teenager she commemorated the tragedy with two poems, one of which still survives. Abijah Prince redeemed her from slavery and married her in 1756. Among their children were two sons, Cesar and Festus, who later joined the Continental army during the American Revolution.

Europe's wars continued to play out in North America, providing more opportunities for slaves and freemen to enlist in the military. The escalating conflict between England and France required militia support during King George's War (1744–1747) to protect New England and Nova Scotia from French attacks on British claims in those regions. An expedition to Canada in 1747 by Captain Thomas Cheney's Eighth Massachusetts Militia saw the enlistment of three men identified only as Will, Cuffee, and Samuel.

FRENCH AND INDIAN WAR (1754–1765)

The French and Indian War, sometimes referred to as the Seven Years' War, contributed most to setting the conditions for the Revolutionary War and the role of Black Patriots in it. Many colonists gained military experience in European-style combat on their own ground. The war also solidified the role and status of colonial militias and sorted out leaders who later served in the Revolutionary War. A number of Black Patriots who later enlisted in the Continental army experienced military life for the first time during this war—service that was useful in the years ahead. After the war, British taxation policies that had paid for the conflict bred resentment in many colonists and prompted closer association between colonies in protest. Braddock's defeat (1755) in the wilderness beyond the Allegheny Mountains saw the rise of a Virginia militia commander, recognized for his bravery and leadership despite the military disaster he tried to prevent, spurned nonetheless by the British military establishment: His name was George Washington.

In the years preceding Braddock's defeat, the French had effectively driven the British from around Lake Erie and the Ohio River Valley. That prompted General Edward Braddock, the new British commander in chief in the Americas, to launch an expedition targeting Fort Duquesne, the French fort at the mouth of the Ohio River (modern day Pittsburgh). Getting there took considerable supplies and required his army to cross the steep Allegheny Mountains and cut a hundred-mile road through the wilderness to the fort.

To haul the army's supplies, at least two hundred wagons and an equal number of drivers were needed. These wagons needed to carry up to two thousand pounds. Braddock sought out laborers and slaves from Virginia and Maryland to hire. A young Daniel Boone enlisted as a wagon driver in the effort. Another driver was Samuel Jenkins.

He was born into slavery in 1734 in Fairfax County, Virginia, and came into the household of Captain Charles Broadwater at his manor house, Springfield (the house was still standing until 1980, when it was demolished by property developers). Captain Broadwater was a close associate of George Washington and George Mason, and both he and Washington were commissioned in the Virginia militia for the Braddock expedition. Jenkins followed Captain Broadwater on the venture, where he tended the horses and kept the wagons rolling.

Also on the Braddock expedition wagon train was Ishmael Titus, a nine- or ten-year-old slave living in Virginia when he joined the expedition under the supervision of his owner. According to his obituary, published nearly a century later, he was assigned to a heavily loaded wagon that required an additional horse, which he needed to ride. Historians also note that other slaves, including Billy Brown, Jack Miner, Abraham Lawrence, and Archibald Kelso, traveled with Braddock's army.

The expedition set off from Fort Cumberland on May 29, 1755. The wagon train typically lagged well behind Braddock's army of 1,300 British soldiers and colonial militiamen. Some of the mountains they crossed were steep on both sides; the rivers they forded were deep and wide. The army had to cut the road for the wagons. They also needed to fight the French and their Indian allies for control of Fort Duquesne. Rather than wait for Braddock's army to arrive, the French went on the offense and set an ambush with a considerably smaller force of 250 French soldiers and 600 Indian warriors.

On July 9, 1755, they sprung their trap just ten miles from Fort Duquesne. Receiving fire from the woods and in the tree lines, the standard British open-field tactics were of little use. When Braddock was shot from his horse and mortally wounded, the army dissolved into disorder. It fell to the twenty-three-year-old George Washington to organize the retreat. Fortunately, the wagon train was nowhere near the scene. When the shattered army finally returned to the wagons, the supplies were dumped and burned to prevent them falling into the hands of the French. Heading back to Fort Cumberland, the wagons now carried the wounded. They were harassed by Indians along the way. Wagon drivers, who were typically not armed, were encouraged to arm themselves, as some became victims to the pursuing French. Braddock died four days later and was buried in an unmarked grave. The British had lost nearly nine hundred men, killed or wounded.

Among the survivors were Samuel Jenkins and Ishmael Titus, who were likely the longest-living survivors of the expedition. Jenkins died in February 1849 at the astounding age of 115. He remained a slave into his old age until he was purchased by an owner who took him to Ohio, where slavery was banned, and there he lived another forty years as a free man, dying in Lancaster, Ohio. Titus died a free man in Massachusetts in 1855, having served in the Revolutionary War as a substitute for his master and participating in many of the major battles of the war's southern campaign.

Braddock's defeat marked the beginning of a string of costly battles for both the British and French in the war. The Hudson and Mohawk River Valleys became a frequent battleground for control of the waterways, namely Lake George, Lake Champlain, and the Hudson River, connecting Montreal and Albany. The key to this area was a string of forts guarding the southern part of the lake and the northern mouth of the Hudson.

Just two months after Braddock's defeat the British launched another expedition to Crown Point, New York, on the southwest shore of Lake Champlain. Listed among those in Captain Edward Moulton's company from Massachusetts was Samuel Deering, who had just moved to Hampden County earlier that year from Woodstock, Connecticut, with his owner, David Wallis. Wallis served as ensign of the company. Both men enlisted in Captain Joseph Blodgett's company in 1756 for another campaign around Lake Champlain. Deering enlisted in two companies during the American Revolution.

Also on the 1756 Crown Point expedition was Cuff Oringo, who later adopted the last name Rosier. Originally a slave of Reverend Samuel Brown of Abington, Massachusetts, an announcement published in the October 5, 1747, edition of the *Boston Evening-Post* indicates that Cuff escaped, and a reward of three pounds was offered for his return. He was eventually recaptured and re-enslaved in the Brown household. His ownership later transferred to Josiah Torrey, who married Reverend Brown's widow. Massachusetts records that another slave of Torrey's, only identified as "Micah," served in the French and Indian War and died during his enlistment. Cuff later married a freewoman and had at least two sons. A history of the town of Abington, Massachusetts, contends that Cuff regularly chaffed under the yoke of slavery and was regularly in trouble with Squire Torrey and the local authorities. Cuff and his two sons, Cuff Jr. and Silas, served during the revolution. Cuff Sr. died in August 1775 during his militia service, making him one of the earliest Black-Patriot casualties of the American Revolution.

The area of Lake Champlain and the Hudson River Valley was still heavily contested by 1757, and in August of that year it was the scene of one of the greatest tragedies of the war: the Fort William Henry Massacre. French General Montcalm had besieged the fort, located at the southern end of Lake George, eventually forcing British Colonel George Munro's capitulation. Montcalm had agreed to allow the British contingent (soldiers, camp followers, children, and slaves) to leave the fort and withdraw to nearby Fort Edward. These arrangements angered the Indian allies of the French, as it denied them the opportunity to take captives and war booty.

Once the British left the protection of the fort, the Indians set upon them, sparing no one. While soldiers were still armed, civilians and slaves were left without any defense. A number of women, children, and slaves were scalped and killed. Most who survived hid in the woods and waited for the savagery to pass. Two survivors were Caesar Cuntea and George Gire, who served in the same militia company from Grafton, Massachusetts. Other slaves and freemen who were captured didn't fare well. Primus Chandler was killed in the massacre, and his son of the same name died in the American Revolution. Ceasar Nero was captured and enslaved in Canada for three years before being released. Prince Goodin of Connecticut was also held captive by one of the French-allied tribes. Others were listed as missing on the muster rolls and were never accounted for or heard from again.

The Fort William Henry Massacre brought an added misery for George Bush and his family. George had been a slave in South America, but at the time was a property-owning freeman in Massachusetts. His son John had been serving in the militia since 1747. Stationed as a soldier at Fort William Henry during the winter of 1755–1756, he originated a specialized folk art decorating gunpowder horns, widely recognized to have inspired many imitators. A few examples of his handiwork still exist and are held by museums. But as John served at Fort William Henry, his brother George was killed in action at the Battle of Lake George in 1755, and another brother, Joseph, also died on the same campaign. Then John was taken captive at the fall of Fort William Henry. His father, George, wrote an appeal to the colonial governor of Massachusetts asking for assistance in obtaining his son's release, but John died the following year on a ship transporting British prisoners of war to France.

British fortunes shifted when General James Wolfe laid siege to Quebec and defeated the French at the Battle of the Plains of Abraham in September 1759. Caesar Pruitt served in the invasion of Canada in the company of Captain Elisha Pomeroy. Both Wolfe and Montcalm were mortally wounded in the battle, and the French evacuated the city. However, the war continued.

A recently republished memoir tells the story of a participant in of one of the last actions of the war, the capture of Havana by the British in 1762. In 1810, former slave Jeffrey Brace sat down with a local abolitionist to tell his life story. His tale begins with his abduction in Africa, progressing to his service at Havana and in the Revolutionary War, then to obtaining his freedom and the trials of life as a freeman. He was born Boyrereau Brinch in 1742 in an area we know today as Mali. At the age of sixteen, he and friends went to the river to swim, where they were abducted by slavers. Enduring the Atlantic crossing on a slave ship, he was purchased in 1759 by Captain Isaac Mills in Barbados. He then lived the life of a sailor. He said that he sailed to Dublin, Savannah, New York City, Newport, Halifax, and then Boston during the French and Indian War. During the British siege of Havana in 1762 he was wounded five times. Having been sold in Connecticut, he suffered from 1763–1768 under a line of sadistic masters until he was purchased in September 1768 by the widow Mary Stiles. He speaks kindly of Stiles, who taught him how to read and write, and he served her son after her death. During the American Revolution, he enlisted along with two of the Stiles sons, joined the Connecticut line of the Continental army, and finally secured his freedom.

The freemen and slaves of the colonies continued to contribute to British success in the French and Indian War. Frequently employed as laborers, they helped to build fortifications to protect the colonies from New York to Georgia. As the war progressed, the hesitation to use them as soldiers diminished. For instance, when the British moved to retake Fort Pitt in 1759, there were forty-two Black soldiers counted among the Pennsylvania militia. Others saw action on the frontier as scouts and rangers. One of the most famous units in the war was Rogers' Rangers, which included two slaves, Boston Burn and Castor Dickinson.

The war also gave colonials serving alongside British troops military experience that was useful in the conflict to come. It also slowly gave them a sense of ownership in their future. Many of the names of those Black Patriots who fought in the French and Indian War reappear in the early battles of the Revolution: Jeffrey Hemmingway, Jonathan Occum, Gershom Prince, John Dimorat, Caesar Robbins, David Lamson, Sandy Onkemour, John Louis Cook, and many others. Barzilai Lew, who spent eight months defending Lake George and Lake Champlain for the British Empire, returned to the same area almost two decades later, fighting under a new flag for a new cause.

AMERICAN OPPOSITION TO BRITISH POLICY (1765–1774)

As the colonies in America resisted British policy, England responded with punitive economic and political measures, and Black Patriots increasingly cast their lot with the American cause. It may seem odd that colonials who were fighting against France for king and country would take up arms against the mother country twelve years later. But heavy-handed British policies that followed in the war's wake—to pay for both the war and for the soldiers to occupy newly won lands—escalated the alienation. First came taxes on sugar and a ban on colonies issuing their own currency. Next the British Parliament, where colonies had no representation, passed the first direct tax on the colonies, the Stamp Act, and the Quartering Act requiring colonies to provide housing and food for troops, including housing them in private quarters if barracks were not available.

There were widespread protests against the Stamp Act, and organizations like the Sons of Liberty began to form and push for boycotts on imported British goods. Most of the colonies sent delegates to New York City in October 1765 to the Stamp Act Congress, which resulted in networks formed between colonies and their leaders to develop a coordinated response to the new measures. The meeting also produced a Declaration of Rights and Grievances that was widely debated in the colonies but ignored by Parliament. Protests against the Stamp Act prompted all of the British agents, appointed to collect the taxes, to resign even before the act went into effect. New York refused to quarter 1,500 soldiers, requiring them to be kept on the ships that brought them. Largely due to the effect of the boycotts on British businesses, within a year the Stamp Act had been repealed.

Startled by American opposition, Parliament passed the Declaratory Act (1766) that asserted their absolute authority to legislate on all colonial matters, effectively ending the ability of colonies to govern their own affairs. Rather than acknowledging the validity of the "taxation without representation" claims made by the colonists, the Crown went the opposite direction and de facto ended colonial self-government. Parliament then made matters worse by passing a series of laws described as the Townshend Acts (1767 and 1768) that taxed a wide range of items and reasserted their right to directly tax the colonies, increased enforcement, and punished New York for failing to quarter troops.

These new laws were detested as much as the previous Stamp Act, inciting more protests and boycotts on British goods. The situation in Boston grew so tense as attacks on customs officials intensified that the fifty-gun ship HMS *Romney* was sent to park in Boston Harbor as a warning, and by the end of 1768 four new regiments of troops (and the colony's obligation to house them) occupied Boston. This was perceived by the colonists as the potential threat of violence that the British intended.

CRISPUS ATTUCKS AND THE BOSTON MASSACRE (MARCH 5, 1770)

The soldiers swelling Boston created a new problem. Off duty, many of them sought work in the city to supplement their income, flooding the job market and depressing local wages. This drove many workers to the cause of the Sons of Liberty. But then on February 22, 1770, a customs official by the name of Ebenezer Richardson shot and killed eleven-year-old Christopher Seider, who was part of a crowd protesting outside Richardson's home. Earlier, Richardson had tried to disperse an early protest in front of the Loyalist business. A public funeral was held for Seider, and he was buried at the Granary Burying Ground in a plot owned by Samuel Adams. Two thousand mourners turned out to pay their respects. Likely among the mourners that day was a man who would become a critical figure in galvanizing resistance to British rule in America: Crispus Attucks.

Very little is known about the life of Crispus Attucks prior to the Boston Massacre, which took place on March 5, 1770. Scholars believe he was born into slavery at some point in the 1720s, in or near Framingham, Massachusetts, the son of an African slave and a Natick Indian mother. It appears he escaped from slavery in 1750, based on a notice published in the *Boston Gazette* and the *Weekly Journal* by William Brown on October 2, 1750. The notice offered a reward for the return of his escaped slave described as "a Mulatto fellow, about 27 Years of Age, named Crispus, 6 feet 2 inches high, short cul'l hair, his knees nearer together than common." Despite two more published notices by Brown, it appears his attempts to recover Attucks were unsuccessful.

Attucks likely took to sea on one of the whaling ships sailing out of Boston Harbor. He may have been a sailor who sometimes went by the name Michael Johnson and sometimes worked on the docks as a ropemaker. What actually transpired in the life of Crispus Attucks between 1750 and the night of the Boston Massacre nearly twenty years later is filled with uncertainty. What we know of his last minutes and hours are details that came out during the trial of the British soldiers who shot and killed Attucks and the other victims of the Boston Massacre.

The events of that night began when a soldier entered a Boston pub looking for work, which angered a group of seamen. A fight several nights before between three British soldiers and local dockworkers contributed to the tensions. A crowd led by Attucks harassed a lone sentry in front of the Customs House. The sentry called for backup after being pelted with rocks and snowballs as the crowd began to swell. Seven soldiers responded to his call. According to court testimony, Attucks wielded a cordwood club and shouted taunts, including urging the mob to "root them out." When the first shot went off he was standing close to the soldiers and took two musket balls to the chest in the volley that followed, killing him instantly.

In a funeral organized by the Sons of Liberty and held at public expense, Crispus Attucks and James Caldwell lay in state at Faneuil Hall for three days. On the day of the funeral a crowd of ten thousand mourners followed the bodies of Attucks and Caldwell. The procession was joined in front of the Old State House by the families bearing the bodies of Samuel Gray and Samuel Maverick. At the time, it was the largest funeral in American history. The procession circled the Liberty Tree on Boston Neck, wound around Boston Common, and ended at Granary Burying Ground, where the dead were interred beside the fresh grave of Christopher Seider. Patrick Carr, who was mortally wounded and died two weeks later, was buried with them.

Notwithstanding the subsequent trial when the eight British soldiers were acquitted of murder, the Boston Massacre galvanized American resistance to the British government. This was fueled by pamphlets and paintings of the event that quickly circulated throughout all the colonies. Most famous was an engraving by Paul Revere of the Sons of Liberty that is one of the most famous American political images before the Revolutionary War (notably, Revere had stolen the image from his friend Henry Pelham, who had sent it to Revere for his review). The anniversary of the Boston Massacre was commemorated annually with speeches by prominent Patriot leaders for years to come, supplanted in American memory only by the Fourth of July after the end of the war.

In time, Crispus Attucks would be recognized as the "first martyr of American Independence," as described by William Cooper Nell.[3] Martin Luther King Jr. would write in his book *Why We Can't Wait* that Black schoolchildren were taught that "the first American to shed blood in the revolution that freed his country from British oppression was a Black seaman named Crispus Attucks."[4] Reverend King lionized his memory, saying, "He is one of the most important figures in African-American history, not for what he did for his own race but for what he did for all oppressed people everywhere."

THE PATRIOT PEN OF PHILLIS WHEATLEY

Another critical figure who lived in Boston during this time and wrote about these events was Phillis Wheatley. Born in West Africa and enslaved at age eight, she survived the Middle Passage and first arrived in Bermuda. Once in Boston, she was purchased by Boston tailor John Wheatley. Her intellectual abilities quickly became evident, as she had mastered the English language sixteen months after her arrival. She was taught to read and write by Mrs. Wheatley and her daughter, Mary. Additional instruction in history, geography, British literature, the Latin classics, and the Bible came from Mr. Wheatley and his son Nathaniel.

At the young age of thirteen she published her first poem in the *Newport Mercury* in December 1767, entitled "On Messrs. Hussey and Coffin." Three years later she gained notoriety when her memorial poem on the sudden death of the prominent Great Awakening preacher Reverend George Whitefield was widely published in Boston, Newport, New York City, and Philadelphia. The Wheatleys were known to associate in Whitefield's circle of supporters on both sides of the Atlantic, and the subject's popularity likely encouraged even greater readership. By 1772, the Wheatleys had sought a Boston publisher for twenty-eight of Phyllis's poems. The assistance of a sea captain that traveled regularly to London, Robert Calef, was enlisted to find a suitable publisher there.

During a May 1773 trip to London with Nathaniel Wheatley, Phillis found a sponsor in Selina Hastings, the Countess of Huntingdon and a Whitefield supporter who had received a copy of her elegy for the late reverend from Mrs. Wheatley. Phillis's book, *Poems on Various Subjects, Religious and Moral*, was published in September 1773, prefaced with a letter signed by the political, religious, and business leaders of Boston, attesting to her veracity and circumstance. The book also bears the only portrait of Phillis made during her lifetime. She was given her freedom by the Wheatleys immediately after her book's publication at the urging of the family's friends in England. The Wheatleys continued to support her until Mr. Wheatley's death in 1778. Remarkably, she became the first enslaved woman—and only the third woman in America—to be published, securing her place as a pioneer in the African-American and overall American literary tradition. An autographed copy of her book of poems and one of her letters where she wrote, "in every human Breast, God has implanted a Principle, which we call Love of Freedom," are on display at the Museum of the American Revolution in Philadelphia.

Coming of age in Boston during the turbulent years immediately preceding the American Revolution, it seems natural that Phillis would set her pen to current political events and controversies. In fact, the Boston Massacre occurred just a few blocks from the Wheatley home. Even before the events of that tragic day, she had already turned to the murder of young Christopher Seider two weeks before. In her poem "On the Death of Mr. Seider Murder'd by Richardson" (1770), she laments the "first martyr for the common good" and notes the "secret rage" of Bostonians against "fair freedoms foes beneath."

Her poem on the Boston Massacre, "On the Affray in King Street, on the Evening of the 5th of March 1770," was published anonymously in the *Boston Evening Post* just a week after the events that occurred on the street where she lived. The poem was likely inspired by the massive funeral for the victims that she very well may have participated in. With "fire enwrapt" and bringing "sudden death," the British muskets still operate with "heaven-directed force." The deaths of these men are part of God's Providence. Though gone from their families and friends, yet from the grave "shall Flames celestial burn":

> Long as in *Freedom's* Cause the wise contend,
> Dear to your unity shall Fame extend;
> While to the World, the letter'd *Stone* shall tell,
> How *Caldwell*, *Attucks*, *Gray*, and *Mav'rick* fell.

For obvious reasons, these works weren't included in her London-published book three years later. But she didn't flinch from tackling one of the controversial issues of the day, one that was immediately personal and consequential for her: slavery.

In one of her earlier poems, "On Being Brought from Africa to America"[5] (1768), she turns to the topic of her abduction and enslavement in the context of the Christian religion, emphasizing the humanity and, tacitly, the equality, of slaves such as herself:

> 'Twas mercy brought me from my Pagan land,
> Taught my benighted soul to understand
> That there's a God, that there's a Saviour too:
> Once I redemption neither sought nor knew.
> Some view our sable race with scornful eye,
> "Their colour is a diabolic dye."
> Remember, Christians, Negros, black as Cain,
> May be refin'd, and join th' angelic train.

EARLY AMERICAN CALLS FOR ABOLITION

By the time Phillis Wheatley wrote those lines, public discussions on the religious and moral hazards of slavery were already well underway in Massachusetts. The arguments on both sides began early in the colony's history, launched when Boston merchant John Saffin signed an agreement in 1694 to free one of his slaves, Adam, after seven years of captivity. After a series of controversies and legal hearings, including an attempt by Saffin to renege on the agreement, Adam was freed by the court in 1703.

As the case progressed and a petition circulated around Boston calling for Adam and his wife to be freed, a three-page tract appeared condemning the slave trade and using biblical arguments to attack the justifications for slavery at the time. The author was a name familiar to many, a local judge named Samuel Sewall, who had previously served as a judge in the infamous Salem witch trials but had publicly repented of his role in those events. Sewall's tract *The Selling of Joseph: A Memorial* (1700) invokes the Old Testament story of Joseph in the book of Genesis, who was unjustly taken captive by his brothers over their jealousies and sold into slavery. Saffin, whose business included slave trading, responded by invoking the accepted arguments of the time in defense of slavery, defending his conduct. While this public interchange did not directly result in any changes in the colony with respect to slavery, it did introduce these abolitionist ideas into culture and make them acceptable in the ruling class.

One of the effects of Black Patriots fighting during the French and Indian War and shouldering the burden of military service on par with White citizens was an escalation in their calls for emancipation. Early abolitionist author William Cooper Nell related a public debate over slavery between Judge Tucker of Virginia and Reverend Belknap, where Belknap cited the decline in the actual number of slaves prior to 1763 to service in the French and Indian war, saying, "because in the two preceding wars, many of them were enlisted either into the army or on board vessels of war, with a view to procure their freedom."

One leading voice in Massachusetts in the years leading up to the Revolutionary War took up their cause. James Otis Jr., one of Boston's leading lawyers, published a defense of the rights of the colonies against the growing powers of the British Empire shortly after the conclusion of the French and Indian War. He introduced a term into the American political discourse that has lasted until today: "taxation without representation."

In *The Rights of the British Colonies Asserted and Proved* (1764), Otis advances the political arguments for liberty by using the language and concepts of the natural rights articulated by John Locke and other British thinkers. The rights of citizens are not bestowed by government, but come from God. He follows this argument to its ultimate conclusion: "The Colonists are by the law of nature free born, as indeed all men are, white or black." Otis then launches into a full attack on slavery itself:

> Can any logical inference in favour of slavery, be drawn from a flat nose, a long or a short face. Nothing better can be said in favor of a trade, that is the most shocking violation of the law of nature, has a direct tendency to diminish the idea of the inestimable value of liberty, and makes every dealer in it a tyrant, from the director of an African company to the petty chapman in needles and pins on the unhappy coast. It is a clear truth, that those who every day barter away other men's liberty will soon care little for their own.[6]

It is hard to overstate the importance of this type of powerful statement coming from one of the most prominent political leaders in Massachusetts and one of the leading lights of liberty in the colonies.

It didn't take long for these ideas to percolate into Boston politics. The issue of slavery was brought up and debated at the city's annual town meeting in May 1766. The citizens resolved to instruct its representatives to the colonial assembly: "That for the total abolishing of slavery among us, that you move for a law to prohibit the importation and purchasing of slaves for the future."[7] The city's representatives in this case were Samuel Adams, known to have strident antislavery beliefs, John Hancock, and James Otis. Since this effort was made at the same time that the colony was resisting the Stamp Act, the measure was obstructed by the Crown and those financially involved in the slave trade.

These ideas and arguments were embraced in Massachusetts and elsewhere in the colonies. Efforts to limit or abolish the slave trade, including by Arthur Lee in Virginia, were repeatedly met with resistance by the Crown. The reluctance by some colonial opposition leaders to incorporate the issue of slavery into their demands of political liberty became an obvious hypocrisy. This was a point made by a writer identified as "A True Son of Liberty" in a January 8, 1768, article in the *Newport Mercury* (Newport was the largest slave-trading port in New England): "If you say you have the right to enslave (Negroes) because it is for your interest, why do you dispute the legality of Great Britain's enslaving you?"

The force of the arguments in favor of liberty and natural rights circulating at the time became undeniable for some. Prince Hall, who became a prominent leader in Boston's Black community and founded the first all-Black Masonic Lodge, was freed by his owner a month after the Boston Massacre and the killing of Crispus Attucks. Prince and his son Primus both fought for liberty in the revolution. Moses Brown, from one of Rhode Island's leading slave-trading families, freed his slaves in 1773 and became a vocal abolitionist. One member of the Massachusetts Provincial Congress was recorded questioning the "propriety, that while we are attempting to free ourselves from our present embarrassments, and preserve ourselves from slavery, that we also take into consideration the state and circumstances of the negro slaves in this province."[8]

Those who were enslaved began to ask that question too. A petition to the Massachusetts legislature in January 1773 by a group of "many Slaves, living in the Town of Boston, and other Towns in the Province," complained that, "We have no Property. We have no Wives. No Children. We have no City. No Country."[9] The intent of the petition, signed with only one name, Felix, was to raise the plight of slaves in the colony and pray for relief. A second petition dated April 20, 1773, signed by four men—Peter Bestes, Sambo Freeman, Felix Holbrook, and Chester Joie—on behalf of "fellow slaves in this province," was more direct. Citing an example from Spain, they requested the ability to work one day a week for themselves and the right to purchase their freedom. Invoking Spain was clearly intended to needle the Massachusetts Puritans, and they sarcastically pressed the point home, saying, "The Spaniards, who have not those sublime ideas of freedom that English men have, are conscious that they have no right to all the service of their fellow-men, we mean the Africans." Their argument was pointed: If surely the Roman Catholic absolutists in Spain could understand this, so should any self-respecting Protestant Englishman.

Later that year the Sons of Liberty would protest British colonial policies with the Boston Tea Party, prompting a British blockade of Boston Harbor and a great military presence in the city. Many Black Patriots began to join local militias to prepare for the colony's defense as other colonies began to mobilize and a Continental Congress convened in Philadelphia to respond to the escalating crisis. Caesar Sarter, a freed slave living north of Boston in Newburyport, proposed a radical measure for Black Patriots in an article in the *Essex Journal and Merrimack Packet* on August 17, 1774: "let the oppressed Africans be liberated." He added, "I need not point out the absurdity of your exertions for liberty, when you have slaves in your houses."

In the heart of Patriot resistance, a Tory by the name of Daniel Bliss of Concord would point out this inherent contradiction in the colonists' cause by composing a tombstone epitaph for a freed local slave, John Jack. At one time he had been owned by one of the accusers in the Salem witch trials, but he eventually bought his own freedom. These words adorned his grave in the Old Hill Burying Ground in Concord after his death in 1773:

> God wills us free; man wills us slaves.
> I will as God wills; Gods will be done.
> Here lies the body of John Jack
> A native of Africa who died
> March 1773, aged about 60 years.
> Tho' born in a land of slavery, He was born free.
> Tho' he lived in a land of liberty, He lived as a slave.
> Till by his honest, tho' stolen, labors,
> He acquired the source of slavery,
> Which gave him his freedom;
> Tho' not long before
> Death, the grand tyrant,
> Gave him his final emancipation,
> And set him on a footing with kings.
> Tho' a slave to vice,
> He practised those virtues
> Without which kings are but slaves.[10]

Daniel Bliss would shortly flee his home forever and join the British army against the Patriots' cause. Meanwhile, Black Patriots continued to rally in defense of the colonies. In March 1775, Winsor Fry enlisted in the Rhode Island militia, eventually serving in the Continental army for the duration of the war, fighting in ten major battles, and being discharged by Washington's own hand in 1783. Just weeks after Fry's enlistment, a British column marched out of Boston headed for Concord to recover cannons, gunpowder, and other military supplies hidden by the Patriots.

On their way, they fired on the Lexington militia gathering on the town commons. Prince Estabrook, a slave serving in the Lexington militia, was wounded in action there.

Marching into Concord on the fateful day of April 19, 1775, the British passed by the Old Hill Burying Ground, site of John Jack's grave with its indicting epitaph. When the British fired at the gathering militia at the nearby Old North Bridge, the Patriots responded with "the shot heard round the world." In the running battle that followed the British all the way back to Boston, they were pursued by Black Patriots serving in units from at least eleven different towns. Several of those fighting along with the Patriots that day, such as David Lamson, had fought for the Crown during the French and Indian War. They were the forerunners of thousands of Black Patriots, slave and free, who enlisted as rightful Sons of Liberty in America's cause for freedom and independence.

Title page for *The Colored Patriots of the American Revolution* (1855) by William Cooper Nell, one of the earliest efforts to document the participation of Black Patriots in the War for Independence. The book's introduction was by Harriet Beecher Stowe, famed author of *Uncle Tom's Cabin*. (Image: Library of Congress)

THE

COLORED PATRIOTS

OF THE

AMERICAN REVOLUTION,

WITH SKETCHES OF SEVERAL

DISTINGUISHED COLORED PERSONS:

TO WHICH IS ADDED A BRIEF SURVEY OF THE

Condition and Prospects of Colored Americans.

BY WM. C. NELL.

WITH AN INTRODUCTION BY

HARRIET BEECHER STOWE.

BOSTON:

PUBLISHED BY ROBERT F. WALLCUT.

1855.

THE

Blind African Slave,

OR MEMOIRS OF

BOYREREAU BRINCH,

NICK-NAMED

JEFFREY BRACE.

Containing an account of the kingdom of Bow-Woo, in the interior of Africa, with the soil, climat and natural productions, laws and customs peculiar to that place. With an account of his captivity, sufferings, sales, travels, emancipation, conversion to the christian religion, knowledge of the scriptures, &c. Interspersed with strictures on slavery, speculative observations on the qualities of human nature, with quotations from scripture.

By BENJAMIN F. PRENTISS, Esq.

ST. ALBANS, Vt.

PRINTED BY *HARRY WHITNEY.*

1810.

Title page for *The Blind African Slave, or Memoirs of Boyrereau Brinch, Nick-Named Jeffrey Brace* (1810). Brace had been born in Africa, abducted at age sixteen, and sold into slavery to a ship's captain in Barbados. He served in the British Navy during the French and Indian War, and participated in the British siege of Havana in 1762. He would serve in the Connecticut Line during the American Revolution, earning his freedom. The memoirs are based on interviews of Brace by Vermont attorney Benjamin Prentiss. (Image: Vermont Historical Society)

THE

RIGHTS

OF THE

Britiſh Colonies

Aſſerted and proved.

By JAMES OTIS, *Eſq;*

The THIRD EDITION, corrected.

Hæc omnis regio & celſi plaga pinea montis
Cedat amicitiæ Teucrorum: & fœderis æquas
Dicamus leges, ſociosque in regna vocemus
Conſidant, ſi tantus amor, & mœnia condant.
VIRG.

BOSTON, NEW-ENGLAND, Printed:

LONDON Reprinted, for J. WILLIAMS, next the *Mitre-Tavern, Fleet-ſtreet*; and J. ALMON, in *Piccadilly*, 1766.

[Price Two Shillings.]

(43)

men to imagine, ſome real general ſtate of nature, agreeable to this abſtract conception, antecedent to and independent of ſociety. This is certainly not the caſe in general, for moſt men become members of ſociety from their birth, though ſeparate independent ſtates are really in the condition of perfect freedom and equality with regard to each other; and ſo are any number of individuals who ſeparate themſelves from a ſociety of which they have formerly been members, for ill treatment, or other good cauſe, with expreſs deſign to found another. If in ſuch caſe, there is a real interval, between the ſeparation and the new conjunction, during ſuch interval, the individuals are as much detached, and under the law of nature only, as would be two men who ſhould chance to meet on a deſolate iſland.

The Coloniſts are by the law of nature free born, as indeed all men are, white or black. No better reaſons can be given, for enſlaving thoſe of any colour, than ſuch as baron Monteſquieu has humourouſly given, as the foundation of that cruel ſlavery exerciſed over the poor Ethiopians; which threatens one day to reduce both Europe and America to the ignorance and barbarity of the darkeſt ages. Does it follow that it is right to enſlave a man becauſe he is black? Will ſhort curled hair, like wool, inſtead of Chriſtian hair, as it is called by thoſe whoſe hearts are as hard as the nether millſtone, help the argument? Can any logical inference in favour of ſlavery, be drawn from a flat noſe, a long or a ſhort face? Nothing

G 2

(44)

thing better can be ſaid in favour of a trade, that is the moſt ſhocking violation of the law of nature, has a direct tendency to diminiſh the idea of the ineſtimable value of liberty, and makes every dealer in it a tyrant, from the director of an African company to the petty chapman in needles and pins on the unhappy coaſt. It is a clear truth, that thoſe who every day barter away other mens liberty, will ſoon care little for their own. To this cauſe muſt be imputed that feroſity, cruelty, and brutal barbarity that has long marked the general character of the ſugar-iſlanders. They can in general form no idea of government but that which in perſon, or by an overſeer, the joint and ſeveral proper repreſentative of a Creole*, and of the D—l, is exerciſed over ten thouſands of their fellow men, born with the ſame right to freedom, and the ſweet enjoyments of liberty and life, as their unrelenting taſk-maſters, the overſeers and planters.

Is it to be wondered at, if, when people of the ſtamp of a Creolian planter get into power, they will not ſtick for a little preſent gain, at making their own poſterity, white as well as black, worſe ſlaves if poſſible than thoſe already mentioned.

There is nothing more evident, ſays Mr. Locke, than "that creatures of the ſame ſpecies

* Thoſe in England who borrow the terms of the Spaniards, as well as their notions of government, apply this term to all Americans of European Extract; but the Northern coloniſts apply it only to the Iſlanders and others of ſuch extract, under the Torrid Zone.

Early Massachusetts Patriot leader James Otis defends racial equality and attacks slavery in his influential tract, *The Rights of the British Colonies Asserted and Proved* (1766), declaring, "The Colonists are by the law of nature free born, as indeed all men are, white or black." (Images: Internet Archive)

Lithograph of a painting by William Champney depicting the killing of Crispus Attucks by British soldiers during the Boston Massacre on March 5, 1770. Attucks would later be described as "the first martyr of liberty." (Image: Library of Congress)

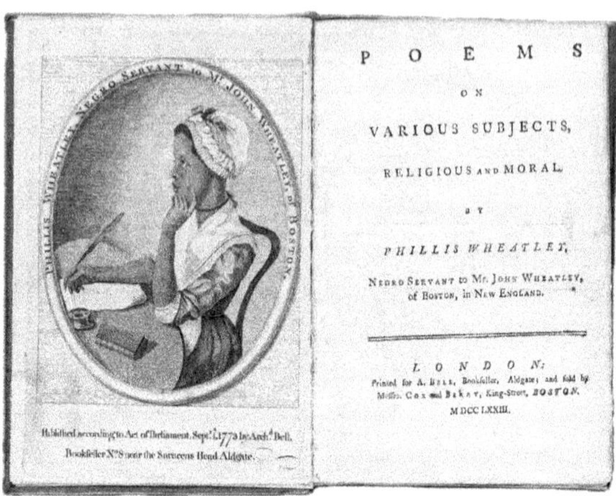

PHILLIS WHEATLEY, NEGRO SERVANT to MR. JOHN WHEATLEY, of BOSTON.

Published according to Act of Parliament, Sept. 1, 1773 by Arch.d Bell, Bookseller No. 8 near the Saracens Head Aldgate.

P O E M S
ON
VARIOUS SUBJECTS,
RELIGIOUS AND MORAL.
BY
PHILLIS WHEATLEY,
NEGRO SERVANT to MR. JOHN WHEATLEY,
of BOSTON, in NEW ENGLAND.

L O N D O N:
Printed for A. BELL, Bookseller, Aldgate; and sold by
Messrs. COX and BERRY, King-Street, BOSTON.
MDCCLXXIII.

Portrait and title page from Phyllis Wheatley's *Poems on Various Subjects, Religious and Moral* (1773). (Image: Smithsonian National Museum of African American History and Culture)

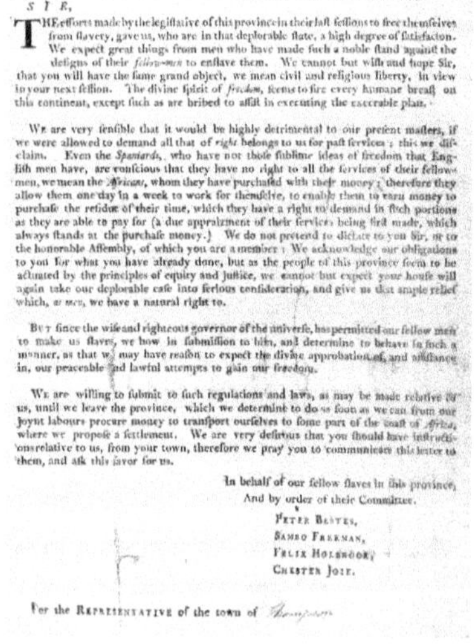

BOSTON, April 20th, 1773.

SIR,

THE efforts made by the legislative of this province in their last sessions to free themselves from slavery, gave us, who are in that deplorable state, a high degree of satisfaction. We expect great things from men who have made such a noble stand against the designs of their *fellow-men* to enslave them. We cannot but wish and hope Sir, that you will have the same grand object, we mean civil and religious liberty, in view in your next session. The divine spirit of *freedom*, seems to fire every humane breast on this continent, except such as are bribed to assist in executing the execrable plan.

WE are very sensible that it would be highly detrimental to our present masters, if we were allowed to demand all that of *right* belongs to us for past services; this we disclaim. Even the *Spaniards*, who have not those sublime ideas of freedom that English men have, are conscious that they have no right to all the services of their fellow-men, we mean the *Africans*, whom they have purchased with their money; therefore they allow them one day in a week to work for themselves, to enable them to earn money to purchase the residue of their time, which they have a right to demand in such portions as they are able to pay for (a due appraizment of their services being first made, which always stands at the purchase money.) We do not pretend to dictate to you Sir, or to the honorable Assembly, of which you are a member: We acknowledge our obligations to you for what you have already done, but as the people of this province seem to be actuated by the principles of equity and justice, we cannot but expect your house will again take our deplorable case into serious consideration, and give us that ample relief which, *as men*, we have a natural right to.

BUT since the wise and righteous governor of the universe, has permitted our fellow men to make us slaves, we bow in submission to him, and determine to behave in such a manner, as that we may have reason to expect the divine approbation of, and assistance in, our peaceable and lawful attempts to gain our freedom.

WE are willing to submit to such regulations and laws, as may be made relative to us, until we leave the province, which we determine to do as soon as we can from our joynt labours procure money to transport ourselves to some part of the coast of *Africa*, where we propose a settlement. We are very desirous that you should have instructions relative to us, from your town, therefore we pray you to communicate this letter to them, and ask this favor for us.

In behalf of our fellow slaves in this province,
And by order of their Committee.

PETER BESTES,
SAMBO FREEMAN,
FELIX HOLBROOK,
CHESTER JOIE.

For the REPRESENTATIVE of the town of Thompson

An April 20, 1773, legislative petition by four enslaved men supporting efforts by the town of Thompson to end slavery in Massachusetts and requesting leave to work one day a week on their own behalf to earn money to buy their freedom. (Image: Library of Congress)

Essex Journal

AND

Merimack Packet:

OR

The *Massachusetts* and *New-Hampshire* General Advertiser.

VOL. I. WEDNESDAY, August 17, 1774. No. 35.

Messrs. PRINTERS,

[illegible] to give the following Address, *To those who are Advocates for holding the Africans in Slavery*, a place in your next, and you will oblige [illegible], who is a well-wisher to his brethren, who [illegible] now in that unhappy state.

AS this is a time of great anxiety and distress among you, on account of the infringement not only of your Charter rights; but of the natural rights and [illegible] of freeborn men; permit a poor, though [illegible] African, who, in his youth, was trapan[ned] into Slavery and who has born the galling yoke of bondage for more than twenty years; though at [illegible] by the blessing of God, has shaken it off, to [illegible] you, and that from experience, that as Slavery [illegible] the greatest, and consequently most to be dreaded, [illegible] all temporal calamities: So its opposite, Liberty, [illegible] the greatest temporal good, with which you can be [illegible] The importance of which, you clearly evince [illegible] world you are sensible of, by your manly and [illegible] struggles to preserve it. Your fore fathers, [illegible] have been often informed, left their native country, together with many dear friends, and came into [illegible] country, then a howling wilderness inhabited, [illegible] by savages, rather choosing, under the protection of their GOD, to risk their lives, among those [illegible] wretches, than submit to tyranny at home: [illegible], therefore, this conduct gives you their exalt[illegible] of the worth of LIBERTY, at the same [illegible] it shews their utmost abhorrence of that [illegible]SE OF CURSES, SLAVERY.——Your [illegible], to their immortal honor be it mention[ed] [illegible] whom WE feel that gratitude, which so high a [illegible] naturally produces, in an ingenious mind [illegible] exerted their utmost abilities, to put a final [illegible] to so iniquitous a business, as the Slave Trade[.] That they have not succeeded in their laudable [illegible] was not their fault: But they were de[illegible] by his late Excellency only.——Now, if you [illegible] sensible, that slavery is in itself, and in its con[illegible], a great evil; why will you not pity and [illegible] the poor, afflicted, enslaved Africans?—[illegible] though they are entitled to the same natural [illegible] of mankind that you are, are, nevertheless, [illegible] in bondage! A bondage which will only [illegible] with life: To them a shocking considera[tion] indeed! Though too little, I fear, thought of [illegible] of you who enjoy the profits of their labour. [illegible] importation of slaves into this Province, is [illegible] laid aside, I shall not pretend a refutation [illegible] arguments, generally brought in support of it; [illegible] you, to let that excellent rule given by [illegible] Saviour, to do to others, as you would, that [illegible] should do to you, have its due weight with [illegible]. Though the thought be shocking—for a few [illegible], suppose that you were trepanned away.—[illegible] husband from the dear wife of his bosom—the [illegible] from her affectionate husband—children from [illegible] fond parents—or parents from their tender and [illegible] offspring, whom, not an hour before, per[illegible] they were fondling in their arms, and in whom [illegible] were promising themselves much future happi[ness]. Suppose, I say that you were thus ravished [illegible] such a blissful situation, and plunged into mi[illegible] slavery, in a distant quarter of the globe: [illegible] you were even parted by your wife and [illegible], parents and brethren, manacled by your [illegible]—harrowing thought! And that after having [illegible] you to keener anguish!—Exposed to sale, with as little respect to decency, as though you were a brute! And after all this, if you were unwilling to part with all you held dear, even without the privilege of droping a tear over your dear friends, who were clinging round you; equally dreading the cruel seperation, which would probably prove an end of one, you must be plied with that conclusive argument, the cat-o'nine tails, to reduce you to what your inhuman masters would call Reason. Now, are you willing all this should befall you? If you can lay your hand on your breast, and solemnly affirm that you should; Why then go on and prosper! For your treatment of the Africans is an exact compliance with the abovementioned rule: But if, on the other hand, your conscience answers in the negative; Why, in the name of Heaven, will you suffer such a gross violation of that rule by which your conduct must be tried, in that day, in which you must be accountable for all your actions, to that impartial Judge, who hears the groans of the oppressed and who will, sooner or later, avenge them of their oppressors! I need not tell you, who are acquainted with the scriptures, that this kind of oppression is discountenanced by them. Many passages, to this purpose, might be adduced, but I shall, at present, mention but one, Exod chap 20 ver. 16 "And he that stealeth a man, and selleth him, or if he be found in his hand, he shall surely be put to death."

Though we are brought from a land of ignorance, it is as certain, that we are brought from a land of comparative innocence—from a land that flows, as it were, with Milk and Honey—and the greater part of us carried, where we are, not only deprived of every comfort of life: But subjected to all the tortures that a most cruel inquisitor could invent, or a capricious tyrant execute, and where we are likely, from the vicious examples before us, to become tenfold more the children of satan, than we should, probably, have been in our native country. Though 'tis true, that some of our wars proceed from petty discords among ourselves, it is as true, that the greater part of them, and those the most bloody, are occasioned, in consequence of the Slave trade.——Though many think we are happier here, than there, and will not allow us the privilege of judging for ourselves, they are certainly in an error. Every man is the best judge of his own happiness, and every heart best knows its own bitterness.——While I feel the loss of my country, and my friends, I can, by sad experience, adopt that expression in Prov. 25th Chap. 20 verse. As he that taketh away a garment in cold weather, and as vinegar upon nitre, so is he that singeth songs to a heavy heart. *Let me, who have now no less than eleven relatives suffering in bondage, beseech you good people, to attend to the request of a poor African, and consider the evil consequences, and gross heinousness of reducing to, and retaining in slavery a free people. Would you desire the preservation of your own liberty? As the first step let the oppressed Africans be liberated; then, and not till then, may you with confidence and consistency of conduct, look to Heaven for a blessing on your endeavours to knock the shackles with which your task masters are hampering you, from your own feet. On the other hand, if you are still determined to harden your hearts, and turn a deaf ear to our complaints, and the calls of God, in your present Calamities; Only be pleased to recollect the miserable* [illegible] *cruel servitude. Remember the fate of Miriam for despising an Ethiopean woman,* Numb. 12 *chap.* 1*st and* 10*th. verses. I need not point out the absurdity of your exertions for liberty, while you have slaves in your houses, for one minute's reflection is, methinks, sufficient for that purpose.—You who are deterred from liberating your slaves, by the consideration of the ill consequences to yourselves must remember, that we were not the cause of our being brought here. If the compelling us, against our wills, to come here was a sin; to retain us, without our consent, now we are here, is, I think, equally culpable, let ever so great inconvenience arise therefrom, accrue to you. Not to trespass too much on your patience; would you unite in this generous, this noble purpose of granting us liberty; Your honourable assembly, on our humble petition, would, I doubt not, free you from the trouble of us by making us grants in some back part of the country. If in this attempt to serve my countrymen, I have advanced any thing to the purpose, I pray it may not be the less noticed for coming from an African.*

CÆSAR SARTER.

Newbury Port, August 12th, 1774.

A writer in the London Advertiser, who takes the signature of Moderator, concludes an ingenious and spirited essay on American affairs, as follows:

SHOULD it happen, and that it may is not beyond the limits of possibility that a coalition of all the provinces of America should be formed into one unanimous alliance to oppose the measures of our government, and join in a determined resolution to cut off all intercourse [illegible] *dependant circumstances* with Great Britain; should the mystic roll of fate bring to pass this, which yet exists but in supposition, how fruitless then would be all our attempts to assert a sovereign right to America, or regain its loss: We might then remain envious spectators of her flourishing situation, and in that situation perceive the visible traces of ill policy and misguided administration. It has been advanced, with a view perhaps to future contingencies, that Great-Britain could suffer no loss, but, on the contrary, be a gainer by the independence of her American acquisitions. This assertion, considering the [illegible] rapid strides of America toward such a [illegible] is, in the true temporising spirit, exhorting a ready compliance with what is foreseen to be inevitable, for without a revolution in nature, or the supernatural aid of miracles, America may (and the belief is not singular) in future times have the seat of empire within herself, and instead of receiving laws from the island of Great Britain, may enforce a code of her own through her almost boundless continent. This conjecture is far from beyond probability; the present appearance of things carry with them an evident tendency towards its completion; the present perhaps is the important crisis, on which depends the continuance of our possession of the American colonies; or their total independence; they know their strength, and will if incensed, call it forth; our policy, therefore, should be to bind them by ties of affection to the mother country, by gentle, by persuasive measures, but on no account to harbour the most distant idea of adopting compulsatory ones; palliative means may possess them with [illegible]

Essay by Caesar Sarter, a former slave, published in the August 17, 1774, edition of the *Essex Journal and Merrimack Packet*, highlighting the contradictions between protests calling for liberty while continuing the horrid practices of slavery. This is an example of the growing abolitionist efforts and feelings taking root in New England immediately preceding the outbreak of the American Revolution. (Image: City of Newburyport)

CHAPTER 2
1775: FIRST BLOOD

ON APRIL 25, 2017, in Brookline, Massachusetts, a special flag-raising ceremony was held to honor three American Patriots who had responded 242 years earlier to the alarm that British troops were on the march headed out of Boston. These three men would take part in one of the most important founding moments of the American nation: the battles at Lexington and Concord, and the sixteen-mile running skirmish between local minutemen and British troops fleeing back to Boston, known as "Battle Road." That day, April 19, 1775, is still celebrated as Patriot's Day.

LEXINGTON, CONCORD, AND THE BATTLE ROAD (APRIL 19, 1775)

The three men being remembered in 2017 were unique. Of the ninety-nine men in the town's militia who left Brookline to confront the British on the Battle Road, Adam, Peter, and Prince were slaves. They marched with their owners to defend liberties they had never enjoyed themselves. Still, they marched and they fought. Adam's owner, Squire Isaac Gardner, would be killed in that fighting. But the only remembrance of their participation in those memorable events is a tablet in Brookline City Hall bearing the name of all the men of town who marched that day, commissioned by the Daughters of the American Revolution and dedicated in 1901. Listed last on the tablet, they are identified only by their first names. Such is the lost history of many who took part in the heroics of that fateful April day almost 250 years ago.

In fact, dozens of Black Patriots shared the honor and sufferings of that day. From the time the British left Boston, headed on the Bay Road toward Concord, freemen and slaves alike were active participants. Among the many riders who, along with Paul Revere and William Dawes, were alerting the local militia of the British movements was nine-year-old Abel Benson of Needham, who according to tradition rode to neighboring towns sounding a trumpet to awaken and muster the area's minutemen. Abel's father, William, obtained his freedom sometime in the 1760s, and his grandfather, Nero Benson, was part of the Massachusetts militia that fought against the Abenaki in 1725. Later, in the French and Indian War, he was a trumpeter in Captain Isaac Clark's militia company. Abel would later follow the family military tradition, enlisting in the Continental army at age fourteen in 1780 and being discharged at the end of the war in 1783.

The first intended destination of the British troops was Lexington. The Provincial Congress had been meeting in the area in defiance of the British, and intelligence was received that Patriot leaders John Hancock and Samuel Adams would be in the area. That proved true, as both men were dining at the parsonage of Reverend John Marrett and his wife, Madame Abigail Jones, having already fled the home of Reverend Jonas Clarke just off Lexington Green. However, the dinner was cut short when news arrived of British patrols roaming the area. The family's slave, Cuff Trot, sprang into action to hide the Patriot leaders. Trot, already a military veteran, had served under Captain William Jones at the end of the French and Indian War. His first task was to hide Hancock's ostentatious coach. He then escorted Hancock and Adams on a little-known path through the woods, delivering them safely to the home of another Patriot and out of the way of the British patrols and the hundreds of redcoat troops advancing toward Lexington. Cuff Trot would finally obtain his freedom in 1783, when Massachusetts courts ruled that slavery was incompatible with the state's constitution.

The contest for that freedom and equality would be launched just hours later at Lexington Green. Having waited for hours following the first alarm, Captain John Parker, the local militia leader, had already dismissed the militia but ordered them to be on alert. Many huddled at Buckman's Tavern across from the town green. When a scout returned around 4:15 a.m. warning that the British advance guard was nearby, Parker had his company drummer beat assembly and call the militia back to the ready. About seventy-five men showed up, including at least one from Woburn, who walked to Lexington on his own after hearing the alarm.

One other member standing with the Lexington militia that morning was thirty-five-year-old Prince Estabrook, one of the town's few slaves. He is believed to have been born and raised in slavery in the home of Benjamin Estabrook. While many colonies had policies prohibiting the enlistment of slaves in the militia, in practice such policies were disregarded in times of emergency. In New England, the presence of freemen and slaves in the militia, as with the earlier French and Indian War, wasn't unusual. So Prince Estabrook waited along with the rest of the Lexington militia to see what exactly the British would do in response to their presence.

It is important to note that Parker's militia company was in no way impeding the progress of the British troops. As they were standing on the town green and not the road, the British could have easily marched on the roads around them on either side and continued on to Concord without incident. Captain Parker made it clear to his men that he had no intention to provoke a fight, famously telling them, "Stand your ground; don't fire unless fired upon, but if they mean to have a war, let it begin here."[1]

It seemed at first that the British would march around, until one of the British officers rode up and ordered, "Lay down your arms, you damned rebels, and disperse!"[2] Rather than escalate the confrontation,

Captain Parker ordered the militia to disband and return home. At some point in the next few moments, a shot was fired from somewhere. Not knowing if it had come from their side or the militia, sporadic fire came from the British troops directed at the disbanding militia, then a full volley. A handful of militia members were able to return fire as they fled. Only one British soldier was wounded. As the smoke cleared the scene, eight men of the Lexington militia were dead or mortally wounded. Jonathan Harrington was able to walk to his house just yards away from the green, where he fell dead at his own doorstep into the arms of his wife.

Among the wounded at Lexington Green was Prince Estabrook, the first Black Patriot casualty of the Revolutionary War. His name was included in a list published by a Boston newspaper of the provincials killed and wounded throughout that bloody Patriots Day. Recovering from his wounds, Prince would continue to serve the Patriot cause in the following year at Fort Ticonderoga and throughout the rest of the war.

As the townspeople of Lexington quickly buried their dead and tended to the wounded, the British continued to march on toward Concord. By the time they arrived later that morning, hundreds of minutemen were assembled on a field on the outskirts of town. Men from Concord, Lincoln, Acton, Westford, and Bedford watched as the British searched around the town for cannons and other military supplies that Loyalist spies had reported were there. Four companies were sent across the North Bridge to the home of the Concord militia commander Colonel James Barrett. Two other companies were left to guard the bridge. The investigations at the Barrett farm were fruitless, as the military stores had been moved days before.

In contrast to numerical superiority the British had enjoyed at Lexington, the combined Patriot militia companies arriving around Concord began to match the strength of the redcoats. Watching from the muster field about three hundred yards from the Old North Bridge, fires could be seen in the town center. Uncertain whether the British were setting fire to the town, some of the local Concord leaders urged the militia to take action. Two leaders, Lieutenant Colonel John Robinson of Westford and Captain Isaac Davis of Acton, agreed to lead the militia column of about four hundred men toward town. The British troops guarding the road on the other side of the bridge withdrew as the militia descended double-file down the hill. Among their ranks marching toward the North Bridge were several Black Patriots, including Caesar Jones, Cambridge Moore, Caesar Prescott of Bedford, and Cesar Bason of Westford. Cambridge Moore accompanied his owner, Captain John Moore of Bedford, to Concord. Caesar Jones had been freed by Lieutenant Timothy Jones, and served that day and until the end of the war as a freeman.

There were less than a hundred British soldiers guarding the bridge, with the bulk of their forces still looking for contraband military supplies in and around Concord. As their commanders watched hundreds of provincial militiamen approaching the bridge, confused orders were yelled out. Soldiers fired warning shots and then a small volley, absent any orders to fire. Captain Davis and Private Abner Hosmer of Acton were killed, and several militiamen were injured. With only fifty yards separating the opposing lines, Major John Buttrick of Concord shouted, "Fire, fellow soldiers, for God's sake fire!"[3]

Fifty years later at the dedication of the minuteman monument at the Old North Bridge in Concord, Ralph Waldo Emerson described what happened next as "the shot heard round the world." Two British soldiers fell dead, and ten more were wounded. The overwhelmed redcoats fled back to the town center, running by their approaching commanding officers who were trying to investigate what had happened. The militia withdrew back up the hill, but other militia elements from other communities continued to flock toward the area.

As the British began their long retreat back to Boston, more militia companies joined the battle, swelling the rank of the Patriots. By the end of the day, thousands of minutemen and militia fighters swarmed the Bay

Road, including other Black Patriots. Caesar Ferrit and his son John caught up with the British as they came back through Lexington from Concord. Caesar was a veteran of the French and Indian War, and they both were enlisted in the Natick militia. One of his other sons, Thomas, headed toward the battle from the town of Dedham. A town historian later recorded that Caesar and John found cover in a home near the Lexington meetinghouse, where they shot at the British from the entryway and concealed themselves underneath the cellar stairs until the column had passed by.

Captain John Parker and the Lexington militia looked to settle the score against the British regulars for the killing of eight of their members earlier that morning by positioning themselves on a high rocky outcrop above the road now known as "Parker's Revenge." From there they fired on the column until British flankers approached. Despite his wounds, Prince Estabrook may have been with those from Lexington exacting the town's vengeance on those who had killed their friends and family earlier in the day. Two Black Patriot cousins from Lexington who are not known to have been in the morning engagement, Eli and Silas Burdoo, joined the later engagement.

By the time the British had reached Meriam's Corner and an area later termed the "Bloody Angle" outside Lexington, fire on the British column grew more intense. And the Black Patriot presence on the Battle Road continued to grow. Peter Ayres and John Chowen arrived from Lancaster, as did Ceasar Bailey from Deerfield. Pomp Blackman joined Samuel Craft from Newton along the way. The commander of the British column sent a rider back to Boston to inform General Thomas Gage of the escalating situation. The British column eventually received word that a relief force was on its way from Boston, but the relief column was delayed as the Committee for Safety ordered the planks taken up from the Brighton Bridge.

Some of the bloodiest fighting of the day occurred at Menotomy (modern day Arlington), which was also where some of the first British prisoners of war were captured by an unlikely crew of colonists. A British support train of wagons became lost and separated from the relief column. With the militia spread out over the area, seven men gathered at Cooper's Tavern to decide how best to capture the stragglers. These seven men were listed as "exempt" in the town militia rolls because of age. They chose from their own number a Black Patriot and veteran of the French and Indian War, David Lamson, to lead them. Hiding behind an embankment, they launched their ambush and demanded that the crew surrender. Attempting to flee the scene, the "Old Men of Menotomy" fired, killing several of the horses and two of the crew. The remainder fled to a nearby pond, where they threw their weapons into the water. They surrendered to an old woman nearby, Mother Batherick, who took them to the home of one of the local militia leaders. Today, a marker memorializes the spot where the Old Men of Menotomy launched their ambush. Today, David Lamson Way in Arlington honors the service and leadership that this Black Patriot gave that day.

The relief column eventually joined up with the ragged column returning from Concord, giving them cover, resupplying them, and caring for the walking wounded. Those British soldiers that could not be transported were left behind and well cared for by the towns that had been terrorized. Among those taken prisoner by the British was a Black Patriot, Caesar Augustus, who may have been one of the last Americans wounded that day. He was released in a prisoner exchange two months later, along with others taken captive along the Battle Road.

While the beleaguered British column was finally able to make it back to Boston, General Gage faced a new dilemma. Thousands of militia soldiers began pouring in from all over Massachusetts, New Hampshire, and Connecticut, including experienced veterans of the colonial wars. Gage and the British were now surrounded, and the siege of Boston was now underway. The Patriot resistance at Lexington and Concord, as well as the hasty retreat of the British back to Boston, energized the Patriot cause up and down the colonies. The British army now trapped in Boston exposed a weakness that could be exploited and emboldened Patriot leaders to consider new possible targets of opportunity.

This wave of patriotism and optimism, along with the demonstrations of bravery of Black Patriots during the historic events of April 19, prompted a fresh round of questioning regarding slavery and the status of freemen and slaves in many New England communities. William Bigelow, commander of the Worcester militia, freed his slaves shortly after the battles of Lexington and Concord. Cuff Ashport of Bridgewater in Plymouth County purchased his freedom from Nathan Mitchell and enlisted in the militia, joining the siege of Boston. Ashport would reenlist multiple times, serving five years during the American Revolution.

One man who was strongly inspired by the events at Lexington and Concord was Lemuel Haynes. He was born a freeman in 1753 to what is believed to be an African slave and a White indentured servant in the home of John Haynes of West Hartford, Connecticut. As an infant of five months he was indentured by his mother to Deacon David Rose of Granville, Massachusetts. A condition of the indenture was the requirement to attend to Lemuel's education. Both Deacon Rose and his wife were dedicated to the task, and he gained in his learning from the church, one of the few segments of colonial society where higher education was demanded.

In his later writings, Lemuel Haynes acknowledges the love and devotion of the couple who in all respects became his adoptive parents. As a learned man he followed the political developments of the day. Shortly after the Boston Tea Party and at the expiration of his indenture, he joined the Granville militia at age twenty-one. They were among the thousands of provincial militia soldiers who crowded around Boston to bottle up the British army in the wake of Lexington and Concord.

It was there at camp in Cambridge amongst common men defying tyranny that Haynes picked up his pen to express his feelings at this moment. What emerged is a thirty-seven-stanza ode to liberty, "The Battle of Lexington." What is remarkable about the poem is that he goes beyond the struggle for political liberty and frames the current conflict as one between human freedom versus slavery and tyranny:

The Awfull Conflict now begun
To rage with furious Pride
And Blood in great Effusion run
From many a wounded Side

For Liberty, each Freeman Strives
As its a Gift of God
And for it willing yield their Lives
And Seal it with their Blood

Thrice happy they who thus resign
Into the peacefull Grave
Much better there, in Death Confin'd
Than a Surviving Slave

This Motto may adorn their Tombs,
(Let tyrants come and view)
"We rather seek these silent Rooms
Than live as Slaves to You"[4]

Political disputes between colonists confronting the evils of slavery was not a new concept. This was an echo of the petitions for freedom by slaves to the colonial authorities both before and after the Boston Massacre. Now the struggle for freedom had begun. Those who pined for acknowledgement of their fundamental liberties not just as citizens but as humans, created equal both before God and the law, saw this nascent tempest as an opportunity to see those hopes realized. The American Revolution would literally mean freedom from bondage for thousands of those enslaved in the colonies.

As the Patriot numbers swelled around Boston, and throughout the entire war for that matter, these soldiers witnessed the sacrifice and heroism of Black Patriots who bore the same burdens and suffered the same hardships as them in the coming years. They too risked their lives facing the greatest military power in the world at that time, but the consequences of defeat for those enslaved was considerably higher. Now, they all had to fight and win, which required boldness and daring.

THE CAPTURE OF FORT TICONDEROGA (MAY 10, 1775)

One man who chose to take up that challenge was an ambitious Connecticut militia leader who presented an audacious plan to the Massachusetts Committee of Safety. His name was Benedict Arnold. Just three weeks after Lexington and Concord he requested permission to take some men from the Patriot forces around Boston to attack the vulnerable but strategic British post of Fort Ticonderoga on Lake Champlain. The fort was lightly manned, and it controlled water traffic on the Hudson River from Canada to New York City. Capturing it would protect New England from being cut off from their sister colonies. He was authorized to recruit troops from around Boston for the attack.

Arnold found himself in a race with another Patriot leader, Ethan Allen of the Green Mountain Boys. Operating much closer to Fort Ticonderoga in the area that would shortly be declared as Vermont, Allen could organize his forces quicker and closer to the intended target. Appraised that he faced competition that was well ahead of him, Arnold sped on horse to Allen's operating base in Bennington. They agreed to co-lead the assault. A joint force headed not just to Ticonderoga but two more strategic points,

Crown Point and Skenesborough. The combined assault unit had several Black Patriots in its number, including two of Ethan Allen's Green Mountain Boys, Primas Black and Epheram Blackman.

What the Patriots found at Fort Ticonderoga was literally an open door. Arnold and Allen stormed in with their soldiers, surprising everyone in the fort's garrison. There was only one injury among the Americans. When Allen burst into the sleeping commanding officer's quarters, he was asked by what authority he had seized the fort. "In the name of the Great Jehovah and the Continental Congress,"[5] was Allen's reply.

The strategy and targets of the assault proved to be brilliant, very likely well beyond anything that Arnold or Allen recognized at the time. First, it gave the early Patriot cause its first victory. Second, the cannons and other military supplies captured at Fort Ticonderoga would later prove critical for the Continental army. Third, a critical iron forge and milling operation commandeered at Skenesborough, along with the slaves and indentured servants who provided the manpower, was used in the coming months to build the first American navy. The occupation of Fort Ticonderoga, command of Lake Champlain, and the slave-built boats from Skenesborough would keep the British army in Canada in place and unable to assist the besieged army in Boston.

FIRST NAVAL ENGAGEMENT AT MACHIAS (JUNE 11–12, 1775)

News of the momentous events in Massachusetts and Fort Ticonderoga spread through the colonies, fueling divisions but raising hopes and fortitude. And patriotic fervor was rising in surprising places.

With the British army surrounded and vastly outnumbered in Boston, their only source of support was now by sea. General Gage dispatched ships up and down the east coast, searching for essential supplies.

One Tory merchant, Captain Ichabod Jones, was dispatched north with two sloops to sell his wares. That money would be used to purchase lumber that would then be sold to the British in Boston. Accompanying them to prevent any problems was the armed Royal Navy cutter *Margaretta*.

Problems quickly arose. Their destination was lumber-rich Machias, Maine (at that time part of Massachusetts territory). An old Boston news item from December 1771 reported that some of the fiercely independent citizens of Machias had assaulted an appointed colonial officer—an appointment they didn't approve of—and threatened the official if he took up the office. These were the townspeople that were to buy Captain Jones's wares. The town gathered to discuss whether to buy the items. Knowing that the proceeds would be used ultimately for lumber for the besieged British in Boston, they agreed to not buy his wares. That was met with a threat that if they did decline, the *Margaretta* would sail in and fire on the town. This didn't have the intended effect. Rather, some of the men hatched a plan to seize the ships, Captain Jones, and the British on board the *Margaretta*. As the plan was about to be executed, a disturbance prematurely alerted Jones to the plot. A race ensued back to the ships, with the villagers firing on the fleeing British officers.

A local man, Jeremiah O'Brien, along with his slave Richard Earle, led the party and seized the two sloops. Sailing one of them up to the *Margaretta*, one of the men shot the captain of the ship, and the warship was quickly boarded by the Machias townsmen. The captured ship was renamed *Machias Freedom* and put into service in the Patriot cause. Richard Earle was counted among the heroes responsible for one of the first American naval victories of the war. London Atus, the slave of the local parson, was dispatched by the town to alert the Committee of Safety to their victory. Atus later enlisted in Colonel John Allen's rangers, protecting the area from the British and their Indian allies. After the war, both the newly freed Richard Earle and London Atus founded an independent Black community called Atusville.

THE BATTLE OF BUNKER AND BREED'S HILL (JUNE 17, 1775)

News of the events in Machias was quickly overshadowed by dramatic events in Boston just days later. With approximately twenty thousand Patriot militiamen now encircling the town, General Gage knew he had to act to protect his position within the city to counter the growing threat. He developed a plan to seize the heights above Charlestown. This would allow operations closer to the Patriot headquarters in Cambridge and prevent the area's occupation by the militias and the threat of artillery from that position firing into British positions in Boston.

The Committee of Safety, however, got wind of the plan. General Artemas Ward, the top commander commissioned by the Massachusetts Provincial Congress, decided to preempt the British plans by seizing the area first and setting up a defensive position. On June 16, 1775, he ordered Colonel William Prescott to take a detachment from his regiment to Bunker Hill in silence and under the cover of darkness to build and man a defensive redoubt. The detachment, composed of Prescott's regiment, the regiments of James Frye and Ebenezer Bridge, and about two hundred men from Connecticut led by Captain Thomas Knowlton—in all, around a thousand men—gathered at Cambridge Common, where Harvard president Dr. Samuel Langdon gave a prayer. The column set off for Charlestown Neck with a day's worth of rations, fifteen musket cartridges per man, and wagons carrying pick axes and shovels.

It's likely that none of the Patriot leaders could have anticipated how important and decisive the next twenty-four hours would be for the American cause.

Once Prescott's column arrived it was decided that Bunker Hill would not be suitable for the redoubt; instead Breed's Hill was chosen, which was closer to Boston. Once the engineers set the boundaries of the redoubt, the men went to work around midnight as quietly as possible to avoid rousing the attention of the British. Men from both Massachusetts and Connecticut were sent down to Charlestown to stand guard to warn of any approaching British units.

A number of Black Patriots crossed Charlestown Neck that night with Colonel Prescott and manned the newly-constructed redoubt: Barzillai Lew, London Citizen, Prince Hull, Cato Tufts, Peter Oliver Philip Abbot, Titus Coburn, Scipio Gray, Cuff Chambers, James Fiske, Pero Hall, Prince Johonnot, Robert Currier, Salem Poor, Peter Poor, and many others. A study commissioned by the National Park Service by George Quintal and published in February 2002 found more than a hundred Black Patriots who fought at Bunker Hill. Quintal found that five were veterans of Lexington, Concord, and the Battle Road: Cesar Bason, Jeffrey Hemmingway, Peter Salem, Cuff Whittemore, and Cato Wood. As many as three dozen are believed to have been with the regiments that built the redoubt.

Sunrise revealed their overnight activity to the surprised British command, alerted by the HMS *Lively* firing its cannons on the Patriot redoubt. First light also revealed to Colonel Prescott the exposed position of the redoubt, vulnerable to being flanked. A breastwork extending to the left of the redoubt by about a hundred yards was quickly started. By mid-morning artillery fire from British ships and from Copp's Hill across the river in Boston landed around the redoubt with little effect. Looking down from Breed's Hill, considerable activity could be seen in Boston, with boats and barges that would soon be filled with redcoats lined up on the shore across the river. A few hundred New Hampshire troops eventually arrived to reinforce the Patriots in the redoubt, with the remainder of the two New Hampshire regiments under Colonels John Stark and James Reed to follow. Even before arriving, Stark ordered a new position to be erected two hundred yards behind the redoubt and the breastwork to the Mystic River, with orders to build a strong fortification on a small stretch of beach along the river. A reinforced rail fence was thrown up and manned by the New Hampshire men, including Jude Hall and Peter Kent.

The redoubt and the adjacent breastwork were attached to the rail fence in the rear by a diagonal position, with several artillery flèches manned by Massachusetts and Connecticut troops. As hundreds of redcoats began arriving on the Charlestown peninsula, additional companies and regiments began to appear, braving the cannon fire raining down on the small strip of land that connected the route from Cambridge to Charlestown. The arrival of new Patriot troops manning new positions prompted a call for British reinforcements. This delay allowed more Patriot reinforcements to arrive. While some companies stalled for fear of the British artillery targeting the Neck, others moved on and took their place among the four positions.

Shortly before the first British attack commenced, Colonel John Stark appeared with the remainder of the two New Hampshire regiments, taking their position at the rail fence that now ran down to the Mystic River along the bottom of Bunker Hill to protect the left flank of the Patriot line. Reed's regiment had just arrived in Cambridge two days earlier, including Jude Hall and Peter Kent. Captain Thomas Knowlton of Connecticut positioned his men on the diagonal line between the rail fence and the redoubt and breastwork, joined by Massachusetts soldiers from Colonel Jonathan Brewer's newly arrived regiment that included James Huzzey, Jacob Speen, and Cuff Nimrod. Some three thousand redcoats had disembarked from the barges and the boats on the riverbank by Charlestown. Facing them were half that number, largely from New England farming stock and many seeing action for the first time. The Patriots readied themselves as Gage's soldiers aligned in battle formation, stepping off around 2:30 in the afternoon. Two British columns set off toward the Patriot line, one headed by General Robert Pigot against the redoubt and the breastwork, and the other led by General William Howe, leading many companies of experienced light infantry, grenadiers, and marines against the rail fence. Howe also sent his best troops to the position on the beach below the rail fence, hoping to turn the Patriot line. Manning the hastily built stone wall in this small space were Peter Brown, Ezra Fuller, Aaron Oliver, and Nathan Weston. Joseph Anthony and Fortune Burnee of Captain Luke Drury's company of Colonel Jonathan Brewer's regiment took their place with the New Hampshire men at the rail fence, as did Thomas Dority, Cato Fair, Caesar Hammon, and Plato Lambert from Colonel Jonathan Ward's regiment. Mark Anthony, Joseph Demas, Charles Jarvis, and Boston Osborn of Colonel Moses Little's regiment were spread out on their arrival amongst the redoubt, breastwork, and the diagonal.

Aware of their limited ammunition, Prescott and other commanders warned to hold their fire until the British were in close range and the order was given to fire. One unlucky soldier fired prematurely and received the flat side of his commander's sword on the top of his head in return for his anxiety.[6] As the British arrived in close range an order was given to fire, and the Patriot defenses erupted in a wall of smoke and fire. The British line wavered, and in moments the redcoats were in retreat, staggering back down the hill, leaving many of their comrades dead and wounded. The British columns had advanced without any field artillery cover, as the wrong ammunition had been sent over. Some British units suffered more than three-quarter casualties.

Having retreated and regrouped, fifteen minutes later another assault following the same plan was launched, but the British troops were again repulsed, leaving behind even more dead and wounded. So far, all of the Patriot positions on the line had held, but ammunition was quickly running out. By the time the third attack came around 3:30 p.m., the British had received the proper ammunition for their field artillery and positioned it to fire into the left flank of the breastwork position, which forced the men there to retreat into the redoubt—the target of the main British effort in this third and final attack. As the red wave moved up the hill yet toward the redoubt, Colonel Prescott withheld the order to fire until they were only twenty yards away. The Patriot volley was true, but not returned. The redcoats charged the redoubt without stopping to fire. The Patriots had few bayonets, and little to no ammunition. Much of the fighting was now hand to hand. While the line at the rail fence held, the redoubt did not. By 4:00 p.m., Colonel Prescott ordered a retreat. Companies from two Massachusetts regiments that had arrived late the battlefield and were positioned between Breed and Bunker Hills were able to cover the withdrawal from the redoubt. Among these troops were Isaiah Barjonah, Jack Briant, Micah Bumpo, Pomp Green, Cornelius Lenox, Nathaniel Small, and Prince Sutton.

It was here, as the redoubt was collapsing and the redcoats crashed over the walls, that some of the most heroic moments were witnessed. Dr. Joseph Warren, the most senior Patriot political leader in Massachusetts, who had shown up at the battle as a volunteer, was instantly killed with a shot to the head. At least three Black Patriots were also among the dead. Philip Abbot of Andover, a slave of Nathan Abbot, was killed. Also counted among the dead that day were Cesar Bason, who had been at the Old North Bridge in Concord for "the shot heard round the world" six weeks before, and Peter Poor from New Hampshire. A town history records Cesar Bason's last moments based on a firsthand witness:

> In the battle he found his powder was nearly gone, and putting in his last charge, he exclaimed, "Now Cesar, give 'em one more." He fired and was himself shot, and fell back into the trench.[7]

Some of the highest honors of the day went to several Black Patriots who fought with extraordinary courage. Jamaica James was wounded in the arm, and one of his officers testified years later to having seen the wound. Prince Johonnot, one of those who crossed Charlestown Neck in the middle of the night with Colonel Prescott to build the redoubt, was also wounded. Jude Hall reported that during the battle he "was thrown headlong by a cannon ball striking near him."[8]

Peter Salem of Framingham was singled out for valor. Fighting first at the breastwork then later in the redoubt, witnesses attest that when British Major John Pitcairn climbed on top of the entrenchment he was immediately cut down by Salem. The pair had previously faced each other in battle. Major Pitcairn had been one of the commanders of the expedition to Concord two months before. Peter Salem entered the fight on the Battle Road with his militia unit in the fighting at Meriam's Corner outside Concord during the British retreat. When the Provincial Council announced in May 1775 that no slave could be enlisted, Salem's owner promptly freed him so that he could continue to fight.

One early Bunker Hill history published by Samuel Swett around the fiftieth anniversary of the battle describes Peter Salem's participation on that day:

> During the action, he with others, was sent from Capt. Drury's company, as a support to Col. Prescott in the redoubt. He reached the redoubt just as Prescott's men had spent their last powder; and with a single charge in his gun, and perhaps another in his powder horn. Just then, in the language of Judge Maynard, "I saw a British officer come up with some pomp, and he cried out, 'Surrender you damned rebels!' But Prescott made a little motion with his hand, and that was the last word the Briton spoke; he fell at once." There is concurrence of testimony which leaves no doubt that this shot was fired by Peter Salem. Maj. Pitcairn fell into the arms of his son, who bore him off to a boat, and thence to a house in Prince Street, Boston, where he died.[9]

When General George Washington arrived in Cambridge to take command of his newly adopted Continental army two weeks after the battle, Peter Salem was reportedly presented to the new commander in chief. For years, the National Park Service displayed a musket that was claimed to be the one used by Peter Salem at Bunker Hill, but the musket disappeared from their inventory years ago after being sent out for repairs.

Seventy-five years after the battle, Peter Salem's heroics were remembered by the celebrated orator Edward Everett, who emphasized that the recently completed Bunker Hill Monument was a testament to all the Patriots who fought that day:

> It is a monument of the day, of the event, of the Battle of Bunker Hill; of all the brave men who shared its perils,— alike of Prescott and Putnam and warrant, the chiefs of the day, and the colored man, Salem, who is reported to have shot the gallant Pitcairn, as he mounted the parapet.[10]

Another Black Patriot noted for his heroics at the battle was Cuff Whittemore of Menotomy. He served with the Cambridge militia on the Battle Road, and shortly thereafter enlisted as an "eight-month man" for the siege of Boston. His unit was in the thick of the battle at Bunker Hill, where his regimental commander Colonel Thomas Gardner was killed. Of Cuff's actions on that day, historian Samuel Swett recorded that he

> fought bravely in the redoubt. He had a ball through his hat on Bunker Hill, fought to the last, and when compelled to retreat, though wounded, the splendid arms of the British officers were prizes too tempting for him to come off empty handed, he seized the sward of one of the slain in the redoubt, and came of the trophy, which in a few days he unromantically sold.

Cuff continued to serve in the Patriot cause after Bunker Hill and, as we will see later demonstrated greater heroism in the war.

It is believed that Asaba Grosvenor, the slave of Thomas Grosvenor of Connecticut, is depicted in the famous John Trumbull painting *The Death of Dr. Joseph Warren at Bunker Hill*, memorializing their respective roles in the battle. Trumbull watched the battle through a looking glass from Roxbury, where his militia regiment was stationed at the time. The painting resides at the Yale University Art Gallery in New Haven, Connecticut.

Another soldier at the battle, fifteen-year-old John Greenwood, wrote in his journal of the encouragement he received on his way to the battle from one unnamed, wounded Black Patriot amidst the blood and death as the battle's casualties were brought back to their lines:

> Everywhere the greatest terror and confusion seemed to prevail, and as I ran along the road leading to Bunker Hill it was filled with chairs and wagons, bearing the wounded and dead, while groups of men were employed assisting others, not badly injured, to walk. Never having beheld such a sight before, I felt very much frightened, and would have given the world if I had not enlisted as a soldier; I could positively feel my hair stand on end.
>
> Just as I came near the place, a negro man, wounded in the back of his neck, passed me and, his collar being open and he not having anything on except his shirt and trousers, I saw the wound plainly and the blood running down his back. I asked him if it hurt him much as he did not seem to mind it; he said no, that he was only going to get a plaster put on it, *and meant to return.* You cannot conceive what encouragement this immediately gave me; I began to feel brave and like a soldier from that moment, and fear never troubled me afterward during the whole war.[11]

One other name has to be mentioned at this point, that of Salem Poor of Andover, because his example on the field of battle likely changed the course of the war. He was born in slavery, but purchased his freedom in 1769. According to local Andover tradition, he was responsible for shooting Grenadier Lieutenant Colonel James Abercrombie, the highest ranked British officer killed during the Battle of Bunker Hill.

THE CONFLICT OVER BLACK PATRIOT TROOPS

The importance of Salem Poor and his importance on the course of the war needs to be seen in the context of how the service of Black Patriots was handled in the opening months of the conflict. As previously mentioned, prior to Bunker Hill on May 20, 1775, the Massachusetts Committee of Safety ordered that "no slaves are to be admitted in this army upon any consideration whatever," making clear their determination that recruiting slaves would "be inconsistent with the principles that are to be supported."[12]

Just days after the Battle of Bunker Hill, the Continental Congress in Philadelphia adopted the militia units around Boston as the new Continental army, with General George Washington appointed as its commander in chief. He arrived in Cambridge to assume command on July 2, 1775, just two weeks after Bunker Hill. The issue of Black Patriot enlistment came up quickly in the newly established headquarters; the day after a July 9 council of war, Washington's adjutant, Horatio Gates, issued instructions to Massachusetts recruiters, saying, "You are not to enlist any deserter from the ministerial Army, nor any Stroller, Negro or Vagabond."[13]

Those instructions, undoubtedly ordered or approved by Washington himself, would seem to have to resolve the matter. But the reality was that dozens of Black Patriots were already serving around Boston, many having already fought at Lexington, Concord, the Battle Road, and Bunker

Hill, and more were arriving every day with units from Rhode Island, Connecticut, and New Hampshire. And some of those already serving, such as Peter Salem and Cuff Whittemore, were the veterans of two battles. Prince Estabrook, who was wounded by the first shots of the war on Lexington Green, had been briefly called up again with his militia company immediately after Bunker Hill. Caesar Augustus had been wounded on the Battle Road and was a prisoner of war. Primas Black and Ephraim Blackman of Ethan Allen's Green Mountain Boys shared in the honor of being part of the stunning victory at Fort Ticonderoga.[14] And Philip Abbot, Cesar Bason, and Peter Poor were killed in action and buried by the British in mass graves with their fellow fallen comrades on the field of battle on Bunker Hill. These recruitment instructions were running headlong into actualities already in place in the new Continental army, which were unlikely to go away, notwithstanding the orders handed down from Washington's headquarters.

As was true during the Colonial era, policies on the matter were regularly contradicted by practice. In the Continental Congress, the stiffest opposition to Black recruitment, regardless of free or slave status, came from the two colonies with the closest attachment to the Crown: South Carolina and Georgia. On September 26 in Philadelphia, Edward Rutledge of South Carolina attempted to force the matter by introducing a resolution to expel all Black Patriots, regardless of status or service, from the Continental army. His motion was promptly voted down, but it did not put the matter to rest.

In correspondence, John Adams inquired of General William Heath about reports of the condition of the army around Boston, namely youths, old men, and Black soldiers who were being paid but allegedly not fit for service. General Heath responded by assuring that the Massachusetts troops were "Robust, Agile, and as fine Fellows in General as I ever would wish to see in the field."[15] An October 24 letter from General John Thomas to John Adams was more direct:

> We have some negroes; but I look on them, in general, equally serviceable with other men for fatigue; and, in action, many of them have proved themselves brave.[16]

Washington brought the matter up during a meeting with three members of the Continental Congress who arrived in Cambridge: Benjamin Franklin, Benjamin Harrison, and Thomas Lynch. The question was whether Black enlistment, and especially enlistment of slaves, should be prohibited altogether. The conclusion was that there should be no such enlistments. This decision was enshrined in a November 12 order to recruiters, stating that neither "negroes, boys unable to bear arms, nor old men unfit to endure the fatigues of the campaign, are to be enlisted."[17] But this order wasn't to last.

Which brings us back to Salem Poor. The local commanders around Boston were likely aware of these discussions and had witnessed firsthand many of the heroics and conduct of the Black Patriots in their units. But now these Black Patriot battle veterans, who were fighting for more than political liberties and facing more dire consequences in the event of defeat, were to be excluded? It's unknown if what happened next was driven by the decisions made by the Continental Congress and the general command, but it seems very likely.

A petition by fourteen officers was sent to the Massachusetts legislature, dated December 5, 1775, singling out Salem Poor's bravery and leadership during the Battle of Bunker Hill:

> The subscribers beg leave to report to your Honorable House (which we do in justice to the character of so Brave a Man), that, under Our Own observation, we declare that a Negro Man, called Salem Poor, of Col. Frye's regiment, Capt. Ames company, in the late battle at Charlestown, behaved like an Experienced officer, as well as an Excellent Soldier. To set forth

> particulars of his conduct would be tedious. We Would Only beg leave to say in the Person of this said Negro Centers a brave and gallant soldier. The reward due to so great and distinguished a character, we submit to the Congress.

Among the petitioners were two colonels, including William Prescott, the overall commander of the Bunker Hill operation. The petition was read in the legislature on December 21, and undoubtedly news of it and perhaps a copy even made its way to the army's headquarters in Cambridge. The implied question posed by the officers' petition put a fine point to the matter: In the early days of this nascent revolution, as winter was beginning to set in and many of the eight-month enlistments were about to expire, was General Washington prepared to sacrifice the continued contributions of "a brave and gallant soldier" such as Salem Poor and other Black Patriots?

LORD DUNSMORE AND THE BATTLE OF GREAT BRIDGE (DECEMBER 9, 1775)

Down south in Washington's home of Virginia, the British were giving yet another reason to reconsider the exclusion of Black Patriots from enlistment. The British colonial governor of Virginia, Lord Dunmore, who had fled Williamsburg in June and taken refuge with his family off the coast of Norfolk on the Royal Navy ship *William*, launched a last-ditch measure on November 14 issuing a proclamation calling for slaves to abandon their Patriot masters and rally to the Crown's standard. It is believed that one thousand to two thousand slaves escaped to the British lines in short order. There were enough able-bodied men from these refugees for the British to form a short-lived all-Black military unit, called the Ethiopian Regiment, which numbered around three hundred members by December 1775.

While much has been made in some quarters about Lord Dunmore's proclamation and the formation of the Ethiopian Regiment contrasted with Continental army policy and the continuation of slavery in the states, the reality was that the regiment never proved any kind of military challenge and largely doomed most of those who responded to Dunmore's hollow edict. Again, his proclamation was issued when he was already effectively in exile. Dunmore had also made no provisions to accommodate the flood of escaped slaves to their lines, leaving most to fend for themselves. The vast majority would be dead from starvation and disease within months and the survivors abandoned when Dunmore eventually fled, never to return.

As for the Ethiopian Regiment, it would be put to the test at the Battle of Great Bridge on the only road that ran between Norfolk, one of the last Tory strongholds, and North Carolina. At the bridge that crossed the Elizabeth River, Dunmore's Loyalist troops had built a fortification called Fort Murray on the south side of the river and fortified the bridge. The Virginia militia, including the Culpeper Minutemen, was established on the north side of the river. The battle that took place on December 9 was unique in at least two respects. First, it was a Patriots-versus-Loyalists affair with Virginians on both sides. Second, it was the first battle of the Revolutionary War where freemen and slaves in both camps would oppose one another.

The battle began with the Ethiopian Regiment being sent down river as a distraction from the main British attack across the bridge. On the Patriot side, sentinels were posted on watch at the bridge, including a freeman, William "Billy" Flora of Portsmouth, serving in the Second Virginia Regiment, who would prove one of the heroes of the battle. Captain Thomas Nash later recounted his actions that day:

> Flora, a colored man, was the last sentinel that came in the breastwork, and he did not leave his post until he had fired

> several times. Billy had to cross a plank to get to the breastwork, and had fairly passed over it when he was seen to turn back, and deliberately take up the plank after him, amidst a shower of musket balls.[18]

Colonial militias were known for firing and fleeing quickly. The British, hoping to exploit this, sent a company of their shock troops, grenadiers under command of Captain Charles Fordyce, over the bridge first. But the Patriots held their fire until they were only about fifty yards away. Fordyce and about half of his men were killed, and their charge dissipated. The Patriots stormed over the bridge in pursuit of the British troops now fleeing back to Fort Murray, with the skilled frontier marksmen of the Culpeper Minutemen harassing the British retreat with their rifles. Overnight, the British retreated back to Norfolk.

At least two enslaved men, James Bass and Ned Streater, participated in the Battle of Great Bridge on the Patriot side. Both later enlisted in the Continental army. As for the Ethiopian Regiment comprised of runaway slaves, most of those who escaped following Lord Dunmore's proclamation were abandoned by the British on Gwynn Island when Dunmore sailed for New York and died of disease within a few months. In March 1777, British General William Howe ordered all Black and biracial soldiers discharged from the British army in America.

The petition of the Massachusetts officers on behalf of Salem Poor had given General Washington an opportunity to reconsider the status of Black Patriots already serving in the Continental army and the state militias. In the very first year of the American Revolution, Black Patriots had shown by their service at Lexington, Concord, the Battle Road, Fort Ticonderoga, Machias, Great Bridge—and in the ongoing siege of the British around Boston—their honor, bravery, utility, and equality. In the coming year, Black Patriots would prove themselves even more indispensable to the American cause.

One of Washington's last orders of 1775 was to allow the reenlistment of Black Patriots. He wrote to John Hancock, the President of the Continental Congress, on December 31, notifying Congress of his order and hoping they would approve:

> It has been represented to me, that the free negroes who have served in this army are very much dissatisfied at being discarded. As it is to be apprehended that they may seek employ in the Ministerial [British] Army, I have presumed to depart from the resolution respecting them, and have given license for their being enlisted. If this is disapproved by Congress, I will put a stop to it.

Additional actions in 1775, including the American invasion of Canada, would expand the war even beyond the siege lines still maintained around Boston. The events of 1776 would prove the wisdom of Washington's change of heart. The Continental army and the American cause needed all the "brave and gallant soldiers" that could be mustered.

Hundreds and eventually thousands of Black Patriots from all over the nascent states answered that call.

A plaque at Brookline (MA) City Hall honoring the militia members from the community that marched to challenge the British column returning from Lexington and Concord on April 19, 1775. The names of three Black Patriots are listed, all slaves, identified by only their first names and their owners: Prince, Adam, and Peter. Adam's owner, Major Isaac Gardner, was killed in the fighting. (Image: Patrick S. Poole)

Monument recognizing the service of the "Old Men of Menotomy," who captured part of the British column headed out from Boston to support and relieve the retreating redcoats from Lexington and Concord. The "Old Men" were led by Black Patriot David Lamson, a veteran of the French and Indian War. (Image: Patrick S. Poole)

Monument honoring three Black Patriots from Bedford, Massachusetts, in the town's Old Burying Ground. Local histories claim that two of the men, Cambridge Moore and Caesar Jones, marched with the militia and minutemen companies to nearby Concord on April 19, 1775, where they engaged the retreating British. (Image: Patrick S. Poole)

Monument in front of Buckman's Tavern honoring Prince Estabrook, a member of Capt. John Parker's militia company who was wounded in the first shots of the American Revolution on Lexington Green. A slave at the time, he would receive his freedom and served throughout the entire war. He died in 1830 and is buried at Ashby First Parish Burial Ground in Ashby, Massachusetts, beneath a military marker. (Images: Patrick S. Poole)

Engraving depicting the fatal shooting of British Major Pitcairn by Peter Salem during the Battle of Bunker Hill. (Image: Wikimedia Commons)

Monument in the town square of Hollis, New Hampshire, honoring their Revolutionary War and War of 1812 dead. At Bunker Hill, a company of Hollis men were in the heat of the battle and suffered eight killed in action—more than any other town represented there. One of those killed in action at Bunker Hill and listed on the Hollis monument is Peter Poor, a Black Patriot. Jacob Danforth, another Black Patriot, also served in the same company at Bunker Hill. (Images: Patrick S. Poole)

Letter signed by eight Bunker Hill commanders sent to the Massachusetts state legislature commending the performance of Salem Poor during the battle, describing him as "a brave and gallant soldier," requesting appropriate recognition for the Black Patriot's service in the battle. (Image: Massachusetts State Archives)

INSTRUCTIONS for the Officers of the ſeveral Regiments of the *Maſſachuſetts-Bay* Forces, who are immediately to go upon the Recruiting Service.

YOU are not to Enliſt any Deſerter from the Miniſterial Army, nor any Stroller, Negro or Vagabond, or Perſon ſuſpected of being an Enemy to the Liberty of America, nor any under Eighteen Years of Age.

As the Cauſe is the beſt that can engage Men of Courage and Principle to take up Arms; ſo it is expected that none but ſuch will be accepted by the Recruiting Officer: The Pay, Proviſion, &c. being ſo ample, it is not doubted but the Officers ſent upon this Service, will without Delay compleat their reſpective Corps, and March the Men forthwith to Camp.

You are not to Enliſt any Perſon who is not an American-born, unleſs ſuch Perſon has a Wife and Family, and is a ſettled Reſident in this Country.

The Perſons you Enliſt, muſt be provided with good and compleat Arms.

Given at the Head Quarters at Cambridge, this 10th Day of July 1775.

HORATIO GATES, Adjutant-General.

Order by Gen. Horatio Gates on July 10, 1775—one week after Washington's arrival in Boston to take command of the Continental Army—prohibiting enlistments of "any deserter from the ministerial Army, nor any Stroller, Negro or Vagabond." Many New England units already had Black Patriots mustered into their ranks, and the order was rescinded by the Continental Congress the following January at Washington's request. (Image: Library of Congress)

Monument erected to William Flora in his hometown of Portsmouth, Virginia. Flora's bravery during the Battle of Great Bridge (December 9, 1775) contributed to the Patriot victory in the first land battle in Virginia. The monument is near where his home and business were formerly located. (Image: Patrick S. Poole)

By his Excellency the Right Honourable JOHN *Earl of* DUNMORE, *his Majeſty's Lieutenant and Governour-General of the Colony and Dominion of* Virginia, *and Vice-Admiral of the ſame:*

A PROCLAMATION.

AS I have ever entertained Hopes that an Accommodation might have taken Place between *Great Britain* and this Colony, without being compelled, by my Duty, to this moſt diſagreeable, but now abſolutely neceſſary Step, rendered ſo by a Body of armed Men, unlawfully aſſembled, firing on his Majeſty's Tenders, and the Formation of an Army, and that Army now on their March to attack his Majeſty's Troops, and deſtroy the well-diſpoſed Subjects of this Colony: To defeat ſuch treaſonable Purpoſes, and that all ſuch Traitors, and their Abetters, may be brought to Juſtice, and that the Peace and good Order of this Colony may be again reſtored, which the ordinary Courſe of the civil Law is unable to effect, I have thought fit to iſſue this my Proclamation, hereby declaring, that until the aforeſaid good Purpoſes can be obtained, I do, in Virtue of the Power and Authority to me given, by his Majeſty, determine to execute martial Law, and cauſe the ſame to be executed throughout this Colony; and to the End that Peace and good Order may the ſooner be reſtored, I do require every Perſon capable of bearing Arms to reſort to his Majeſty's STANDARD, or be looked upon as Traitors to his Majeſty's Crown and Government, and thereby become liable to the Penalty the Law inflicts upon ſuch Offences, ſuch as Forfeiture of Life, Confiſcation of Lands, *&c. &c.* And I do hereby farther declare all indented Servants, Negroes, or others (appertaining to Rebels) free, that are able and willing to bear Arms, they joining his Majeſty's Troops, as ſoon as may be, for the more ſpeedily reducing this Colony to a proper Senſe of their Duty, to his Majeſty's Crown and Dignity. I do farther order, and require, all his Majeſty's liege Subjects to retain their Quitrents, or any other Taxes due, or that may become due, in their own Cuſtody, till ſuch Time as Peace may be again reſtored to this at preſent moſt unhappy Country, or demanded of them for their former ſalutary Purpoſes, by Officers properly authoriſed to receive the ſame.

GIVEN under my Hand, on Board the Ship William, *off* Norfolk, *the 7th Day of* November, *in the 16th Year of his Majeſty's Reign.*

DUNMORE.

GOD SAVE THE KING.

Proclamation dated November 7, 1775, issued by exiled Virginia royal colonial governor Lord Dunmore, promising freedom to slaves of "rebels" who defect to British lines and fight for the Crown. Many, if not most, who acted on Dunmore's proclamation would be dead by the time Dunmore sailed for England in June 1776. (Image: Wikimedia Commons)

CHAPTER 3

1775–1776: INDEPENDENCE AND THE CRISIS

AT GENERAL GEORGE Washington's headquarters in Cambridge, Massachusetts, the morning of January 1, 1776, marked an important moment as the new Grand Union flag was raised for the first time. Since his arrival at Cambridge the previous July, just two weeks after the pivotal Battle of Bunker Hill, he immediately faced the monumental task of turning a gaggle of varied New England militias into a Continental army. While he had the British bottled up in Boston and had more than twice the number of soldiers (sixteen thousand to Britian's seven thousand), he confronted several seemingly insurmountable problems. First was that many of the "eight-month men" who had enlisted following the battles of Lexington and Concord were now returning home as their enlistments expired. The Continental Congress meeting in Philadelphia had also promised supplies for the army, but most of the colonies were preparing for their own defense with few supplies to spare for the army.

That same day news arrived from England. King George III's proclamation outright rejected the Olive Branch Petition sent by Congress after Bunker Hill, making clear that British policy with respect to its rebellious colonies would be war to put a decisive end to the uprising. Soon, hundreds of British ships and thousands of new troops would likely be headed toward Boston Harbor to reinforce General Howe. Short on artillery and gunpowder, and Washington's numerical majority soon to be negated, the nascent Continental army faced a real crisis in maintaining its siege of the British in Boston.

HENRY KNOX AND THE "NOBLE TRAIN OF ARTILLERY" (NOVEMBER 17, 1775–JANUARY 27, 1776)

Two men that Washington had come to rely on as advisors and leaders on his arrival to Boston were Nathanael Greene and Henry Knox. Both were self-taught with no prior military service. Greene was a Quaker from Rhode Island. He first attempted to join the siege as a private with the Rhode Island Kentish Guards after the Lexington Alarm, but they were turned back at the border. He returned in May 1775 as the general of the Rhode Island Army of Observation. Knox was a twenty-five-year-old Boston bookseller who had escaped across the siege lines with his wife to join the army. Knox had just met Washington in Roxbury in September, but was now in the general's circle of closest confidantes. Wanting to put an end to the siege and drive the British from Boston before they could be reinforced, Washington sought the advice of his war council. He intended a full assault on the city, but his subordinates convinced him that an attack on the British fortifications would carry a horrible cost. What the Continentals needed was firepower, but from where?

Henry Knox, the newly appointed chief of artillery, made an audacious proposal. There was plenty of artillery available, but it was three hundred miles away at Fort Ticonderoga, which Ethan Allen and the Green Mountain Boys had seized shortly after the battles at Lexington and Concord. Getting it back to Boston would be a logistical nightmare, but Knox and his men left camp on November 17, 1775, to do just that.

In Knox's contingent were Caesar Robbins and Cuff Ashport, two Black Patriots. Robbins was a logical choice for the mission, as he had previously served at Fort Ticonderoga during the French and Indian War and would have been familiar with the fort and the route they needed to take back to Boston. He had been born into slavery in 1745 in Chelmsford, and may have been freed at the time of his enlistment in the Revolutionary War. We do know that he lived as a free man after the war and during his three terms of service in the conflict. Cuff Ashport was also a slave from Bridgeport, near Plymouth, when the war broke out. He was able to purchase his freedom from his owner in the spring of 1775, and promptly enlisted in the Continental army, one of several Black Patriots joining from Bridgeport, including Jupiter Richards, Toby Torbett, Elias Sewall, and Joel Smugmug. Since Ashport was with the Knox expedition to Ticonderoga when his eight-month enlistment expired, he voluntarily extended his service to help complete the mission.

Bravery and fortitude were needed for this expedition. Getting to Ticonderoga was the easy part. Sailing to New York City, they took the Hudson River north to the fort. They arrived there on December 5 and began building sleds to transport the cannons, and Knox began to negotiate for eighty teams of oxen to pull the sleds. After haggling with locals, he ended up having to employ 124 pairs of horses instead of oxen for most of the trip. Selecting sixteen mortars, two howitzers, thirteen eighteen-pounders, ten twelve-pounders, and two twenty-four-pound cannons (weighing five thousand pounds each), Knox and his team waited for snow to begin the trek. In total, they would haul sixty tons of artillery three hundred miles through snow and mud, fording frozen rivers and attempting to cross the Berkshire Mountains of western Massachusetts.

When the snow finally came it was close to two feet deep, causing problems moving sleds with cannons weighing several tons. But it was enough for the water to freeze. They had to cross the Hudson River four times before they even reached Albany. There, one of the largest cannons fell through the ice, but the citizens nearby helped to recover the piece. Once at the Berkshires, the descent on the other side proved just as treacherous as the push up the mountains. By the time the Grand Union flag was first raised at Washington's headquarters on January 1, 1776, the Knox expedition was already on their return journey.

Henry Knox and the artillery arrived in Framingham, twelve miles outside of Boston, on January 25. It had taken the expedition just fifty-six days to reach the army's lines—an astounding accomplishment for the bookseller colonel and his troops. John Adams saw the column as it snaked toward Boston, calling it "the noble train of artillery." Within days some of the smaller pieces were placed on the Continental fortifications. How the larger artillery should best be deployed was still being debated.

CLASHING CULTURES IN THE RANKS

Meanwhile, the atmosphere among the Continental lines was an interesting mix of contrasts. Alongside New England militias were Virginia riflemen under Dan Morgan, who arrived the previous August having marched twenty-one days to join the Boston siege. The frontier dress of Morgan's men stood out, causing some friction with the local troops. This was particularly true for the rough seafarers of John Glover's Marblehead Regiment from the northern Massachusetts coast. The Marblehead unit was an integrated unit, with both slaves and freemen among its number. Life on the sea was one of the few vocations in the New World where Black men could receive both rank and respect. It's no wonder then that as much as one quarter of the crews serving in the Continental and state navies, as well as Patriot privateers, were eventually manned by Black Patriots. Virginia men, however, were not accustomed to having such familiar associations with Black men, and at least a few of their officers had brought their slaves with them to Boston. One Continental officer, Alexander Graydon of Philadelphia, later wrote about Glover's Marblehead unit, "In this regiment there were a number of negroes, which, to persons unaccustomed to such associations, had a disagreeable, degrading effect."[1]

Insults and jibes from both sides finally boiled over. One day on Harvard Yard a snowball fight quickly escalated to an all-out brawl between the two units, with hundreds of soldiers joining the fray. Israel Trask, an eleven-year-old young man acting as his father's personal servant, later described the brawl and its sudden end:

> Their first manifestations were ridicule and derision, which the riflemen bore with more patience than their wont, but resort being made to snow, which then covered the ground, these soft missives were interchanged but a few minutes before both parties closed, and a fierce struggle commenced with biting and gouging on the one part, and knockdown on the other part with as much apparent fury as the most deadly enmity could create. Reinforced by their friends, in less than five minutes more than a thousand combatants were on the field, struggling for the mastery.
>
> At this juncture General Washington made his appearance, whether by accident or design I never knew. I only saw him and his colored servant, both mounted. With the spring of a deer, he leaped from his saddle, threw the reins of his bridle into the hands of his servant, and rushed into the thickest of the melee, with an iron grip seized two tall, brawny, athletic, savage-looking riflemen by the throat, keeping them at arm's length, alternately shaking and talking to them.
>
> In this position the eye of the belligerents caught sight of the general. Its effect on them was instantaneous flight at the top of their speed in all directions from the scene of the conflict. Less than fifteen minutes' time had elapsed from the commencement of the row before the general and his two criminals were the only occupants of the field of action.[2]

What transpired afterward and what, if any, punishments were meted out is unknown. But the incident captures the considerable cultural differences of the troops comprising the nascent Continental army. John

Glover's Marbleheaders repeatedly played a crucial role in the survival and success of Washington's forces in 1776, and Dan Morgan's Virginia riflemen distinguished themselves throughout the conflict in both the northern and southern theaters of the war. But the friction from the many regional differences was just one added obstacle that Washington faced during the siege, on top of the British army looking up from their fortifications in Boston at his army's positions.

A PATRIOT SURPRISE ON DORCHESTER HEIGHTS (MARCH 5, 1776) AND THE BRITISH EVACUATION OF BOSTON (MARCH 17, 1776)

The arrival of Colonel Knox and his "noble train of artillery" in Cambridge on January 27 presented the best chance to evict the redcoats from the city, and with the expectation that British reinforcements may already be heading across the ocean, time was of the essence. In late February, curious activity was underway south of the city. Spirits among the Continental lines had been buoyed as hopes for some kind of break in the siege spread.

One source of inspiration for General Washington during these uncertain days was correspondence from poetess Phillis Wheatley. She had sent a letter and a poem dedicated to him months before overflowing with praise for the commander in chief. Hailing the fictional goddess Columbia as the patron of freedom's cause, she concluded her ode by urging the general to be directed by divine wisdom and the certainty that the American cause was just:

> Proceed, great chief, with virtue on thy side,
> Thy ev'ry action let the Goddess guide.
> A crown, a mansion, and a throne that shine,
> With gold unfading, Washington! Be thine.

His letter in reply, dated February 28, apologized for the delay in receiving her correspondence at his Cambridge headquarters and the understandable extended delay caused by his military duties. Offering his sincere thanks and extending to her the offer to visit him, he admitted his desire to see her work published to let others share in her talents, but demurred to prevent any accusations of vanity (in fact, Washington had already sent a copy to his friend Joseph Reed, who saw to its publication; it subsequently received wide distribution).

Within days, General Washington had ordered offensive demonstrations from the existing siege lines of the Continental army to draw the attention of the British. The moves continued for the next three days but were a ruse. A secret plot was underway to capture the empty Dorchester Heights that overlooked Boston from the south. Curious construction had been underway for weeks in the area. The army was pre-building fortifications to reinforce artillery positions on the heights, positions that were being simultaneously constructed featuring cannons provided by Colonel Knox and his "noble train of artillery."

Seizing Dorchester Heights before the British was essential, as was maintaining secrecy for the operation. Militia units from nearby, which had returned home at the end of their eight-month enlistments at the end of 1775, were now quietly being recalled. The Continental army siege lines could not be weakened. Washington's plan was for 1,200 troops in a vanguard to seize the area and erect the fortifications and artillery positions while another eight hundred men protected the operation.

Included in the vanguard were some familiar Black Patriot names. Cuff Ashport, who went with Colonel Knox to Ticonderoga and helped drag the artillery three hundred miles back to Boston, participated in the completion of the mission by helping take the hill. David Lamson, the French and Indian War veteran who led the "Old Men of Menotomy" to take the first POWs of the conflict as British retreated from Lexington and Concord, also took his place in the vanguard. James Easton, a blacksmith, was one of the many Black Patriots who enlisted from Bridgewater, along with Cuff Ashport from Plymouth County. Caesar Robbins arrived in the area with the Acton militia under Captain Israel Heald. Dozens more held the siege lines.

On the evening of March 4, the operation launched with some of Ticonderoga's cannons opening up from Cobble Hill, Lechmere, and Roxbury as a diversion. With frozen ground, digging was impossible. Seizing the hill in the dark of night, the men set to work dragging the prefabricated pieces and the cannons up the slope and placing them in position overlooking the city of Boston below. As work progressed, Washington encouraged the men by invoking Crispus Attucks and the other victims of the Boston Massacre, an event that had happened exactly six years earlier to the day, telling them, "Remember it is the fifth of March, and avenge the death of your brethren."[3]

By morning, the cannons were in place and secure on Dorchester Heights and defenses constructed for the anticipated response. General Howe, commander of the British garrison in Boston, was reported to say, "My God, these fellows have done more work in one night than I could make my army do in three months."[4] The admiral of the British fleet warned that the occupation of Dorchester Heights directly threatened his ships in Boston Harbor and would likely prevent any assistance to British troops in Boston with any counteroffensive. Howe needed to immediately retake the position and began making plans to attack the Continental's position on Dorchester Heights a few nights later. But a winter storm began on the evening of March 5 that continued for several days, convincing Howe that openly attacking Dorchester under artillery fire up icy slopes would be more damaging to his army than surrendering Boston to Washington and the Continental army and surviving to fight another day.

On March 8, an unsigned note was sent to General Washington from inside the city, indicating that the British were willing to leave Boston without setting fire to the town as they left, as long as they could leave in peace, not under unrelenting Continental artillery fire. As General Howe awaited favorable tides, his army and a thousand Loyalist citizens prepared to leave Boston. The day finally arrived on March 17, when the British and their supporters boarded the ships of the British fleet, loaded with all that could be carried from the town, and sailed off to Halifax. Years of British rule in Massachusetts had come to a seeming end. The siege of Boston was over.

As the victorious commander in chief and his troops entered the ransacked city, they still undoubtedly felt a feeling of accomplishment and pride at the first great victory of the Continental army in the war. The Black Patriots had played a role from the beginning of the struggle, from the martyrdom of Crispus Attucks to Lexington Green and the Old North Bridge in Concord, the bottling up of the British army in Boston and the manning of the siege, the surprise victory at Fort Ticonderoga, the heroic stand on Bunker Hill, and the miraculous transport of the Ticonderoga artillery back to Boston, concluding with the taking of Dorchester Heights and the British evacuation of Boston. They played a part at every point and earned their role in the story in the early and uncertain days of the American Revolution. There would be more suffering and sacrifice required in the months and years ahead, but now was the time for celebration. But the celebration was short.

Washington knew that, having allowed Howe and the British to leave unscathed, he was likely to face the same redcoats again. He didn't know when or where, or even how many more would arrive. The other states were working to put themselves on a war footing, anticipating the next British move. Shortly after the British evacuation of Boston, Continental army troops were on the move, anticipating a reappearance of the British somewhere around New York. By April, slaves were constructing defensive fortifications ordered by Washington around New York City and the Long Island Sound. By June, there were nineteen thousand Continental army troops stationed around the area, awaiting the British return.

Boston, however, had not been the only front in the expanding American conflict against King George's forces.

A DISASTROUS EXPEDITION TO CANADA (SEPTEMBER 1775–JUNE 1776)

Nearly a year earlier in September 1775, Washington had approved a plan to invade Canada with Richard Montgomery, a former British officer, approaching from the south out of New York, and Benedict Arnold leading a force of one thousand men through the Massachusetts wilderness (now Maine), following the Kennebec and Chaudière Rivers for a surprise attack on Quebec. A number of Black Patriots participated in the Canadian campaign.

The strategy behind the invasion was to seize key British supply nodes and occupy the major transport routes into the northern colonies. Believing that many Canadians were friendly to the Patriot cause and would join in support of the Continental army's invasion, Americans hoped that a potential fourteenth colony could be added. Montgomery's column saw initial success when they took Montreal on November 14, 1775, gaining a base to launch a joint assault on Quebec and avenging a loss there by Ethan Allen just weeks before (where Allen was captured). Benedict Arnold's column was still slogging through the wilderness, where hunger, dysentery, and smallpox were the most lethal enemy. They finally reached the southernmost villages south of Quebec at the end of November. Black Patriots Asa Gardner and Thomas Reynolds were among those who survived the wilderness with Arnold. Their company commander, Captain John Topham, wrote a journal chronicling the arduous journey that is still in print today. Prime Wheeler was part of a New Hampshire ranger regiment that traveled with Montgomery, and military records place him near Montreal at the end of September.

Finally, on December 31, 1775, the Continental army columns converged on Quebec, but the attack quickly went awry after column commander Richard Montgomery became one of the first fatalities. With their leader dead, his column was never fully engaged. Arnold's troops took part of the lower town, along with dozens of prisoners, only to be taken prisoners themselves. Nearly five hundred Continental troops were now prisoners of war, including Captain Topham. Several captured American officers would gain fame later in the war, including Lieutenant Colonel Christopher Greene and Captain Daniel Morgan. Arnold was wounded but determined to carry on by besieging the city.

In the first months of 1776, New Hampshire authorized new regiments to assist the Canada campaign. Army pay records trace Black Patriots' progress into Canada among the New Hampshire troops, including London Dow, Primus Black, and Stephen Lovewell. Benajah Blackman and Fortune Negro were present in late February at Orford, the Continental headquarters for the campaign located at the northern part of Lake Champlain. Titus Freeman received one month's wages, with additional payments for bounty, blankets, and billeting, on March 28. He and John Blackman were paid again at Montreal on April 25.

In May 1776, British reinforcements arrived in Quebec, forcing Arnold to abandon the siege and begin a retreat. On May 19, Primus Chandler was taken captive by Indian allies of the British at the Cedars southwest of Montreal, in a skirmish between American troops and a force of British soldiers, Canadian Loyalists, and Iroquois. He and other American prisoners were forced to run the gauntlet. Primus Chandler eventually died from his injuries from the ordeal. His father, also named Primus, had been killed at the Fort William Henry massacre during the French and Indian War.

The retreating Americans took refuge on the Isle aux Noix, an island in the Richelieu River. Titus Freeman, John Blackman, and Benajah Blackman were reported present on June 24. Over the ten days the army was encamped there, these Black Patriots likely helped bury more than nine hundred of their fellow soldiers who had died from smallpox in two large mass graves. Nearly a month later, on July 22, John Blackman received his monthly wages at Fort Ticonderoga, marking the end of the retreat. At the end, the Continental army had five thousand men killed, wounded, or captured during the Canada campaign.

One of those who may have greeted the arriving troops at Fort Ticonderoga was Barzillai Lew, a veteran of the French and Indian War who had served at the fort during that conflict. After the battles at Lexington and Concord, Lew enlisted for eight months and fought at Bunker Hill. After serving out his enlistment in December 1775, his militia unit was called up again in February for two months for the conclusion of the siege of Boston and the evacuation of the British. They were called up again to serve at Fort Ticonderoga to cover the retreat from Canada and reinforce the positions still held around Lake Champlain. A portrait believed to be Barzillai Lew hangs in a diplomatic room at the State Department in Washington DC.

TACTICAL LOSS BUT STRATEGIC VICTORY AT VALCOUR ISLAND (OCTOBER 11, 1776)

The British were keen to maintain their advantage after the humiliating retreat of Arnold from Canada. General Guy Carlton was amassing a force of nine thousand men and a fleet of twenty-five armed ships, intent on pushing the Americans out of the Lake Champlain area and possibly even further south toward Albany. Benedict Arnold, who was put in charge of the American fleet, had to contend with a smallpox outbreak, likely brought back by his own troops, among the shipbuilders in Skenesborough, where slaves had been building the first American navy since the area came under their control with the taking of Fort Ticonderoga by Ethan Allen and the Green Mountain Boys in May 1775.

In October 1776, it was clear that the British would soon set off to challenge the American presence on the lake. Within a few days the British were sighted, and Arnold set up his small and outmatched flotilla of schooners, sloops, and galleys in a battle line in the bay between Valcour Island and the New York Coast. One of those involved in the fight at Valcour Bay was Plato Turner, a slave who had enlisted for three years in the Third Massachusetts Regiment in the spring of 1776 at the age of twenty-eight. He was freed after serving his term of enlistment and continued to serve until the end of the war. Robin Starr of Danbury, Connecticut, was also at the battle on Lake Champlain in his first combat action and continued to serve to the end of the war, receiving the Badge of Merit for his years of service.

The battle was a tactical loss but a strategic victory for the Americans. Both the presence of the Continental army on Lake Champlain and the battle had seriously delayed their offensive. While many of the ships were lost, and Arnold was forced to burn down the nearby fort at Crown Point to deny it to the British, they still held Fort Ticonderoga after the British troops withdrew north back to Canada as an early snow began to fall several days after the battle.

PATRIOT VICTORIES AT MOORE'S CREEK (FEBRUARY 27, 1776) AND SULLIVAN ISLAND (JUNE 28, 1776)

Nearly nine hundred miles further south, Patriots were trying to hold off British advances. The American victory at the end of 1775 at the battle of Great Bridge in the Virginia Tidewater area effectively ended British rule there. Lord Dunmore, the British governor of Virginia living in exile on a British ship, ordered the bombardment and burning of the town of Norfolk, the last Loyalist stronghold in the state, on January 1, 1776. He eventually abandoned the state altogether in April 1776, leaving behind the bodies of hundreds of escaped slaves he had enticed to flee their masters with the promise of freedom. Most had died from disease, but Dunmore had made virtually no effort to feed or care for the escaped slaves lured by his proclamation. Dunmore failed even to free his own slaves before setting sail for New York—a sad testament to hollow British promises of emancipation.

One other important event might have inspired Lord Dunmore to totally cut his losses. Josiah Martin, the British colonial governor of North Carolina, had been notified in early January 1776 that two thousand British soldiers were being sent from Ireland to help put down the rebellion in the Carolinas. Martin issued a call for Loyalist militias to prepare to supplement the arriving force, due in mid-February. The bulk of his supporters who responded were Scottish Highlanders who arrived here after the failed Jacobite Rebellion of 1745. When 3,500 arrived at the February 15 muster, they had to march to the coast to meet the arriving British force.

The Patriot militia intended to intercept them and hotly pursued them along the way. The Patriots gained the advantage when they arrived first at Moore's Creek Bridge, near Wilmington, on February 27, 1776. The Loyalist commander was urged to give battle even though their numbers had dwindled to around eight hundred. On reaching the bridge they discovered that most of the boards had been taken up. They had to cross single file. Many of the Loyalists did not have firearms, only broadswords. A company charged across the bridge to the other side of the creek, where the Patriot militia was waiting behind an embankment. Much like at Bunker Hill, as the Highlanders charged forward, a volley erupted from the Patriot lines, breaking the charge and forcing an immediate retreat. Governor Martin fled North Carolina when the British fleet arrived with reinforcements, which headed for Charleston.

At least four Black Patriots of the First North Carolina participated in the Patriot victory at Moore's Creek Bridge, all slaves and identified only by their first names: Billy, Gears, George, and Jack. Shortly after the battle, all four deserted. Like many other Black Patriots, they abruptly pop up in the story of the fight for American independence and disappear from the record without any further trace.

Such is true for slaves from Charleston, hired by Patriots to build fortifications on Sullivan Island off the South Carolina coast in anticipation of the arrival of the British fleet. When they were finally sighted in late June, Fort Sullivan Island was ready to greet them. Among those defending Charleston at the fort was Spencer Bolton, a freeman drafted in 1776 to the company commanded by Captain John King. Edmund Davis had enlisted in 1775 in the First South Carolina under Captain Thomas Pinckney. Valentine Locus was present as part of his two-year enlistment with the Third North Carolina in Captain James Emmett's company under command of Colonel Jethro Sumner. George Perkins was present for the battle, serving as a substitute for James Johnson in Captain Elle LeBush's company.

When the British fleet opened fire, Fort Sullivan Island's construction of palmetto logs and sand prevented any significant damage. Many cannonballs bounced off harmlessly. The fort's guns, however, were effective against the British ships. British troops landed on an island to the north in an attempt to flank the fort, but the water in the channel between was too deep to cross. The battle was not without Patriot casualties, however. Included among the few dead was a young slave, the personal servant of the fort's commander, Colonel William Moultrie. With several ships heavily damaged, the British fleet disengaged. The date was June 28, 1776—less than a week before the Continental Congress declared the independence of the United States in Philadelphia.

News quickly reached Charleston, and the British fleet raised anchor, setting off for New York. The attention of the British Empire was largely directed to the northern states for the time being. While Patriot and Loyalist militias in the Carolinas continued to clash over the next few years, it was three years before the British turned their attention south again.

The Patriot victories at Boston, Great Bridge, and Moore's Creek Bridge inspired Americans and the Continental Congress to push for independence. It would be a long hard road ahead. The Continental Congress and the army under Washington would shortly learn the determination of King George to end the rebellion and hopes for American independence.

Black Patriots who would soon be fighting for American independence were also fighting for a more fundamental cause: their personal freedom. Some of them still lived in slavery, their future freedom conditioned on their military service. Many wives and children also remained in bondage. What, if any, difference would independence make for them?

PRINCE WHIPPLE: AN EYEWITNESS TO INDEPENDENCE

One Black Patriot who witnessed the proceedings of the Continental Congress in Philadelphia was Prince Whipple, the slave of New Hampshire delegate William Whipple. Born in Anomabu, Ghana, in 1750, it appears that he was from a family of means, as he and his brother Cuffee were sent by their parents to America for an education. Then tragedy struck. The two boys fell victim to an unscrupulous captain in charge of transporting them to America. They were sold as slaves upon reaching Baltimore, where Prince was purchased by William Whipple, and Cuffee by William's brother, Joseph. They then sailed to Portsmouth. In the years that followed, Prince, though enslaved, became a trusted agent for William Whipple, responsible for much of his business affairs and conducting transactions on his behalf.

In Philadelphia, he likely would have waited near the door of the Pennsylvania State House (now known as Independence Hall), awaiting direction from his master, who served on a number of important committees of the Continental Congress. When in town, William and Prince lodged with Captain Robert Duncan, where John Adams also boarded while in town. Undoubtedly, Prince would have listened to the delegates debate for and against independence while Congress was in session, and afterward in the taverns, where the debates and negotiations continued well into the night. He may have heard the reports from General Washington of the progress of the Continental army constructing defenses around New York City in anticipation of the British army's return. Deep into the debates over Virginia delegate Henry Lee's resolution calling for American independence, Prince would have undoubtedly noticed the reaction of the delegates to the news that the first British ships had been sighted approaching New York. In the days that immediately followed, Prince Whipple, the slave, would be privy to the concluding arguments and, finally, the vote to declare the independence of the United States from Great Britain. How much did he take to heart the text of the Declaration of Independence and its affirmation that "all men are created equal" as the Continental Congress debated the final wording—including striking Jefferson's strong condemnation of slavery due to the objections of southern delegates? Finally, the Declaration was publicly read from the very steps he had occupied for months. It must have meant something, for when William and Prince returned home to Portsmouth, they together planted an acorn from a Philadelphia horse chestnut tree at the Whipple homestead—a Liberty Tree that still grows today.

In New York, General Washington had the Declaration of Independence read to his troops. There was now more at stake than just political and economic concerns. For the Continental army and all the states, the fight was over the fate of a people and what shape this new nation would take if, in fact, it could survive the immediate ordeal ahead. And for Black Patriots, slave and freemen alike, what changes would it mean? The Declaration of Independence and the language of liberty it employed rippled from Philadelphia north and south, and out to the farthest settlements on the frontier. It also made an impact at the birthplace of the American Revolution in New England.

POMP JACKSON: FIGHTER FOR INDEPENDENCE

Jonathan Jackson was a prominent Patriot businessman who served on the Massachusetts Committee of Correspondence and in that role regularly communicated with General Washington. Toward the end of the war he would be sent as a delegate to the Continental Congress. As independence was debated in Philadelphia in 1776, the implications of the American struggle for freedom were much on Jonathan Jackson's mind. How could he work for liberty while denying it to his own slave? The answer he arrived at was that he couldn't reconcile the two. On June 15, 1776, his slave Pomp enlisted in Colonel Edmund Phinney's regiment, presumably with Jackson's permission. Four days later, Jackson formally signed Pomp's manumission papers, finally freeing him. In them he explains the struggle he felt:

> Know all men by these presents, that I, Jonathan Jackson, of Newburyport, in the county of Essex, gentleman, in consideration of the impropriety I feel, and have long felt, in beholding any person in constant bondage,—more especially at a time when my country is so warmly contending for the liberty every man ought to enjoy,—and having sometime since promised my negro man Pomp, that I would give him his freedom, and in further consideration of five shillings, paid me by said Pomp, I do hereby liberate, manumit, and set him free; and I do hereby remise and release unto said Pomp, all demands of whatever nature I have against said Pomp.

In witness whereof, I have hereunto set my hand and seal, this nineteenth June, 1776.

Jonathan Jackson.

This document was also signed by two witnesses and filed with the Suffolk County Probate office. The five shillings that Pomp paid for his freedom is comparable to forty dollars today. He also took Jackson's last name for his own. Within weeks, his regiment marched north to reinforce the army around Lake Champlain and Lake George. The main action of this campaign was the battle of Valcour Island, but the most lethal enemy to the Continental soldiers was disease and exposure, with thousands dying before the British withdrew back to Canada in early November.

After the campaign, Pomp Jackson reenlisted for the duration of the war at a time when the fortunes of the Continental army were at their lowest. He was honorably discharged in June 1783 and settled in Andover, Massachusetts, in an area still known as Pomp's Pond. Jonathan Jackson lost most of his fortune during the war but was named as the first US Marshal for the District of Massachusetts by President Washington.

THE NEW YORK CAMPAIGN (JUNE–OCTOBER 1776)

At the time of the final debates on Henry Lee's motion for declaring independence in late June 1776, British ships from Halifax had already begun arriving off the coast of New York City. On July 3, the British landed on Staten Island, which lay undefended, with about ten thousand men. Eventually, more than four hundred British ships arrived carrying thirty-two thousand British and Hessian soldiers. Washington's dilemma was that he lacked intelligence about where the British troops might attack, and yet there were hundreds of miles of coastline in the New York City area that could have been a landing point for an assault.

Over the next three months, the Continental army under General Washington was pushed by the British from defeat to disaster, and then to desperation. It began in late August when General Howe landed fifteen thousand troops on Long Island. Washington's intelligence, however, claimed only eight to nine thousand, convincing him that this was not the main point of attack. After arranging their troops on the flatlands, the British columns set off, with one marching around the left flank of the Americans and attacking from the rear. Over the next few days, the battle turned into a British rout.

Several Black Patriots are known to have been in the battle, including Julius Cesar, London Citizen, and Timothy Prince. In the thickest of the fighting was Samuel Sutphen, a slave who had been sold to a New Jersey man, Casper Berger, to serve as his substitute in the militia. In the spring and summer of 1776, he served in a "flying camp" patrolling the New Jersey coast, anticipating a possible British attack. When it became clear that the activity on Long Island was not a diversion, Washington ordered more troops. Sutphen landed with his unit just as the right flank began to collapse. Years later, he described in a pension deposition the march to Flatbush on Long Island:

> And in two hours after their arrival the engagement commenced between the British and Hessians on one side and the Americans on the other side, the Americans were obliged to retreat and being pursued by the enemy suffered considerable loss. Lord Stirling, General Sullivan and several other officers were taken prisoner, the battle continued about six hours. Deponent fought in this battle, and as the company was dismissed immediately after the retreat, he returned home.

He describes how he and two other members of his company escaped:

> I found a colored man with a skiff, who took us across to Staten Island. The black man piloted us through the bye ways across Staten Island and we crossed the sound over to Elizabethtown point—thence through the town, and by the Wheat Sheaf Tavern, Short Hills, Quibble Town, Bound Brook, and home.

Near escape from the enemy was common for those in the American lines. Lord Stirling's action helped delay the British advance, as did a heroic series of charges by the First Maryland and Delaware Regiments on the opposite flank against three times their number. The few that survived and weren't captured had to wade through a creek to what was left of the American camp around Brooklyn Heights. On the other side of the Continental battle line was Timothy Prince of Connecticut, serving in Colonel John Tyler's regiment that unsuccessfully tried to hold the Gowanus Pass and had to fall back. An illustration of how close the British were to the American lines: Richard Stanhope, a slave of George Washington who served him throughout the war, was shot in the right leg above the knee. Trapped against the East River, Washington ordered a full retreat to Manhattan.

The Continental army's saviors from total defeat were John Glover's integrated Marblehead Regiment and the weather. After dark on August 29, Glover's men removed what was left of Washington's troops on Long Island using a thrown-together flotilla moving against the tide. With British war ships nearby, their movements were miraculously concealed by a fog. At least nine thousand soldiers escaped without a single casualty from Brooklyn to Manhattan Island, surviving the largest engagement of the Revolutionary War and giving the Continental army a chance to fight another day. They would not have to wait long.

One tragic postscript to the Battle of Long Island was a claim that the British buried dead Black Patriots apart from their comrades. Years later when these remains were discovered, a local parson reported that the bones were carelessly thrown into the sea.

During the summer months of 1776 after the evacuation of the British from Boston, the failed invasion of Charleston, and the vote for American independence in Philadelphia, hopes for the Patriot cause were high. A number of Black Patriots enlisted during this time, particularly in the South, and served in the catastrophic New York campaign.

Charles and James Ailstock of Louisa County, Virginia, enlisted in 1776, in the company commanded by Captain Thomas Johnson in the Third Virginia, and marched north to join the Continental army. Thomas Camel was the slave of Colonel Martin Picket of Culpeper, Virginia, when the news of the Long Island defeat arrived, prompting the recruitment of new regiments to be sent north. In his pension application, Thomas explained that Picket "gave me my choice to either remain a slave as I was or to go into the army, and I chose the latter and enlisted."

Luther Jotham, a freeman, volunteered for the Massachusetts militia even before the battles at Lexington and Concord, and served in Roxbury during the siege of Boston, agreeing to extend his service when his term expired in January 1776 until the British evacuated. He reenlisted in the summer of 1776, and was marched to New York to prepare for the anticipated return of the British. Marlin Roorback was a slave who enlisted in October 1776 in the New York troops with the permission of his master and served under General Schuyler in upstate New York, protecting from British attacks from Canada. Nace Butler of Annapolis enlisted in the Second Maryland and would serve seven years until the war's end, as would Joel Taburn of North Carolina, who joined the Patriot cause in the spring of 1776 in North Carolina.

General Washington would need every Patriot who could bear arms, and casualties, prisoners, and deserters from Long Island had thinned the ranks. General Howe landed on at Kip's Bay north of New York City with four thousand troops on September 15, just two weeks after the retreat from Long Island, forcing another retreat of the Continental army north to Harlem Heights. Howe attacked Washington there the following day, and a counterattack that included Luther Jotham's regiment forced the British back. Other Black Patriots shared the honors of victory at Harlem Heights, including Fortune Freeman, Primus Hall, Richard Rhodes, Enoch Freeman, James Keeter, Anthony Gilman, and Aaron Brister. The temporary victory at Harlem Heights bolstered the army's spirits.

It was another month before the British attempted another major amphibious landing at Pell's Point on October 18, with four thousand troops intent on flanking Washington and trapping the army on Manhattan. Heavily outnumbered, a brigade commanded by John Glover, including the integrated Marblehead Regiment he commanded before his promotion, executed a collapsing retreat behind a series of stone walls to slow the British advance. Also present for the Battle at Pell's Point was Nathaniel Small, a Black Patriot who enlisted in June 1775, fought at Bunker Hill, and was part of the siege of Boston. Pay records show that he traveled with his unit to New York before May 1776. He later died in his country's service.

The delaying action by Glover's brigade allowed the army to move into Westchester County, and defensive positions were eventually established at White Plains. It's there that a force of seven thousand British and Hessians attempted to storm the entrenchments of the Continentals on October 28. The first two attempts were repulsed, but Hessians eventually turned the right flank of the Continental line. American artillery forced back an attack on the left flank, and rain the following day gave time for Washington to redeploy the troops in White Plains and nearby New Castle. An unsuccessful attack on the American lines at New Castle prompted Howe to return to Manhattan to mop up what was left of the Continental army on the island, while Washington and the bulk of his troops traveled north to cross the Hudson River into New Jersey at Peekskill. Again, Black Patriots were well represented in the units that held their ground at White Plains, including Samuel Dunbar, Artillo Freeman, Phillip Rodman, Titus Hayward, Scipio Shaw, Jethro Freeman, Cornelius Lenox, and Caesar Shelton, who was a slave of John Shelton and was serving as a substitute for Shelton's son in exchange for the promise of his freedom.

While most of the army was now on the other side of the Hudson from the British, at least three thousand Continental troops sat inside Fort Washington on the Manhattan side of the Hudson River in the area now occupied by the George Washington Bridge. The fort was poorly constructed, and on November 15, the British and Hessians assaulted it from all sides. Washington had to watch helpless as Fort Washington quickly fell, its three thousand occupants killed or taken prisoner. Among the American POWs were William Luckens, who was part of the flying camp under Colonel Michael Swope, and Polydore Redman, a drummer for the Fifth Pennsylvania Battalion. It was one of the largest disasters of the entire war.

Howe set his sights on Fort Lee opposite Fort Washington on the other side of the Hudson and, guided by some local Loyalists, crossed the river unnoticed. Disaster was only averted because the British advance guards were spotted by Polly Wyckoff, a slave working in a farm kitchen, who quickly warned of their approach. Washington had time to remove his two thousand troops stationed there but had to leave much of their supplies. Thanks to Polly Wyckoff's warning, Washington kept intact what was left of his army following the losses at Fort Washington. Today, a New Jersey chapter of the Daughters of the American Revolution bears her name in memory of her invaluable service to the Patriot cause.

"THE CRISIS" AND THE PATRIOT RETREAT THROUGH NEW JERSEY (NOVEMBER 19–DECEMBER 26, 1776)

Seizing all the boats they could find and burning the bridges behind them, Washington's dwindling army slowed the British pursuit as they retreated south through New Jersey until they were able to cross over the Delaware River into Pennsylvania. With winter setting in, Howe returned to New York City, having let the Continental army escape for the time being, likely hoping that disease and desertions would weaken Washington's army over the winter.

But there was no cause for the Patriots to celebrate. In fact, it was at this time that Thomas Paine, traveling with the army, wrote his pamphlet "The Crisis," writing of the "times that try men's souls." The Continental Congress had moved to Maryland in case the British tried to move on Philadelphia. They were protected there by the Maryland Flying Camp, who had at least five Black Patriots on their rolls. Washington had also called on reinforcements from the northern army around Lake Champlain. One of those who arrived was Titus Coburn, a Black Patriot veteran of the Battle of Bunker Hill, who marched in December with Captain Fortunatus Eager's company to join Washington's command. With his army depleted by casualties and desertion from 13,000 to 2,500, he was also facing the expiration of enlistments for a large part of his army at the end of December.

Many military historians agree that facing these grim circumstances, Washington's proposal to cross the Delaware River on Christmas night, attacking the 1,500-man Hessian garrison stationed in Trenton before enlistments expired, ranks among the most decisive military decisions in Western history. Black Patriots served an outsized role in the success of the operation.

CROSSING THE DELAWARE AND A SURPRISE PATRIOT VICTORY AT TRENTON (DECEMBER 26, 1776)

The backbone of Washington's plan was for the Marblehead Regiment to ferry the army over the Delaware. It is important to review the essential role the regiment had played over the past year, both as sailors and infantry. They were present for the siege of Boston, which eventually forced the British to evacuate and gave Washington his first victory. At the Battle of Long Island, the Marbleheaders moved the army across the East River in the dark of night within range of British warships without a single casualty. Without their efforts there, the Continental army faced destruction. At the Battle of Pell's Point, they delayed the British amphibious invasion to allow the army to retreat in an orderly fashion. And now they were the keystone to the Continental army's future existence.

As mentioned at the beginning of this chapter, the Marblehead Regiment was an integrated unit, with slaves and freemen serving together with all ranks of Massachusetts society. Pomp Devereaux, a slave who helped ferry Washington's troops across the Delaware, served with his master. Caesar Glover, a freeman who served John Glover in peacetime, was there with him in wartime. Other Black Patriots, including Romeo Johonnot, Aesop Hale, and others who remain unknown, were tasked with carrying an oversized burden: the very survival of the Continental army and American independence.

In the face of snow and an icy Delaware River, they were true to their task in ferrying Washington's column safely across. From there, other Black Patriots from at least half a dozen states marched silently in the cold the eight miles toward Trenton. Scipio Dodge marched with Nathaniel Small in Colonel Loammi Baldwin's Twenty-Sixth Continental Regiment, while Thomas Semor and Luther Jotham did their service with Colonel John Bailey's regiment. Primus Coffin was present with the Second New Hampshire men. Dick Fortune, Cesar Cipeo, Samuel

Pompey, John Pompey, Abraham Pharaoh, and Cudgo Shepherd represented Connecticut. Oliver Cromwell fought on his home turf with the Second New Jersey.

One of the best soldier accounts of the Battle of Trenton and the days that immediately followed comes from Peter Jennings, who served with the Fifth Regiment of Artillery Blacks from Rhode Island. In his pension affidavit, he describes firsthand the great Patriot victory at Trenton:

> The enemy so little expecting an attack from us, was thrown into great confusion, and we obtained a complete victory over them, killing many of them, and taking several hundred prisoners, who were principally Hessians. We also took a large amount of military stores, and number of pieces of cannon, and a great many small arms.

The expedition was a tremendous success, and several Black Patriots served with distinction in the battle. John Sidebottom's unit was one of the first to cross the Delaware and was in the vanguard attacking Trenton from the north. At a critical moment of the battle, his unit, led by Captain William Washington (a distant relative of the commander in chief) and an eighteen-year-old Lieutenant James Monroe, charged a group of Hessians preparing to fire several artillery pieces. Both Washington and Monroe were severely wounded. One of those who carried Lieutenant Monroe to the field hospital was John Sidebottom. James Monroe survived his near-fatal wound and continued to serve his country's cause throughout the war, later becoming the fifth president of the United States.

A surprise victory in hand, the Continental army gathered the weapons, supplies, and prisoners and returned to their crossing point. The Marbleheaders ferried the triumphant army back across the Delaware. With less than a week left on many enlistments, General Washington called a council of war to plot their next move.

The Bridge at Moore's Creek, North Carolina. Here on February 27, 1776, Patriot militias won an overwhelming victory against Loyalists who were marching to join with British forces at Wilmington. At least four Black Patriots—all slaves—are known to have fought at the battle. British hopes were dashed of using Loyalist colonist supporters to help subdue the southern states in the early years of the war. (Image: Patrick S. Poole)

THE LIBERATOR

We had no intention, however, of dwelling on this subject at the length we have, when we took pen in hand. Our object was, simply to introduce a scrap, copied from our Suffolk Probate Record, of what in our new country may pass for antiquarian lore, to the readers of the Liberator; and here it is—which, without preface, will speak for itself:

'Know all men by these presents, that I, Jonathan Jackson, of Newburyport, in the county of Essex, gentleman, in consideration of the impropriety I feel, and have long felt, in holding any person in constant bondage—more especially at a time when my country is so warmly contending for the liberty every man ought to enjoy—and having sometime since promised my negro man Pomp, that I would give him his freedom—and in further consideration of five shillings, paid me by said Pomp, I do hereby liberate, manumit and set him free; and I do hereby remise and release unto said Pomp, all demands of whatever nature I have against said Pomp.

In witness whereof, I have hereunto set my hand and seal, this 19th June, 1776.

JONATHAN JACKSON. [Seal.]

Witness, Mary Coburn, Wm. Noyes.'

It only remains to say a word respecting the two parties of the foregoing indenture.

Jonathan Jackson, of Newburyport, we well remember to have heard spoken of, in our boyish days, by honored lips, as a most upright and thorough gentleman of the old school, possessing talents and character of the first standing. He was the first Collector of the Port of Boston, under Washington's administration, and was Treasurer of the Commonwealth of Massachusetts for many years, and died in 1810. A tribute to his memory and his worth, said to be from the pen of the late John Lowell, appeared in the Columbian Centinel, March 10, 1810. His immediate descendants have long resided in this city, are extensively known, and as widely and justly honored.

Pomp took the name of his late master, upon his emancipation, and soon after, enlisted in the army, as Pomp Jackson, served through the whole war of the revolution, and obtained an honorable discharge at its termination. He afterwards settled in Andover, near a pond, still known as 'Pomp's Pond,' where some of his descendants yet live. In this case of emancipation, it appears, instead of 'cutting his master's throat,' he only slashed the throats of his country's enemies. J.

Boston, Feb. 1, 1847.

The Boston-based antislavery newspaper, *The Liberator*, recounts in their February 12, 1847, edition the June 1776 manumission and enlistment of Pomp Jackson into the Continental Army, citing Suffolk County, Massachusetts, probate records documenting his freedom. His former owner, Jonathan Jackson, described his motivation for freeing his slave, saying that he couldn't in good conscience fight for his freedom while he kept Pomp in slavery. Pomp Jackson enlisted in the Continental Army several days after being freed. (Image: Internet Archive)

Tradition holds that William Whipple and his slave, Prince, planted this horse chestnut Liberty Tree beside their home in Portsmouth, New Hampshire, in 1776 upon their return from Philadelphia, where William had voted for American independence as a delegate to the Continental Congress for his home state and signed the Declaration of Independence. Prince served with William at the Patriot victory at Saratoga and at other times during the war, eventually being freed in 1784. His grave at the North Cemetery in Portsmouth is marked with a military headstone recording his military service. (Images: Patrick S. Poole)

The USS *Philadelphia* was a Continental navy gunboat that was sunk in the naval battle near Valcour Island on Lake Champlain on October 11, 1776. The *Philadelphia* was built July to August 1776 in Skenesborough by slaves and indentured laborers, along with seven other gunboats that patrolled the lake. Plato Turner of the Third Massachusetts participated in the battle at Valcour Island. While a loss, the battle delayed a British invasion from Canada until the following summer. The remains of the *Philadelphia* were discovered in 1935, and it was raised the following year. It is now on exhibit at the Smithsonian Institution's National Museum of American History. (Image: Patrick S. Poole)

CHAPTER 4

1777: THE PRECARIOUS BALANCE OF LIBERTY

IN THE DAYS BEFORE Washington's all-or-nothing gamble, Thomas Paine, traveling with the Continental army, termed the situation "the American crisis." The surprise Patriot victory on December 26, 1776, at Trenton offered a needed promise of hope for American independence. The damaging losses in New York had shrunk the army, but the retreat through New Jersey ahead of the pursuing British meant the survival, at least for the moment, of Washington's army. The heroic crossing of the Delaware and the capture of the Hessian garrison at Trenton with few casualties had been a desperate measure that had paid off for Washington and the Patriot cause.

But he still faced the end-of-year enlistments that would deplete the army even further. The column led by John Cadwalader that had failed to make the Delaware crossing for the Trenton operation had crossed into New Jersey the following day and was harassing small British units. On December 29, the rest of the army crossed the Delaware and reoccupied Trenton. But many enlistments were still set to expire. Washington made a passionate plea to those who would leave at year's end:

> You have done all that I asked you to do and more. But your country is at stake, your wives, your houses, and all that you hold dear. You have worn yourselves out with fatigue and hardships, but we know not how to spare you. If you will stay on one month or longer, you will render that service to the cause

> of liberty and to your country for which you would probably never do under any circumstances.[1]

To increase the enticement to stay on, Washington offered a bounty of ten dollars in hard cash to those who extended their enlistments. The appeal worked, with many pledging to stay. Washington still, at least temporarily, had a semblance of an army.

THE TEN CRUCIAL DAYS (DECEMBER 25, 1776–JANUARY 3, 1777)

Then word came that Lord Cornwallis was headed to Trenton with five thousand British soldiers. An American force under Edward Hand was dispatched to delay his approach as Washington gathered to meet the threat. On January 2, 1777, Hand's troops engaged the British column, utilizing riflemen at longer distances, collapsing defenses, and street fighting in Trenton. Late in the day, Hand's column reached a bridge over Assunpink Creek, with Cornwallis close behind, no doubt relieved to be greeted by Washington's column on the other side of the bridge.

Cornwallis's troops were met at Assunpink Creek with Continental artillery that pushed back three separate charges at the bridge. With night approaching, Cornwallis retired to Trenton intent on dealing a fatal blow the following day. While holding off the British at the bridge, Washington knew that his position there was untenable. The boats used to cross the Delaware had been sent further upriver and were not available, and the creek had several points on his right flank that could be easily forded. One of Washington's aides, Arthur St. Clair, proposed secretly leaving their positions and marching during the night to attack the British rear guard in Princeton. Just as they had at Long Island, the army kept their fires burning as they quietly slipped away on a back road headed north.

Marching with the Continental army that night was a contingent of recently recruited marines under the command of Major Samuel Nicholas, who tradition claims had used Tun Tavern in Philadelphia as his recruiting office. The three hundred men who joined Major Nicholas in 1776 represented the first US Marine Corps battalion in history. Two Black Patriots who had joined just weeks before were Isaac Walker and a man identified only as "Orange," both Black Patriots serving among the 130 marines fighting with the Eleventh Continental Line at Princeton.

Also marching toward Princeton was Primus Hall. He was born into slavery, the child of Delia and Prince Hall, his father a prominent Black Patriot leader in Boston who was also the first Grand Master of an all-Black Masonic Lodge in America. Their owner sent Primus at a very early age to live with Ezra Trask of Danvers to learn the shoemaking trade, with the promise that he would be freed at age twenty-one. He later related that he was treated as an adopted son, and he later took the family name of Trask. But he never took to the trade, and instead worked as a farmer and wagon driver. He enlisted in January 1776 in the Continental army in the midst of the siege of Boston, serving at Winter Hill. During the New York campaign, his unit served first at Governor's Island in New York harbor but removed to Manhattan after Washington's retreat from Long Island. He was present for the Battle at White Plains and retreated with the army through New Jersey to Pennsylvania. His brigade had intended to cross the Delaware River and attack Burlington as a distraction while Washington attacked Trenton, but they were unable cross the river at that time due to ice. They rejoined Washington in New Jersey at the end of the year, and Primus agreed to extend his service in response to the general's plea. At Princeton he reportedly captured two British soldiers that he had pursued for half a mile. He later reenlisted and served through the end of the war, including two years as part of Washington's "military family."

Another Black Patriot veteran serving with the Fourth Massachusetts was Cato Smith. Born in Ghana in Africa, he was taken as a slave when he was ten years old. A profile published by the National Park Service notes he was enslaved by the Smith family, whose home is now part of the Minute Man National Historical Park. When word of the British approach toward Lexington and Concord arrived in nearby Lincoln, where they lived, Cato's owner led the Lincoln minuteman company to fight at the Old North Bridge in Concord. It's not known if twenty-five-year-old Cato was part of the company on that historic day, however, he did enlist with his owner a few days later until the end of 1775. With the anticipated invasion of New York by the British looming, Cato reenlisted in summer 1776. He may have served as a substitute for his owner. Fighting at Long Island, Harlem Heights, and White Plains, he survived the Battle at Princeton but died in service a few weeks later of unknown causes on January 24, 1777, at New Castle, New York. He was likely buried in an unknown grave, having received his freedom only in death.

Nathaniel Small of Gloucester, Massachusetts, was a veteran who responded to General Washington's call to extend his enlistment. Having fought at Bunker Hill and served during the siege of Boston, he fought at Pell's Point alongside the Marblehead Regiment, helping delay the British attempt to trap the Continental army on Manhattan. Just before agreeing to extend his enlistment until the end of the war (well beyond the six weeks that Washington had asked for), he fought at Trenton and was now marching with his regiment toward Princeton.

Just after sunrise on the morning of January 3, troops under General Nathaniel Greene were spotted moving toward Princeton on the Saw Mill Road by the tail end of a British column led by General Mawhood, heading south on the King's Highway to reinforce Lord Cornwallis at Trenton. Until then they were entirely unaware that the Continental army was on the move. Mawhood ordered his column to turn around, and in less than a half hour the British were engaged against troops under General Hugh Mercer. John Cadwalader was advancing in support of Mercer when Mawhood ordered a bayonet charge that broke Mercer's line. Mercer himself was repeatedly bayoneted and left mortally wounded. With Mercer's men in full retreat, Cadwalader's line also began to waver.

It was at this point, as the Continental flank was collapsing, that General Washington arrived with reinforcements. On a white steed and holding up a flag, with the British charging, he placed himself in front of his men and urged them forward. The moment has been recreated in a number of paintings from the era. Washington's push forward and artillery brought to bear on the charging redcoats broke their line. Nearly surrounded, Mawhood ordered retreat, which left his men fleeing the battlefield with the Continentals in hot pursuit. Two to three hundred fled back to Princeton and took refuge in the college's Nassau Hall, which still stands today. It was at this point that Samuel Sutphen's unit arrived on the scene and eventually forced their surrender.

Peter Jennings of the Fifth Artillery of Blacks from Rhode Island left his detailed eyewitness account of the Princeton battle in his pension statement years later. His unit's cannons helped to hold back Cornwallis's charges at Assunpink Creek and the silent march north:

> The firing from our artillery, somewhat checked their advance upon us, and night coming on, they halted on the opposite side of a creek from us, and ceased firing. It was then supposed that they intended making a general attack upon us the next morning. We were ordered to light fires along our lines in our front, for the purpose, as declarant afterwards discovered, of deceiving the enemy; for instead of remaining at the fires we were marched off with all possible expedition towards Princeton where some regiments of the British troops were quartered. We reached there very early the next morning and made a vigorous attack upon them. Declarant has a perfect recollection of an occurrence which took place during this engagement, which will never be effaced from his memory. A part of our troops

> were driven back by the British and were thrown into much confusion. Gen. Washington perceiving it, seized a standard and rushed in front of our troops, and dashed several paces ahead towards the enemy, exclaiming "come on boys," or some such expression. His example had the desired effect of rallying our troops, and they followed the Commander with renewed ardor. While Gen. Washington was between the two armies at least one round was fired on each side, and he remained untouched.
>
> Soon after this occurrence, the British troops gave way and retreated into some public building, where we pursued them and kept up such a play of artillery upon them, that all those who had taken refuge, were compelled to surrender to us. In this engagement, the British were completely routed and defeated. Many of them were killed and wounded, and a great number taken prisoners. The loss on the American side he thinks was inconsiderable.[2]

Decades after the fact, Washington's personal battlefield heroism in the face of imminent danger between the two lines still seemed fresh to Peter Jennings and many others who witnessed it.

From Princeton, Washington marched his army to Morristown, where they would quarter for the winter. There were discussions about making another attack, but the victories at Trenton and Princeton had their intended effect for the army and the country. The Continental army could stand against the British regulars. The New York campaign in late 1776 was still painful, and the losses were still significant, but the desperate gamble to go on the offense and win gave many Americans reason to hope.

Militia raids during the winter would push the British further back out of New Jersey and toward New York. It would still also cause more Continental casualties. Anthony Shaswell, a Black Patriot who fought in the heat of the Battle at Bunker Hill along the rail fence, was listed as taken prisoner on January 24, 1777. He is not named in any further record, and he may have died in captivity with thousands of other American POWs. British prison ships were frequently more lethal than the battlefield.

REBUILDING THE ARMY: VETERANS AND NEW RECRUITS

After the men who had extended their enlistments were released, Washington didn't have much of an army left. The Continental Congress issued a call for states to raise eighty-eight more battalions, and encouraged longer enlistments to avoid the year-end manpower drain of experienced veterans being replaced by green recruits. But now green recruits were needed for the coming year.

Some Black Patriot veterans returned to the army. Three veterans who rejoined had served at Bunker Hill and the siege of Boston: Charlestown Lyndes, Jude Hall, and Eden London. Lyndes enlisted for three years in the Massachusetts line on February 20. With only a few intermittent breaks, Jude Hall served through the end of the war. Having served in both 1775 and 1776, he apparently returned to his home in Exeter, New Hampshire, but reenlisted in the Second New Hampshire in April 1777. Renowned for his great strength, his service became legendary. George Quintal, who wrote the definitive study of Black Patriots on the Battle Road and at Bunker Hill, notes that Eden London had been enslaved by eleven different owners in eighteen years. On December 7, 1776, he enlisted for three years in the Tenth Massachusetts, which would see action at Saratoga later in 1777.

Philip Rodman of Providence, Rhode Island, was at the battles of White Plains and Trenton in 1776. In his pension application he notes he extended his enlistment "by the request of General Washington," and fought at the Battle of Princeton.

One man who declined Washington's offer to extend his enlistment at the end of 1776 was Jacob Francis. But his reasons were personal. His story is the subject of a recent book-length study by William Kidder. Born in New Jersey, as a teenager he was bound out and served several different men. He ended up in Salem, Massachusetts, and was taken out to sea, traveling to New York and the Isle of St. John's in the spring of 1768. Months after his term of indenture was complete, he enlisted in October 1775 as Jacob Gulick (his last name taken from a previous man who owned his time). Serving at Long Island and Trenton in 1776, being camped so close to his mother in New Jersey enticed him to leave at the end of the year to seek her out. After a decade's absence, he found her in Hunterdon County. He later served with New Jersey militia for several turns of service and applied for a pension in 1832, when he recounted his military experience.

On his death in 1839, the *Flemington Gazette* lamented the loss of "Another Hero of the Revolution"—a fitting epitaph for Jacob Francis and many other Black Patriots:

> In this village, on Tuesday the 26th of July, Jacob Francis, a colored man, in the 83rd year of his age. He has resided in this place thirty-five years; has been an orderly member of the Baptist Church for thirty years; he has raised a large family, in a manner creditable to his judgement and his Christian character, and lived to see them doing well; and has left the scenes of this mortal existence, deservedly respected by all who knew him. Jacob Francis was a soldier of the Revolution—he served a long tour of duty in the Massachusetts militia, and was some time in the regular army in New Jersey; and we have learned from those who knew him in those days of privation of peril, that his fidelity and good conduct as a soldier were the object of remark, and received the approbation of his officers. For the last few

> years he received a pension from the government; an acknowledgement of his services to his country which, though made at a late day, came most opportunely to minister to his comfort in the decline of life, and under the infirmities of old age.[3]

The unexpected victories at Trenton and Princeton provided an added degree of hope to the American cause, and inspired new recruits to enlist. During 1777, Black Patriots would flock to Washington's army unlike any other period during the Revolutionary War. In the previous two years they could be seen smattered in small numbers in some units, mostly from New England, but not in any consistent way. That changed dramatically as the ranks of companies and regiments swelled, including in southern states, such as Virginia and Maryland. One Hessian officer observed in the fall of that year that, "One sees no regiment in which there are not Negroes in abundance, and among them are able-bodied, sturdy fellows."[4] In fact, of the nearly three hundred Black Patriots identified by historian David O. White as enlisting in Connecticut during the war, more than half (157) enlisted in 1777 alone.

One of those was Cash Africa of Litchfield, Connecticut, who had already served a term of service in 1775 with his brother Jeph Africa. But he still wasn't a free man, a problem he resolved before reenlisting by successfully suing Deborah Marsh for illegally enslaving him for three years. Now freed by the courts, he reenlisted in the Fifth Connecticut and served until the end of the war. Caesar Shelton was born into slavery when his mother gave birth to him on a slave ship on the Middle Passage from Africa, and he enlisted in the Fourth Connecticut to obtain his freedom. Chatham Freeman was the slave of Noah Yale of Wallingford, and he agreed to enlist with the promise of his freedom after his service for Yale's son, who had been drafted. He fought with the Sixth Connecticut in one of the last major engagements of the year that proved the reliability and bravery of Black Patriots and prompted even more recruitment. Fighting with him was Jeffrey Brace (enlisting at age thirty-five as Pomp London), whose later memoirs of his enslavement and war service discussed in chapter 1 were one of the most detailed and rare looks into the life of a Black Patriot. Prince George joined the Connecticut Line at age thirteen as a drummer for the duration of the war, and left the army at the war's end with a discharge signed by George Washington.

In February 1777, Prince Ames and Scipio Bartlett both enlisted in the Fifteenth Massachusetts, the former serving as a substitute for Benjamin Ames. They served in several battles before year's end. Adam Adams enlisted in the famed First Maryland that had made the heroic and costly stand at Long Island to save the Continental army the year before. He was one of sixty Black Patriots in that regiment. Primas Coffin joined the Second New Hampshire, having been enslaved by the Coffin family for many years. He became good friends with another Black Patriot, London Dailey, during their service together. William Wanton, London Hazard, and Esek Roberts mustered in with the Rhode Island Line, Wanton and Hazard serving as substitutes, exchanging their service for freedom. Roberts became a prisoner of war during the conflict. Thomas Lively joined the Fifth Virginia, lost an eye at the Battle of Monmouth, and later become a prisoner of war, only to return as a substitute at Yorktown. David Ivey became a wagoner for the Tenth North Carolina and served three years.

Cuff Rosaria Jr. and his brother, Silas, both signed up for three-year enlistments in the Massachusetts line. Their father, Cuff Rosaria, had been a slave of Josiah Torrey in Abington and was the subject of a runaway slave notice in 1747. He was later sent by his owner's second husband to fight in the French and Indian War. After the battles of Lexington and Concord, at age forty-eight, Cuff Sr. joined the militia and was stationed in Roxbury in the early months of the siege of Boston. From their position, they could likely watch the battle on Breed's and Bunker Hills. According to records, Cuff Sr. died in camp on August 6, 1775. Two years later, Cuff Jr. and

Silas took their place as the second generation of Black Patriots that their country would accept as soldiers but not citizens.

William and Ben Franck were also second-generation Black Patriots, joining the First Rhode Island within weeks of each other in the spring of 1777. Shirley Green, a descendant of William who wrote her doctoral dissertation on the Franck brothers and their Revolutionary War experience, records that their father, Rufus Franck, served in both the French and Indian War and the 1762 British siege of Havana. Enlisting in the Continental army, William and Ben assumed a proud military legacy, but during the course of the war the brothers unexpectedly took divergent paths.

Sipp Ives, Peter Brewer, and Prince Douglass cast their lots with the American cause in early 1777. Sadly, by the end of 1777 all three were killed in action in service to their country.

THE DANBURY RAID AND THE BATTLE OF RIDGEFIELD (APRIL 22–APRIL 28, 1777)

One of the first engagements for these new Black Patriot recruits came when British General William Tryon crossed the Long Island Sound, landing with 1,800 troops at Compo Beach near Westport, Connecticut, intending to raid Continental army supplies stored further inland in Danbury. Raiding nearly twenty storehouses, the supplies they found were tossed into the streets of Danbury and burned. Local militia leaders alerted their troops, and a barricade was established on the main street of Ridgefield under the command of David Wooster and Benedict Arnold. Tryon was likely mindful of the thousands of minutemen who had responded to Lexington and Concord and knew that his raiding party could quickly be outnumbered. Pushing through the spirited Patriot defense (Wooster, who regularly corresponded with Phyllis Wheatley in Boston, was mortally wounded, and Arnold had his horse shot from under him), the British continued to press on back to their boats. The British soldiers still took time to loot and pillage the local citizens along the way. The Patriots' pursuit pushed Tryon's troops back to the beach with their boats, where a small skirmish saw them on their way. The Danbury raid deprived the Continental army of valuable supplies, but the Battle of Ridgefield and the haste with which the British had to make their departure were valuable reminders that in the countryside, away from the major cities and the protection of the Royal Navy, things could turn against them rapidly. While the British continued attacking towns along the coast throughout the war, they never made another inland raid in Connecticut. Arnold was promoted to major general for his role in repelling the British.

One of those in the Battle of Ridgefield was Jack Congo, who had enlisted in the Fifth Connecticut just days before Tryon's arrival. A slave of Nathaniel Baldwin, he might have served as a substitute for someone in the Baldwin family with a promise of freedom after his term expired. The following year he fell sick at Valley Forge and died at a military hospital in Fishkill, New York, on October 30, 1778. Jack Congo's only freedom came in death, in an unmarked grave on behalf of his country's cause. Years after the war, Baldwin unsuccessfully tried to collect his dead slave's back pay.

Robin Starr of Litchfield reenlisted with the Second Connecticut on the first of January and claimed in his pension application to have been at Danbury, among many other battles during his six years of service, receiving the Badge of Merit at the end of the war. Other Black Patriots in Danbury and Ridgefield may have been inspired by the brave Patriot stand against the Tryon raid, encouraging them to enlist. John Dimorat had served with David Wooster in the French and Indian War, and in March 1778 at the ripe age of forty-four he enlisted in the Third Connecticut. Local historian Jack Sanders records that several members of the Jacklin family in the Ridgefield area, including Ebenezer and Thaddeus, also served.

One story about the Tryon raid, told by historian David White, involves Ned, a slave of Samuel Smith of Redding, who mustered with Major Daniel Starr of Danbury to oppose the British as they moved into the town. Overwhelmed, these Patriot defenders retreated to a house. Discovered there by the British, an officer ordered the men killed and the house set afire. Ned was run through with a sword, and, rising up mortally wounded to shoot his assailant, another officer beheaded him. Samuel Smith said that Ned was "a very zealous friend to the American cause," but appealed to the General Assembly to reimburse the loss of his slave. A monument placed in 2002 honors the citizens of Redding who were taken hostage by Tryon in the raid and concludes noting Ned's heroic sacrifice.

The wave of enlistments continued into the summer months. Juba Freeman was one of six Black Patriots who enlisted from the town of Milford, Connecticut—the others being Job Caesar, Pomp Cyrus, William Sowers, Congo Zado, and Peter Gibbs. All six men from Milford served in a Connecticut company of Black Patriots initially commanded by Captain Charles Pond, and later by Captains David Humphrey and Zebulon Butler. There are several payment vouchers for Juba Freeman held by the Library of Congress from his service during the war. One fascinating document dated July 2, 1777, records an agreement between Freeman, identified as "Juba Negro," and his master, Richard Law, who served in the Continental Congress for Connecticut, consenting to his enlistment in exchange for payment of half of Juba's wages to Law, presumably the purchase price for his freedom.

THE PRESCOTT RAID (JULY 10, 1777)

Black Patriots also played a role in one of the most daring commando raids of the whole war. It began with the British capture of Continental General Charles Lee in December 1776, the second highest ranking American officer. A prisoner exchange could only occur if the Continentals had a prisoner of similar rank, and in early July 1777, they had none. To address that problem, Lieutenant Colonel William Barton of the First Rhode Island asked for forty volunteers to accompany him on a secret mission into occupied territory. The British had seized the valuable port city of Newport, Rhode Island, unopposed the previous December, shortly before General Lee's capture and after their success against the Continental army at Long Island, Harlem Heights, and White Plains. The target of the raid was none other than Major General Richard Prescott, the commander of all of the British Forces in Rhode Island.

Information from spies inside the city and a runaway slave, Quako Honeyman, identified the home that Prescott stayed in at night and details about the movements of his guard. Honeyman had been hired out to the owner of the home where Prescott slept. Barton's volunteers traveled at night in five whaling boats, using muffled oars to avoid alerting British ships in the harbor. On landing they had to travel unnoticed more than a mile to the house and disarm Prescott's guard without alarming their intended captive. Having successfully crossed the bay, they found a lone sentry at the house, who was promptly disarmed and subdued. Barton and some of his party surrounded and entered the house. Entering Prescott's bedroom, Barton informed him that he was now a prisoner of the Continental army.

Decades after the Prescott raid, considerable lore circulated about several Black Patriots on the mission. Several versions relate that either Jack Sisson, Guy Watson, or Prince Godwin put his head through the door of the residence, or Prescott's locked bedroom door, to reach their target. The three men were likely present and are documented as being part of the First Rhode Island. Jack Sisson had been the slave of Thomas Sisson of Tiverton. When the regiment was reorganized the following year, composed entirely of Black Patriots, Sisson reenlisted and served until the end of the war. Guy Watson was also a slave serving to obtain his freedom.

Like Jack Sisson, he also reenlisted in the reorganized First Rhode Island and served five more years, obtaining a pension from the state for disabilities from his battle wounds. Years later he was elected "Black Governor" of South Kingstown, the leader of the freemen and women of the community. An obituary published on his death recounted his participation in the Prescott raid.

Another likely participant was Richard Rhodes, who was abducted in Africa and sold into slavery on his arrival. When he enlisted, he was the teenage slave of Nehemiah Rhodes. He was shot through the arm with a musket ball at the Battle of Monmouth, fought at Yorktown, and served honorably until the end of the war. He froze to death in 1821, and his obituary noted his honorable service in the Revolutionary War and identified him as one of Barton's raiders. Quako Honeyman faced attempts by the family of his late owner to re-enslave him even before the war's end. Appealing to the Rhode Island legislature, they declared him manumitted from slavery and, noting his service as a Patriot spy, therefore forever free.

THE SARATOGA CAMPAIGN (JUNE 14–OCTOBER 17, 1777)

While there were no major military campaigns in the first half of 1777, that quickly changed. The British had devised a plan to split New England from the rest of the colonies by taking control of the Hudson River through New York with a three-pronged attack. General John Burgoyne marched south from Quebec with a combined force of British and Hessian soldiers and captured the forts around Lake Champlain and Lake Edward held by American forces. General Barry St. Leger in Montreal approached from Lake Ontario in the west with his column and the Indian allies of the British and marched along the Mohawk River. The third column under General Howe marched north up the Hudson

River Valley from New York City, intending for all three columns to converge somewhere around Albany.

New England was providing much of the men and supplies for the Continental army. Disrupting or altogether depriving General Washington of those critical resources with complete control of the Hudson River would force a speedy end to the war. There was sound logic to the plan, but an unspoken danger was that the British columns would be operating so close to the manpower and military supplies that they intended to stop. While the Northern Department of the Continental army, under the command of General Horatio Gates, fielded only seven to eight thousand men at the time, those numbers quickly swelled as the alarm and calls for militiamen went out. By the time of the culminating battle of the campaign at Saratoga just a few months after Burgoyne departed, he faced twice his numbers.

Black Patriots were well represented in the battles to come and participated in some of the fiercest fighting of the campaign. The majority of Black Patriots who served in the Revolutionary War came from New England—Massachusetts, New Hampshire, Connecticut, and Rhode Island. And by the summer of 1777, many of them were already serving or had just enlisted when Burgoyne marched out. In the fight to come, they played an important role in turning the tide of American fortunes in the war.

Burgoyne's first targets were the Continental positions at Fort Ticonderoga and Mount Independence on opposite sides of Lake Champlain. While Benedict Arnold's ragtag fleet had lost the Battle of Lake Champlain the previous October, the British army had returned to Canada as winter had set in, leaving the forts in the area in American hands. Continental General Arthur St. Clair maintained four thousand troops occupying the forts, and Burgoyne was quickly bearing down with considerably more numbers. On July 5, St. Clair ordered a retreat rather than face a bitter battle defending their positions or risk being surrounded and losing the entire force as casualties and prisoners, surprising Burgoyne. Several units were left in the rear to cover the retreat and slow the British pursuit.

BATTLES OF HUBBARDTON (JULY 7, 1777) AND FORT ANNE (JULY 8, 1777)

The first major engagement occurred at Hubbardton on July 7, when the Eleventh Massachusetts under Colonel Ebenezer Francis made a stand, forcing the British to try to turn the flanks of the Americans and slowing the redcoats' pursuit of the rest of the army. Prince Ames, Scipio Bartlett, and Lonnon Rhode, all three of whom had enlisted earlier in the year, were in the heat of the battle serving under Colonel Francis. Other Black Patriots present at the Battle of Hubbardton—the only Revolutionary War battle occurring in what is now Vermont—included Pompey Woodward, Simeon Grandison, and Peter Brewer, who had been stationed at Fort Ticonderoga; and Primas Coffin, George Evans, Cato Wallingford, and Gloster Watson of the Second New Hampshire.

Several Black Patriots were casualties in the battle. Nicholas Vintrom, also of the Second New Hampshire, disappeared entirely from the military record after the battle, presumably because he was either killed or captured. Some records indicate that Titus Wilson was wounded in action, became a prisoner, and died in captivity; or, he was killed in action. Asa Perham was mortally wounded in the battle. Aaron Oliver, a veteran of the Battle of Bunker Hill, was captured and sent to a British prison ship moored in Wallabout Bay in New York, where he languished until he was released in April 1778. Apparently weakened by his captivity, he died four weeks after his release. In a cruel blow for his widow and three orphans, the town of Temple, New Hampshire, "warned out" the family (meaning they would no longer receive public support) in December 1778, just months after his death and as winter approached. In 2017, parts of Aaron Oliver's military kit, including priming horn, cartridge pouch, wooden cask, and shaving mirror, were donated by his descendants for permanent display at the Hubbardton Battlefield State Historic Site.

With the British still in pursuit of the Continentals, another brutal battle occurred the following day (July 8) at Fort Anne, involving a small American force that was moving the sick and wounded from Fort Ticonderoga to Fort Edward. As they rested at Fort Anne they encountered some of Burgoyne's reconnaissance troops. Seizing on a numerical advantage, the Americans engaged the British until Burgoyne's reinforcements began to arrive on scene, forcing them to retreat to Fort Edward. Peter Abbott, Cato Moulton, and Peter Pomp (who had been a slave of Major Andrew McClary of Epsom, killed at the Battle of Bunker Hill) of the Third New Hampshire participated in the battle.

THE SIEGE OF FORT STANWIX AND THE BATTLE OF ORISKANY (AUGUST 6, 1777)

The western column led by British General Barry St. Leger was not faring well in their progress along the Mohawk River Valley, having been stalled by the stubborn Patriot defense at Fort Stanwix, now at Rome, New York. One concerning development for St. Leger was that militia units from all over the area were headed to relieve Fort Stanwix and raise the siege. One of those relief columns was headed by Benedict Arnold. Traveling with him were Brister Bennet and Prince Douglass, who had enlisted in the Second Massachusetts just weeks before, had already been on the retreat from Fort Ticonderoga, and now were heading back toward battle.

Another American militia relief column led by General Nicholas Herkimer, including some Oneida allies, were also headed to Fort Stanwix. The British were alerted to their approach by their Iroquois allies and prepared an ambush comprised of Loyalists, Mohawks, and Seneca to attack Herkimer's militia in a ravine near Oriskany, about six miles from Fort Stanwix. What followed on August 6, 1777, was one of the bloodiest battles of the entire war.

Louis Cook had command of a detachment of Indian Rangers of the First New York traveling with Herkimer. The son of a Black man and an Abenaki wife, Cook had spent much of his youth with his mother among the Caughnawaga people. In the French and Indian War he had fought against the British at Braddock's defeat. His experiences during that war developed into a deep hatred of the British, and he quickly took up the Americans' cause. He had already met with Washington (his adversary from the previous conflict), twice offering assistance. Cook's experience in frontier fighting—as well as that of Han Yerry of Stockbridge and his wife, Polly Cooper (Tyonajanegen), an Oneida leader in her own right, and their sixty Oneida fighters—was critical to the survival of Herkimer's column.

When the ambush at Oriskany began, Herkimer was one of the first casualties, being shot in the leg. He propped himself against a tree, where he continued to direct the counterattack. Three messengers were sent to alert the garrison at Fort Stanwix, requesting help. As the Patriot militia regained some order by taking a defensive position, a thunderstorm created a pause in the battle. This gave Herkimer's troops time to regroup. As the battle resumed, much of it was hand-to-hand fighting. Soon, many of the Indian allies of the British began to retreat, and sounds of an attack on the undefended Loyalist and Indian camps nearby—attacked by a sortie from Fort Stanwix led by Colonel Marinus Willett—largely ended the fight. The Americans suffered heavy casualties, considerably more than the Loyalist and Indian ambushers, but successfully fought their way out of the ambush and held the field at the end of the battle. General Herkimer died days later from an infection caused by the amputation of his leg. General St. Leger continued the siege of Fort Stanwix, which prevented any further progress toward joining up with Burgoyne. As General

Arnold's relief column approached, St. Leger abandoned the siege on August 22, just over two weeks after the Battle at Oriskany, and retreated back up the Mohawk River toward Lake Ontario, never coming close to joining up with Burgoyne. Louis Cook eventually received an American commission and was the highest ranked person of color on the American side during the entire war.

THE BATTLE OF BENNINGTON (AUGUST 16, 1777)

As Burgoyne's push down the Hudson was blocked, supplies were running low and American forces facing him were growing larger. His invasion plan assumed that his column heading south out of Canada would receive considerable support from Loyalists in the area, including men and supplies, but that support never materialized. Burgoyne's intelligence told him that supplies had been stored nearby, and he dispatched Hessian Lieutenant Colonel Friedrich Baum to head east to forage. He ended up headed toward Bennington, in what is now in Vermont, where General John Stark, one of the heroes of Bunker Hill and the man later responsible for New Hampshire's "Live Free or Die" motto, had amassed a considerable militia force, including from the Berkshires in Massachusetts, New Hampshire, and the Green Mountain Boys under Colonel Seth Warner. Following some skirmishes between Baum and Stark's militia, Stark decided on a daring plan to envelop many of the Hessian troops entrenched on top of a hill. Two columns marched around the Hessian position and approached from the flanks. Before the battle, Stark reportedly pointed to the Hessian position and told his troops, "They are ours or Molly Stark sleeps a widow tonight."

The Battle of Bennington on August 16, 1777, resulted in a resounding Patriot victory. The attack on the Hessian positions on the hill resulted in a desperate two hours of hand-to-hand combat that saw most of the

Hessians captured or killed. Nearby, Stark drove off a Loyalist force of two hundred men in minutes, mortally wounding Baum, but he and his troops were pushed back nearly a mile into a ravine by an arriving relief force of five hundred men under Lieutenant Colonel Heinrich Breymann, sent by Burgoyne. At the very moment it appeared that Stark's line might begin to falter, five hundred men of Warner's Green Mountain Boys joined the battle, which continued until darkness fell and what was left of the Hessian troops retreated.

It is likely that at this dramatic moment of the battle a Black Patriot, Sipp Ives, was killed. He was the only member of the Green Mountain Boys who died at the Battle of Bennington, one of fourteen Patriots killed in the fighting, but other Black Patriots were present that day. Historians Lion G. Miles and Phil Holland have found that Adam Negro, Zephy Negro, Simeon Grandison, and Charles Grandison were part of the same company with Sipp Ives. Peter Blanchard served under Colonel Thomas Stickney, and Charles Bowles was part of Colonel David Hobart's militia, with both regiments making the main assault on Hessian Hill. Jesse Brown and Thomas Griffin approached from the rear with David Hobart's regiment. Peter Blanchard was part of Colonel Thomas Stickney's regiment that also made the main charge up Hessian Hill but also joined the Green Mountain Boys to reinforce Stark's position at the ravine.

Fourteen-year-old Pompey Woodward had already served at Fort Ticonderoga and Mount Independence when Burgoyne's invasion began, and he was at the Battle of Hubbardton. While he was not present at Bennington, he was near the battle and watched the Hessian prisoners being brought into town immediately following the battle. In his pension affidavit, Woodward claims to have witnessed an attempt by some of the Hessians to escape. A traditional account claims that a Mrs. Moses Robinson offered rope to transport the prisoners if her slave could lead them on her old mare—a moment depicted in a mural painted by Leroy Williams that hangs in the Bennington Museum.

The Patriot victory at Bennington is considered by many historians to represent the founding event of Vermont. Shortly thereafter the Republic of Vermont was proclaimed, and its new constitution abolished slavery. Burgoyne was not only deprived of the supplies he intended Baum to forage, but many of Baum's Brunswick Dragoons were either killed or captured. With the retreat of St. Leger's column, supplies dwindling as Stark's militia brigades prevented any further British raiding parties, and Patriot militias pouring in from all over the region, Burgoyne lost more than men and supplies. The victory boosted morale and provided hope that the northern army under General Gates might successfully stand against the British invasion.

The surprise victories at Trenton and Princeton at the beginning of the year had breathed new life into Washington's army at the time described by Thomas Paine as "the American crisis," and it inspired many Black Patriots to cast their lots with the American cause. Their participation in the raid in Rhode Island capturing British General Prescott and repelling Tryon's troops from Connecticut at Ridgefield were bright moments in what was an otherwise quiet period during the first half of 1777. But the battles at Hubbardton, Oriskany, and Bennington were just a prelude to the coming conflict between Burgoyne and Gates. And further south, General Washington and his army were about to face a new threat that endangered American independence just a year after the Declaration. The service and sacrifice of Black Patriots would be needed on all fronts.

Two monuments marking a large-scale British raid of Connecticut in April 1777 targeting Continental army stores in Dansbury. The first monument in Redding memorializes citizens taken prisoner during the raid and held for ransom. It also honors the sacrifice of a slave from Redding, identified as Ned, who was killed by the British in Danbury while trying to prevent the raiders from burning the town. The second monument in Westport honors the minutemen and militia who responded to the raid and drove the British back to their boats. Black Patriots taking part in repelling the invasion were Jack Congo, Robin Starr, John Dimorat, and members of the local Jacklin family. (Images: Patrick S. Poole)

ARREST OF GENERAL PRESCOTT.

On July 10, 1777, a small group of volunteers under the command of Continental Major William Barton conducted a nighttime raid to capture British General Richard Prescott, who commanded the forces occupying Newport, Rhode Island. Evading British warships and patrols, the party surprised Prescott in bed and captured him without firing a shot. Several Black Patriot soldiers, including Guy Watson and Jack Sisson, were part of the raiding party. Prescott was eventually exchanged for the release of Continental General Charles Lee. (Image: Internet Archive)

Items from the field kit of Black Patriot Aaron Oliver, including powder horn, cartridge pouch, cask, and mirror. Oliver enlisted on April 23, 1775, in Temple, New Hampshire, and marched with his company to join the siege of Boston. There he fought at the Battle of Bunker Hill. In 1776, he served at Mount Independence and Fort Ticonderoga. It was near there on July 7, 1777, that he was taken prisoner by the British at the Battle of Hubbardton. Weakened by starvation during his captivity, he died on April 30, 1778, shortly after his release. These items were donated by his descendants to the Hubbardton Battlefield State Historic Site, where they are on display. (Image: Vermont State Historic Sites)

CHAPTER 5

1777 CONTINUED: VICTORY, DEFEAT, AND SURVIVAL

THE ARCHIVES OF THE Massachusetts Historical Society contain several important documents related to the service of Cato Baker, a Black Patriot from New Hampshire who enlisted in Captain John Drew's company of the Second New Hampshire Battalion in May 1777. The first document is dated December 6, 1763, and it is a bill of sale for Cato between Henry Ward of Rhode Island, his owner at the time, and Otis Baker of Dover, New Hampshire, his new owner, for the amount of 1,400 pounds. The bill of sale identifies Cato as a "negro boy" and a "negro lad," indicating that he was not yet a man. The reverse side of the document is dated thirteen years later, and it records Otis Baker freeing Cato from slavery. The June 1777 date of his manumission coincides with his enlistment just weeks earlier, and the witness was Reverend Jeremy Belknap, who had served as chaplain to the Dover-area militias. Though not explicitly detailed, it seems that he was granted his freedom in return for his service in the Continental army. Cato Baker participated in the battles around Saratoga, New York, in September and October 1777, one of the most consequential battles of the entire American Revolution, and his unit was involved in some of the thickest action of the campaign.

Prince Bailey also enlisted earlier in the year with the Second Massachusetts Regiment. Abducted from Africa and enslaved at age eight, he said his original name had been Prince Dunsick, which he used after the war. This caused some confusion when he applied for his veteran's pension years later. He, too, was in the hottest fighting at Saratoga.

John Reed of the New Hampshire militia had already served three short tours, including participating in the Patriot victories at Trenton and Princeton and reinforcing Fort Ticonderoga earlier in the year. He was also part of the assault from the rear of the enemy's position with Colonel Nichols on Hessian Hill at the Battle of Bennington. But with Burgoyne trying to cut off New England from the rest of the country, Reed enlisted with the First New Hampshire Regiment, which defended the American position at the Battle of Bemis Heights just weeks later. Overall, the New Hampshire and Massachusetts regiments and the Black Patriots fighting with them were heavily engaged in the battles around Saratoga.

The Saratoga campaign was the first action seen by Prince Whipple, slave of Declaration of Independence signer William Whipple, who had waited on his owner during the deliberations of the Continental Congress in Philadelphia in 1776. Much folklore surrounds Prince Whipple's war record, including claims that he is the Black Patriot depicted in Emanuel Leutze's famous painting, *Washington Crossing the Delaware*, but William Whipple was not present at Trenton at the time, and Prince Whipple was likely with his owner at the time. William Whipple would, however, command a brigade of four regiments at Saratoga.

Another oft-repeated apocryphal anecdote records the following exchange between William and Prince earlier in the war:

"Hurry up, Prince, we've got to go fight for our freedom."

"But I have no freedom to fight for," Prince replied.

Whipple, it is said, looked into the young fellow's eyes and proclaimed, "From this moment on you are a free man, Prince. Hurry up now and we will fight for our freedom together."

Prince Whipple, however, was not freed until after the war in 1784, at the time of his marriage. But he was intimately involved in William's personal and business affairs, and in 1781 he was given the rights of a freeman. And he served honorably in the Saratoga campaign in defense of the independence and freedoms he heard much about the year before in Philadelphia.

Agrippa Hull also saw his first combat at Saratoga. Born a freeman and raised in the mixed community of Stockbridge, Massachusetts, at age eighteen he enlisted and served as the orderly to General John Paterson, who commanded a brigade of Massachusetts regiments. He later developed a close relationship with the volunteer Polish engineer Tadeusz Kosciuszko, who was responsible for the excellent defenses of the American position at Saratoga. Both men later collaborated on the defenses at West Point and visited each other after the war.

THE BATTLES OF SARATOGA

There was a change of leadership in the American camp. General Horatio Gates assumed command of the northern army in late August after the Continental Congress and General Washington grew dissatisfied with Philip Schuyler. Gates was born in England and served in the British army during the French and Indian War but married an American woman and settled in Virginia on a small plantation. His task at Saratoga was markedly different than Burgoyne. Gates needed only to play defense and delay, or stop altogether, the British army's progress toward Albany. Burgoyne had left Canada with limited supplies and men. He was stalled nearly forty miles from his intended objective of Albany. St. Leger's column approaching from the west had been stopped at Fort Stanwix. His Indian allies abandoned him after the Battle of Oriskany, forcing him to retreat back up the Mohawk River. The foraging party Burgoyne dispatched to Bennington had cost him at least a thousand men, either killed or captured. Without reinforcement, resupply, or retreat, time was Burgoyne's enemy unless they could make it to Albany. For Gates, all he had to do was prevent that.

BATTLE OF FREEMAN'S FARM (SEPTEMBER 19, 1777)

With the loss of his Indian allies, Burgoyne lost much of his intelligence on the Americans' strength and position. To probe the American lines, on September 19 he divided his army into three columns, with General James Hamilton in the center. General Simon Fraser took many of the elite British troops to the right, with the hope of flanking the American lines, and the Germans to the left, moving along the Hudson River. British skirmishers encountered Dan Morgan's Virginia sharpshooters on a field that was part of John Freeman's farm. Morgan's troops initially pushed back the skirmishers but were repelled when British reinforcements arrived. Benedict Arnold, Gates's second in command, asked to move troops forward to protect the American position. For several hours both lines fought back and forth between the farm fields and a thick woods. Approaching darkness, the German column moved up and began firing into the American right flank, forcing them to withdraw. As night fell, the British still commanded the field but had suffered twice the casualties of the Americans, further shrinking Burgoyne's already depleted army.

In addition to Morgan's men, the First and Third, and later the Second New Hampshire (that had borne the brunt of the Battle of Hubbardton), did much of the fighting at Freeman's Farm. Cato Baker's unit fought there, as did Agrippa Hull. Other Black Patriots who fought in New Hampshire units that day included Cato Marcy, John Cook, Jude Hall, Oliver French, Samuel Wier, and Caesar Thompson. Serving in Massachusetts units that day were Obed Coffin, Fortune Freeman, Luke Nickelson, and John Wheeler. There were hundreds of Black Patriots who served during the Saratoga campaign. (See Appendix 3)

Shortly after the Battle of Freeman's Farm, Burgoyne received word from Sir Henry Clinton in New York City that he would be headed north up the Hudson, hoping to force Gates to divide his army and face a fight on two fronts. This encouraged Burgoyne, who halted any advances on the American lines and began improving his defense, awaiting further word from Clinton. There is much debate about Burgoyne's response at this point, on whether his overconfidence from the tactical victory at Freeman's Farm and his hope that Clinton would actually be able to aid him blinded him to the possibility of retreating back to Canada.

ATTACKS ON FORT MONTGOMERY AND FORT CLINTON (OCTOBER 9, 1777)

On October 6, General Clinton landed and made a coordinated attack on Fort Montgomery and Fort Clinton, near West Point. Both forts stood on the west bank of the Hudson River and were manned by less than a third the number of Clinton's troops. The Americans were commanded by recently elected New York Governor (and later, the fourth vice president of the United States) George Clinton, prompting some to describe the fight there as the "Battle of the Clintons."

Fortunately, we have the firsthand account of the battle from a Black Patriot, Benjamin Latimore of the Fifth New York, who recounted his experience in his pension affidavit years later:

> In the early part of the month some vessels belonging to the enemy came in sight and when within five miles of the Fort the wind being slackened they disembarked at a place called Dunderberg on Thunder Hill and marched from thence to the Fort. Before they arrived at the Fort Geo. Clinton sent out different detachments of men to meet them and fire was kept up between them and the enemy until our men returned to the Fort.
>
> Shortly after orders were given by Gen Clinton to stop firing as the enemy had sent a flag by Col. Campbell. The Col.

> Approached near to one of the gates of the Fort near too me of the gates of the Forts and was met on the outside of the Fort by Gen Clinton & Dr. Cook after the usual salutations had passed between them and Col Campbell the Col. Was asked by Gen. Clinton the nature of his business who replied that he came to demand a surrender of the Fort which of done within one hour and our troops presented their arms they would be permitted to go as it was not wished to take them prisoners because they (the enemy) had more men with them than could be accommodated in the fort. Gen. Clinton replied that the Fort would not be surrendered as long as he had a man able to fire a gun. Col. Campbell then said he would eat his supper or would sleep & which it is not collected in the fort that night or in hell. They then parted. An attack was made in the fort by the enemy and was defended until ten or eleven o'clock when it was taken. Gov. Clinton, Gen James Clinton, Col. Dubois, De Cook made their escape Col Bryan or Brown, Stephen Lush aid to Clinton and others and this declarant were made prisoners.
>
> In taking the fort Col. Campbell was killed. He was stabbed on the walls of the fort by Capt. Ronorane of Fishkill. The enemy and the prisoners of whom this declarant was one remained until the latter part of October when the Fort was destroyed by the Enemy and they all went by water to New York.[1]

Latimore's application was supported by a witness statement of General Abraham Godwin of the same regiment, who recounted that he remembered hearing that Latimore had been taken prisoner at Fort Montgomery, had later returned to the regiment on his release by the British, and observed "that he conducted himself as a good and faithful soldier."

Tobias Gilmore of Raynham, Massachusetts, was also present for the battle. He had been abducted in West Africa as a child, his original name being Shibodee Turry Wurry. Brought to America on the slave ship *Dove*, he was sold in Rhode Island to pay for the ship's repairs before it sailed off again to its intended destination of Virginia. He fought in several more battles and was freed from slavery on the completion of his term of service in December 1781. Back home in Raynham, he became a successful and respected figure. Each July 4 the town gathered as he fired off a cannon that he reportedly had brought back from the war. Two homes that he built still stand in town, and the cannon and other personal artifacts, including items from his Continental army kit, are on display at the Old Colony Historical Society. Some of his descendants are now members of the Daughters of the American Revolution.

Sir Henry Clinton made short work of Fort Montgomery and Fort Clinton and would later burn down the town of Kingston on October 17, eventually getting as far up the Hudson as Tivoli in his attempt to reinforce Burgoyne. But it would come too late as events continued to unfold further north, and he would be recalled back to New York City, never having got closer than seventy miles from Burgoyne's army in Saratoga.

BATTLE OF BEMIS HEIGHTS (OCTOBER 7, 1777)

The day following Clinton's victory at Fort Montgomery and Fort Clinton, Burgoyne's waiting had come to an end. Pressured by dwindling supplies, having imposed reduced rations, and with American militias continuing to arrive in the area, he sent out a reconnaissance force of 1,500 soldiers and ten pieces of artillery to scout Gates's western defenses, hoping to find a way to punch through the American lines. This second Battle of Saratoga around Bemis Heights on October 7, 1777, was one of the most consequential in American history and certainly among the most important of the Revolutionary War.

Notified of British movements, Gates responded by sending out six thousand men—considerably more than Burgoyne's scouting force—including the First, Second, and Third New Hampshire Regiments that had seen heavy action at Freeman's Farm. An artillery barrage was unable to dislodge the Americans, and while leading a bayonet charge on the right flank of the deployed Continentals, General Simon Fraser was mortally wounded by one of Dan Morgan's riflemen. The first phase of the battle cost Burgoyne hundreds of troops and the artillery that he had sent out with them, and what was left of his scouting forces retreated back to their defensive positions. At this critical point, Benedict Arnold arrived on the battlefield and took command. Leading New York and Massachusetts units, he directed a charge on one of the British redoubts. While initially repelled, they were able to move to the left and take the position from the rear. This exposed the westernmost redoubt of Burgoyne's line, which was also surrounded and taken, at which time Arnold was shot twice in the leg. Burgoyne's entire army was now exposed, and a hasty retreat to the "Great Redoubt" close to the Hudson River ensued.

The next day, Burgoyne began retreating north. A few days later General John Stark, already the hero of both Bunker Hill and Bennington, and his militia crossed the Hudson River and blocked the only remaining route of escape available to Burgoyne, a spot now known as Stark's Knob. One member of Stark's militia that participated in this critical moment of the Saratoga campaign was Sampson Battis. He had been offered his freedom by his owner, Colonel Archelaus Moore, if he enlisted, and he responded with his local militia to the Lexington Alarm and served a month during the siege of Boston in 1775. Already a veteran, he reenlisted with General John Stark's New Hampshire militia immediately following the Battle of Bennington, joining the march to Fort Edward where they countered British foraging parties and continued to deprive

General Burgoyne of necessary supplies for his continued campaign down the Hudson River to Albany.

SURRENDER OF BURGOYNE'S ARMY (OCTOBER 17, 1777)

The New Hampshire militia's actions on October 12 closed the American loop around the British army at Saratoga, forcing Burgoyne to open surrender negotiations the following day. William Whipple led those negotiations for the Americans, presumably with Prince Whipple present most of the time. On October 17, Burgoyne and his entire army surrendered to General Gates. Both of the Whipples escorted their British and Hessian prisoners to Winter Hill near Boston.

The National Park Service estimates that there were approximately four hundred Black Patriots at Saratoga who served either in Continental army units or in state militias that had been called out to check Burgoyne's invasion. Salem Poor, whose bravery and leadership at Bunker Hill had prompted a number of officers to publicly praise his conduct, was present. Another hero of Bunker Hill, Peter Salem, was in the thick of the battle at Bemis Heights. David Lamson, the French-and-Indian-War veteran who had led the "Old Men of Menotomy" to attack the British reinforcements headed toward Lexington and Concord, capturing the first British prisoners of the war, was there too, having responded to the call for troops. Pomp Magus, serving in the Eighth Massachusetts, was in the center of the Continental line at Bemis Heights with Benedict Arnold in the attack on one of the redoubts. Primus Hall later testified that he saw two of his officers killed in the attack on the British positions, as did John Brown of the same unit.

Cuff Whittemore left Saratoga with a fascinating battle story. At one point during the campaign he had been captured by the British and was put to service in Burgoyne's camp. Ordered to hold the general's white horse, he waited until Burgoyne's entourage was safely distant, climbed aboard the steed, and galloped off back to the American camp, dodging British fire.

Other Black Patriots never left Saratoga. Prince Douglass enlisted for three years in the Second Massachusetts in June 1777, a slave of a member of the Asa Douglass family and possibly a substitute for one of them. He was with Benedict Arnold in the relief of Fort Stanwix, and with the retreat of St. Leger, he quickly returned with his unit to the main army near Saratoga. His regiment was engaged in the battle at Freeman's Farm, and he was one of five members of his unit killed in action that day. Peter Brewer also fought at Freeman's Farm with the First New Hampshire. He had been drafted in January 1777, but agreed to enlist for the entire war. He had earlier retreated with his regiment from Fort Ticonderoga and Mount Independence in advance of Burgoyne's troops earlier that summer. His regiment had the highest number of casualties on the American side from the fight at Freeman's Farm, but he was killed weeks later in the subsequent action at Bemis Heights. Prince Negro had enlisted earlier in the year in the Third Connecticut, and was also killed fighting at Bemis Heights. All three of these Black Patriots killed in action at Saratoga are likely buried in unmarked graves on the battlefield.

Others left with severe wounds. Sidon Martin of the Third New Hampshire was reported dead on November 12 as his regiment marched south after the battle, possibly of battle wounds from Saratoga. Luke Nickerson of the Sixth Massachusetts had enlisted early in the year, survived smallpox that summer, and was wounded in the thigh by a musket ball at Bemis Heights. He was later taken prisoner and rejoined his unit on his release, continuing to serve until January 1780. Sampson Brown was present at Saratoga with the Fifteenth Massachusetts, and was wounded in the hip by a cannon ball. He was transferred to the Invalid Regiment and was granted a disability pension by the US government in 1792.

The impact of the American victory at Saratoga is hard to overstate. For the first time, the Continental army had captured an entire British army. Having transported his British prisoners, General Whipple sent a note, likely carried by Prince Whipple, to Captain John Paul Jones, who was about to set sail for France. Jones was able to relay news of the Saratoga victory to the Continental Congress ambassador in Paris, Ben Franklin, on December 4. The Franco-American alliance concluded on February 6, 1778, with France promising to increase its military aid to the American cause. France officially declared war on Great Britain on March 17, 1778. Spain followed with its own declaration of war in June 1779. General Howe resigned in the spring of 1778 as British commander in chief in America, and his second in command, Sir Henry Clinton, assumed the position and shifted British military strategy to the southern states.

THE PHILADELPHIA CAMPAIGN

American General Horatio Gates was leading the northern army around Saratoga as General Washington was simultaneously trying hold off General Howe's attempt to take Philadelphia. On August 24, 1777—nearly a month before the Battle of Freeman's Farm—Howe had landed with thirteen thousand British troops and five thousand Hessian mercenaries in Maryland, intent on marching north to seize the seat of the Continental Congress and the de facto American capital. Aware of Howe's intentions thanks to intelligence conveyed by Cato, a slave of Hercules Mulligan in New York City who repeatedly risked his life moving through the British lines, Washington established strong defenses south of Philadelphia along the Brandywine Creek.

BATTLE OF BRANDYWINE (SEPTEMBER 11, 1777)

The Battle of Brandywine on September 11, 1777 (eight days before Freeman's Farm, the first Battle of Saratoga), was the largest one-day land battle of the entire Revolutionary War, with thirty thousand soldiers engaged over ten square miles and both armies evenly matched. There were heavily forested areas around Brandywine Creek, so the only places to cross were the existing fords along its course. These fords are where Washington concentrated his troops. Howe discovered through intelligence, likely from Loyalist supporters, that two of the northernmost fords were left undefended. Following the same tactics he had successfully executed at Long Island the year before and several times since, Howe divided his army to flank the Americans. Hessian General Knyphausen feigned an attack at one of the lower crossings, Chadds Ford, while Howe and General Cornwallis took nine thousand troops on an extended seventeen-mile march north on the Great Valley Road to the undefended fords, planning to flank the American positions on the other side of the creek. Throughout the day on September 11, Washington had been repeatedly warned of Howe's movements but failed to act, a heavy fog concealing the British march. Only when local Patriot Thomas Cheney appeared at Washington's headquarters, saying that he had narrowly escaped capture by the British, was the general finally convinced to act, but it was too late.

There were three main areas of action at Brandywine: the main Continental defensive position at Chadds Ford; Birmingham Hill, where an attempt was made to stall Howe's flanking column; and later, General Nathanael Greene's position covering the retreat of the army.

Seeing his first action of the war at Brandywine was a thirteen-year-old Prince George, who served that day with the Sixth Connecticut. John Emery of the Fifth Pennsylvania was part of the brigade under the command of General Anthony Wayne near Chadds Ford. When the British column under Howe and Cornwallis was discovered to have crossed the Brandywine Creek on the exposed American right, posing an immediate threat to the entire American line, the brigades of General John Sullivan, which were guarding the upper fords, were redirected to defend against the flanking action around Birmingham Hill. Adam Adams of the First Maryland was in the middle of the action there, as was Stacey Williams, John Francis, and Ned Hector, serving with Pennsylvania units.

Ned Hector's heroics on the battlefield at Brandywine have rightly become legendary. A teamster of the Third Pennsylvania Artillery, he began the day near Chadds Ford but was ordered to assist moving the artillery to the middle of the defensive line on Birmingham Hill. The cannons were fired with devastating effect until their position was about to be overrun by the British and Hessian troops and the order to abandon their equipment and "save yourselves" was given. Disobeying that order, Hector reportedly shouted that he would not abandon his team of horses and wagon to the enemy. Gathering up some of the muskets that had already been abandoned, he put them into his wagon and sped off under fire from the enemy. He later received a reward from the Pennsylvania legislature for his heroism.

The Marquis de Lafayette was wounded in the fighting on Birmingham Hill and brought off the battlefield by Colonel Heman Swift of the Seventh Connecticut, which had several Black Patriots fighting in its ranks at Brandywine: Lemuel Cumber, Prime Hubbell, Jabez Pottage, Lemuel Pete, Cuff Niger, brothers Samuel and Jeruel Phillips, and Robin Starr all saw action that day. The powder horn of Prince Simbo, also of the same unit, is now part of the collection of the Smithsonian Institution and one of the few known artifacts from the military service of Black Patriots during the war.

Peter Jennings, who provided detailed narrative of his prior exploits at Trenton and Princeton, also recounted his experience with the Fifth Artillery of Blacks at Brandywine, including seeing Lafayette wounded:

> This engagement commenced early in the morning, and the attack was brought on by the British who were under the command of Lord Cornwallis. They crossed the creek about a mile above our forces, and made an attack upon our rear. We were about the same time attacked in front by a British general whose name is now not remembered. The American troops were compelled to retreat with great loss. He well remembers seeing Gen. Lafayette in this engagement, and saw him receive a wound, which he thinks was in his right leg. He also remembers that there was another American General wounded, but he has forgotten his name.[2]

John Francis had his leg shattered by grapeshot during the British attack on Birmingham Hill, and Stacey Williams was wounded in his right thigh. Francis received a disability pension for his war wounds. After the battle, Joseph Townsend, a local Quaker, commented that Birmingham Hill "exhibited a scene of destructions and waste." The Birmingham Friends Meetinghouse was used as a hospital, and a mass grave containing American, British, and Hessian dead was made on the meetinghouse grounds. Among the dead buried on or near the battlefield was Thomas Dring of the Second North Carolina.

With the right flank collapsing, the Continental army began to retreat southward to Chester. To prevent the army from being encircled, the brigade under General Nathanael Greene, made up mostly of Virginia regiments, made a fighting retreat on the main road south to buy time for the army to find its way out of Howe's trap. The North Carolina troops under Colonel Francis Nash, including Anthony Garnes and Willis Boon, joined Greene to protect the Continental army's retreat. The First Virginia Brigade, led by General Peter Muhlenberg, included around one hundred Black Patriots. Shadrach Battles and Drury Scott served with the Tenth Virginia. Anthony Chavers and Daniel Williams, also part of the Virginia Line, tried to hold the British at bay as long as possible. It was during this fighting retreat that the British suffered some of their heaviest casualties.

Washington's failure to act in response to the early intelligence reports about possible British movements around the right flank of his army was a major blunder that contributed to the loss at Brandywine. The army itself fought bravely against heavy odds. At Birmingham Hill, the Continentals faced three times their own number and put up a fierce fight. The fighting retreat by the Virginia and North Carolina troops allowed much of the army to escape. Though having lost at Brandywine, Washington reported to Congress that, "despite the day's misfortune, I am pleased to announce that most of my men are in good spirits and still have the courage to fight the enemy another day."

THE BRITISH OCCUPATION OF PHILADELPHIA AND THE BATTLE OF GERMANTOWN (OCTOBER 4, 1777)

The Americans fought several skirmishes in the weeks following, but Howe crossed the Schuylkill River north of Philadelphia on September 25 and camped at Germantown, sending a column under Cornwallis into Philadelphia itself the following day, occupying the city. The northern army under General Gates had just fought the first Battle of Saratoga at Freeman's Farm a week before, three hundred miles to the north. The Continental Congress had already evacuated the city, and the town's bells (including the Liberty Bell) had been taken down and removed to prevent them from being melted down by the British and used for making musket and cannonballs.

Though Howe now held Philadelphia, Washington was not going to let him keep it without a fight. Having received reinforcements from several states since Brandywine the month before, his army, combined with the local militias, was now larger than Howe's force camped at Germantown several miles north of Philadelphia. That's where Washington ordered an attack at sunrise on October 4. His plan was to divide the army, with four columns hitting Howe's forces all at once, while another column demonstrated in front of Philadelphia to hold Cornwallis's troops in place to prevent them from reinforcing Howe during the attack. It was a complicated and very risky plan, with the various columns marching for hours in the dark to arrive at their appointed positions in the Continental line, ready to launch a simultaneous attack. Nathanael Greene's column, which was supposed to hit the right flank of the British line, got lost during the night but was eventually able to find its way back to the right road—now behind schedule.

Just a few minutes after sunrise, the first shots of the Battle of Germantown were fired as American troops opened up on the British pickets. Many of Howe's troops were just waking up and preparing their breakfast. Taken by surprise, some of the British units were rolled up quickly. The Continentals were also concealed by a heavy fog in the area that initially gave them an advantage. However, the respective columns didn't have sight of each other, hampering communication. As the Americans continued to push forward, seemingly toward a victory as British units began to retreat, a series of unplanned incidents and errors began to unravel Washington's plan.

In the course of the American assault, several British companies took refuge in a two-story stone building, the Cliveden House, about one hundred yards from one of the main roads into Germantown. That house had been bypassed by the advance troops. In all, there were about 120 British soldiers there. Continental riders were being fired at from the Cliveden house as the reserve column, which would bring fresh troops into the attack, moved up. A debate emerged as to whether the house should be bypassed or, as Henry Knox successfully argued, whether it should be dealt with to prevent those inside from causing trouble later in the army's rear. Cliveden, which still stands today, proved a formidable obstacle. Troops that attempted to storm the house were shot down. The light artillery available at the time couldn't penetrate the stone walls. Men who attempted to set fire to the house were also killed on their approach.

Those columns that had advanced heard the commotion behind them, unaware of what was happening. Some stopped; others turned around to make sure they were not being attacked from the rear. It was at this point that the fog which had concealed their approach began to add confusion to the American ranks, creating a literal "fog of war." Several units unknowingly exchanged fire with each other in the spiraling chaos, causing friendly-fire casualties. Greene's column discovered that they were now on their own and exposed, prompting a fighting retreat. The pause gave time for the British to regroup and mount a counterattack. The fortunes of war that had been with the Americans shortly before quickly shifted, and now Washington's army was in full retreat. Howe pursued the routed Continentals for ten miles. The British would hold Philadelphia for the winter to come.

Again, Peter Jennings provided his firsthand account of the battle in his pension application:

> Two or three weeks after the battle of Brandywine, Gen. Washington having received a considerable reinforcement from Virginia, marched us to Germantown and made an attack upon the British stationed there. The attack was made early in the morning, and from its sudden & unexpected character, the British forces were thrown into great disorder; but it being a cloudy, foggy morning it was difficult for our troops to keep in regular order, which caused considerable confusion amongst us; and the enemy rallying from the confusion into which they

> had first been thrown, drove back our troops, and were in at length compelled to retreat with great loss. In this engagement an American General Nash was killed.[3]

General Francis Nash commanded all of the North Carolina regiments, and a cannonball struck his horse and tore off his thigh, mortally wounding him. Washington ordered all available officers to attend his funeral several days later. The same cannonball killed Major James Witherspoon, Nash's aide-de-camp and the son of Reverend John Witherspoon, the president of Princeton College and signer of the Declaration of Independence. Brothers Samuel and Caleb Overton served in the First North Carolina under Nash during the battle (Samuel was wounded), as did Isaac Perkins in the Tenth North Carolina.

Germantown was the first battle for a number of Black Patriots. Jack Green was enlisted by his owner in May 1777 in exchange for his freedom. He was at the fight at Cliveden House with other members of the Fifth Connecticut, including Pharaoh Hart, Jack Rowland, and Kay Cambridge. Jack Negro of that regiment was taken prisoner at Germantown but escaped. Retired National Park Service ranger Joe Becton has identified other Black Patriots from the same unit who were present at Germantown: Cash Africa, Jack Congo, Cato Cuff, Ned Negro, Phillip Negro, Plymouth Negro, John Brister, Caesar Fiddler, and Ebenezer Jacklin. William Anderson of the Sixth Maryland enlisted after Brandywine. Sherard Going and William Clarke also experienced their first battle as part of the Virginia reinforcements. Joseph Sidebottom, who had come to the aid of the wounded future president James Monroe at Princeton, was already a battle veteran when he was present at Germantown with the Third Virginia.

SIEGE OF FORT MIFFLIN AND THE BATTLE OF FORT MERCER (OCTOBER 22, 1777)

Even though Howe now held Philadelphia, trying to control his supply lines without complete control of the Delaware River was problematic, with Washington and his sizable army still in the area. Occupying the city without continual support and supply from the Royal Navy would be perilous. One of the biggest problems were two forts on the Delaware that blocked their way: Fort Mifflin, or Mud Fort, on the Pennsylvania side, and Fort Mercer at Red Bank on the New Jersey side. The two forts stood opposite each other, and the river was filled with dangerous obstacles called *chevaux de frise,* solid wooden spears driven into the riverbed beneath the water's surface, intended to pierce boat hulls. Only select Patriot pilots knew how to navigate the obstacles. Any column crossing by land risked being attacked by elements of Washington's army. Securing the Delaware was essential for the British to hold Philadelphia.

Just days after Germantown, General Washington wrote to Colonel Christopher Greene of the First Rhode Island (a cousin of General Nathanael Greene), sending him and his regiment to Fort Mercer, which had been built earlier in the year, emphasizing the importance of holding his position:

> Upon the whole Sir, you will be pleased to remember that the post with which you are now intrusted is of the utmost importance to America, and demands every exertion you are capable of, for its security and defence. The whole defence of the Delaware absolutely depends on it, and consequently all the enemy's hopes of keeping Philadelphia, and finally succeeding in the object of the present campaign. Influenced by these considerations, I doubt not your regard to the service and your own reputation, will prompt you to every possible effort

> to accomplish the important end of your trust and frustrate the intentions of the enemy.[4]

Greene replied to Washington that upon arriving he discovered that Fort Mercer was too large to defend with his numbers and that he was in the process of reducing its size for better defense, but acknowledged the significance of holding his post:

> The post I have in charge I am Determined to defend with the small Number I Command to the last extremity. Yet I doubt my Number is much too small to Answer your Excellency's expectations.[5]

Intelligence from inside Philadelphia indicated that an attack on Fort Mercer was in the works. American troops labored every day to prepare for the awaited attack. Fortunately, a French engineer had been tasked to assist Colonel Greene in improving its defenses. His earlier conclusion that the fort was too large for the men he had was correct, and an outside wall that would be lightly defended concealed a new wall in the fort's interior, a more compact and defensible position unseen by the enemy.

In all, Greene had four to five hundred troops, mainly from his First Rhode Island and some troops from Connecticut. At this time, the First Rhode Island was an integrated unit, with about fifty-six Black Patriots mustered in the regiment. Several were already familiar names, including Jack Sisson and Guy Watson, who had participated in the successful commando raid near Newport earlier in the year to seize British General Prescott to exchange for captured American General Charles Lee. Caesar Shelton was a veteran of the New York campaign the year before and was present at Red Bank with the Fourth Connecticut under Colonel John Durkee, who had commanded his company at Bunker Hill.

Gershom Prince also served under Colonel Durkee and by now was a veteran of three conflicts. Born in Connecticut in 1733, he fought in the French and Indian War as a ranger with Israel Putnum, then served in the expedition to Havana in 1762. During his prior service he had become acquainted with Colonel Durkee and now had fought with him at Brandywine and Germantown. Prince Greene had escaped slavery the year before in Rhode Island, and Fort Mercer was his first taste of actual combat, as it was for Prosper Gorten and freeborn brothers William and Ben Franck. The First Rhode Island took on an entirely different character the following year as a result of the actions of the Black Patriots who fought to defend Fort Mercer.

Early in the morning of October 22, a Hessian column of at least 1,200 men set off for Red Bank and Fort Mercer, but wouldn't arrive until early afternoon. As the Hessians moved to encircle the fort, their commander, Colonel Carl Emil von Donop, sent a delegation to demand the fort's surrender, warning that no quarter would be given. The resounding answer that came from the Americans was, "By God, no!"

As the attack began, the Hessian troops on the south side of the fort were met with heavy grapeshot and musket fire from the Americans, cutting many down. The fortifications there were nine feet high, surrounded with an abatis and a fosse, or deep ditch, making their approach even more difficult. As planned, the Hessians moving on the north side met little resistance, and Colonel Greene had pulled back the few troops manning the old walls. The Hessians crawled up the old breastworks believing they were on the verge of a rout, only to discover that they were not inside the fort but inside the trap. Behind the newly constructed wall nearly one hundred yards away, Greene's men opened up and made short work of the Hessians. There were 138 casualties in that section alone, most dead or dying. Three Hessian colonels, including Donop, were killed or mortally wounded. As what Hessian leadership was left tried to rally their men, hidden American galleys on the river, mounted with cannons, began firing on the attackers. The larger Hessian numbers only made for more casualties. Slipping back into the woods after just forty minutes of battle, they loaded up what wounded they could for the ten-mile march back, leaving hundreds of dead, dying, and wounded behind. Colonel Greene saw no need to pursue the enemy, as it would weaken the defenses. The Battle of Fort Mercer was one of the worst defeats of the war for the Hessians, with ninety killed, 227 wounded, and sixty-nine more taken prisoner. The Americans suffered only fourteen killed and nineteen wounded. Among the dead were William Sharper and William Buskirk of the Rhode Island troops. While no descriptions of the men exist, some have speculated that they may have been Black Patriots.

Across the river on Mud Island, Fort Mifflin was besieged for six weeks by the full might of the Royal Navy, which was able to get within cannon range. Among the four hundred Americans manning the position were Prince Duplex, Pero Mowry, Caesar Cook, and Jeffrey Brace. By delaying the resupply and reinforcement of Howe in Philadelphia, these men were buying time for the rest of Washington's army to make their way to winter quarters and preventing any further British attacks before cold weather set in, making any pursuit by Howe unlikely. British ships being able to resupply Howe's army would also have dissuaded Washington from setting up a siege. Leaving the American garrisons at Fort Mercer and Fort Mifflin was not an option.

On November 15, three British ships armed with 158 cannons parked off Fort Mifflin, along with three other ships with fifty-one cannons, and unleashed the heaviest bombardment of the Revolutionary War. After weeks of siege, the Americans only had ten cannons to respond to the fury, but almost no ammunition left. One Black Patriot, Richard Sowers, was killed in action. In the darkness, Major Simeon Thayer ordered the Fort Mifflin garrison to retreat to Fort Mercer and set the fort on Mud Island ablaze. A few days later, Lord Cornwallis marched a column toward Fort Mercer and unleashed his artillery. Colonel Greene ordered it abandoned and blew up the fort's magazine as they departed. By their valiant defense, a performance praised by their commander in chief, they had largely served their purpose by allowing Washington's army to remove to Valley Forge. The battles at Fort Mercer and Fort Mifflin had proved the bravery and fortitude of large numbers of Black Patriots.

The opening of the Delaware River to British ships allowed Howe's army to be resupplied before operations during winter became unfeasible. In early December Howe made one final attempt to strike at Washington's army before the end of the year. The result was a series of skirmishes over several days north of Philadelphia known as the Battle of White Marsh, or Edge Hill, with several dozen casualties on both sides during the fighting, after which Howe retreated back to the city. Private Robert Fox, a Black Patriot serving in the Second Connecticut, was killed in action on December 7. He had enlisted in the regiment on May 28. Other Black Patriots in this action included John Emery of the Fifth Pennsylvania; Thomas Carney of the Fifth Maryland; Jack Green, Timothy Prince, and Bristol Budd of the Connecticut line; Anthony Garnes of the Seventh North Carolina; and Thomas Mason of the Virginia line.

In 1777, the Continental army had experienced great victories at Saratoga and Bennington and great defeats at Brandywine and Germantown. A large part of the northern army at Fort Ticonderoga and Mount Independence, who had fled from Burgoyne's invasion, had survived due to the rear guard action at Hubbardton, and the sturdy defense of Fort Mercer and Fort Mifflin by elements of the main army near Philadelphia allowed Washington to keep his army from danger at Valley Forge. In victory, defeat, and survival, at each action, Black Patriots served with honor, dignity, and commitment. When America needed men to stand in the breach after the disastrous campaign in New York in 1776 and the ten crucial days that saw victories at Trenton and Princeton, Black Patriots responded overwhelmingly to the call. As the Continental army began to encamp at Valley Forge and Washington planned to build a professional army that could stand against the British, they would be there too. In the trials, tribulations, and triumphs of 1777, Black Patriots shared in them all.

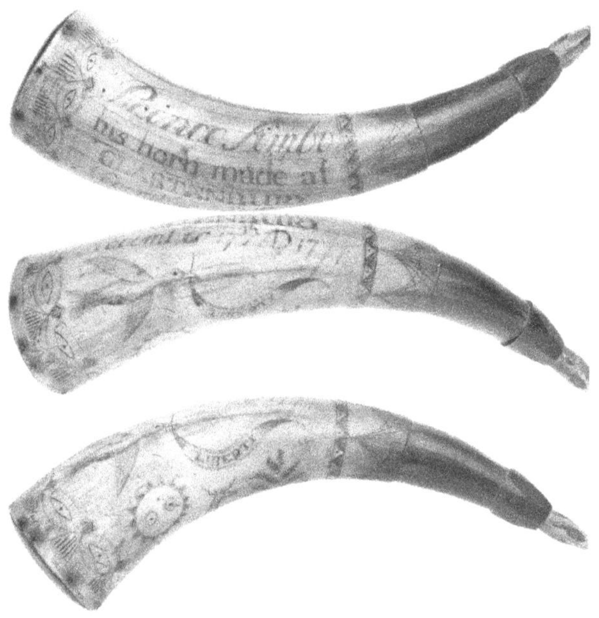

Powder horn owned by Prince Simbo, a private with the Seventh Connecticut who enlisted in February 1778. The carved cow's horn features his name, hometown of Glastonbury, and the date November 17, 1777. It also features a dove with a banner inscribed *LIBERTY*. He would have joined the regiment at Valley Forge and served at the battle of Monmouth in June 1778. Other Black Patriots serving in his company included brothers Samuel and Jeruel Phillips, Mingo Treat, Prince Crosley, and Sampson Freeman. (Image: National Museum of African American History and Culture)

Revolutionary War reenactor Noah Lewis portraying Edward "Ned" Hector, one of the heroes of the Battle of Brandywine, who disobeyed orders to retreat in order to bring his artillery wagon, horses, and ammunition back under British fire to the Continental army lines. A historical marker was erected in 1967 commemorating Hector's military service in his hometown of Conshohocken, Pennsylvania. A street in the town is also named after him in his memory. (Images: National Park Service, Patrick S. Poole)

The remnants of Fort Mercer in the Red Bank Battlefield State Park in Red Bank, New Jersey. It was here in October 1777 that heavily outnumbered Rhode Island troops commanded by Col. Christopher Greene withstood and repelled an assault by Hessian mercenaries. More than fifty Black Patriots, including Dick Potter, Prince Bent, Windsor Fry, and brothers William and Ben Franck are known to have participated in the fort's defense. (Image: Patrick S. Poole)

CHAPTER 6

1778: FROM THE FIRES OF VALLEY FORGE

THE TOWN OF WINDHAM, Maine, was settled by hearty seafaring pioneers from Marblehead, Massachusetts, used to the wind, wet, and cold. The spark of the American Revolution ignited the patriotism of its inhabitants, many of whom enlisted during the war. One of those was Lonnon Rhode, who had been the slave of one of the town's earliest inhabitants, William Mayberry. In 1763, he married another of Mayberry's slaves, Chloe, and the marriage was duly reported in the town's records. But at the time of Mayberry's death two years later, they were divided as property between two sons in the settlement of the estate. While the couple had four children, at the time of his enlistment in January 1777 only one, five-year-old Lucy, was still alive.

With his enlistment came his freedom, though at a price, as he had to use most of his bounty to pay his owner. His manumission was recorded with the town two days after his enlistment, declaring, "I hereby certify that the above named Lonnon is free and his own man." Other Black Patriots from Windham would also enlist, including Flanders and Ruminah (Romeo) Smith. His regiment, the Fifteenth Massachusetts, fought at Hubbardton, where a member of his company also from Windham was killed in action, and they were present at the great American victory at Saratoga.

In November 1777, they were reassigned to the main army under Washington and headed toward Philadelphia. Howe already occupied the city before their arrival. Washington selected Valley Forge for winter quarters for its high ground and good defensive position. With twenty miles distance from the city, they were far enough away to respond to any attempted attack by the British on their camp or the Continental Congress now meeting in York, but close enough to hold Howe and his troops inside the city. It was also important to protect the farm-rich Pennsylvania countryside from foraging raids.

The Fifteenth Massachusetts entered Valley Forge with an impressive contingent of Black Patriots. Pomp Blackman, Titus Coburn, and Prince Sutton had been at the Battle of Bunker Hill, the siege of Boston, and at Saratoga just weeks before. Others entering the encampment with the regiment were Jethro Jones, Phillip Allen, Jupiter Free, Brister Freeman, James Barret, Sampson Brown, John Hill, Robert Jackson, Primus Jacobs, Philip Boston, and Jethro Townsend. But Lonnon Rhode was missing, having died even before reaching camp on December 9. He was not alone in death. Titus Hayward had enlisted as a substitute for Simon Tuttle, responding to the Lexington Alarm, fought at Bunker Hill, Crown Point, White Plains, and Saratoga, but also died before reaching Valley Forge on November 15, as did Isaac Barbadoes on December 1. Titus Coburn, a Bunker Hill veteran, would die in camp on April 14, 1778.

DEATH, SURVIVAL, AND REVITALIZATION AT VALLEY FORGE

When the army arrived at Valley Forge on December 19, 1777, the first task was to build enough housing to shelter at least ten thousand soldiers. Over the next forty days, the army constructed nine hundred twelve-man huts with fieldstone fireplaces. Hospitals and other necessary amenities were needed to care for the exhausted army. Supplies and clothing were scarce. Continental surgeon James Thacher wrote in his journal:

> In the month of December the troops were employed in erecting log huts for winter quarters, when about one-half of the men were destitute of shirts, shoes and stockings. Some thousands were without blankets, and were obliged to warm themselves over fires all night, after the fatigues of the day, instead of reposing in comfortable lodgings. At one time nearly three thousand men were unfit for duty from the want of clothing; and it was not uncommon to track the march of the men over ice and frozen ground by the blood from their naked feet.[1]

Some would not live to see the huts completed. In a December 26, 1777, letter, surgeon's mate Jonathan Todd of the Seventh Connecticut wrote to his father, "Since Writing Yesterday—Jethro A Negro from Guilford belonging to Capt. Halls Compy. Died in his Tent the first man that hath died in Camp belonging to our Regt." That same day Joseph Anthony of the Ninth Massachusetts, who had served at Bunker Hill and both battles at Saratoga, also died.

Death claimed more American lives at Valley Forge than the British army did at any of the major battles of the war. At least two thousand soldiers died from disease, exposure, or famine. Dozens of Black Patriots were among their number. Smallpox, dysentery, typhoid, and typhus were all present in the camp.

Despair was also a killer. On January 14, 1778, Private John Day, a Black Patriot from Captain Robert Fenner's company of the Second North Carolina, either overdosed or committed suicide in camp "by taking a dose of physic and quickly afterward drank freely of spirits which caused his death." More than two hundred soldiers from North Carolina who had been a part of the Philadelphia campaign, including the battles of Brandywine and Germantown, died in winter quarters at Valley Forge—the equivalent of two companies of men. Jackson Hull of the Third North Carolina, a free man from Halifax, died in January, and

Brutus Johnston of the Tenth North Carolina died on February 15, 1778. A Black Patriot drummer for the Second North Carolina, identified only as Frederick, died of fever early in 1778 according to Benjamin Robinson, who was quartered in the same hut. Other Black Patriots from North Carolina who endured and survived the hardships of Valley Forge were Squire Dempsey, William Stewart, Martin Black, Isaac Perkins, Ishmael Roberts, and David Ivey. Black and Perkins had enlisted together at New Bern in May 1777 and were promptly inoculated for smallpox, which had been raging through the Continental army at the time.

New recruits began to arrive at Valley Forge, ready to join their country's cause. Ephraim Hearn, a free man of color from Gloucester, Virginia, had been drafted, served with the First Virginia, and was later captured as a British prisoner of war, but escaped captivity and returned home. James Harris enlisted in the same regiment. Shadrack Chavis enlisted for three years in the Second Virginia. Andrew Pebbles was born a freeman and arrived at Valley Forge to join with the Fifteenth Virginia, as did several brothers of the Goff family of Chesterfield County. Born to freeborn parents, Abraham, Daniel, and John were in the Fifteenth Virginia at Valley Forge; Samuel and Zachariah had enlisted the previous year; and Moses, the youngest brother, also served in the Continental line. John died at Valley Forge on May 16, and Samuel was killed in action later in the war. Decades after the war, Daniel moved to Kentucky with a White comrade he had met during the war and remained friends with for more than forty years. Thomas Pinn arrived in camp with the First Virginia State Regiment, but died shortly thereafter on January 11.

Nero Hawley was still a slave when he was enlisted in the Second Connecticut to serve as a substitute for his owner, Daniel Hawley, who had acquired him when marrying the daughter of his original owner. Jack Congo of the Fifth Connecticut had fought to repel Tryon's Danbury raid the previous year, and was among eighteen Black Patriots of his regiment at Valley Forge. He, too, was still enslaved and likely serving as a substitute for his owner. Prince Simbo and Sampson Freeman of the Seventh Connecticut had fought at Brandywine and Germantown and marched into winter camp with the Phillips brothers, Samuel and Jeruel, and eleven other Black Patriots. The First Connecticut began the winter with thirteen Black Patriots mustered, but lost Pomp Free to sickness on February 26. The town of North Stratford documented donations they sent to fifteen of their soldiers at Valley Forge, including three Black Patriots: Toney Turney, Caesar Edwards, and Nero Hawley.

More than one thousand New Hampshire troops entered Valley Forge having participated in most of the major action during the Saratoga campaign, including the decisive battles at Freeman's Farm and Bemis Heights. Among them were Jude Hall of the Second New Hampshire, already a legendary veteran, having served since the beginning of the war. Cato Baker, who had only become a freeman when he enlisted the previous July, had now seen the face of battle at Hubbardton and Saratoga in just a few short months. William Nelley and Samuel Wier arrived with the First New Hampshire, but Cato Marcy of the regiment succumbed to disease on May 27. Peter Abbott, Ezra Fuller, and Peter Pomp were mustered in winter quarters with the Third New Hampshire. Pomp died on March 15, about the time that Fuller returned from furlough and quickly fell ill, eventually dying on July 14.

By far the largest contingent of Black Patriot soldiers at Valley Forge was from the two Rhode Island regiments. Many of those encamped in an area known as Chester Woods had participated in the valiant defense of Fort Mercer and Fort Mifflin, which significantly delayed the Royal Navy from resupplying and reinforcing General Howe in Philadelphia. That delay prevented the British from making any additional major assaults on the Continentals before winter set in. Winsor Fry was likely one of the most senior of the Rhode Island soldiers, having enlisted in 1776. Those who arrived in camp in mid-December following the failed Philadelphia campaign had enlisted in 1777 and seen action. Cesar Cole,

James Edwards, Richard Pomp, Jack Allen, Abraham Isaacks, Francis Tifft, Peter Bristol, Prince Jackson, William Archer, and Amos Stedman all succumbed to camp conditions.

Suffering and sacrifice, however, were not the only elements of patriotism exhibited at Valley Forge. Communities rallied from all over to collect supplies for the Continental army. Polly Cooper and her husband, Han Yerry, were Oneida leaders who had fought together at the bloody Battle of Oriskany the previous summer, preventing British General St. Leger from joining forces with General Burgoyne at Saratoga. The British retreat and the surrender of Burgoyne's army had protected Oneida lands. When word of the situation at Valley Forge reached Chief Skenandoah, he directed Polly Cooper and forty Oneida warriors to transport six hundred baskets of corn from their autumn harvest to Washington's deprived army. She then remained with the army to tend to the sick.

Cyrus Bustill had been born into slavery in Burlington, New Jersey, and secured his freedom before the war, having learned the baking trade from his last owner, a Quaker. With the Continental army encamped nearby, Burlington became an important port for essential supplies. Christopher Ludwick, a successful baker appointed as the superintendent of baking for the army, recruited Bustill to use the flour arriving at the port to bake bread for the soldiers. Two documents, at one time possessed by the Bustill family, were later used by his descendants to verify his patriotic service for their membership in the Daughters of the American Revolution. Both items were certificates by two known quartermaster officials responsible for contracting in Burlington, confirming that Bustill had been contracted by the Continental army:

> I certify that Cyrus Bustill has been employed in the baking up of all the flour at the Port of Burlington and that he has behaved himself as a faithful honest man, and has given general satisfaction; such as should recommend him to every good inhabitant!

Given under my hand at Burlington May 1st 1782,
Thomas Falconer
Contractor for supplying the Troops at the above port

An additional note by Thomas Ives, one of Falconer's agents, communicates the same endorsement of Bustill's service on behalf the Continental army. After the war, he used proceeds from his bakery to open a school for Black children and was one of the founders of Philadelphia's Free African Society. Several of his descendants were active in the Underground Railroad.

Two civilians present in the Valley Forge camp, giving direct service to General Washington, were Hannah and Isaac Till. Hannah's services as a pastry chef and servant had been leased by the commander in chief from her owner, Reverend John Mason, beginning in 1776; he served as a cook to Washington with his wages paid to Captain John Johnson. They had both arranged for payments to be made to their respective owners to purchase their freedom. During their time in Valley Forge they were both still enslaved, freed only after their sojourn at the army's winter quarters in October 1778. Thus, when their son, Isaac Worley Till Jr., was born, he was the first of their four children to be born free. They eventually had seven children. Hannah and Isaac worked for Washington for six and a half years. After the victory at Yorktown, Washington consented to them working for the Marquis de Lafayette for six months. When Lafayette returned to the US in 1824, he visited Hannah, now more than one hundred years old, at her home in Philadelphia, paying off her debts and providing money for her care and support.

Also in the Washington household at Valley Forge was his body servant, William (Billy) Lee, whom he had purchased in 1768. Billy served Washington in the field for the duration of the war, acting as one of his most trusted aides in addition to his duties maintaining the general's appearance and dress. In that latter role, he would have been associated with Washington's laundress, Margaret Thomas, a freewoman employed in the general's retinue since his time in Cambridge during the siege of Boston. In 1784, Billy and Margaret were married, somewhat to the consternation of Washington. At the time, she was living with Hannah and Isaac Till in Philadelphia. It appears that she died shortly thereafter. Around the same time, just after the end of the war, Billy Lee suffered a knee injury while surveying with Washington and was permanently crippled. He remained enslaved until Washington's death, at which time he was freed in the will and endowed with an annual pension from the late president's estate. He is buried at the slave cemetery at Mount Vernon.

Several Black Patriots at Valley Forge served as angels of mercy to their fellow soldiers. A June 1778 muster roll shows Samuel Phillips of the Seventh Connecticut assigned to tending to the sick in the encampment. Cuff Wells had been born in Africa, abducted and enslaved, and instructed in medicine by his owner, Deacon Israel Wells, a doctor in Hartford, Connecticut. After Cuff enlisted in the Fourth Connecticut in May 1777, his talents came to the attention of Dr. Philip Turner, who served as surgeon general of the Northern Division of the Continental army. Dr. Turner employed him as an attendant in an army hospital. Cuff Wells entered Valley Forge with his regiment, which had fought at both Brandywine and Germantown. There, he tended to the sick. A regiment document dated May 8, 1778, identifies him as "Cuffee Wells Doct'r." When the army left camp to pursue the British, evacuating Philadelphia in June, he was left in camp to care for the sick. Later in the summer of 1778, he was still at the army hospital at Yellow Springs, then spent the rest of his enlistment continuing his medical service for his regiment on command in Danbury. He was discharged at the end of his term of service on May 5, 1781. The testimony of two witnesses, John Nutter and Richard Lamb, dated a few days prior on April 30, 1781, confirms that the bounty and wages Wells earned in the army's service purchased his freedom. Once freed, he changed his family name to Saunders. After the war he married and died of influenza in December 1788. His son, Prince Saunders, attended Dartmouth College and served as a teacher in a school for Black children in Boston.

Cuff Wells probably knew and worked with John Cook of the Second New Hampshire. Cook had enlisted at age seventeen to reinforce the defeated army returning from Canada in 1776, and after reenlisting his unit saw action during the Saratoga campaign at Hubbardton, Freeman's Farm, and Bemis Heights. After Burgoyne's surrender, the New Hampshire regiments marched south to join the main army for winter quarters. When the army left Valley Forge in mid-June 1778, Cook was also left behind to continue caring for the sick and wounded. At year's end he was in Danbury, as was Cuff Wells. He went south with the army for the victory at Yorktown and continued to serve until the end of the war.

Tobias Pendall was a freeman from Norwich, Connecticut, who enlisted in 1777 and was with his regiment at Valley Forge but wouldn't live to leave winter camp with the army. The muster rolls of his company show that he was tending the sick at the army hospital at Yellow Springs in April 1778. The next muster roll records his death on May 10, with no indication of whether he died from something he caught while caring for his ill comrades.

Things began to improve at Valley Forge with the appointment of General Nathanael Greene as quartermaster general of the army. He created a supply system to bring in food, equipment, and weapons to revitalize the army. Sanitation at the encampment was improved. Inoculations for smallpox lessened fatalities and protected the army in the years to come.

The February 23, 1778, arrival in camp of Baron Friedrich von Steuben, a veteran of the Prussian army, marked the beginning of a military revolution in Valley Forge. As the newly appointed inspector general he implemented a training regimen that brought military discipline and consistency to the Continental army. Until this point in the war there had been no standardized training for the dozens of regiments from eleven different states that comprised the army. Very few American commanders had any actual experience in European strategy and tactics, including Washington, who had only served as a colonel in the Virginia colonial militia and was denied a commission in the British army. On the Grand Parade at Valley Forge, von Steuben oversaw instructions in maneuvering in formation and weapons practice. The army also became experienced in using the bayonet, the feared weapon used to devastating effect by the British against the Americans many times before. These trainings were summarized in a short book, *Regulations for the Order and Discipline of the Troops of the United States*, known less formally as the "Blue Book." Elements of this manual are still in use by American troops today. The army that emerged from Valley Forge was better trained and better equipped, ready to test their skills against the professional training of the British and Hessian soldiers.

THE ALL-BLACK FIRST RHODE ISLAND REGIMENT

In order to match the British head to head, the Continental army had to grow. General James Varnum had a radical plan to address a shortfall in the troops of his adopted home state of Rhode Island. He submitted his plan in a letter to Washington dated January 2, 1778:

> The two Battalions from the State of Rhode Island being small, & there being a Necessity of the State's furnishing an additional Number to make up their Proportion in the continental army; The Field Officers have represented to me the Propriety of making one temporary Battalion from the two, so that one entire Core of Officers may repair to Rhode Island, in order to receive & prepare the Recruits for the Field. It is imagined that a Battalion of Negroes can be easily raised there.[2]

There appears to have been some prior discussion between the Rhode Island commanders in the field and the political leadership back home about the prospect of raising a regiment of Black Patriots. No copy of Washington's reply has been found, but Christopher Greene, who had led the valiant defense of Fort Mercer, and several fellow officers quickly headed back to Rhode Island to begin recruiting and training the new regiment. Governor Nicholas Cooke sent a letter to Washington on February 23 informing him that the legislature had approved the plan along the following lines:

> I laid the Letter before the General Assembly at their Sessions on the Second Monday in this Month, who considering the pressing Necessity of filling up the Continental Army, and the peculiarly difficult Circumstances of this State which rendered it in a manner impossible to recruit our Battalions in any other way, adopted the Measure. Liberty is given to every effective Slave to enter the Service during the War, and upon his passing Muster he is absolutely made free, and entitled to all the Wages, Bounties and Encouragements given by Congress to any Soldier enlisting into their Service. The Masters are allowed at the Rate of £120 for the most valuable Slave, and in Proportion for those of less Value. The Number of Slaves in this State is not great, but it is generally thought that 300, and upward will be enlisted.[3]

The Slave Enlistment Act was a dramatic turnaround in Continental army military policy from just two years prior, when Washington's headquarters issued an order prohibiting any recruitment of Black Patriots (an order that was quickly withdrawn and widely ignored). Now at least one state was not only going to actively recruit them but emancipate slaves to fill their quotas and pay owners out of the State Treasury for their freedom. The proposal didn't pass without some resistance from pro-slavery voices in the legislature, and the recruiting of slaves only lasted until the end of June.

The day following the bill's passage, William Greene submitted his slave Cato to be the first enrollee in the "Black Regiment." Shortly thereafter, Greene assumed the governorship of Rhode Island after the resignation of Governor Nicholas Cooke. By the end of March 1778, ninety-six slaves were enlisted and freed. In all, 140 Black Patriots enlisted in the First Rhode Island Regiment of the 225 men mustered. A state treasurer's accounting of the payments made to slave owners indicates that £10,437 were spent freeing the former slaves of the new First Rhode Island Regiment.

Back in Valley Forge, the existing Black Patriot veterans in the Rhode Island units in winter encampment with the main army were consolidated into a large company of the First Rhode Island under Captain Thomas Arnold, with fifty-five privates. Most of these had participated in the defense of Fort Mercer, such as Winsor Fry, Jack Sisson, and Guy Watson. Sisson and Watson had participated in the capture of British General Prescott. Nine of these Black Patriot veterans died at Valley Forge. This detachment company was attached to Colonel Israel Angell's Second Rhode Island for the time being while the new regiment was stood up and trained back at home. Several veterans had left Valley Forge on command and returned to Rhode Island with Colonel Greene, including Richard Allen and Ceasar Sabins, joining the newly formed companies and adding at least a few combat veterans to their ranks. Captain Arnold's detachment company left Valley Forge in June with the main army and participated in one of the largest battles of the war. The rest of the First Rhode Island stayed close to home for the time being as the political leadership of the state wanted the newly raised troops to prevent any further encroachments by the British beyond their continued occupation of Newport, the only British base in New England. With this task the green recruits saw their first action later that summer.

The recruitment of Black Patriots wasn't on the mind of just Rhode Islanders. Colonel John Laurens wrote to his father, Henry Laurens of South Carolina (who had succeeded John Hancock as President of the Continental Congress), raising the suggestion of Black Patriot recruitment for southern states. John Laurens had attended law school in London, coming under the influence of the Patriot arguments of his homeland and the European Enlightenment. As an aide-de-camp to Washington, he had served during the Philadelphia campaign and developed a reputation of "running to the roar." Following the Battle of Brandywine, Lafayette had expressed surprise that Laurens hadn't been killed with his repeated (and some thought reckless) exposure to danger. Laurens had been struck by the inconsistencies of slavery with the rhetoric of liberty. He too wanted to form Black battalions, recommending in his February 2, 1778, letter to his father "5,000 black men, properly officer'd, to act as light troops, in addition to our present establishment." On completion of their service, they would be given their freedom. He forwarded this idea despite the fact that Laurens's father had built a large part of his fortune on the slave trade. That notwithstanding, John Laurens advocated for not just Black Patriot recruitment but the abolition of slavery itself. His own slave Shrewsbury was present with him at Valley Forge and continued to serve with him throughout the war. Andrew Pebbles, a freeman of Virginia who joined the army at Valley Forge, witnessed John Laurens's death in one of the last military actions of the Revolution.

News soon arrived in Valley Forge that would change the course of the war. On May 5, 1778, Washington was notified that the Continental Congress had ratified a treaty forming a military alliance with France, negotiated by Benjamin Franklin in Paris. The American Revolution was now part of a larger global war between two of the world's largest empires, and the British now had to devote resources away from the fight in America. The following day, Washington ordered the army to muster on the parade grounds at Valley Forge to celebrate the new French-American alliance. Army prisoners were pardoned, and soldiers received an extra ration of rum that day. In light of the rigorous training and the physical hardships endured, in addition to the more than two thousand dead, there was good cause to receive the news with joy.

THE BRITISH EVACUATION OF PHILADELPHIA (JUNE 18, 1778)

For Henry Clinton, the new British commander in chief in the Americas sitting in Philadelphia, the news was not so good. He had reluctantly assumed command following the dismissal of General Howe. Notwithstanding the decisive victories at Brandywine and Germantown and the occupation of Philadelphia that had forced the Continental Congress to flee, his situation there was now in doubt. Washington had been rebuilding his army and receiving new troops. And with the French entry into the war, specifically French ships headed toward America, his situation in Philadelphia was now untenable. A French fleet could appear on the Delaware River and cut his army off from New York, which was also now a likely target for a joint French-American attack. He had to return to New York to consolidate his forces and prepare defensive positions, but the question was, how would they get back? He could sail his army without any difficulty but not take all of the camp followers and Loyalists in the city that had been supporting them all winter. Abandoning them and leaving them entirely at the mercy of the returning Patriots and the army would be disastrous, so they—Clinton's army, the camp followers, and Loyalist refugees—would have to travel to New York City overland and be vulnerable to an attack by Washington. This decision would alter the course of the war.

Clinton snuck out of Philadelphia with his army of fifteen thousand soldiers in the middle of the night on June 18, 1778. The British train grew to nearly twelve miles long as it began snaking through New Jersey. Their destination of Sandy Hook provided a good defensive position as they boarded British ships for the rest of the trip back to New York. Aware from intelligence inside Philadelphia of the planned evacuation, Washington and the army left Valley Forge the following day in pursuit. He directed General William Maxwell and General Philemon Dickinson of the New Jersey militia to set off ahead of the main army to harass the British rear guard while Washington shadowed the army farther north. The pace of the British column was slowed by sweltering heat and intermittent rain. Washington later tasked Colonel Dan Morgan and his group of hand-picked riflemen to join the harassment effort. Some historians believe that General Clinton might have been deliberately taking his time, hoping that Washington would attempt a major direct engagement. In three days the column had only reached Mount Holly, just eighteen miles from where they had crossed the Delaware River.

Also slowing their progress was the harassment campaign by the New Jersey militia. One of the first clashes on the British march was on June 22, at a critical bridge at Crosswicks Creek, controlled by several hundred Patriots. One Black Patriot, Adam Pierce of the Second New Jersey, mentioned participating in this engagement in his pension application decades later. Likely there, too, were Oliver Cromwell, also of the same regiment, as well as Amos Thomson and Primus Tyng of the New Jersey militia. The action delayed the march of the British column even further as Washington's army continued the pursuit. One problem that Clinton faced, much like Burgoyne the previous year at Saratoga, was a limited amount of supplies. Several days later he camped the column at Freehold, now known as Monmouth, which was surrounded by a number of farms that were perfect for foraging and resting his army.

BATTLE OF MONMOUTH (JUNE 28, 1778)

Meanwhile, the Continental army remained close by. Some intelligence indicated that there were only two thousand soldiers in the British rear guard at Freehold. Not worried about a direct engagement with the whole of Clinton's army, Washington decided that now was the time to act. He ordered his second-in-command and rival, General Charles Lee, a former British officer in the French and Indian War, to lead a vanguard of 4,500 troops out toward the remaining British position early in the morning of June 28, 1778. Lee had been captured by the British before the Battle of Trenton and had only recently been exchanged for British General Richard Prescott, captured in Newport in July 1777. Lee's mission kicked off the longest battle of the war and one of the largest around Monmouth Court House.

Hundreds of Black Patriots participated in the thickest of the action at Monmouth. American historian George Bancroft wrote in his *History of the United States* of their participation: "Nor may history omit to record that, of the 'revolutionary patriots' who on that day periled life for their country, more than 700 black men fought side by side with the white." As discussed earlier, some of these Black Patriots had joined the Continental army at Valley Forge and were seeing battle for the first time. Many others, however, were now battle-hardened veterans, having served at Bunker Hill, Dorchester Heights, Fort Ticonderoga, Long Island, Harlem Heights, White Plains, Trenton, Princeton, Brandywine, Germantown, Bennington, and the great Patriot victory at Saratoga. They had survived the brutal winter at Valley Forge that had claimed the lives of many of their fellow soldiers, including dozens of their Black Patriot comrades. The Battle of Monmouth would demonstrate whether von Steuben's training and discipline would allow the Continental army to match the British, and whether the service and suffering in this cause of liberty was worth the sacrifice.

Marching out with Lee in the vanguard were largely Virginia, Connecticut, and Rhode Island troops. The latter included the detached company of the First Rhode Island Black Patriot veterans under Captain Thomas Arnold, serving with the Second Regiment while the new Black Patriot recruits of their own reorganized regiment were still being trained back home. Much of Clinton's column had already moved out of Freehold even before Lee left. A group of officers, including Baron von Steuben and John Laurens, rode forward to scout the existing British positions but were spotted and came under fire. As Lord Cornwallis brought up his two thousand troops, Lafayette was ordered to move his positions to attack the British left flank to possibly encircle and trap the British rear guard. Lee, never having fought before with many of the officers now under his command, lost control in the chaotic situation, failing to communicate orders to commanders already in the thick of the battle. British troops that had already left Freehold conducted a counter march back to the fight, and Lee realized that he was now facing many more British troops than he initially believed. Lee ordered a general retreat about a mile back to reorganize and await the main American body under Washington.

It was during the retreat that the Third New Hampshire under Lieutenant Colonel Henry Dearborn maintained formation and withdrew in an orderly manner. Among the regiment were Peter Abbott, Jockey Fogg, Fortune Moore, and Cato Moulton. The regiment received special recognition from General Washington for their performance under fire. New Hampshire historian Glenn Knoblock notes that later in the battle Washington ordered a counterattack—with the First and Third New Hampshire and the First Virginia—through the woods against the British right flank, pushing them back. Charles Bowes, Anthony Gilman, Silvanus Hastings, Jesse Knott, George Knox, and Robert Miller, of the First New Hampshire, and Sylvester Beverly and Daniel Cumbo of the First Virginia, would all have been part of that effort. Prince Bailey and Fortune Fogg of the Second Massachusetts also fought in the center during the battle.

It was during the Battle of Monmouth that Jude Hall of the Second New Hampshire earned his nickname of "Old Rock," likely due to his coolness and bravery under fire. Three years into his service, he had already served at Bunker Hill, Trenton, Fort Ticonderoga, Hubbardton, and both battles of Saratoga, and survived the winter at Valley Forge. Caesar Wallace of the same regiment had fought at the Battle of Oriskany the previous year. Cato Fisk had participated in the regiment's battles at Hubbardton and Saratoga, as had Gloster Watson. Zach Kelsey may have been one of the oldest privates on the battlefield that day, having enlisted as a freeman in 1777 at the age of fifty-two. At Monmouth, the Second New Hampshire proved their reputation as one of the most experienced and hard-fighting regiments in the Continental army.

As Lee failed to keep control, Washington arrived at the front ahead of the main army, amazed to find some of the troops in retreat. An infuriated commander in chief immediately took full command. A roar went up in reply when he asked the retreating troops if they were able to fight. The main body of the army was still not near the battle, so a defensive line was established along a hedgerow with about eight hundred men, including the Fourth Connecticut and the Rhode Island Regiments. Clinton urged his men forward to try to catch the Continental troops against a creek in their rear. The fight at the hedgerow lasted only minutes, but it was some of the fiercest combat of the entire war as both lines fired at near point-blank range, then turned to hand-to-hand fighting.

One of the men wounded in the blazing exchange at the hedgerow was Benajah Abro of the Fourth Connecticut, who was shot in the neck and left for dead as the Continentals retreated from the hedgerow. Years later, Captain Lemuel Clift described finding Abro alive when they returned to the area later in the battle:

> [I] was a Captain in the fourth Regiment of the Connecticut Infantry during the Revolutionary War...in the year ad 1778 at

> the Battle of Monmouth. Benajah Abro a black man was a private soldier in the Company then under my command and that during said action while the American troops were retreating they said Abro was wounded in the Neck by a musket ball from the Enemy. I then supposed the wound to be mortal and he was left on the ground. We afterwards occupied the same ground on which Abro was shot and found him alive and he was sent to the Hospital and recovered.[4]

After recovering in an army hospital in Princeton, Abro later rejoined his unit and continued to serve until the end of the war, receiving a soldier's pension in 1819.

The Rhode Island troops at the hedgerow included Captain Arnold's detached company of Black Patriot veterans. Arnold was wounded and his leg required amputation. Richard Rhodes, one of the veterans of the Battle at Fort Mercer the previous October, was wounded in the arm. Rhodes had been born in Africa, abducted and enslaved as a child, and enlisted to obtain his freedom. Decades later he testified that, "he is very much crippled in one arm in consequence of a wound received in the Battle of Monmouth."

Seeing Washington's fresh troops gathered on the heights of Perrine Hill facing them, and with soaring temperatures now reaching a hundred degrees, the British brought up artillery to drive off the Patriots. Washington responded in kind, and what followed was the "Great Cannonade," the longest artillery duel of the war. The Second New Jersey, including Oliver Cromwell and Adam Pierce, began forming the defensive line on the hill, later joined by Edward Harman of the Delaware line. Participating in the fierce cannon exchange was Ned Hector of the Third Pennsylvania Artillery, one of the heroes of the Battle of Brandywine. Many veteran officers recalled that it was the loudest and longest sustained barrage they had ever heard.

As the Great Cannonade continued through the afternoon, it provided sufficient time for General Nathanael Greene to move his troops and four artillery pieces to Combs Hill on the American right flank. Once set and the cannons readied, they opened fire on the British left flank, catching the British soldiers on the field in a deadly crossfire. Lord Cornwallis led a charge of British and Hessian troops to push the Continentals off the hill. Anthony Garnes of the First North Carolina and Daniel Goff of the Fifteenth Virginia were just two of the soldiers who drove back the enemy charge. Unable to dislodge Greene and break the crossfire, Cornwallis was ordered to withdraw to Monmouth Court House. One of the last actions of the day was an attack by General Anthony Wayne against the British rear guard, with James Hamilton of the Third Pennsylvania participating. The Battle of Monmouth concluded around six o'clock in the evening, the longest battle of the Revolution finally at an end, with the Americans in command of the field.

With hundreds of Black Patriots at Monmouth involved in the hardest fighting of the day, they were represented among the battle's casualties. Caesar Spragues of the Fourth Massachusetts had his left foot shot off by a cannon during the battle. Thomas Lively of the Fifth Virginia lost an eye but continued to serve until the end of the war. Drury Pettiford of the Second Virginia was wounded in the leg by a cannonball. Thomas Camel of the Fourth Virginia was one of the many soldiers overcome by the heat during the battle (thirty-seven Continental soldiers reportedly died of heat exposure). He was put in the hospital and unable to walk. Once on his feet, his doctor allowed him to live with a family nearby when the Continental army left the area. In his pension affidavit he noted "that the company to which he belonged were mostly killed in the battle at Monmouth." William Nealey of the First New Hampshire was wounded in the battle and furloughed shortly afterward to recover. Margaret Houck, the slave of a local farmer, helped Continental doctors tend to the wounded.

Caesar Jowler of the Eighth Connecticut, who had enlisted in April 1777, was mortally wounded at Monmouth and died on August 7 in the hospital. Jesse Knott of the First New Hampshire, which had been recognized for its actions at Monmouth, died several weeks after the battle on July 18 of unknown causes, possibly of wounds or illness. Nathaniel Small of the Ninth Massachusetts died two weeks after the battle, on July 15. He had enlisted as an "eight-month man" following the battles of Lexington and Concord and fought at Bunker Hill. Completing his term of enlistment at the end of 1775, he reenlisted for another year, during which time he participated in the siege of Boston and the disastrous New York campaign, and crossed the Delaware with Washington for the Patriot victory at Trenton. With his enlistment expiring, he responded to Washington's desperate appeal to extend his term for an additional six weeks and was undoubtedly at the Battle of Princeton. After a brief break, he reenlisted yet again in March 1777 and fought at Saratoga. After the surrender of General Burgoyne, he marched south to join with the main army at Valley Forge. His cause of death is not mentioned in the subsequent muster roll.

There were heroes made at Monmouth as well, such as William Condo of the First New York. A slave of Joseph McCracken who was mustered into the company commanded by his owner, Condo entered Continental service in March 1777. A bout of smallpox kept him from the campaigns in the spring and summer of that year, but he rejoined his company before they entered winter quarters at Valley Forge. During the Battle of Monmouth, Joseph McCracken was knocked over by the concussion of a cannonball. As he rose, he was struck with grapeshot that took his arm. Condo carried him off the battlefield, and they took shelter in some bushes. After McCracken resigned his commission in 1780, he asked Washington if Condo could be released from the army in order to assist him at home, a request that was granted. Research from the National Park Service indicates that Condo never left McCracken's service, notwithstanding a promise made to him before the war to be freed in 1787.

An incident at Monmouth told by George Washington Park Custis, Washington's step-grandson, many years after the general's death concerned Washington's right-hand man, Billy Lee, and other valets. In his *Recollections and Private Memoirs of Washington* published in 1860, Custis relates the following "ludicrous occurrence" at Monmouth:

> The servants of the general officers were usually well-armed and mounted. Will Lee, or Billy, the former huntsman, and favorite body-servant of the chief, a square muscular figure, and capital horseman, paraded a corps of valets, and, riding pompously at their head, proceeded to an eminence crowned by a large sycamore-tree, from whence could be seen an extensive portion of the field of battle. Here Billy halted, and, having unslung the large telescope that he always carried in a leathern case, with a martial air applied it to his eye, and reconnoitered the enemy. Washington having observed these manoeuvres of the corps of valets, pointed them out to his officers, observing, "See those fellows collecting on yonder height; the enemy will fire on them to a certainty." Meanwhile the British were not unmindful of the assemblage on the height, and perceiving a burly figure well-mounted, and with a telescope in hand, they determined to pay their respects to the group. A shot from a six-pounder passed through the tree, cutting away the limbs, and producing a scampering among the corps of valets, that caused even the grave countenance of the general-in-chief to relax into a smile.

No doubt the moment of battlefield levity allowed a very temporary respite to the chaos and carnage of the day. In the end, both Washington and Clinton accomplished what they had set out to do in the engagement. For Washington, the Continental army had taken on the British, standing toe to toe, and were left in command of the field. The Patriots could claim a well-fought victory. On the other hand, Clinton had conducted his risky march through New Jersey largely unscathed. Washington was prepared to renew the fight the following morning, but the British column slipped away in the night, headed toward Sandy Hook and ships bound for New York City.

The Battle of Monmouth was the last large-scale engagement between the Americans and the British in any of the northern states until the end of the war. For the next few years, Washington and Clinton's armies continued to eye each other warily around New York with regular skirmishes, raids, and intrigues. There would be battles in the years to come, but the military center of gravity in the war shifted toward the southern states.

Clinton's abandonment of Philadelphia was an acknowledgement that the situation for the British in America had radically changed. The French-American alliance and France's declaration of war against its old enemy, England, changed the scope of the war. Soldiers and supplies that had been dedicated to the colonial rebellion were now needed for a global war between empires. The threat from the French fleet in American waters diminished to a degree the British sea-power advantage. An added change was the professional training program and influx of European officers to the American cause in support of the Continental army. Saratoga and Monmouth had showed that in the right circumstances, the Patriots could get the better of the British. Clinton needed to exercise an extra degree of caution in his use of military power.

For the Black Patriots, there was more fighting than at any time before in the war. With Clinton's troops now back in New York City, Washington and the main body of the Continental army camped nearby at White Plains. One of Washington's aides, Alexander Scammell, the adjutant general of the army, conducted a return of Black soldiers encamped there. The return, dated August 24, 1778, counted 755 Black Patriots in the fifteen brigades of the more than twenty thousand collective rank and file at White Plains. Of those, 586 were present in camp, ninety-eight were sick and absent, and seventy-one were on command elsewhere. The Connecticut brigade under the command of Samuel Parsons had 117 Black Patriots present of the 1,589 men mustered—the largest presence of any of the brigades. The three Massachusetts brigades counted 124 Black Patriots present.

Scammell's "Return of Negroes" provides a helpful snapshot of Black Patriot participation at one of the most pivotal points in the war. The original is held by the Library of Congress as part of the George Washington Papers collection. Sadly, the return only records the raw numbers of those mustered without identifying who they were. A number of historians and researchers have been working to reconstruct those records, as much as possible, to identify as many as possible.

There were other Black Patriots who were part of the army at the time who were not present at White Plains and could not be included in the count, even some who had survived the winter at Valley Forge and fought at Monmouth. One example is the detachment company from Rhode Island of Black Patriot veterans who fought at Monmouth and were now with the rest of the newly reformed First Rhode Island Regiment of new recruits, including those who had been freed from slavery in return for their military service. These soldiers were undergoing training with the officers who had left Valley Forge to recruit and command the regiment. At the very same time that Alexander Scammell was completing the return, the newly segregated First Rhode Island Regiment was about to face their first military test.

BATTLE OF RHODE ISLAND (AUGUST 29, 1778)

One reason that the First Rhode Island hadn't joined the main army under Washington was that the state's legislature wanted action about the British occupation of Newport. A plan to force the British out in 1777 was scuttled. General John Sullivan of New Hampshire was put in command of a new effort to liberate Newport that would be the first joint military venture with the French. Washington sent several of his senior officers, including Nathanael Greene, John Laurens, and the Marquis de Lafayette, to support the effort. Both Rhode Island regiments participated, as did the brigades of Generals John Glover and James Varnum (who had proposed the formation of the Black Regiment to Washington earlier in the year).

The French fleet under Admiral d'Estaing arrived in the area with four thousand French soldiers in early August. The agreed plan was for the joint force to move on Aquidneck Island, where Newport is located, and lay siege to the city while the French fleet, comprised of twelve ships of the line, provided cover and fought off any relief attempts by the Royal Navy. But in the following weeks several of the French ships were damaged by a storm and skirmishes with the British off the coast. After attempting to regroup, the French fleet sailed for Boston to repair the ships, leaving the Americans alone. But Sullivan's troops had already been digging entrenchments on the island for the siege. Without French support, Sullivan ordered the siege entrenchments abandoned on August 28, and the troops withdrew to the northern part of the island for transport back to the mainland.

Seeing the entrenchments empty, the British commander of the six-thousand-man Newport garrison, General Robert Pigot, who had led the British left wing at Bunker Hill, decided to harass the Americans during their withdrawal and possibly trap them. On August 29, he sent four British regiments up the east road, against the American left flank, and Hessian regiments up the west road, against the right flank. Both columns were ambushed by American skirmishers, which retreated back to the main defensive line. The British attack on the left flank was repulsed by Glover's brigade. Pigot moved to turn the American right flank with his Hessian troops against Varnum's troops, including the First Rhode Island, who were holding strong positions behind stone walls and a redoubt, but to no avail. A second attempt also failed. In the face of a third charge by the Hessians, the First Rhode Island held long enough for reinforcements to arrive. After the attack, word arrived from Washington that thousands of British reinforcements had already sailed from New York City, headed toward Newport. In the night, the army's baggage was moved to the mainland, followed by the troops themselves, without incident. The Battle of Rhode Island was over.

The British losses on both American flanks was enormous—even greater than at Bunker Hill. Several Black Patriots present at both Bunker Hill and Rhode Island included James Arcules of the Fourth Massachusetts, serving as a substitute for Nathaniel Coolidge, and Jeffrey Hemmingway in the regiment of Colonel Nathaniel Wade, also a veteran of Bunker Hill, who would have taken part in his regiment's turning the right flank of the enemy. Prince Whipple was likely present at the scene, as his owner, William Whipple, was one of Sullivan's direct subordinates in the expedition. James Anthony of the Fourth Massachusetts, Samuel Dunbar of the Tenth Massachusetts, and Joseph Johnson of the Fifth New York were also Black Patriots that were part of the battle.

The performance in the battle of the First Rhode Island Black Regiment has been the subject of much mythology over the years, and a debate on the subject began almost immediately after the action. No Continental field commander was going to risk the entire defense of their position on the performance of a single green, untested, undermanned regiment, regardless of the background of its soldiers. Claims that they singlehandedly repulsed successive Hessian charges appear unfounded. But it is clear that they took part in the action of the day.

Historian Dan Popek, who has written the definitive history of the First Rhode Island, *They "...fought bravely, but were unfortunate"*, finds evidence that they were engaged against the Hessians but, being heavily outnumbered, retreated back beyond the redoubt and likely regrouped to reinforce the Second Rhode Island in fighting from the redoubt. Popek notes a statement in a pension application from one White soldier stating, "I was in the Battle of the Orchard with the Black Regt. commanded by Col. Green," confirming they had seen action. A handful of deaths in the regiment in the days before and after the battle were from men already listed as being sick. A letter sent by the acting commander to his wife following the battle states, "I believe that a couple of the blacks were killed and four or five wounded but none badly."

Popek suggests that the Black Regiment wounded included George Thomkins, Solomon Wanton, Thomas Nichols, and Jack Sisson. William Babcock died three days after the battle, and Primus Jencks died on October 11, perhaps from battle injuries. He also notes the account of one Massachusetts officer, Samuel Lawrence of Groton, who found himself between the battle lines during the repeated Hessian charges and was rescued from capture by one company of the Black Regiment. In his orders the day after the battle, General Sullivan deflected any criticism from Colonel Greene's troops, concluding that they were "entitled to a proper share of the honor of the day."

The First Rhode Island Black Regiment would fight another day. But in the months ahead, the attention of the British turned toward the southern states, believing that Loyalist support there would divide the Americans and break the stalemate that had developed with Washington's army in the North. Compared to the string of major battles in the North since 1775, the South had largely been free of such large military engagement since the battles of Sullivan Island off Charleston and Great Bridge near Norfolk in 1776. Now, the experience and support at Valley Forge had produced a more disciplined, cohesive force that could match the British, such as at Monmouth.

For the next two years of fighting in the South, the Patriot cause was carried on by militias operating in areas with which they were intimately familiar. The Black Patriots who joined this fight participated in a new way of fighting. Many enlisted as slaves, some even returning to slavery after the war, highlighting the most glaring contradiction in the American war for freedom. They fought against their own Loyalist neighbors. Everyone needed to choose sides, and no one was spared from the horrors of war. That was the strategy of the British southern campaign: to leverage conflict between Patriot and Loyalist Americans to recover their colonial control.

Their first target was Savannah, Georgia, which they occupied in a surprise attack with three thousand troops on December 29, 1778. The war for the South, and ultimately the fate of America and the prospect for permanent independence, had begun.

Hannah Till was an enslaved cook and servant hired by George Washington who served at the Isaac Potts House at Valley Forge, which served as Washington's headquarters during the Winter of 1777–1778. Her service to the commander in chief allowed her to purchase her freedom later that year, and she continued to cook for Washington of her own volition. She is depicted here by reenactor and National Park Service Ranger Ajena C. Rogers. Hannah Till died in 1826, and her remains now rest at Eden Cemetery, Collingdale, Pennsylvania. (Images: National Park Service, Patrick S. Poole)

Letter from General James Varnum of Rhode Island to George Washington proposing that a battalion could be raised by the state by freeing slaves in return for their military service. Washington's reply is unknown, but officers were sent back to Rhode Island days later to begin recruiting for what became the all-Black First Rhode Island Regiment. (Image: Library of Congress)

Certified copy of the act passed by the Rhode Island legislature in February 1778 authorizing the purchasing of the freedom of "every able-bodied Negro, Mulatto, or Indian Slave in this State" willing to enlist in the state's battalions fighting against the British.

The Patriots of African Descent Monument at the Valley Forge National Historical Park honors the hundreds of Black Patriots who encamped there during the winter of 1777–1778. The nine-foot-tall monument was sponsored by the Valley Forge Alumnae Chapter of Delta Theta Sorority and features an image by artist Cal Massey. It was dedicated on June 19, 1993. Peter Pomp enlisted in the Third New Hampshire in February 1777, served at Fort Ticonderoga, fought at Fort Anne and Saratoga, and encamped for the winter with his regiment at Valley Forge. It was there that he died on March 15, 1778, one of dozens of Black Patriots who died from sickness and exposure there. This military marker at the McClary Cemetery in Epsom, New Hampshire stands as a cenotaph in his honor, but he was likely buried in a mass grave at or near Valley Forge. (Images: Patrick S. Poole)

A monument dedicated to the service of Dick Pointer, a slave at the time of the attack of British-allied Mingos, on Fort Donnally near present day Lewisburg, West Virginia, on May 29, 1778. Pointer and another man together fought off the initial surprise assault and rallied the rest of the fort's occupants. They continued to hold until the arrival of a relief column later that afternoon. Dick Pointer was freed shortly after, and the town constructed a home for their hero. He is buried in the cemetery behind the monument. (Image: Patrick S. Poole)

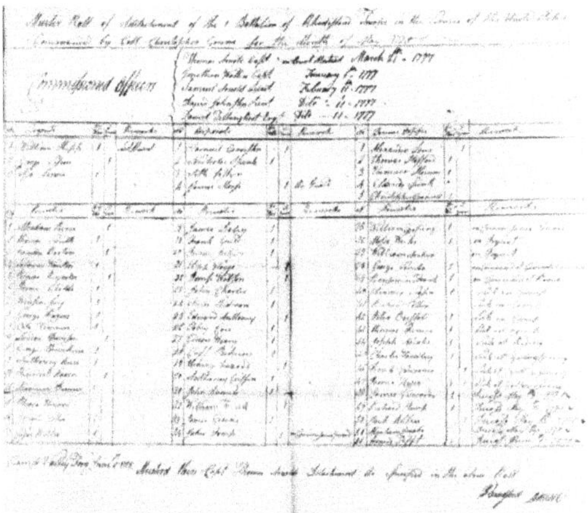

June 1778 muster roll of Captain Thomas Arnold's company of the First Rhode Island. This all-Black company was created at Valley Forge of Black Patriots who were already serving in the state's two regiments. These men were all likely veterans of the valiant defense of Fort Mercer and the Battle of Monmouth just weeks before this July 10, 1778 muster was taken. The "Arnold detachment" would march to Rhode Island shortly afterward to join the rest of the newly recruited all-Black regiment. (Image: National Archives)

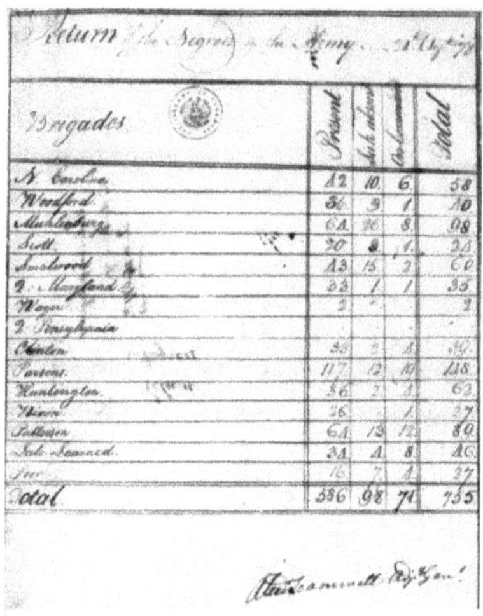

Return of the Negroes in the Army — 24th Augt 78

Brigades	Present	Sick absent	On command	Total
N. Carolina	42	10	6	58
Woodford	36	3	1	40
Muhlenburg	64	26	8	98
Scott	20	3	1	24
Smallwood	43	15	2	60
2. Maryland	33	1	1	35
Wayne	2			2
2 Pennsylvania				
Clinton	33	2	4	39
Parsons	117	12	19	148
Huntington	56	2	4	62
Nixon	26		1	27
Patterson	64	13	12	89
Late Learned	34	4	8	46
Poor	16	7	4	27
Total	586	98	71	755

Alexr Scammell Adjt Genl

"Return of the Negroes in the Army," dated August 24, 1778, prepared by New Hampshire Col. Alexander Scammell, recording 755 Black Patriots immediately under Washington's command in the fifteen brigades encamped at White Plains. This would not include the First Rhode Island "Black Regiment" and other Black Patriots serving in units in the South or garrisons elsewhere. (Image: Library of Congress)

Monument dedicated to the all-Black First Rhode Island that fought at the Battle of Rhode Island on August 28, 1778. Many were fighting for the first time, having been purchased by the state legislature from their slave owners in exchange for their military service. Dozens other were experienced veterans of the Battles of Red Bank and Monmouth. The monument, dedicated in May 1976, stands at Patriots Park in Portsmouth, Rhode Island, on part of the battlefield where they fought. (Image: Patrick S. Poole)

CHAPTER 7

1779: THE WAR EXPANDS NORTH, SOUTH, EAST, AND WEST

THE SURPRISE LOSS of Savannah in the last days of 1778 and Augusta on January 29 shook the American leadership, awakening them to the fact that the southern states, which so far had largely been spared from the conflict, were going to be a new front in the war. With France casting their military support to the Americans and Spain following suit later in the year, British troops that were now needed overseas had to be replaced with American Loyalists to continue the war. To that end, British Colonel James Boyd of South Carolina was dispatched by British commander Archibald Campbell to recruit Loyalists from Georgia, South Carolina, and North Carolina to join with the British army in Augusta. In addition to British troops under General August Prevost up from St. Augustine, Florida, the plan was to take the battle to Patriot strongholds in the southern backcountry. Judging by the seven hundred recruits that quickly joined as a result of his efforts, it seems that Boyd had quite an appeal.

BATTLE OF KETTLE CREEK (FEBRUARY 14, 1779)

Notwithstanding their smaller numbers, Patriot militia leaders in the area were not going to let the enemy efforts go unchallenged. Elijah Clarke and John Dooly of Georgia and Andrew Pickens of South Carolina determined to launch a surprise attack on Boyd's encampment on Kettle Creek near the Georgia–South Carolina border before his column of Loyalists reached Augusta. Facing a force twice their size, the joint Patriot militias attacked the camp on top of a five-hundred-foot hill on the morning of February 14, 1779. Pickens took the bulk of the men up the middle, with Clarke and Dooly trying to turn the flanks of the Loyalist position. Pickens was able to push the pickets back into the camp while the other two columns were hung up in swampy land. Likely fighting with him was his trusted slave, Old Dick, who fought with Pickens against both the Indians and the British in the war. The tide of the two-hour battle turned when Boyd was shot and mortally wounded and the two flanking Patriot columns broke out of the swamp and engaged in the battle. The Patriots continued to push until Boyd's troops abandoned the camp and fled. Over one hundred of Boyd's men were captured, and several dozen Patriot prisoners held by the Tories were freed. Only seven Patriot soldiers were killed to forty Loyalists killed, including Boyd. Also taken were six hundred horses and considerable supplies. Only 270 of Boyd's recruits made it to Augusta, and as word of the extent of the Patriot victory became clear, virtually every single member of the Tory regiment deserted. Lieutenant Colonel Campbell was forced to abandon Augusta for the time being, denying them an important base of operations in the area. With Boyd's Loyalist regiment destroyed and Boyd's recruiting influence dying with him, the intended British occupation of Georgia was abandoned.

Among the Patriots in the victory at Kettle Creek was Austin Dabney. He was serving as a substitute for his owner, Richard Aycock, who offered Austin in his place when he was drafted for the militia. Later in the war during the siege of Augusta, Dabney was severely wounded by a musket ball that went through his thigh, breaking the bone. He recovered in the home of a fellow militia member, David Thurman. Still enslaved, he continued to live and work for Thurman, establishing a friendship with Thurman's son-in-law, Giles Harris. Permanently disabled by his battle wound, Austin Dabney received a pension for his disability. Through the efforts of many prominent citizens he received a land grant of fifty prime acres—the only Black Patriot from Georgia to receive land for his military service. Only after his owner, Aycock, died would the state legislature pass an act in August 1786 freeing Dabney from slavery and granting him all the rights and privileges of a citizen. Austin Dabney became prosperous and owned race horses but remained devoted to the Harris family. He even paid for the college education of William Harris, one of the Harris sons, and cried tears of joy when the young man was accepted at the bar as an attorney. On his death in September 1830, Austin Dabney was buried in the Harris family cemetery outside Zebulon, Georgia. William Harris, who named his own son after the family friend, was later buried by Dabney's side.

A story told by Georgia Governor George Gilmer demonstrates the esteem that many had for Austin Dabney. He relates that on the occasion of Austin's annual trip to Savannah to collect his disability pension payment, he came upon a fellow former soldier, Colonel Wiley Pope. Riding together, as they entered town Pope suggested that it wasn't proper to be seen riding with a Black man, and Austin obliged by taking a position behind him. As they rode past the house of General James Jackson, who was serving as Georgia's governor at the time, the general ran out to greet his old friend Austin Dabney, shook his hand, and welcomed him to stay in his home on his trip as Colonel Pope continued to ride away unrecognized. Another local history relates that Judge Dooly, the son of John Dooly, who led one of the columns at Kettle Creek and was later killed at his home by Tories, would regularly sit and listen to Austin Dabney tell stories about the Revolutionary War in the tavern whenever he was in town for his judicial duties.

Stephen Heard was also at Kettle Creek, serving under John Dooly. As an adventurous young man, he had joined George Washington's company during the French and Indian War. In 1780 he assumed the office of state governor, though most of the state's population—in Savannah and Augusta—were under British occupation. The Patriot victory at Kettle

Creek set back the British cause in Georgia, but enraged the Loyalists living there. Heard's home was attacked by Loyalists, and his wife and adopted daughter were thrown out into a snowstorm and died of exposure. Heard himself was captured and set to be executed by the British. One of his slaves, Mammy Kate, visited him twice a week with food and fresh clothes and took away his dirty laundry in a large basket she carried on her head. She was accompanied sometimes by her husband, Daddy Jack. As the time for Heard's execution approached, Mammy Kate and Daddy Jack hatched a plan. Positioning two of Heard's best horses nearby, she visited her master in his cell in Augusta at her regular time and secreted him in the laundry basket, carrying him out of the prison and allowing his escape. Delivered from death by his faithful slaves, he gave both Mammy Kate and Daddy Jack their freedom, and they were cared for by the Heard family for the rest of their lives. They are both buried in the Heard family cemetery beneath marble ledger stones bearing their names at the former Heard family plantation now owned by the Daughters of the American Revolution.

Given the different nature of the war in the South, it became clear to many leaders that the participation of Black Patriots was essential for the fight ahead, even if only to prevent them from defecting to the British side in the hopes of freedom. Lord Dunmore had tried to lure Virginia slaves away with his Ethiopian Regiment in 1776, but most were dead within a few months from starvation and disease. That the British would continue their attempts to encourage slave defections to weaken the Patriot cause was a point raised by Alexander Hamilton in a letter to John Jay dated March 14, 1779, carried by Colonel John Laurens, who himself had been advocating for widespread enlistment of Black Patriots:

> Col Laurens, who will have the honor of delivering you this letter, is on his way to South Carolina, on a project, which I think, in the present situation of affairs there, is a very good one

> and deserves every kind of support and encouragement. This is to raise two three or four batalions of negroes; with the assistance of the government of that state, by contributions from the owners in proportion to the number they possess. If you should think proper to enter upon the subject with him, he will give you a detail of his plan. He wishes to have it recommended by Congress to the state; and, as an inducement, that they would engage to take those batalions into Continental pay.
>
> It appears to me, that an expedient of this kind, in the present state of Southern affairs, is the most rational, that can be adopted, and promises very important advantages. Indeed, I hardly see how a sufficient force can be collected in that quarter without it; and the enemy's operations there are growing infinitely serious and formidable. I have not the least doubt, that the negroes will make very excellent soldiers, with proper management; and I will venture to pronounce, that they cannot be put in better hands than those of Mr. Laurens.[1]

Hamilton was aware of the opposition that the effort to enlist Black Patriots on a large scale would face:

> I foresee that this project will have to combat much opposition from prejudice and self-interest. The contempt we have been taught to entertain for the blacks, makes us fancy many things that are founded neither in reason nor experience; and an unwillingness to part with property of so valuable a kind will furnish a thousand arguments to show the impracticability or pernicious tendency of a scheme which requires such a sacrifice. *But it should be considered, that if we do not make use of them in this way, the enemy probably will; and that the best way to counteract the temptations they will hold out will be to offer them*

> *ourselves.* [emphasis added] An essential part of the plan is to give them their freedom with their muskets. This will secure their fidelity, animate their courage, and I believe will have a good influence upon those who remain, by opening a door to their emancipation. This circumstance, I confess, has no small weight in inducing me to wish the success of the project; for the dictates of humanity and true policy equally interest me in favour of this unfortunate class of men.[2]

The Laurens project was not just ideological but a military necessity. Washington had determined that there were no more Continental troops to send south for now. For the time being, the battle in North Carolina, South Carolina, and Georgia would be carried by militias and whatever regiments the states could raise. Henry Laurens, the President of the Continental Congress, favored his son's proposal and recommended it in his correspondence to General Washington following the news of the Patriot victory of Kettle Creek:

> Our affairs in the Southern Department are more favorable than we had considered them a few days ago. Nevertheless, the country is greatly distressed and will be more so unless reinforcements are sent to its relief. Had we arms for three thousand black men such as I could select from Carolina, I should have no doubt of success in driving the British out of Georgia and subduing East Florida before the end of July.[3]

The Continental Congress passed a resolution on March 29, 1779, calling on South Carolina and Georgia to raise three thousand armed Black Patriots, but to no avail. Neither state moved on the proposal, making the Laurens project a dead letter. Yet just as they had in the northern states in support of the Continental army, Black Patriots in the South flocked to the Patriot cause. They took their place in the ranks, fighting in battles and skirmishes of all sizes in the next few years. Some became casualties, either dead or wounded, and many more became prisoners of war. Some of these Black Patriots serving in the South fought in as many engagements as the most battle-hardened vets in the North and saw the fortunes of the Patriot cause wax and wane during the brutal war in the South.

One of those was Jim Capers, who claimed to have begun his military service as a slave in June 1775. As a drum major he grew famous among the Patriot soldiers, even mentioned in unrelated pension applications from battle comrades decades later. By the time of the Battle of Kettle Creek, he had already fought in two engagements of the southern campaign at St. Helena Sound (December 31, 1778) and Port Royal Island/Beaufort (February 3, 1779). At the latter engagement, the Patriots fighting under General William Moultrie were able to prevent the British from seizing the largest deep-water harbor in the South, thereby delaying an invasion of Charleston. Capers continued to serve until after Yorktown, being wounded multiple times and narrowly averting death in battle.

Two weeks after Kettle Creek on March 3 the British got their revenge at Brier Creek. Following the evacuation of Augusta, the Patriots followed the column, hoping for an opportunity to attack, and were stalled at Brier Creek after the British pulled up the boards from the bridge. The British launched a surprise attack, routing the Americans. William Taburn of the North Carolina Line was there as a teamster and served in several subsequent battles, even witnessing historic scenes. Drury Walden was also serving with a North Carolina unit and would be of great service to the Patriot cause by building gun carriages for the Commissary General. Isham Carter of the Fourth South Carolina was also at Brier Creek and a number of future engagements. He would also be taken as a prisoner of war.

Brothers Berry and Osbourne Jeffers were at Brier Creek with their cousin, Allen Jeffers, in the Third South Carolina, also known as "Thomson's Rangers." Several other Black Patriots that were friends from their neighborhood or otherwise related to the Jeffers family also enlisted in 1778 and served with the unit. This included Morgan and Gideon Griffin, Benjamin Holley, Drury and Edward Harris, and John Busby. Several other Black Patriots enlisted in the Third South Carolina are identified only as Negro Adam, Negro Bob, and Negro Isaac.

ESCALATING ATTACKS ALONG THE FRONTIER

The southern states were not the only field of action in 1779, as the war expanded to the farthest reaches of the American frontier. Attacks by British, Loyalist, and Indian forces had targeted American settlements from upstate New York to South Carolina since 1777, including the attacks on Fort Stanwix and the Battle of Oriskany in upstate New York as part of Burgoyne and St. Leger's unsuccessful invasion from Canada during the Saratoga campaign.

Indian attacks on Fort Henry, located in what is now downtown Wheeling, West Virginia, occurred in September 1777 around the same time as the Battle of Brandywine. The men grew frustrated at having to defend the fort instead of proactively dealing with the Shawnee Indians attacking them. Henry Dorten was a freeman drafted into the Pennsylvania militia who served under Captain William Foreman, and they were at Fort Henry when fire was spotted several miles south on the river at what they believed was the abandoned fort at Graves Creek (near modern day Moundsville, West Virginia).

Foreman was given permission to leave Fort Henry to investigate. But the party was being observed by the Shawnee on the other side of the river. In his pension affidavit, Dorten details what happened:

> Foreman was soon ordered to a fort at Grave creek, on the Ohio river, twelve miles below Wheeling—upon arriving there

> we found the fort burnt, and we commenced a march back to Wheeling along the bank of the river—in the narrows of Grave creek, we were attacked by about seventy Indians, and Capt. Foreman and twenty of his men were killed, twenty two were saved—that he made good his escape back to Wheeling, and in ten days after, he went with others to bury the dead, putting fourteen in one hole and seven in another.[4]

Henry Dorten was later drafted for six months and helped build Fort McIntosh in Beaver Falls, Pennsylvania, and Fort Laurens in eastern Ohio, one of only twenty-two men who survived the Foreman Massacre.

Another Black Patriot account of the incident exists. Rachel Johnson was a slave of Yates Conwell, present at Fort Henry at the time. She was interviewed twice by historian Lyman Draper in 1845 and 1846, where at an advanced age (likely over one hundred years old) she gave this account:

> Foreman's and Linn's companies came [to Wheeling], the next day went down to see if there were any signs of Indians at Grave Creek, where there was a deserted blockhouse. 46 turned out to go, camped [that night]; next morning [set out to return]. Linn, Daniel McLane and a few others went up [over] the hill, the others marching in Indian file. The Indians had made blinds and were under the river bank, etc.; when the whites were opposite [they rose and fired]. Foreman at the head was first shot down by a single fire; the others stopped suddenly and were fired on and shot down. McLane said he rant part way down the hill [when he heard the firing] and said he heard the tomahawks as if the Indians were cutting up beef. In the afternoon a fugitive with his gun, but without his hat gave the first mournful intelligence [at Wheeling] of the defeat, not knowing of any beside

himself who had escaped. Others between that and night kept dropping in.

In 1778, the attacks continued in New York, Pennsylvania, and Virginia territory along the Ohio River as Ranger companies patrolled vulnerable frontier settlements. One of those was at Fort Donnally in Greenbrier County, Virginia (now West Virginia), where Shawnee made an attack on the small settlement on May 29, 1778. Having killed a settler that left the fort and left the gate unlocked, the warriors charged the fort. Finding the gate partially blocked, they attempted to force their way in with their tomahawks. One of the few defenders to respond to that first attack was Dick Pointer, a slave of Colonel Andrew Donnally, who used an old musket to kill two of the lead Shawnee warriors, scattering the rest and giving the other fort inhabitants time to arm themselves. After repeated attacks, a relief column arrived outside the fort. In return for his valiant defense at the beginning of the battle, the local inhabitants built a cabin for Dick Pointer, and he was granted his freedom in 1801. At his death in 1827, he was buried with military honors. A monument at the African Cemetery in Lewisburg was built in his honor, and in 1982 his eroding tombstone was fitted with a bronze plate bearing the original inscription:

Dick Pointer
Hero During Indian Attack
On Fort Donnally
1778
Died 1827

A pension petition sent to the Virginia Assembly in 1795 on behalf of Dick Pointer, supported by the local residents and testimonies of those who fought there, was rejected.

On July 3, 1778, Gershom Prince, a Black Patriot who had fought in the French and Indian War and the British siege of Havana, participated with Connecticut troops at Brandywine, Germantown, and Fort Mifflin, and endured the winter at Valley Forge, was killed in the Wyoming Massacre in Luzerne County, Pennsylvania, when Loyalists and Indians ambushed Patriot militia, killing three hundred. After the battle, a local farmer discovered Prince's engraved powder horn on the battlefield. Today, a large monument stands above the mass grave where Gershom Prince and the other Patriots killed that day in the Wyoming Massacre now rest. His recovered powder horn is one of few preserved items from Black Patriots killed in action during the war. It is currently on display at the Museum of the American Revolution in Philadelphia, on loan from the Luzerne County Historical Society.

The Shawnee under Chief Blackfish, allied to the British, struck Fort Boonesborough (modern day Richmond, Kentucky) in September 1778, laying siege to the fort established by Daniel Boone and his company shortly before the outbreak of the American Revolution. Several days into the siege a slave of Nathaniel Henderson was on post and was killed in action while defending the fort. The Shawnee abandoned the siege after eleven days. Henderson petitioned the legislature for the loss of his unnamed slave. A replica of Fort Boonesborough was constructed on the site by the state of Kentucky and is now a state park.

Francis Dewitt was the slave of Captain Jacob Dewitt, who commanded a company of rangers patrolling against Indians and Loyalists in New York. Francis served three years with the Rangers, which had been formed in May 1777 to defend against the British invasion from Canada by the two columns of Generals Burgoyne and St. Leger. Even after Burgoyne's defeat in Saratoga in October 1777, he continued to defend the area against attacks, as he recounted in his pension affidavit:

> In that year 1777 a fort was built of pickets around Dewitt's house to protect the neighborhood from the incursion of the Indians and Tories, and Captain Dewitt's Rangers when not called out were engaged in protecting and defending this fort and other forts of similar kind.
>
> In 1778 Fort Dewitt was attacked by the Indians & Tories while I was stationed there. I was wounded in the leg with a bullet at this attack.
>
> When the Rangers were at the fort, they were ordered out frequently in squads of 10 to 15 as scouts and spies to look out for and follow the tracks of the Indians. And I was sent out very often as one knowing the woods. In 1779 Capt. Wood commanded Fort Dewitt and the troops there.[5]

Francis was living at Fort Defry when it was attacked and burned in October 1778, requiring the inhabitants to flee to Fort Dewitt, which also came under attack, with four or five houses burned by the enemy. Benjamin Defry testified that Dewitt and another soldier had rescued "with great difficulty and danger" a soldier caught alone by the Indians between Forts Defry and Dewitt. James Tellinger testified that Francis helped rescue one Esther Van Aukan when Fort Dewitt was attacked, and also that Dewitt was in the battle where Tellinger's father was killed.

One of the most consequential engagements on the frontier during the entire war occurred in February 1779. George Rogers Clark was tasked by Virginia Governor Patrick Henry to take his Illinois Regiment down the Ohio River on a secret mission to attack British forts in the Northwest territories obtained from their victory in the French and Indian War. Clark was informed in January 1779 that British governor Henry Hamilton had occupied Fort Sackville in modern-day Vincennes, Indiana, with British regulars and had begun reinforcing the fortress, threatening the balance of power on the frontier. Clark and the Illinois Regiment set off from Fort

Kaskaskia near the Mississippi River, today in southwestern Illinois, to travel more than 180 miles away in winter to lay siege to Fort Sackville. A number of Black Patriots described only as "negroes" (presumably slaves) were with Clark's Illinois Regiment. Paul Quibo, also a Black Patriot, is described in regiment documents as a matross (an artilleryman), but nothing more is known about him.

On their march toward Vincennes, Clark's men frequently had to wade in cold chest-high waters for hours at a time, as the Wabash River had overflowed its banks. It took several weeks to reach the fort. The British were entirely unaware of their approach or their arrival until they opened fire on the fort on February 23, 1779. It only took a day and a half for Hamilton to capitulate, surrendering the fort, which was promptly renamed Fort Patrick Henry. Another Black Patriot named Boston Damewood is named in later muster rolls of Clark's regiment, but there is no indication of when he enlisted or whether he participated in the taking of Fort Sackville.

In addition to a strong American foothold deep in the interior, the victory at Fort Sackville proved to both the French and Spanish that Patriot frontiersmen and militias could successfully conduct a siege against British regulars. The Spanish declared war against the British on May 8, 1779. They built Fort San Carlos on the Mississippi River (modern-day downtown St. Louis) the following year, and had to defend it against an attack by the British and their Indian allies on May 28, 1780. A number of freemen participated in the fort's successful defense, which ensured the British could not control the Mississippi. Spanish military commander Bernardo de Galvez also launched a campaign to seize British-controlled West Florida in 1780, taking what are now Baton Rouge, Mobile, and Pensacola. De Galvez's army included dozens of freemen. The Daughters of the American Revolution has identified the names of seventy Black Patriots who aided the American cause by their service with the Spanish against the British during the West Florida campaign.

Notwithstanding the Patriot victory at Saratoga in October 1777, a year later in November 1778 a mixed force of Loyalists, British regulars, and allied Indian tribes launched an attack in the Cherry Valley of New York. Several hundred soldiers of the Seventh Massachusetts manning the fort in Cherry Valley included Black Patriots Cato Hart, John Wheeler, Luke Nickerson, Joseph Johnson, and Bunker Hill veteran Charlestown Lyndes. Dozens of civilians were murdered, and many more, mostly women and children, were taken captive by Seneca and Mohawk fighters. Virtually all of the homes in the valley were burned out, and half those taken were never seen again.

SULLIVAN'S CAMPAIGN AGAINST THE SIX NATIONS (JUNE–OCTOBER 1779)

In response to continued attacks in upstate New York, General John Sullivan, who had led the unsuccessful effort to oust the British from Newport, Rhode Island, in 1778, was ordered by General Washington to conduct an expedition against the hostile Six Nation tribes allied with the British, intending to break their morale in the hope of ending attacks on American settlements along the frontier. Washington made his objective for the expedition clear in his orders to Sullivan: "The immediate objects are the total destruction and devastation of their settlements, and the capture of as many prisoners of every age and sex as possible. It will be essential to ruin their crops now in the ground and prevent their planting more." During the summer of 1779, Sullivan and his Continental troops engaged in a number of small-scale skirmishes targeting Mohawk, Cayuga, Onondaga, and Seneca villages.

One of those returning to service for Sullivan's expedition was Benjamin Lattimore, who had been taken as a prisoner of war at the fall of Forts Montgomery and Clinton on the Hudson River nearly two years earlier in October 1777. The American POWs were taken to New York City, where the notorious British prisons and prison ships awaited them. Lattimore was months later taken as a slave to a group of British officers. According to his pension affidavit, he was freed when one of the British officers he accompanied on a mission was captured. His former unit, the Fifth New York, was encamped nearby, and he was sent by General Israel Putnum back to the regiment.

They joined up with Sullivan's column at Tioga, New York, having earlier marched up the Mohawk River to Lake Otsego. The lake was dammed to raise the water level, and once the dam was broken the Patriot boats were taken by the current down the Susquehanna River to Tioga.

Samuel Sutphen, a Black Patriot from New Jersey and a slave serving as a substitute for his owner in the expedition, later recounted in detail his participation in the expedition following the trail of destruction and deaths from Indian and Tory raids just days before:

> We were Marched through Sussex, Goshen in Orange County, to West Point. Here I recollect there was a huge chain of Iron stitches across the north river, anchored into the rocks, to prevent vessels passing up and down. We marched through N. Windsor, Newburg, Esopus Utica at or near which place there was a fort, called Fort Stanwix or Fort Schulyer, perhaps I am wrong in the name. We remained here a few days. The Indians had just left the place, having massacred some of the inhabitants. The bodies of three children were found here, that had been massacred by them. We marched through a place called Cherry Valley, which the Indians had also visited and destroyed, as well as Fort Montgomery. I think the name of our General was Sullivan, and he joined the expedition and took the command somewhere over the North river, I believe at West Point. The Indians had destroyed most of the new settlements and

> villages through which we passed, only a few days before. We found them deserted and burnt. We pursued them through the wilderness Country to the Lake Country the Indians retreating as we advanced. We had some 4 or 5 small field pieces with us. When we arrived near the lake, it was about husking corn time in the fall, and we did not begin to march homeward.... [A]fter the new year began we returned by the same route, or nearly the same.[6]

From the meeting point of Tioga, the expedition set off on August 26 up the Chemung River toward the Indian settlement of Newtown. It was there, three days later, that the Indians and Tories planned to ambush Sullivan's troops. Discovering the hidden fortifications, American artillery pounded their position and columns were sent around both flanks to try to trap the enemy. The Second New Hampshire, including Jude Hall, Caesar Wallace, and Dan Woodman, were heavily engaged and nearly trapped themselves when the enemy was driven into their position by an American bayonet charge and heavy artillery fire. With the support of the Third New Hampshire, the enemy was forced to retreat from the area, ending the only battle of the entire Sullivan expedition. The Americans continued to attack Indian towns, destroying crops and winter stores. The devastation of the expedition was so complete that most of the survivors from the hostile tribes abandoned their towns and retreated north to Fort Niagara.

On Samuel Sutphen's return from the expedition, his regiment stopped at West Point on the Hudson River. He recounted how, on guard duty one night, his post was attacked and he was wounded in the action:

> One cold night, when the snow was knee deep, as I was standing sentry, a party of Hessians or Highlanders, who had crossed the river on the Ice came upon us by surprise. I hailed the first I

saw, and he giving us answer, I fired by moon light and saw him fall. I loaded my gun, and as they fired and rushed upon me, I fired again and retreated to the main guard who were coming to my relief. They immediately fired, killing and wounding 16 of the enemy. Our light horse had rallied for our relief and coming in their rear, they soon surrendered and we [had] 70 prisoners. They were dressed in short wide plaid trousers and wore broad swords. I received a bullet upon the button of the gaiter of my right leg. Both bullet and button were driven into the leg just above the outer ankle bone. The wound was dressed by Doctor Parrott, the surgeon of our Regiment, who extracted both ball and button from the leg, with the knife, the next morning. The fight was in the fore part of the night. In the same affair, I received a wound just above the heel, as high as the ankle, which appeared to be a cut, almost dividing the legs cord behind the ankle, in the same leg. Both these wounds and scars, are yet plain to be seen and felt, and a lameness has remained from them to this day. I was confined 2 weeks and 5 days by this wound at West Point, Doctor Parrott attending and dressing the wounds daily. Capt. Younglove was wounded in the fleshy and back part of the thigh, the same night, by a ball. The Regiment remained here about 3 weeks, as I believe, when we took up our homeward march, and I hobbled along with them as well as I was able. We reached home late in the winter and were discharged but a little before the spring season began, having served out the full time our engagement.[7]

This would be Sutphen's last action of the war. His service began in 1776, fighting in the thick of the Battle at Long Island and only escaping the disaster with a few of his comrades thanks to a Black man with a skiff who sailed them back safely to New Jersey. He continued in the militia, patrolling the coast, and marched into battle in the Patriot victory at Princeton in January 1777. Several weeks later he fought with the militia in the Battle of Millstone, where they captured forty wagons of supplies, more than a hundred horses, and close to fifty prisoners. In reward for his service in that action, he was given a musket by General Philemon Dickinson. His unit was in the area during the Battle of Monmouth, though it did not participate, but it had been involved in a nearby skirmish at Crosswicks.

On his arrival home he was returned to slavery. He had originally been sold to Casper Berger to serve as his substitute for militia service, with the understanding that he would receive his freedom after the war. As he later said, "I believed the white man's word, hoping to be free when the fight was over. I took no paper to show the bargain, but trusted my master." Returning from the Sullivan expedition Sutphen raised the issue of his freedom with Berger but was informed shortly after that he had been sold to Peter Van Eyck. Attempts by Colonel Frelinghuysen and others to stop his sale were unsuccessful in the absence of any documentation of the prior agreement. He remained enslaved until 1805. In his old age, he applied for a federal pension but was repeatedly denied, as he could not secure witnesses to his service. His fifth application was denied, notwithstanding support by his congressman and Senator Frelinghuysen, the son of his former commander. The New Jersey legislature finally intervened by passing an act for an annual pension on his behalf on March 10, 1836—nearly sixty years after he began his service to the American cause. The home he and his wife, Caty, occupied in Branchburg, New Jersey, remains standing.

BATTLE OF STONY POINT (JULY 16, 1779)

Samuel Sutphen's final militia service and wounding at West Point was part of the defense of American positions in the valuable Hudson River

Highlands. In his pension application, Sutphen mentions that, while they were on the march during Sullivan's expedition, they were informed of the Patriot victory at Stony Point, a fortified British position 150 feet above the Hudson River, thirty miles north of New York City. He noted seeing the "Great Chain" that extended from West Point to the other side of the river, anchored into the rock, preventing any boats from sailing up the Hudson. Stony Point and Verplanck's Point on the opposite bank had been seized by the British in May 1779 with the hopes of drawing some of Washington's troops away from the Continental camp in New Jersey. The commanding heights of both positions gave the British effective control of the river, which could now be used to advance further up the Hudson.

To counter this threat, Washington directed General Anthony Wayne to take 1,350 soldiers on a surprise nighttime raid to retake the position. Rather than attack the point directly from the causeway with a full frontal assault straight into the British artillery positions, a likely fatal move, they charged up the steep hills from the riverbank. To maintain the element of surprise, the soldiers were directed to keep their muskets unloaded to prevent any premature firing and charge with their bayonets. Prior to the attack, great efforts were made to collect intelligence from the British camp on numbers and artillery placements. To this end, General Wayne had a secret weapon: a local slave named Pompey Lamb.

A regular visitor to Stony Point, Pompey Lamb regularly brought fruits and vegetables to sell to the British. He was also given the constantly changing countersign to enter the camp. His activities came to the notice of General Wayne in the course of intelligence gathering, and he was approached to serve as a spy for the Patriots. Pompey brought his wares to the British camp several times a week. Instructed by Wayne, he shifted his visits to nighttime, explaining that he was needed to hoe corn during the day. This continued for more than a week. On July 16, Wayne's troops set off to take Stony Point. Arriving at the rendezvous point, they waited for nightfall. Two columns climbed the rocky slope from both the north and the south, and two hundred men demonstrated on the causeway to distract the British from the main attack.

The south column was piloted by Pompey, and the north column was guided by another Black Patriot whose name is lost to history. Traditionally it is claimed that Pompey approached the sentry post with two beefy soldiers disguised as farmers, and having given the countersign, both sentinels were subdued, bound, and gagged. Both columns charging up the cliffs attacked nearly simultaneously and quickly overwhelmed the British fortifications. In the melee, General Wayne was shot in the head. Having fallen to the ground still conscious, he is claimed to have said, "March on, boys. Carry me into the fort! For should the wound be mortal, I will die at the head of the column." Fortunately, the ball had only grazed his head. In the early morning hours just after the battle, he wrote a quick note to Washington: "The fort and garrison with Col. Johnston are ours. Our officers and men behaved like men who are determined to be free."

Washington visited the recaptured fort that same day. On his visit he saw a number of Black Patriots among the victors, one especially. Richard Stanhope was one of his own slaves and part of his "military family" serving him in the field. He had previously been wounded with a musket ball just above his right knee at Long Island, served at Brandywine, and at Stony Point he received a wound to his left hand from a sword slash. Others may have been familiar to the commander in chief from their long service in his army. Peter Salem, who had served as a minuteman at Concord, been acclaimed as one of the heroes of Bunker Hill, and fought at Saratoga, saw his last action of the war at Stony Point. Many other battle-hardened Black Patriot veterans were among those in action under "Mad" Anthony Wayne, including Julius Cezar of New York, who had already fought at Long Island, Trenton, Princeton, and Brandywine. He served until the end of the war. Hamet Achmet had been born in Africa, enslaved and transported to Virginia early in life. He enlisted in the First Connecticut as a drummer in 1777 and had been wounded at Germantown. Other Black Patriot participants from Connecticut included Bristol Budd, Chatham Freeman, Jack Arabus, and Cuff Liberty. Nero Hawley of the Second Connecticut fought at White Marsh, wintered at Valley Forge, and had been at Monmouth, but in the taking of Stony Point he suffered debilitating injuries that required months of care in the hospital. Nathan Fry began his service in 1775 fighting Creek Indians in Georgia, joined the Continental army at Valley Forge, fought at Monmouth, and served at Stony Point as bat man (a personal servant or orderly) to Baron von Steuben. Shadrack Battles and John Roe, both from Virginia, also saw action, as did Drury Pettiford, Cato Copeland, and Martin Black of North Carolina. Primus Tyng of Salem, Massachusetts, years later added an unexpected nugget of information about the battle to the historical record: Rather than the officers long since named as first to enter the British camp, Tyng claimed that a regular soldier by the name of Daniel Drury had that honor.

The Patriot victory at Stony Point lifted the spirits of Washington's men and, with nearly five hundred British prisoners and all the supplies and arms captured, bolstered the Continental army's position in the north. Having learned from previous failures, Washington knew that British ships coming up the Hudson would make holding Stony Point impossible. So he ordered all the fortifications destroyed and the location abandoned. The British returned three days after the battle. The Patriots employed the same strategy a month later at Paulus Hook (modern day Jersey City), successfully attacking the British fort there in a surprise action led by Major Henry Lee on August 19, just a few miles from the British headquarters in New York City. The fort had been used by the British to conduct raids nearby. Lee withdrew in just a few hours with more than one hundred prisoners of war. One of the few American soldiers killed in that action was Samuel Goff of the Sixth Virginia, one of six Black Patriot brothers who had enlisted in 1777 and the second from the family to die in service (brother John died at Valley Forge). The result of the attacks on Stony Point and Paulus Hook was that British General Henry Clinton was dissuaded from continuing to force his way up the Hudson. His southern campaign strategy was where British hopes for better fortunes lay for now.

American prospects in the South were mixed. General Benjamin Lincoln had been dispatched by Washington to take charge of the Southern Department, and on his arrival he found the British occupying Augusta and Savannah, but Charleston—the most prosperous port city in the country—was still in Patriot hands. British General Augustine Prevost had led an expedition to take Charleston in May 1779, but informed of the British approach, General William Moultrie began throwing up defenses around the city. This convinced Prevost to abandon the expedition. Lincoln attacked the British rear guard at Stono Ferry southwest of Charleston on June 20, using militias largely from North and South Carolina.

The attack, unfortunately, was not well planned, poorly executed, and hampered by bad weather. While hard fought, the assault was unsuccessful, and Lincoln had to withdraw on the appearance of British reinforcements, suffering more casualties than Prevost. Black Patriots at Stono Ferry included Isham Carter of the South Carolina Fourth Artillery, whose commander, Colonel Robert Owen, was mortally wounded. Other South Carolinians in action included Lazarus Chavis, Gideon Griffin, Edward Harris, and Lemerick Farr. Many men from the Third North Carolina served in action, including Hardy Jones, Thomas Bibby, Elisha Parker, and Charles Roe (who lost an eye in the battle). The British were able to get close enough to Charleston to survey the difficult terrain in the area and scout out potential paths for a future attack on the city.

SIEGE OF SAVANNAH AND THE HAITIAN VOLUNTEERS

The next move for Patriot forces in the South was to link up with the French in an attempt to retake Savannah. Lincoln, still in Charleston, was informed that French Admiral d'Estaing was headed for Savannah with his ships and four thousand troops. He arrived off the coast of Georgia with thirty-three French ships of the line and began landing his troops near Savannah even before Lincoln could arrive with his forces. The militia, which had been called out, began to appear too. On September 16, d'Estaing offered terms of surrender to the British garrison inside Savannah, a request that was rebuffed the following day after a British column from Beaufort slipped inside the siege lines unnoticed during the night. Now reinforced, the Americans and French were not facing just Loyalist militias but British regulars. The city was also quickly reinforced with cannons and strongly fortified redoubts. During the aborted British march toward Charleston a few months before, they had raided a number of plantations along the way and took away as many as three thousand slaves, who were put to work building the British defenses at Savannah. The chief engineer responsible for the defenses, British Major James Moncrief, was later accused of selling hundreds of captured slaves in the West Indies after the siege for his own personal benefit.

The combined French-American force also began building their siege lines, creeping closer to the city each day. When they were close enough, they began firing artillery into the city. The British, with more than eighty cannon in their lines, responded in kind. As days turned into weeks, pressure began to mount on d'Estaing. Established siege tactics indicated drawing out the siege, but it was hurricane season, and the French ships were as vulnerable to nature's fury as the British. D'Estaing's fleet needed to depart shortly, so he urged an attack on the city. Lincoln agreed, and he ordered an assault with two columns, with the main point of joint attack focused on a well-built and heavily defended point known as the Spring Hill Redoubt. Polish volunteer Casimir Pulaski led a cavalry charge between the redoubt and a nearby battery to hopefully drive into the city itself. Lincoln was not aware that the Spring Hill Redoubt (which was rediscovered in 2005 and is now a city park) was manned by the entire force of British regulars from Beaufort. An American deserter from the Charleston militia absconded into the British lines, informing them of Lincoln's battle plan and allowing them to reinforce intended points of attack.

The attack was launched in the morning of October 9. Fog covered the area, making the approach of the French-American forces difficult. The first wave of the attack on the Spring Hill Redoubt was met with withering fire, killing many. The trenches of the redoubt were already filled with the bodies of the Patriot wounded and dead by the time the second wave attacked, which also suffered heavy casualties. One Black Patriot in the battle, Allen Jeffers, claimed to have seen Pulaski mortally wounded during his cavalry charge. Within an hour a general retreat was ordered. The losses from the attack were among the worst of the entire war for the Patriots, with nearly four times more killed and wounded than the British. Admiral d'Estaing, who was wounded in the attack, set sail with his ships days later. Lincoln abandoned the siege on October 18, adding yet another loss for the Patriot cause in the South.

Some traditional accounts claim that the entire force risked being completely routed on their retreat as they were pursued by the British regulars from the Spring Hill Redoubt. It was only through a defensive rear guard action by the St. Domingo Legion, a unit of 750 Black and biracial freemen recruited in the French colony of St. Domingo (what is now Haiti), which according to these accounts saved the allies. The reality of their role in the attack is mired in myth and mystery. What is known is that these "volunteer chasseurs" served in a number of locations along the siege lines in the lead up to the failed October 9 attack and likely suffered heavy casualties, as did many other allied units. As part of the reserve on the day of the battle, they would have covered the allies' retreat. As historian George P. Clark observed more than four decades ago, virtually all of the documentation and official accounts of the St. Domingo recruits has been lost due to successive fires at the Haitian National Archives. The volunteers were intermixed with other units, French and American alike. But with the possible exception of the First Rhode Island Regiment, the St. Domingo Legion was likely the largest Black Patriot military presence of the entire Revolutionary War. A monument to their service and sacrifice in the American cause stands in Franklin Park in Savannah.

It is debated to what degree the American Revolution inspired Haiti's later independence. Some of the heroes of the Haitian insurrection are claimed to have been a part of the St. Domingo Legion, including the first king, Henri Christophe. At least one member of the legion, Monsieur de Bordeaux, returned to Savannah after the war. He was wounded in the October 9 battle, claiming to have seen Pulaski fall, and lived in the city until his death.

Other Black Patriots from Virginia, North Carolina, and South Carolina took part in the siege and the battle. Drury Harris and his cousin, Edward Harris, were part of the Third South Carolina, as was their neighborhood friend Gideon Griffin. John Davis, the first sergeant of their platoon, later testified in support of Drury's pension claim, saying:

> In the fight at Savannah I saw no man, officer, or private more active nor braver than Drury Harris. Who also seeing and knowing him, to receive two wounds, a shot wound in the thigh and a bayonet in the arm, in trying to seal the walls of his enemy, which I will say, now he is old, of course not able to labor hard, if there is any old soldier deserves any assistance from the public, Drury Harris does.[8]

Randal Bowers of the same regiment died the day following the battle, likely of his wounds. Shadrack Battles of the Tenth Virginia was already a veteran of the fights at Brandywine, Germantown, and Monmouth when he served at the siege of Savannah. John Womble of the Tenth North Carolina likely saw his first action of the war, having enlisted the previous June, as did Aaron Hathcock. Other Black Patriots from their regiment included Isaac Perkins, Jack Rock, James Smith, and John Weaver. Billing Lucas, a new recruit, died on September 5 even before the siege began, and Francis Jack was omitted in the October 1779 muster roll, presumably killed in action. Jim Capers, already gaining fame as a drummer, was present, as was Isham Carter of the Fourth South Carolina Artillery. These were all part of approximately three hundred Continental troops under Lincoln's command, in addition to the 750 militiamen called up specifically for the siege.

The year 1779 saw the Revolutionary War expand beyond its previous limits. Raids by the British Indian allies and Loyalists along the New York frontier were met with the Sullivan expedition that saw dozens of Indian communities destroyed. Attacks beyond the Allegheny Mountains brought about the construction of American forts deep into the northwest wilderness beyond the Ohio River. George Rogers Clark and the Illinois Regiment took the battle to the Mississippi River at Kaskaskia, and then captured the British outpost of Fort Sackville at Vincennes. Continued action in the Hudson River Valley necessitated the surprise Patriot attack at Stony Point. The southern campaign launched by the British brought the war to Georgia and the Carolinas. Many of those battles pitted American Patriots against their Loyalist neighbors, resulting in small victories (Kettle Creek) and heavy losses (Brier Creek, Stono Ferry, Savannah).

British General Henry Clinton raised the potential cost to Black Patriots by publishing the Philipsburg Proclamation on June 30, 1779, an edict threatening to enslave any freeman or slave captured with the

Americans—a threat they later carried out. It also promised to protect any slave "who shall desert the Rebel Standard" and reach the British lines. That notwithstanding, the names of Black Patriots continued to swell the muster rolls of Continental regiments and local militias, increasing their stake in the hopes of American independence. Every one of them would be needed, as some of the most difficult and costly fighting of the war still lay ahead.

The nature of the stakes was evident in a message that General Clinton received from London on December 29, 1779—a year to the day after he had taken Savannah. The message directed him to take Charleston, the richest port in the southern states. Soon, one hundred British ships filled with thousands of British soldiers would set sail to expand the war even further in the South.

The Haitian Monument commemorates the hundreds of free men recruited by the French in Haiti who served at the Siege of Savannah. These "chasseurs-voluntaires" (volunteer infantry) were stationed throughout the allied siege lines, supplementing American and French units. Many of these men covered the Allied retreat after a disastrous October 9, 1779, charge on the British lines, with as many as two dozen killed while protecting the retreating troops. Sixty-two of these Black Patriot fighters from Haiti were captured at the fall of Charleston in May of the following year, with most being sold into the slavery by the British in the West Indies. (Image: Patrick S. Poole)

Wyoming Massacre monument in Luzerne County, Pennsylvania, built over the mass grave of Continental soldiers killed in the battle. Among those killed in action was Gershom Prince, who had been a slave of Robert Durkee, an officer of the Connecticut line. He served with Durkee in the French and Indian War at the Battle of Lake George (1755) and the Siege of Havana (1762), and took the field again in the Revolutionary War in Durkee's company of the Fourth Connecticut. They both died together at Wyoming. His inscribed powder horn dated September 3, 1761, at Crown Point from the French and Indian War was found afterward on the battlefield. (Image: Patrick S. Poole)

CHAPTER 8

1780: INDEPENDENCE IN THE BALANCE

THE WAR IN THE NORTHERN states was largely a stalemate as Washington's army encamped at Morristown, New Jersey, for the winter. In the South, the costly failure of the joint French-American attack to take back Savannah left that city and its valuable port firmly in British hands. Soon, one hundred ships would be headed south to take Charleston. The defense of the major cities in the North, as well as the worst winter on record at the time (even worse than at Valley Forge two years previous), would prevent Washington from reinforcing Benjamin Lincoln, who already had suffered defeats at Savannah and Stono Ferry. The defense of Charleston would be an even greater test for the hapless general from Massachusetts. Losing the southern states would divide the country and likely provide the British with sufficient supplies to further pressure Washington and the hard-pressed northern army. Entering into 1780, American independence was in the balance.

The Black Patriots fighting in both the northern and southern theaters had even more at stake. General Clinton had announced in his Philipsburg Proclamation the previous year that any Black man, slave or free, fighting for the Patriots and taken prisoner by the British would be sold into slavery. But Clinton's corresponding offer of freedom and protection for any slaves who deserted their Patriot owners and made it to the British lines created an opportunity for some that may not have existed even if the Patriots were victorious. Some grew impatient with the lack of action by most of the states to address the contradiction of a continued fight for freedom while enslaving others.

"NATIVES OF AFRICA, NOW FORCIBLY DETAINED"

One expression of this impatience was a petition signed by twenty leaders of the Black community in Portsmouth, New Hampshire, that was submitted to the state's legislature sitting in Exeter and subsequently published in the *New Hampshire Gazette.* Addressing themselves as "Natives of Africa, Now Forcibly Detained," they asserted, perfectly in line with the sentiments of the Declaration of Independence, that "the God of Nature gave them Life and Freedom upon the terms of the most perfect Equality with other men." Slavery, the state in which they now found themselves, violated the fundamental Laws of Nature and Religion that were now the source of American law and government. The dictates of divinity and humanity demanded "that the Name of Slave may not more be heard in a Land gloriously contending for the Sweets of Freedom."

The petition is remarkable in that the signers were enslaved by some of the most prominent and wealthy families in Portsmouth, some actively involved in the slave trade. One name is of particular note: Prince Whipple, who by this time had already served at the battles of Saratoga and Rhode Island. He was still enslaved by Continental Congress delegate William Whipple, a signer of the Declaration of Independence that the petitioners clearly drew inspiration from. He would remain enslaved until after the end of the war. The petition was received by the legislature on April 25, 1780, and the body voted to have the petition published for public comment, but any action on their plea was tabled. Most of the signers would die in slavery. No legislative action was taken on the matter until a bill was passed and signed into law by New Hampshire Governor Maggie Hassan on July 11, 2013, posthumously emancipating all of the petition signers 233 years later.

In neighboring Massachusetts, a constitutional convention held in 1780 adopted a Declaration of Rights that included in its first article that, "All men are born free and equal, and have certain natural, essential and inalienable rights, among which may be reckoned the right of enjoying and defending their lives and liberties..." While much of the state's constitution was drafted by John Adams, this particular provision was introduced and championed by delegate John Lowell, who had served in the Revolution and would shortly thereafter represent Massachusetts in the Continental Congress. Lowell believed that this article would end slavery in the state, and according to the recollections of his son, he offered his legal services pro bono to any slave who wanted to sue for his freedom on the basis of this constitutional acknowledgement.

THE FELIX CUFF AFFAIR

One Black Patriot who took these words seriously was Felix Cuff of Waltham, Massachusetts, who enlisted in the state militia shortly after the state constitution was approved by voters. But days later a man named Edward Gearfield showed up, claiming that Felix was his slave and that he had been forced to enlist without his knowledge or permission. A letter from the town's selectmen contradicted his account, saying that Gearfield was present when the enlistment occurred and that Felix was already a free man. Unconvinced by the selectmen's appeal, the militia's commanding officer directed one of his subordinates to return his new recruit to Gearfield. But Felix and two other men liberated themselves and hid in a local cave called the Devil's Den. When a posse showed up, attempting to take them by force, they asserted their freedom and successfully fought them off. Felix then went back into town and promptly sued the posse for assault, a claim that was supported by the town. Felix Cuff subsequently served out the term of his enlistment and was paid for his services.

THE ORDEAL OF SILAS ROYAL

Being a freeman and a war veteran didn't protect Black Patriots from potential abduction, as Silas Royal of Dracut, Massachusetts, found out. He had enlisted during the siege of Boston, was discharged after the British evacuation, and then served on board a privateer targeting British shipping. But on their return to port, a man named Joshua Wyman claimed most of Royal's prize money. In 1777, he sued to recover his prize money from Wyman (John Lowell, who had authored Article 1 of the state's Declaration of Rights, was Royal's attorney in the suit). The following year as the lawsuit was still progressing, Royal was taken captive by a John White, who claimed that he had purchased Silas from Joshua Wyman. Fortunately, the powerful Varnum family, whom Royal had previously served as a slave, moved quickly to intervene. Protesting to General William Heath, then in command of Boston, they secured Royal's release. What was revealed by the affair was that Wyman conspired with John White to have Royal transported to the South to be sold as a slave, which would have effectively ended the lawsuit over his prize money. Silas Royal remained close to the Varnum family for the rest of his life and was buried in the family cemetery in 1826. But few Black Patriots had powerful protectors to come to their aid in such situations.

Fifteen-year-old Andrew Ferguson, a freeman from Dinwiddie County, Virginia, found protection from General Nathanael Greene in January 1780, two weeks after he and his father had been taken captive by two British officers, who beat them with whips. As recounted by Ferguson years later in his pension application, having escaped their captors they ran into Greene, who was recruiting in their area, and told him their story. Ferguson recounts Greene's reply, "that if the British ever got us again they would killed us and he had better draft us and so he…told us we should go with him and must fight the British." In his first battle, Ferguson faced the very same British officers that had beat him and his father. Over the next two years, he fought in virtually every major battle of the southern campaign leading up to the Patriot victory at Yorktown. Though severely wounded in combat, he lived to a ripe old age, dying in 1855 in Bloomington, Indiana, where his grave is marked with a military marker.

An honorable discharge for one Caesar Fiddler was filed with the town of Wethersfield, Connecticut, in May 1780, attached with a copy of his manumission papers freeing him after three years of service with the Fifth Connecticut. Enlisting in June 1777 to obtain his freedom from slavery, the manumission was dated to that time, but only submitted three years later after his term was honored and ended. Soon after his enlistment, the regiment marched to Pennsylvania to support Washington's attempt to prevent the British from seizing Philadelphia. His unit fought at Germantown, and the record shows that Fiddler wintered at Valley Forge. He then fought at the Patriot victory at Monmouth and entered the northern army's winter camp at Morristown. He likely would have known the other Black Patriots in his regiment, including Cash Africa, Cudjo Clark, Jack Congo, Jack Green, Cezar Black, Cato Hunt, Cato Cuff, John Brister, Ebenezer Jacklin, and Pharoh Hart, among others. But his discharge and manumission belie a darker reality. In fact, Caesar Fiddler was never freed in life, having died in the service on February 19, 1780, likely succumbing to illness or disease. There's no explanation of why his brigade commander issued a discharge to a dead soldier, or why his former owner formalized his manumission after his death, but it may have been a late recognition of his fulfilled commitment, or perhaps an attempt to memorialize a life that mattered to some in his community and to the country he served.

CONTESTED LINES IN NEW JERSEY

The Continental army under General Benjamin Lincoln in the South needed every man it could muster with General Henry Clinton and one hundred ships headed toward Charleston. But there were few or none available to be sent by Washington from his army in the North. At his winter camp in Morristown, the army had been reduced to about eight thousand men, and as many as one-third that number were deemed unfit. What soldiers he had fit for duty were keeping Clinton's army in place inside New York City and defending against the roaming Loyalist militias raiding the countryside for supplies. One of those raids struck Elizabethtown and Newark, New Jersey, on January 25, 1780. A British raiding party crossed the ice from Staten Island, targeting homes of Continental officers and known Patriots in the area. Elizabethtown, a port city on the Hudson River, was the largest city in New Jersey at the time and would be the site of dozens of raids throughout the war. Reverend James Caldwell, the pastor of the Presbyterian church in Elizabethtown, was specifically targeted, with raiders burning down the church and the parsonage, leaving he, his wife, and their nine children homeless. The attack on the church had been led by a former Loyalist resident of the town whose father was an elder of the congregation. The courthouse and the Presbyterian school, where both Aaron Burr and Alexander Hamilton had been educated, were also torched. The Presbyterian church and academy in Newark were also burned down during the raid. The wife of Justice Joseph Hedden was bayoneted as her husband was taken from their home. Local Patriot militias drove the raiders out of Newark.

The small-scale British raid on Elizabethtown resulted in the capture of five American officers and forty-seven privates in addition to stores and supplies that were taken. Several Black Patriots were taken prisoner in the raid. Philip Savoy of the First Maryland had enlisted in May 1778 and fought with the regiment at Monmouth the following month. Captured at Elizabethtown, he was taken to New York City, where he was imprisoned. He was exchanged or paroled at some point several months later, being discharged from the service in August 1780. After his return to Maryland he was drafted and served at the siege at Yorktown. George Dias of the Fifth Maryland, who had been at the taking of Stony Point the year before, was also taken prisoner during the raid. Though wounded during the skirmish, he was able to escape from his British captors later that night. He continued to serve until the end of the war. James Due, another Black Patriot in the same regiment as Dias, was also taken as a prisoner of war, spending eleven months in captivity. Sharp Camp testified to his participation in the action at Elizabethtown in his pension application, and was likely present with other Black Patriots serving in his company, including James Dinah and Andrew Jack. There were thirty-six Black Patriots who served in the Sixth Connecticut Regiment, all of whom enlisted in 1777 and 1778. Two of those, Pomp Cherry and Gift Freeman, died during their service.

Elizabethtown was the staging area for a large-scale attack by British and Hessian soldiers just months later under Hessian General Wilhelm Von Knyphausen. Their objective was to attack Washington's weakened army in Morristown. Washington's camp was wisely shielded by the Watchung Mountains, and the only reasonable attack point was through Hobart's Gap, which was stoutly defended by the Continentals. Landing with five thousand troops in Elizabethtown on June 7, 1780, Knyphausen moved out toward the mountain gap in two columns, but they were met by Continental troops and the New Jersey militia and stopped at Connecticut Farms (now Union, New Jersey). They set about burning the town. Reverend Caldwell and his family had relocated to the area after his church and home in Elizabethtown were burned the previous January. This time too, his new church and parsonage were targeted for destruction, but in the attack, his wife, Hannah, was shot and killed by a British soldier. Today, the seal for Union County, New Jersey, depicts her murder. Facing determined Patriot resistance, Knyphausen retreated back to his landing site.

Two weeks later, Knyphausen landed with six thousand troops in a second attempt to push through Hobart's Gap to attack Washington's camp. At least as many troops had been positioned elsewhere in the event that Washington emerged from behind the mountains to attack the British right flank. They quickly reached and secured the ruined remnants of Connecticut Farms and pressed ahead toward Springfield. It was there that a force of only 1,500 Continentals and New Jersey militiamen tried to stall the advance. The Second Rhode Island made a heroic stand at a bridge, where they faced an assault by five times as many men. General Nathanael Greene, commanding the force, eventually withdrew from Springfield, and the British and Hessian soldiers set fire to the entire town. One nearby house that was struck by cannon fire still stands, and the cannonball hangs outside in front of the hole it made during the battle. Seeing growing numbers of militiamen gathering on the mountains in front of them, Knyphausen ordered a retreat. The rear guard of the column faced a fighting retreat all the way back to Elizabethtown, where the British and Hessians crossed a pontoon bridge back to Staten Island in the dark. In his pension affidavit years later, Oliver Cromwell of the Second New Jersey recalled seeing, during the course of the battle, the burned-out Caldwell home at Connecticut Farms where Hannah Caldwell had been murdered weeks before. George Dias of the Fifth Maryland, who had briefly been a prisoner of the British at Elizabethtown in January but had escaped, also served in the Patriot victory at Springfield.

Another Black Patriot who participated in several battles in New Jersey was Jack Cudjo Banquante, a slave serving as a substitute for his owner, Benjamin Coe of Newark. Drafted in 1777, he fought at Germantown, suffered the winter at Valley Forge, endured the oppressive heat at Monmouth, and repelled the British at both Elizabethtown and

Springfield. He was freed at the end of his term of service after the siege of Yorktown, given ten acres of land in what is now downtown Newark, and became a prosperous businessman in the area. His service is memorialized with a plaque at the New Jersey Performing Arts Center in Newark, which is built on a former graveyard where Banquante was buried in 1823.

The Battle of Springfield on June 23, 1780, represented the last major action in the northern theater of the war. Just a few weeks later more than five thousand French troops under command of the Comte de Rochambeau arrived in Newport, Rhode Island, to reinforce Washington's army. The British never staged another invasion of New Jersey again. Raids and skirmishes continued, however, such as an attack by DeLancey's Cowboys at Horse Neck, New York, on May 23, 1780. Cesar Shelton of the Fourth Connecticut was wounded in that action by a musket ball to the shin and a sword thrust to his back. Caesar Wallace of the Second New Hampshire also mentioned participating in the action at Horse Neck. At the end of the war he received the Badge of Merit for his six years of service in the war. His regiment had the largest representation of Black Patriots enlisted from New Hampshire.

The presence of the Continental army in New Jersey provided an opportunity for Peter Williams to escape his Loyalist master, John Heard of Woodbridge, who had defected to the British side. An act of the New Jersey legislature passed on September 1, 1784, notes that Williams had joined the state militia defending the state's frontiers, and then joined the Continental army, serving until the war's end. The legislature's action declared that "said Peter William is hereby declared to be manumitted and set free from slavery and servitude as fully to all intents and purposes, as though he had been freeborn and continued in such a state of freedom, any law, usage or custom to the contrary notwithstanding." In the eyes of the law, Williams had never been a slave and no man had any claims on him. Another slave freed by the state of New Jersey was Cato, whose master had also defected to the British. In freeing the man, the legislature acknowledged "that the said Cato had rendered essential Services both to this State and the United States in the Time of the last War."

One Black Patriot helping to keep Washington's men supplied during this time was Caesar, the former slave of Isaac Drake. Born in Africa in 1702, abducted there and enslaved, he was given his freedom in 1769. Well into his seventies at the time, he served as a Continental wagon master driving a team of four horses. A respected member of his church, his grave at the Scotch Plains Baptist Church in Connecticut Farms is marked with a finely carved stone restored in 2011 by the Alpha Kappa Alpha sorority, and a recently placed military marker now records his patriotic service.

THE CAPTURE OF BRITISH MAJOR JOHN ANDRE (SEPTEMBER 23, 1780)

A monument at the Peekskill Museum in New York honors the contribution of one Black Patriot veteran who played a critical role in one of the most famous episodes of the entire war. John Jacob Peterson was a formerly enslaved man who had served a three-year term in the Second New York, serving at the battles of Saratoga, Monmouth, and Newtown and surviving the winter at Valley Forge. After his discharge, he continued to serve in the Westchester County militia. One morning while he and Moses Sherwood were at Croton Point making cider, the British ship *Vulture* anchored nearby in the Hudson River. An article on the incident by Erik Weiselberg notes that as a barge attempted to land with twenty British soldiers, Peterson and Sherwood opened fire, forcing it to return to the *Vulture*. The men hastily raced to nearby Fort Lafayette, reporting the activity. The commander rushed several cannon back to the scene and fired at the ship the following morning, requiring the *Vulture* to sail back downriver. The date was September 22, 1780.

Unbeknownst to both men at the time, the ship had brought Major John Andre, the head of the British Secret Service in America, upriver to meet with General Benedict Arnold, who had communicated with the British high command in New York City of his intention to defect to their side. During the late-night meeting between the two men, Arnold offered to betray his friend General Washington and the American fort at West Point, which protected the Hudson River Valley from British naval incursions upriver. By forcing the *Vulture* to retire from the area, it effectively stranded Major Andre in Patriot territory. Dressed in civilian clothes, he was captured by three militia members near Tarrytown, New York, the following day. Documents found on Andre's person implicated Arnold, though Washington was reluctant to believe his friend's treason. Sending a note to Arnold, Washington unwittingly tipped him off that his cover was blown and gave him time to flee to the British. A late attempt by Washington to have Arnold arrested failed. An investigation led by General Nathanael Greene found that Andre had been found in civilian, not military, dress and was traveling under an assumed name, rendering him a spy under the laws of war.

Andre's execution on October 2, 1780, is mentioned in the pension narratives of several Black Patriots. The widow of Peter Hunter of the Sixth Connecticut reported that her husband stood guard over Andre during his short detention. John Foy of the Second Massachusetts reported that he did the same. At Andre's execution, Primus Coburn of the First Massachusetts was one of five hundred infantrymen surrounding the gallows, preventing any rescue attempts. Prince Light of the Second New Hampshire made note of the remarkable shine of Andre's shoes. Whereas Arnold had left the defenses at West Point in dilapidated condition, and the traitor had provided a map of the installation to Andre, the Sixth Connecticut with its three dozen Black Patriots was one of the regiments stationed at West Point to defend the fort in the event of a British attack.

THE FALL OF CHARLESTON (MARCH 29–MAY 12, 1780)

The stalemate in the northern campaign was matched by desperation in the southern theater in 1780. The war in the South for the next two years saw the fortunes of both armies wax and wane—sometimes unexpectedly changing course within days. The Patriots suffered catastrophic defeats but continued to keep their hopes alive with small but important victories.

The first act of the southern theater in 1780 took place in Charleston, where General Benjamin Lincoln anticipated the arrival of Henry Clinton and the British fleet carrying its army of invasion. With 13,500 troops arriving by sea with Clinton, the heavily outnumbered southern army under Lincoln also faced the British force already operating in the area under Lieutenant Colonel Mark Prevost, who had already bested him the previous year at Stono Ferry and Savannah. A request by Lincoln to the South Carolina government to arm 1,500 slaves in defense of the city was rebuffed.

In 1776, General William Moultrie had successfully defended the city against a British fleet at the Battle of Sullivan Island, where the cannonballs bounced off the fort's walls reinforced with palmetto logs and sand. Lincoln had no such luck when Clinton's fleet sailed past the same fort (now renamed Fort Moultrie after its former commander) and into Charleston Harbor in early April. This was the beginning of Clinton squeezing Charleston and Lincoln's army.

Two important figures who played a major role in the fighting in South Carolina, British Lieutenant Colonel Banastre Tarleton and Major Patrick Ferguson, surprised a small Patriot force of five hundred men at Monck's Corner on April 14. Defending the area were militias and men from the Third South Carolina, including several Black Patriots, including Edward Coleman, Gideon Griffin, and Edward Harris. Not only did Tarleton capture supplies and four hundred horses, but by seizing the crossroads there and also Biggins Bridge, Lincoln's communications from the north were effectively cut off and the British could stall any reinforcements headed toward Charleston. With the British fleet in Charleston Harbor within range of the city and Clinton's siege lines creeping closer to the Continental lines by the day, the loss of Monck's Corner put a stranglehold on Lincoln's army by closing off any possible escape route.

At a parlay between the two commanders after two weeks of British bombardment, Lincoln offered to surrender the city if his men were allowed to leave under arms. Clinton's response was to continue to bombard the city. Lincoln believed that escape was still possible and wanted to attempt an evacuation of his army, but city leaders threatened to burn any boats to prevent the army from abandoning Charleston. On May 11, Clinton opened fire on the city, using hot shots to set it on fire. There were no options left for Benjamin Lincoln but to accept Clinton's harsh terms of unconditional surrender on May 12, 1780.

In material costs, the American loss was steep: three hundred cannons, six thousand muskets, and gunpowder. These would all be used in the British push to subdue the South Carolina backcountry. In personnel costs, the results were catastrophic. The Continental army's presence in the South ceased to exist. Five thousand Patriots were now facing the rough mercy of the British army. Most would be held prisoner.

The costs were also high for Black Patriots serving in Charleston. For the Jeffers family and their friends in the Griffin and Harris clans, and several others serving in the Third South Carolina from their neighborhood, the biggest loss was Osbourne Jeffers, who was killed in action. Allen Jeffers was paroled, leaving their brother, Berry, to continue the fight by joining the state forces under General Thomas Sumter. Elisha Hunt of the Second North Carolina lost an arm during the siege. Thomas Lively of the Fifth Virginia had lost an eye at Monmouth but had reenlisted. At Charleston he was wounded in the leg and became a prisoner of war for fourteen months. He returned to the fight after his exchange. Buckner Thomas of the Tenth Virginia was near the end of his enlistment at the time of the siege, having already served at the raid of Sandy Hook and the taking of Stony Point. He remained a prisoner for eighteen months until he was finally exchanged.

Dozens more Black Patriots were imprisoned, many at Haddrell's Point in sight of the now-ruined city of Charleston. Among the POWs was Jasper Browngard, William Burnett, Isham Carter, Cato Copeland, Edmond Davis, Adam Ivey, Hardy Jones, William Kersey, Israel Pearce, and Arthur and Matthew Wiggins. John Edward Carter became a prisoner but was never heard from again. Ephraim Hearn was transported to New York, where he was imprisoned on one of the notorious British prison ships but was able to escape and return home. Martin Black, who had earlier fought at Monmouth and Stony Point, was only held a week before he escaped and returned to his regiment. Isaac Perkins also escaped and joined the state militia. William Lomack joined back up with General Horatio Gates, who was dispatched south to rebuild the southern army. John Freeman of the Fifteenth Virginia, who had enlisted in December 1776, died in captivity, as did many Patriots who became prisoners after the fall of Charleston. The costs were steep for sixty-two Haitian volunteers who had arrived the previous year with the French to fight for Savannah and had remained with the Americans to defend Charleston. Now prisoners, they were sold by the British back into slavery in the West Indies, fulfilling Henry Clinton's vow that that any Black man taken fighting with the "rebels" would be enslaved regardless of whether they had been born slave or free. For his part, however, Benjamin Lincoln was paroled and allowed to stay in Philadelphia until he was exchanged, the British perhaps wishing he would get another command.

The fall of Charleston was one of the greatest American military losses not only of the Revolutionary War but in our country's history. Now holding Savannah and Charleston, the British were able to move into the backcountry of the Carolinas and eventually Virginia. Clinton left General Charles Cornwallis in charge of the British southern campaign.

But others still had hope for an American victory and independence. When news of the fall of Charleston reached Halifax County, North Carolina, Mark Murray's father came to him while he was mauling rails, relating the recent events. "Mark, I have bad news to tell you," his father told him. "The British have taken Charleston. You must go and fight for your country. You are a free man and you serve your country, and never do you return unless you get an honorable discharge and bring it home to me." Murray served two successive three-month terms in the militia under the direction of General Thomas Sumter. And he returned home, having fulfilled his father's challenge, bringing him his honorable discharge.

WAXHAWS MASSACRE (MAY 29, 1780)

But more bad news was to quickly follow. Colonel Abraham Buford was leading a column of Continentals from Virginia south down the Catawba River Valley to reinforce Lincoln at Charleston when news reached him of Lincoln's surrender and the city's fall. The column then began marching back north to defend North Carolina and Virginia from any British incursions. On May 29, 1780, just a few weeks after the disaster at Charleston, the fast-moving British legion led by British Lieutenant Colonel Banastre Tarleton caught up with Buford near the Waxhaws settlement, just a few miles from the border of North and South Carolina. Tarleton's unit was composed largely of trained American Loyalists divided into light infantry, cavalry, and artillery. In fifteen minutes, Buford's column was cut to shreds. More than one-third of his regiment were killed. As Continental soldiers tried to surrender, they were massacred by Tarleton's troops with swords and bayonets.

British casualties were slight; Buford's losses were catastrophic—113 dead, 150 injured, and 53 taken prisoner. Very few Patriots were able to escape. Eighty-four Continental soldiers were buried in a mass grave that is now the center of a battlefield preservation trust. Twenty-six of Buford's supply wagons were captured shortly thereafter. The Patriot wounded (many who subsequently died) were treated by the civilians of the Waxhaws settlement, including a boy by the name of Andrew Jackson. The enemy's brutality began to forge in him a lifelong hatred of the British.

Several Black Patriots were part of the Waxhaws Massacre. Robert Owls of the Third Virginia was wounded in the head. James Cooper served in the same company, and their captain, Gustavus Brown Wallace, was killed in the action. William Clark had already served three years in the Continental army and was a member of the First Regiment of Artillery at Waxhaws. Asher Crockett, later known as James Anderson, escaped from slavery in Virginia in 1776 and removed to Pennsylvania, where he eventually fell in with Washington's army as a camp servant. Later returning to Virginia, he enlisted as a substitute in 1778, concerned about his former owner's attempts to return him to slavery. He later reenlisted and served until 1783 and the end of the war. After the war he fought with General George Rogers Clark in Kentucky. He eventually settled in Cabell County, in what is now West Virginia. George McCoy successfully petitioned the Virginia legislature for a land warrant in consideration of the wounds he received at Waxhaws.

The massacre by the British did not have the intended effect. Instead of being seen as victors, they were deemed murderous oppressors by many of the backcountry folk who had left Great Britain to escape such tyranny. The horror of "Tarleton's Quarter" became a rallying cry that animated many to the Patriot cause. Without any organized opposition, Loyalist militias behaved as if they had been given carte blanche to wage terror in their neighborhoods and mete out revenge against Patriots. British garrisons were established in places such as Camden and Ninety-Six, with even more outposts to reach deeper into the interior.

Captain Christian Huck, a Philadelphia Loyalist, was one of the more notorious leaders operating in the Carolina backcountry. Lieutenant

Colonel George Turnbull, commander of the New York (Loyalist) Volunteers, ordered Huck to leave the outpost at Rocky Point, South Carolina—the furthest outpost of the Camden garrison—to recruit and organize Loyalists and to suppress "rebel" activity. Arriving at the home of militia leader William Bratton and not finding the known Patriot leader at home, Huck threatened Bratton's wife, who rejected his request to convince her husband to change sides. Huck and his men spent that night at the neighboring Williamson plantation. Bratton's wife dispatched their slave, Watt, to locate her husband and inform him of Huck's mission and location. William Bratton was camped on the other side of the Catawba River with General Sumter and received the message from Watt. Immediately springing into action, the Patriots arrived at the plantation in the early hours and plotted a three-pronged attack to cut off any escape. The assault began at first light on the morning of July 11, 1780, and the surprised Loyalists, many of whom had been at Waxhaws, were quickly routed. Huck was shot and killed trying to flee on a horse. Bratton's slave, Watt, was clearly acknowledged as the hero of "Huck's Defeat" at Williamson's Plantation, the first Patriot victory following the fall of Charleston. Watt is buried in a marked grave at the plantation's slave cemetery.

Loyalist militias continued to harass Patriots in the backcountry, confiscating livestock and burning plantations, prompting General Sumter to convene a council of war to confront the raids. The next day, August 6, Sumter and Major William Davie of North Carolina led a column to attack a larger Loyalist militia encamped at Hanging Rock on the road between Camden and Charlotte. Traveling with Sumter and Davie was Asher Crockett, one of the Black Patriot survivors of the Waxhaws Massacre. Again, the Loyalists were quickly put to flight, their camp looted, and two counterattacks were repelled. Two hundred Loyalists were killed, while the Patriots lost only forty men.

"OVERMOUNTAIN MEN" ON THE MARCH

The Patriot victories at Williamson's Plantation and Hanging Rock did much to briefly boost the morale in the backcountry and encourage recruitment. These victories showed that, while the British still had an advantage when they confronted Continental regulars, the Patriots could utilize hit-and-run tactics with smaller, more mobile forces. Meanwhile, the British campaign of terror continued. Word of the Waxhaws Massacre had prompted some militia leaders west of the Allegheny Mountains in what is now eastern Tennessee to band together to defend their communities. These "overmountain men" were under the leadership of John Sevier and Isaac Shelby, who joined forces with Colonel Elijah Clarke from Georgia. Their target was British Major Patrick Ferguson, who commanded 1,800 Loyalists and whose mission was to subdue the Carolina backcountry. The respective units commanded by Ferguson and Tarleton served as the eyes and ears of General Cornwallis.

One of Sevier's captains was John Scott, who traveled with his slave, Benjamin, who became separated from his owner and was captured by Ferguson's troops at some point before or after the Battle of Cedar Springs in early August 1780. According to accounts, Benjamin was hung three separate times in an attempt to get him to divulge the location of Captain Scott and the Patriot militias. He refused to give them any information. Benjamin Scott, who was born free in Africa and subsequently enslaved, came to be owned by Scott, who lived at Piney Creek, Maryland, at the time. He would serve the Scott family until his death in 1829, never again a free man. Some records indicate that he received an award or medal for his heroism. The Patriots successfully held off an assault by Ferguson at Cedar Springs on August 8, fighting fierce hand-to-hand combat with the Loyalist dragoons. Despite a running battle, they were able to remove themselves across the Pacolet River with British prisoners before Ferguson halted his pursuit.

GATES'S DEFEAT AT CAMDEN (AUGUST 16, 1980)

Also operating in the area was a column of 1,500 Continental regulars from Maryland and Delaware under the command of General Horatio Gates, the hero of Saratoga. They were joined by militias from North Carolina and Virginia. Gates had been appointed the new Continental commander in the South following the surrender of Benjamin Lincoln and his entire army. From Charlotte, Gates headed toward Camden, one of the main British garrisons.

It was in the early hours of August 16 when the two armies unintentionally ran into each other in the dark near Camden. A furious cannonade between the two lines followed. When the two armies finally met in the field, Gates positioned the militia on his left flank and two Maryland regiments on his right. When attacked, the militia on Gates's left quickly collapsed. On his right, Tarleton charged into a gap between the First and Second Maryland, while the rest of his dragoons attacked their rear. Gates's whole army was put to flight and pursued by Tarleton for miles.

One of the Black Patriots seeing action for the first time at Camden was Andrew Ferguson, who had joined up with the Continentals earlier in the year after he and his father had been whipped by British officers in Virginia, later escaping. Dozens more served in the battle. Asher Crockett testified that he saw Baron DeKalb, a volunteer from Germany and the second in command under Gates, mortally wounded. Adam Adams faced down Tarleton's charge with the First Maryland, as did Thomas Carney of the Second Maryland. James Carter and Lucas Valentine served with the Second Virginia artillery, with Carter wounded in action. Solomon Bibbie, James Harris, Thomas Mason, and Israel Pearce all served with North Carolina units. Francis Freeman and Edward Harman were with the Delaware Regiment. The Second Virginia was in the thick of the battle with Ambrose Lewis (who had already served a three-year term in the Virginia state navy), who survived five bayonet wounds and was taken prisoner, and Ed Sorrell, who took a musket ball to the shoulder. Sorrell recounted that he had tried to take the wounded Colonel Charles Porterfield from the field of fire, but had to leave him to be taken prisoner as the British pursued. Tim Jones of the Third Virginia found himself serving under unique circumstances; he was a slave enlisted as a substitute for his owner, Rolling Jones, who had signed up as a recruit while he was drunk and later regretted his decision when he sobered up, sending his slave to serve as his substitute.

Gates's defeat at Camden is highlighted in the pension narratives of a number of Black Patriots. It was a defining moment in the southern campaign. Gates was replaced by Washington confidante Nathanael Greene, the Quaker general from Rhode Island. Greene had seen his predecessors move from disaster (Savannah) to catastrophe (Charleston) to rout and defeat (Camden). The Continental army operating in the South had to take a lesson from the Patriot militias, who were continuing to rack up small victories in the backcountry. Three days after the defeat at Camden, two hundred Patriot militiamen set a successful ambush for a Loyalist column camped at Musgrove Mill, a fight where Black Patriot Lemerick Farr of the Second South Carolina Spartan Regiment served. Greene understood that the army he now commanded had to alter how his troops maneuvered in the field and when and how the enemy were to be engaged. This was the beginning of a uniquely American way of war.

BATTLE OF KINGS MOUNTAIN (OCTOBER 7, 1780)

It was the Patriot militias who were responsible for the first major victory after the fall of Charleston. It came in response to threats by Patrick Ferguson directed at the overmountain communities who supported the Patriot cause. He warned, "If you persist in your opposition to the British

I will march this army over the mountains, hang your leaders, and lay waste to their country with fire and sword." This had the opposite effect than he had intended. General Cornwallis had divided his force, with Ferguson and Tarleton operating their own columns on the west and east wings respectively, raiding and gathering intelligence, which was sent back to Cornwallis with the main southern army in Charlotte. With the British force divided, Ferguson was vulnerable. Taking his threats seriously, overmountain militias gathered at Fort Watauga at Sycamore Shoals (near present day Elizabethton, Tennessee), determined to hunt down Ferguson and his column. They elected Colonel William Campbell from Virginia as their leader.

Joining together Patriot militias from Georgia, South Carolina, North Carolina, Virginia, and the overmountain settlements, they pursued Ferguson's column, which eventually camped on top of Kings Mountain on the border of North and South Carolina. With his column isolated so close to joining up with Cornwallis in Charlotte, time was of the essence. Leaving any militiamen behind who did not have horses, the Patriots rode overnight in the rain to Kings Mountain.

On the morning of October 7, 1780, the Patriots surrounded Ferguson's camp at the bottom of the mountain. Attacking uphill from all sides, the Patriots fired their rifles behind trees as Ferguson's men responded with muskets standing in the open. Twice the Patriots were driven back, but on the third charge they reached the top and the battle became a rout. Patrick Ferguson was shot by a hail of bullets and was killed. Virtually the entire force was killed or taken prisoner. Ferguson was buried on top of Kings Mountain, where he still rests today, never having reached the overmountain lands or fulfilling his threats. The west wing of Cornwallis's army was destroyed.

Several Black Patriots shared the victor's honors at Kings Mountain. This included Benjamin Scott, who had been thrice hung by the British in the failed attempt to elicit the Patriot militia's location. Ishmael Titus of

Virginia, who had served under General Washington at Braddock's defeat in the French and Indian War, fought as a substitute for his owner in exchange for his freedom. Esaias Bowman, a free man from North Carolina, was directly beneath Ferguson's camp fighting uphill under the command of Colonel Benjamin Cleveland. Andrew Ferguson, having escaped the aftermath of Gates's defeat at Camden, arrived at Kings Mountain toward the end of the battle. John Broddy was the slave of Colonel William Campbell, the overall commander of the Patriot militia. While protecting the horses during the battle, he was shot at and was able to see much of the action. Joseph Sidebottom had been fighting since 1775 when he served as a minuteman, and his brother John had saved future President James Monroe at the Battle of Trenton. He had previously served two years with the Third Virginia, fighting at Brandywine and Germantown, and was at Kings Mountain with the Virginia militia. Primes, erroneously identified in subsequent federal documents as "Record Primes," had been a prisoner of war at Charleston but violated his parole by rejoining the army. He was wounded in the head at Camden and continued to fight in all of the major battles in the South until Yorktown. There is a monument to the Black Patriots who fought at Kings Mountain, erected on the battlefield by the Daughters of the American Revolution.

RIDING WITH THE SWAMP FOX

The destruction of the western wing of Cornwallis's army left him vulnerable, forcing him to return to South Carolina. Ferguson's loss deprived him of valuable intelligence about Patriot movements. And in addition to the victorious militias who fought at Kings Mountain, Cornwallis also had to deal with Francis Marion, who was now causing havoc in the South Carolina low country. Fighting with the "Swamp Fox" was his slave, Oscar Marion. Researcher Tina Jones discovered that both men had grown up together, and due to her research Oscar was honored in a ceremony held December 2006 at the US Capitol, with a proclamation signed by President George W. Bush. In 2009, he was remembered at a ceremony at Arlington National Cemetery, where military honors were rendered in commemoration of his service.

Other Black Patriots rode with the Swamp Fox, including George and James Kersey of North Carolina. George had been at the Patriot defeat at Brier Creek in March 1779, then marched to Charleston, where he remained until the fall of the city. He remained a prisoner of war on a British prison ship until a smallpox outbreak, when he and several others were taken ashore and were able to make an escape. He fell in with troops that later came under command of General Marion, conducting raids targeting British shipping in the South Carolina low country. He later fought at Eutaw Springs, the battle that forced Cornwallis to retreat to Yorktown. Spencer Bolton was at the fall of Charleston; his company was able to evade capture but abandoned their baggage and belongings in the city, eventually joining up with Marion at Bowling Green. Jasper Browngaurd of the First South Carolina was also a prisoner of war after Charleston, but he and his captain were exchanged in January 1781, at which time he joined the cavalry under Colonel Peter Horry and General Marion. John Rawls served in the Fourth Virginia, which became attached to Marion's Brigade when it came to South Carolina. Adam Ivey volunteered at the age of fifteen in North Carolina and became a prisoner of war at Charleston. Paroled and exchanged in August 1781, he joined with Marion at Parker's Ferry on the Edisto River in South Carolina. Ivey likely arrived in time for an ambush planned by Marion for notorious Loyalist commander William "Bloody Bill" Cunningham, who was traveling to join a larger column of British, Hessian, and Loyalist troops. Springing the trap, Marion's men inflicted heavy casualties, forcing the British cavalry to retreat to Charleston. Ivey continued to serve with Marion's forces until the end of the war.

Jim Capers was also with Francis Marion in the raids and skirmishes of 1780 and 1781, but he was already a seasoned veteran by that time. Born enslaved on a South Carolina plantation, he enlisted as a drum major in June 1775 in the Fourth South Carolina with his owner and fought through the end of the war. He participated in the battles at Beaufort, the siege of Savannah, Camden, Biggin Church, and Eutaw Springs, as well as the action with General Marion. At Eutaw Springs he was wounded by two saber cuts to his head and one to his face, and was shot through his side. One soldier's pension application years later noted his fame and reputation, testifying that he had heard that "the famous drummer Jim Capers" had been wounded in the battle. Despite his injuries he was able to march north in pursuit of Cornwallis and serve during the siege of Yorktown. When he was discharged in 1782, he was among the longest-serving Black Patriots of the entire war. Having finally obtained his freedom, after the war he married his wife, Milley (a slave), and moved to Alabama. Over one hundred years old, he applied for a pension in 1849 and died in 1853. The Sons of the American Revolution erected a monument in his honor in 2015 in Orion, Alabama.

Marion's raids after the Battle of Kings Mountain concerned Cornwallis enough that he sent Tarleton south to deal with him. But this now left him alone camped at Winnsboro. It was at this point that General Thomas Sumter reappeared in the area, having reformed his militia after being defeated by Tarleton at Fishing Creek shortly after the Camden disaster. Cornwallis dispatched Major James Wemyss to deal with Sumter with part of the British Legion of Loyalists and a detachment of mounted infantry. Sumter had ordered his men to sleep prepared to fight at a moment's notice, so when the British attacked their camp at Fishdam Ford on November 10, the Patriots were able to surprise their attackers. Wemyss was wounded early in the engagement, and the British retreated after twenty minutes. Among the few American wounded at

Fishdam Ford was Moses, the slave of Colonel David Hopkins, who was shot and received three bayonet wounds.

Sumter's victory, following up on the victory at Kings Mountain, electrified the Patriots in the region. Within days he had gathered as many as a thousand militia troops from South and North Carolina and Georgia. Cornwallis sent a messenger to Tarleton, recalling him from his pursuit of Francis Marion to deal with the growing threat to British control in South Carolina now posed by Thomas Sumter. The two forces met at Blackstock's Farm on November 20, ten days after Sumter's victory at Fishdam Ford. Fighting in the battle were Black Patriots Edward Coleman of the Third South Carolina and Lemerick Farr of the Second Spartan Regiment. William Blackstock's plantation was chosen by Sumter for the strong defensive position it provided. Even without all of his infantry and artillery brought up, Tarleton pressed ahead with his attack on the Patriot's position. Tarleton's officers were targeted by Sumter's sharpshooters, their loss creating confusion in the British ranks. Tarleton in desperation tried a cavalry charge as one of his flanks came under attack but was repulsed. Tarleton's men began a disorderly retreat. Sumter, the victor, was seriously wounded in the attack and had to hand over command. In the months ahead the general was cared for and nursed by his faithful slave, Soldier Tom.

At Blackstock's Farm, "Bloody Ban" Tarleton had suffered his first loss of the British southern campaign. Many of the Patriot militia units who fought at Blackstock's Farm would face Tarleton again two months later at the Battle of Cowpens in January 1781. The dramatic reversal of momentum away from the British following their seemingly decisive victories at Savannah, Charleston, and Camden was accomplished by the Patriot victories at Williamson's Plantation, Musgrove Mill, Fishdam Ford, Blackstock's Farm, and of course, Kings Mountain, where Major Patrick Ferguson's column was completely destroyed. British brutality at Waxhaws had built resentment in the backcountry, and Ferguson's threats against the overmountain communities directly led to his demise at Kings Mountain. General Nathanael Greene and Colonel Daniel Morgan would soon take charge of the Continental army operations in the South, working closely with the militia commanders who had already found success against the British with guerilla warfare tactics they had employed throughout 1780.

While the fortunes of war weighed heavily throughout the year in favor of the British with their victories, entering 1781 the momentum had clearly shifted, and the Black Patriots of the South had done their part to restore the prospect of American independence. Personal acts of heroism by Benjamin Scott and William Bratton's slave, Watt, averted potential disasters for the Patriot cause; Andrew Ferguson and Benjamin Scott had suffered torture at the hands of the British; Elisha Hunt, Thomas Lively, Ambrose Lewis, George McCoy, and Robert Owls all suffered serious battle wounds; dozens became prisoners of war after the fall of Charleston, including Ephraim Hearn, taken to New York and imprisoned on a British prison hulk; John Edward Carter was missing in action after becoming a British captive, never to be heard from again; and Osbourne Jeffers sacrificed his life for his country, killed in action at Charleston. In maintaining the military stalemate in the northern theater and persevering through the cycles of defeat and victory in the southern theater, the contributions of Black Patriots in keeping America's hopes alive going into the seventh year of war helped to tip the balance in the Patriots' favor.

THE
NEW-HAMPSHIRE GAZETTE;
OR,
STATE JOURNAL, and GENERAL ADVERTISER.

A petition sent to the New Hampshire legislature by twenty members of the Portsmouth slave community, identifying themselves as "Natives of Africa, now forcibly detained," was published in the July 15, 1780, edition of the *New Hampshire Gazette*. The petitioners asserted their equality and denounced slavery as contrary to the laws of nature and religion that formed the basis of the state's new government. A bill was passed in 2013 and signed into law retroactively granting them their freedom. (Image: Library of Congress)

Monument on the battlefield of Kings Mountain, South Carolina, honoring three Black Patriots who participated in the decisive victory on October 7, 1780. Several other Black Patriots are known to also have served in the battle, which destroyed one whole wing of the army under Lord Cornwallis and marked the beginning of the end of British control of the Carolina backcountry. (Image: Patrick S. Poole)

Cannon from Fort Lafayette, New York, mounted on a monument dedicated to the military service of John Peterson, a Black Patriot who with comrade Moses Sherwood discovered the HMS *Vulture*, which had carried Major John Andre up the Hudson River to meet with traitor Benedict Arnold. The cannon may be one of those from the fort used to bombard the *Vulture*, forcing it to depart and stranding Andre in Patriot territory. Andre's subsequent capture revealed Arnold's treason, and many Black Patriot pension affidavits mention being witness to Andre's execution. The Peterson monument stands in front of the Peekskill Museum in Peekskill, New York. Peterson is buried nearby at Bethel Cemetery in Croton-on-Hudson. (Images: Patrick S. Poole)

CHAPTER 9
1781: THE TIDE TURNS

AS THE WAR ENTERED 1781, the area between Sir Henry Clinton's army in New York City and George Washington's army at West Point had become a violent no-man's-land where skirmishes between Loyalist "Cowboys" and Patriot "Skinners" and attacks on the respective enemy's supporters were now a regular feature. Small unit raids by the British and the Americans, and the arrival of the French force of 450 officers and 5,300 men under the Comte de Rochambeau the previous July, heightened the tension even further. After the British had evacuated Newport in October 1779, New York City and the immediate surrounding area was King George's last remaining stronghold in the North.

PATRIOT RAID ON MORRISANIA (JANUARY 22, 1781)

One particular hotspot was Morrisania, now a neighborhood in the Bronx, which at that time served as the headquarters of Colonel James DeLancey, a Loyalist commander responsible for a number of violent raids in the area. On January 22, 1781, men from several units attacked DeLancey's camp at Morrisania, taking prisoners and burning down the Loyalist barracks. Primus Coburn of the First Massachusetts participated in the assault and was wounded in the leg. He was one of several dozen Black Patriots from Plymouth County who had joined the Continental army during the war, with Coburn enlisting during the summer of 1780.

Also present at the Battle of Morrisania was Anthony Gilman of the famed First New Hampshire. A freeman, he first enlisted for one year in the Sixth Massachusetts in December 1775, serving during the siege of Boston. After the British evacuation of the city, the regiment was sent in May 1776 to New York in anticipation of the British return. He fought in the battles of Long Island, Harlem Heights, and White Plains later that year, reenlisting at the end of his term in the First New Hampshire, which was in the heat of the battles of Freeman's Farm and Bemis Heights in the Patriot victory at Saratoga in September and October 1777, and then at Monmouth in June 1778. Gilman was unfortunately taken prisoner at Morrisania. In his pension application he relates how, as a prisoner of war, he was sold as a slave by the British and later taken by his new master to Canada:

> I was one of the men and was with about 40 more taken by the British and carried into New York, and then kept a few weeks prisoner. Being a man of color I was sold for a slave to John Falkingham and left as a slave for more than a year there, then sent to St. John's and to Annapolis-Royal [in Nova Scotia], from when after about 6 or 7 month I made my escape and came away. The war was over.[1]

Enslaving captured Black Patriots regardless of their previous status as freemen was the official policy of the British Empire explicitly stated in Henry Clinton's Philipsburg Proclamation two years prior to Gilman's capture. Anthony Gilman became a victim of that policy but was fortunate to escape back to America after the war had concluded. How many other Black Patriot prisoners of war were enslaved under Clinton's policy but unable to escape their captivity is unknown.

LOYALIST RAID ON PINES BRIDGE (MAY 14, 1781)

DeLancey and his Loyalist marauders would have their revenge for the attack on their Morrisania headquarters. Their rage was directed at the First Rhode Island Black Regiment, which by that time had merged with the Second Rhode Island to form one entirely integrated Rhode Island Regiment, still under the command of the hero of Fort Mercer, Colonel Christopher Greene. General William Heath had ordered the unit to guard the Pines Bridge over the Croton River (near modern-day Yorktown Heights, New York). The Pines Bridge was a strategic asset for both sides. It was needed for any British or Loyalist attempt to cross the Croton River from Morrisania to attack the American camps at West Point and Fishkill, as well as to raid any of the American-held areas nearby. While other units were stationed at other bridges and fords in the area, the Pines Bridge outpost was isolated and vulnerable. The Rhode Island Regiment camp, known as "Rhode Island Village," was fourteen miles away.

DeLancey struck the outpost in the early morning of May 14, 1781, with one hundred cavalry and nearly two hundred infantry. One of the main points of attack was two miles from Pines Bridge at the Davenport House, where the regiment's officers were quartered. DeLancey's men approached unseen and surprised the sentries. Colonel Greene and Major Ebenezer Flagg, who had recruited, trained, and led the Black Regiment, attempted to defend themselves with pistols and swords, but Flagg was killed inside the house and Greene was mortally wounded. A dragoon took the wounded Greene away, and his body was later found more than a mile away, stripped and having bled to death. While the officers were well cared for by their captors, the privates were housed in the infamous British Sugarhouse prison. The Rhode Island prisoners were exchanged in September 1781.

As with other previous actions related to the Black Regiment, considerable embellishments have attached themselves to the attack, but the casualties at Pines Bridge were very real. In addition to Greene and Flagg, six Rhode Island privates were killed in the attack, including four Black Patriots: Cato Bannister, Africa Burke, Jack Minthorn, and Jeremiah Greene. Two others were mortally wounded: Nathaniel Weeks and Prince Childs. Bristol Arnold was wounded but survived. Among the twenty-four prisoners taken by DeLancey's marauders were Peter Daley, John George, Ichabod Northup, Primus Watson, and Prince Jencks. It is important to note that the casualties included both White and Black privates, following the integrated nature of the Rhode Island Regiment after the consolidation earlier in the year. Command of the regiment fell to Captain Stephen Olney after Pines Bridge, and he continued his command until the regiment was disbanded at the end of the war. A monument was erected over the graves of Colonel Greene and Major Flagg in the churchyard of the Presbyterian Church in Yorktown Heights, New York, and a separate monument to the Black Patriots who fell at Pines Bridge now stands beside it. A Pines Bridge battle monument was erected in 2018 in the town's Railroad Park, depicting three figures: Colonel Greene, a Black soldier, and a Wampanoag soldier of the regiment fighting in defense of their position.

The DeLancey raid was a major blow to the Black Patriots of the regiment, which had already been wracked with sickness, deaths, and desertions since the Battle of Rhode Island nearly two years prior. One of the most prominent desertions was by Ben Franck, a freeman veteran who had enlisted along with his brother William in the spring of 1777 before the passage of the Slave Enlistment Act and the formation of the Black Regiment. A living descendent of Ben Franck, Shirley Green, conducted extensive research on her ancestors for her PhD thesis on the brothers' service and life history. She documents that their father, Rufus Franck, served honorably in the French and Indian War. They both fought in the heroic defense of Fort Mercer and wintered at Valley Forge, and were in the brutal fight at the hedgerow at Monmouth. But Ben Franck's departure was not just a desertion but a defection to the British side; he also abandoned his wife and child back home in Rhode Island. His movements immediately after his desertion are unknown, but he reappears in Long Island in 1782 under the assumed name Ben Frankham. He joined the British forces and left the country in October 1783 as part of the British evacuation at the end of the war. He was awarded fifty acres of land and remained in Canada until his death. His brother William Franck fought at Yorktown and remained with the Rhode Island Regiment until their discharge in June 1783, one of only sixteen Black Patriot veterans from Rhode Island prior to the formation of the Black Regiment that continued their service until the end of the war. William also received a land warrant for his service following the war.

The desperation by some in the Black Patriot ranks of the Rhode Island Regiment is seen in a rare artifact recently discovered, specifically a letter from Thomas Nichols dated January 18, 1781, to his former owner. He had enlisted for the war in March 1777, before the formation of the Black Regiment. The letter, now in the archives of the Varnum Armory Museum, pleads for his discharge, as he finds the war "very disagreeable to my mind as well as destructive to my health" and he "not having any money or clothes fit to wear." A postscript to the letter by a surgeon's mate (likely written by Nichols) notes that he "has been for some time attended with fits," and regimental records show he had several previous turns in the hospital in 1778 and 1779. He agrees to return to serve his owners if they can obtain his release from the regiment. On February 1, Nichols was transferred to the Corps of Invalids.

BENEDICT ARNOLD SACKS RICHMOND (JANUARY 1–19, 1781) AND NEW LONDON (SEPTEMBER 6, 1781)

One of the most notorious raids of the year wasn't conducted by DeLancey's marauders but by the traitor Benedict Arnold, now a British brigadier general, who launched an attack in September 1781 on his home state of Connecticut. At the beginning of 1781, just months after his defection to the enemy, he had sailed up the James River in Virginia with 1,200 troops, sacking and setting fire to Richmond. With most of the Continental troops and militias in the southern theater tied up in South Carolina, there were few men available to respond to Arnold's sacking of Richmond. In his pension application, Kenaz Ralls recounts how he was part of two militia companies from Prince William County called up to respond to the threat. Tracking the traitor's movements for two weeks, he helped remove baggage wagons from Richmond and watched as Arnold's troops set fire to warehouses in nearby Manchester. William Barber of Dinwiddie County was also called up and spent several weeks in the Great Dismal Swamp near Norfolk watching for the enemy column. A notice sent from Colonel George Muter, Virginia's Commissioner of the War Office, to Governor Thomas Jefferson testified that during the sack of Richmond one "Jupiter" was able to save four cannons from the British, which he delivered to Muter, noting no reward had yet been approved for the man's heroic service.

But Arnold's attack on Connecticut nine months later was a more deliberate action. Henry Clinton hoped that unleashing Washington's former friend on New England would prevent the commander in chief from moving his forces in the North to assist in the southern campaign. But by the time Arnold attacked New London on September 6, 1781, Washington had already begun to direct American and French troops south toward Yorktown weeks before. During most of the war, Connecticut had been known as the "storehouse of the Revolution," which had prompted the British attack on Danbury in April 1777, an attack which Arnold himself had led his troops to help repel when he was still committed to the Patriot cause. New London was also a valuable port and a station for American privateers attacking British shipping. In 1781, two positions on either side of the Thames River, Fort Griswold and Fort Trumbull, protected the harbor that is today the home of a US Navy submarine base and the US Coast Guard Academy. Most American efforts to confront the assault were directed at Fort Griswold on the east riverbank at Groton across from New London. Colonel William Ledyard defended the fort with less than two hundred militiamen and civilians, while Arnold landed with 1,700 British, Hessian, and Loyalist troops.

At Fort Griswold, two Black Patriots distinguished themselves in action against the overwhelming foe. Eight hundred of Arnold's troops assaulted Fort Griswold, with the defenders making a determined but brief stand. Leading one of the British columns was Major William Montgomery, who attacked the ramparts but was killed by Jordan Freeman, who thrust a ten-foot pike into the invader. Freeman had previously been a slave of Colonel Ledyard but had been manumitted before the war and was fighting that day as a free man. Despite the loss of their commander, Montgomery's men breached the fort. Overrun and quickly running out of ammunition, Colonel Ledyard ordered his men to ground their arms. According to some accounts, when Ledyard offered his sword in surrender, the British officer who received it ran Ledyard through with his own sword. It was at this point that one of the fort's defenders, Lambo Latham, ran the British officer through with a bayonet, and was instantly set upon and killed by watching British soldiers. Latham's body bore thirty-three separate wounds. The clothes that Colonel Ledyard wore that day—complete with a sword cut on the left side—are in possession of the Connecticut Historical Society, a gift from his family. Most of the fort's defenders were killed, including Jordan Freeman. A monument to his killing of Major Montgomery is placed on a parapet of Fort Griswold and was unveiled on September 4, 2022, during the 241-year commemoration of the battle. Both Lambo Latham and Jordan Freeman are listed on a bronze plaque noting their place among the eighty-eight men killed at Fort Griswold, which is a state park today.

Benedict Arnold's attack on New London and Groton left both towns desolated and was the largest military action in Connecticut during the entire war. But both slaves and freemen alike responded to the series of coastal attacks throughout the conflict, some—such as Lambo Latham and Jordan Freeman—paying with their lives. Ned was a slave killed and beheaded while defending civilians during the burning of Danbury in 1777. Pomp was killed in July 1779 in a raid on New Haven; his small headstone stood in the West Haven Green Cemetery for decades until it eventually disappeared. His grave remains unmarked. Sharper Michael was born into slavery in Massachusetts at the estate of Zacheus Mayhew in 1742 and removed from Chilmark to Gay Head on Martha's Vineyard around 1775. His father, Caesar, who had been abducted from Africa, served in the militia prior to the Revolution. According to the facts uncovered by local historian Andrew Pierce, Michael was killed on September 1777 when the British privateer *Cerberus* sailed close to the coast of Martha's Vineyard as it pursued an American ship. He had procured a cannon and commenced firing at the ship, during which he was killed by a musket ball to the head. Sharper Michael was married in 1775, but it is unclear whether the freedom promised him by Mayhew was in effect when he died on the cliffs of Squibnocket two years later.

As with Massachusetts, New Hampshire, and Rhode Island, Black Patriots were found throughout Connecticut's Continental regiments. A consolidation of Connecticut regiments at the beginning of 1781 saw the creation of a company of the Fourth Connecticut comprised of all Black Patriot privates under Captain David Humphrey. The day-to-day command of the Second Company of the regiment fell to other officers, as

Humphrey had also been assigned as aide-de-camp to General Washington and was regularly away. Almost all had enlisted for the duration of the war. More than a dozen of these men had participated in a highly successful raid of a British garrison at Sag Harbor, Long Island, in May 1777. They helped construct defenses at West Point while there during the winter of 1777–1778. Many of them had been attached to General Anthony Wayne as part of the light infantry regiment that stormed the heights at Stony Point in July 1779, and they all endured the harsh winter of 1779–1780 at Morristown.

During their years of service from 1777–1780, the men of Captain Humphrey's company had fought and served beside regiments from Virginia, Maryland, Delaware, and North Carolina, who also had Black Patriots among their ranks. In 1781 many of those other regiments were now fighting in the southern theater to maintain the independence of those states in the face of the ongoing British campaign that had wrought catastrophic losses on the Americans at Savannah, Charleston, Waxhaws, and Camden, only to see Patriots rally after critical victories at Musgrove Mill, Kings Mountain, and Blackstock's Plantation.

BATTLE OF COWPENS (JANUARY 17, 1781)

The death of British Major Patrick Ferguson and the destruction of his entire command at Kings Mountain in October 1780 left Cornwallis without one of his crucial wings to conduct reconnaissance and protect his army as he tried to operate in the South Carolina backcountry. Having learned the lessons from the failures of his predecessors Benjamin Lincoln and Horatio Gates, the new commander of the Continental southern army, General Nathanael Greene, knew that a direct confrontation with his army against Cornwallis at this time would be yet another disaster. Departing from conventional military doctrine, Greene divided his army to be more mobile so that he could counter any movements against his position by Cornwallis or the remaining British wing under Banastre Tarleton. The other part of Greene's army was led by Colonel Daniel Morgan of Virginia, who would lead his troops in one of the most decisive battles of the war.

Tarleton discovered Morgan's column in early January 1781 near the Pacolet River in western South Carolina. Morgan withdrew to nearby Cowpens. His column was composed of militiamen under Colonel Andrew Pickens and about five hundred Continentals from battle-hardened units from Maryland, Delaware, and Virginia. Three Black Patriot veterans from Maryland were waiting together at Cowpens for "Bloody Ban" Tarleton and his troops to arrive. Boston Medlar and David Wilson were drum majors for their respective companies. Medlar's first battle was at Staten Island in August 1777. Since then he had fought at Brandywine, Germantown, Monmouth, and Stony Point. Norman Bezaleel had been at Monmouth, and all three men had served at Camden. These men knew each other, as Medlar and Norman served in the same regiment and Wilson's pension petition would be supported by an affidavit from Medlar. These three men played a vital role in setting a trap for Tarleton at Cowpens that in many respects was the beginning of the end of the war.

Morgan understood that the militia was very good at fast movement and backcountry fighting but not trained or equipped to stand toe to toe with British regulars or mounted dragoons. This was proven at Camden, where retreating militiamen had collapsed Gates's left flank. Morgan's sharpshooters had been effective at the great victory at Saratoga three years before, and they were put to good use at Cowpens. The Continental troops were under the direct command of famed Maryland commander Colonel John Eager Howard.

On the crisp morning of January 17, Morgan arranged his men in three separate lines to draw in Tarleton. First were the sharpshooters, who could hit targets one hundred yards away but took longer to reload their rifles. They were the first part of the bait, and their main targets were officers, to deprive the British units of their commanders. They retreated and reformed behind the second line of militiamen, who only fired several volleys then also retreated. As Tarleton's men came over a rise in Morgan's position, they were confronted with the third line of Continental regulars. At that point, the militia came around to attack the British left flank, while cavalry under Colonel William Washington (a distant cousin of General Washington who had been wounded at Princeton) rode to flank the British on the right.

John Biddie and Lemerick Farr were at Cowpens as part of the Second South Carolina "Spartan" Regiment. Francis Freeman, who had enlisted in 1776 and been serving since, was present with the Second Maryland of the Continental line. Andrew Ferguson and his father, Andrew Peleeg, who had fallen in with Greene in Virginia the previous year, were also present. Ferguson and the soldier erroneously identified later by pension authorities as "Record" Primes, who was also at Cowpens, had served at the great Patriot victory at Kings Mountain three months before. Gideon Griffin, Morgan Griffin, and Edward Harris of the Third South Carolina had likely been exchanged as prisoners of war just before the battle, allowing for their participation. Thomas Jordan and William Taburn of North Carolina and Daniel Strother of Virginia were also part of the battle.

Dan Morgan's plan worked almost perfectly. The retreating lines of sharpshooters and militiamen may have convinced Tarleton that he had encountered the rear of the column, tempting him to press his troops forward into the trap, where they slammed into the unseen Continental regulars. One part of the regulars, misunderstanding orders, began a retreat, at which point Morgan and Howard ordered them to stop and turn around. They fired at near point-blank range into their British pursuers, staggering Tarleton's line and prompting many to surrender on the spot. The militia units that had previously retreated reappeared on Tarleton's left, as did

Washington's cavalry on his right. Morgan's trap had been sprung and captured his prey.

One of the Black Patriot heroes at Cowpens was part of one of the most dramatic moments of the battle during Colonel William Washington's cavalry charge. Virginia Continental officer and future Chief Justice of the Supreme Court John Marshall later recounted the action:

> In the eagerness of pursuit, Washington advanced near thirty yards in front of his regiment. Three British officers, observing this, wheeled about, and made a charge upon him. The officer on his right aimed a blow to cut him down as an American sergeant came up, who intercepted the blow by disabling his sword arm. The officer on his left was about to make a stroke at him the same instant, when a waiter, too small to wield a sword, saved him by wounding the officer with a ball from a pistol. At this moment, the officer in the center, who was believed to be Tarleton, made a thrust at him which he parried; upon which the officer retreated a few paces, and then discharged a pistol at him, which wounded his horse.[2]

The man who saved Colonel Washington is believed to be the fourteen-year-old bugler for the Third Continental Light Dragoons, who some later historians have identified by the name Collin. The incident was witnessed by John Eager Howard, who related the details in a letter to Marshall. The scene was recreated in an 1845 painting by William Ranney, which is now part of the collection at the National Portrait Gallery in Washington DC.

Daniel Morgan and John Eager Howard received gold medals from the Continental Congress for their victory at Cowpens. While Tarleton escaped—pursued from the battlefield by William Washington for thirteen to fifteen miles—his legion was destroyed. Andrew Ferguson later recounted, "While we were at the river Pacolet the British under Col. Tarleton came upon us and Col. Morgan marched us up toward the Cowpens but before we got there we made a stand and whipped the British completely..." Morgan's tactics are still demonstrated at West Point today. Unfortunately, Cowpens was Morgan's last battle, as sciatica caused him constant pain, forcing him to resign his commission just a few weeks later to return home to Virginia to recuperate.

THE RACE TO THE DAN (JANUARY 18–FEBRUARY 15, 1781)

Rather than see his army continue to be destroyed piecemeal, Cornwallis decided that leaving South Carolina and finding Greene's army to destroy it was his best option. Notwithstanding the Patriot victory of Cowpens, Greene understood that his undermanned and undersupplied army was still no match for Cornwallis, who had burned his wagons and ordered his men to only carry what they needed to quickly pursue the Americans. Thus began what has been termed "the Race to the Dan" toward the Dan River that ran from southern Virginia into North Carolina. On the north side of the river Greene could recruit and resupply. But he had to reach the Dan River and the protection it afforded before Cornwallis reached him.

To slow the British movements, Greene dispatched parts of his army to oppose Cornwallis as he tried to move through the North Carolina Piedmont country. One of those delaying actions was at the Catawba River at Cowan's Ford on February 1, just two weeks after Cowpens. One thousand Patriots under General William Davidson faced the entire five-thousand-man army of Cornwallis. William Taburn, a Black Patriot from North Carolina who was in the battle at Cowan's Ford, described what happened in his pension application:

> From Hillsborough we marched through Salisbury to the Catawba about Beattie's Ford and joined our army under Gen. Davidson. The enemy were on the opposite bank of the river. I was stationed at Cowan's Ford when the attempt was made to cross the river at this place as well as at Beattie's Ford three miles above. I was stationed very near General Davidson who rode upon a black horse, when he received the ball that put a period to the life of the ablest, kindest, and best officer that ever commanded an army. As soon as he was struck by the ball he called out, "Help me down, boys, I am a Dead man—give the news to the men at the Island and above" and expired. We were soon thrown into confusion by the death of our beloved General, the Enemy took advantage of it, crossed the river overpowered our men and put us to flight. We scampered for life and made our way as well as we could to the Widow Torrance's land where we were stopped and formed into order of battle by our company and field officers. It was raining like a torrent, Tarleton with his light horse pursued and here overtook and charged upon us. Our guns were so wet we could not discharge them and we were all put to flight in the utmost confusion. I ran and escaped as well as I could.[3]

The skirmish that started at Cowan's Ford became a running rout that extended toward nearby Tarrant's Tavern, where some of Davidson's men had sought shelter and were found by Tarleton. The battle was no doubt a bit of revenge for Tarleton, having narrowly escaped from his devastating loss at Cowpens. But the race to the Dan River continued, with both sides using decoys and deception to mask their movements and river crossings where they would be more vulnerable. Greene's decoys added exhaustion to the cold and wet already experienced by the lightly supplied troops of Cornwallis. As the two armies raced north, the chief engineer of the Continental army, Theodore Kosciuszko, and his trusted aide, Agrippa Hull, who had been with the Polish colonel since Saratoga, made preparations to move the army across the Dan River and erected defenses to protect their crossing. At times Greene's army moved just hours ahead of Cornwallis. The Continentals arrived at the Dan River on February 13 and had moved most of the army across by the end of the following day. By the time Cornwallis arrived, he found Greene and his army, as well as all of the boats in the area, on the other side of the river. He had failed to catch the Americans and draw them into a full-scale battle that Greene knew he could not win.

Ten days later, Greene and his resupplied Continental southern army crossed back over the Dan River to give chase to Cornwallis. Reinforced by Virginia and North Carolina militia, Greene now had the numerical advantage, while the British troops experienced difficulty recruiting and foraging during the interlude. One new recruit to the Continental army was Ned Griffin, a slave who had been purchased from his owner by William Kitchen, who had deserted the army and was faced with being forcibly returned to the ranks. He offered Griffin as his replacement. Promised freedom in return for serving out Kitchen's term of service, Griffin willingly took his place in Greene's army and shortly saw action at the Battle of Guilford Court House.

BATTLE OF GUILFORD COURT HOUSE (MARCH 15, 1781)

Greene chose his location to confront Cornwallis on March 15, 1781, because of three successive ridges at Guilford that his army could occupy. Utilizing the tactics successfully used by Daniel Morgan at Cowpens, Greene aligned his troops in three ranks along the New Market Road. The British approached the first American line comprised of North

Carolina militiamen, Virginia riflemen, and Delaware regulars arrayed behind a rail fence, who fired several devastating volleys into their ranks, killing and wounding many. Edward Going and Francis Coley of the North Carolina militia were likely among this first rank, which, having inflicted damage to Cornwallis's advancing troops, retreated back to the second American line about 350 yards back. Sylvester Beverly of the First Virginia Regiment would have been a part of the Virginia militia largely holding this position. They nearly broke the British right flank, and the American cavalry under Henry "Light-Horse Harry" Lee and William Washington directly took on the British dragoons. During this action Banastre Tarleton was shot in the hand, losing two fingers. Lazarus Harman was part of a bayonet charge of the First Maryland at this point of the battle. With his losses mounting, Cornwallis sent in his reserve toward Greene's third line, composed of Continental regulars. British cannons fired into the chaotic fight, killing and wounding both Americans and their own soldiers. Much as he had at Brandywine, Greene conducted an orderly retreat, leaving the battered British in command of the field. The tactical victory at Guilford Courthouse was of little comfort to Cornwallis. Having lost one quarter of his army at Cowpens, after finally fighting Greene he had lost another quarter. These losses meant that in just a few months he no longer had an effective fighting force that could challenge Greene's army.

Black Patriots were among the American casualties in the Battle of Guilford Court House. Zacharia Jacobs of the North Carolina militia and Ambrose Month of the Virginia militia were both wounded in action. Edward Coleman of the Third South Carolina took a musket ball to the knee and needed six months to recover. Andrew Ferguson, who was previously at Kings Mountain and Cowpens, was wounded in the head. Elisha James and Frederick James of the North Carolina militia, Negro George of the Second Maryland, and Tim Jones of the Third Virginia were taken as prisoners but exchanged shortly thereafter. Thomas Carney and Bazaleel

Norman of the Maryland line; Isaac Brown, George Kendall, John Rawls, and Henry Hill of the Virginia line; and Solomon Bibbie and William Lomarck of the North Carolina regiments were all part of the battle. Willis Boon had enlisted with the Second North Carolina in 1776, serving three and a half years, including wintering with the regiment at Valley Forge, until he later reenlisted with Colonel William Washington's Corps of Light Horse, later fighting at Guilford Court House.

Though the field had been left to the British, Cornwallis decided to retreat to the safety of the coast and the British Navy. With Greene in pursuit, he fast marched toward Wilmington two hundred miles away. As the Patriots got closer to his shattered army, the "victorious" Cornwallis abandoned his sick and wounded to speed up his pace, at which point Greene broke off the chase. The British retreat to Wilmington emboldened the Patriots in the Carolinas. Absalom Bibby, Patrick Mason, Hill Scipio, Isham Scott, and Absalom Martin were all Black Patriots who enlisted in the Third North Carolina following the Patriot "loss" at Guilford Court House. It also demoralized the Loyalists in the Carolinas, which much of the British southern campaign strategy had relied upon to supplement Cornwallis's army, effectively ending recruitment.

Seizing the momentum, Greene determined to return to South Carolina to clear out the fortified strongholds the British needed to operate away from their coastal bases at Charleston and Savannah, as well as the smaller garrisons needed to resupply and communicate. Greene's first target was Camden, the site of Gates's defeat the previous year, which was now a fortified town occupied by around one thousand British soldiers. He tasked "Light-Horse Harry" Lee and Francis "Swamp Fox" Marion to direct their attention to the forts between Camden and Charleston in the South Carolina low country.

BATTLE OF HOBKIRK'S HILL (APRIL 25, 1781)

In late April, Greene and 1,500 troops of largely Virginia and Maryland Continental regulars set up on a sandy ridge several miles north of Camden called Hobkirk's Hill, hoping to draw the British out from behind their fortifications to attack his position. Lord Rawdon, the commander at Camden, did exactly that on April 25, leading about nine hundred men south out of the fortified Old Town then heading north to Hobkirk's Hill on a concealed creek bed, coming up almost on Greene's position. Alerted by his sentinels, Greene arranged his troops with the Maryland regiments on his left and the Virginia regiments on his right, supported by William Washington's cavalry. All went according to plan, with Greene observing perilously close to the action with the Virginia regiment of Lieutenant Colonel Richard Campbell, the unit of Jesse Peters (who had already fought at Guilford Court House). John Pipsico and Henry Hill were also part of the Virginia line near the center of the battle. But the death of one of the Maryland commanders caused the Maryland line to waver, where David Wilson, Thomas Carney, Boston Medlar, and Bazaleel Norman were fighting, and Rawdon was able breach the Continental line. Unwilling to take more unnecessary casualties, Greene conducted an orderly withdraw from Hobkirk's Hill. Later in the day, William Washington set up an ambush that caught by surprise some British dragoons that were searching for abandoned American artillery pieces.

Hobkirk's Hill had been a costly affair for Lord Rawdon. He had lost one quarter of his men during this "victory," was still outnumbered, and had gained nothing but pushing Greene from the field. Following Rawdon's return to the fortifications at Camden, Greene reoccupied the area he had just been driven from. At the same time, Light-Horse Harry Lee and Francis Marion were attacking smaller garrisons down the Santee River. Andrew Pebbles was part of Lee's light infantry, and nearly a dozen other Black Patriots were riding with the Swamp Fox at the time. Just days before Hobkirk's Hill, they besieged Fort Watson and its 150 men. George Kersey placed himself with Marion's troops at the fort, identified by other soldiers as Scott's Lake or Wright's Bluff. Several days into the siege a plan was suggested to build a thirty-foot tower so that sharpshooters such as Harden Denham (a Black Patriot rifleman riding with Marion at the time) could fire down into the stockade. The tower was quickly constructed and put to effective use, and the fort surrendered on April 23, two days before the battle at Hobkirk's Hill.

Two weeks later Lee, Marion, and their men were laying siege to Fort Motte, the house of a Patriot commander that had been confiscated and turned into a British outpost. It was during this time that Lord Rawdon, still pressured by the presence of Nathanael Greene and the news of the loss of Fort Watson, decided to abandon Camden, burning the fortifications and spiking any of the cannons they could not take with them. Several of the spiked cannons abandoned by the British are still on display at Old Town Camden. The evacuation of Camden occurred on May 10. Lee and Marion were still at Fort Motte, and they set fire to the outpost before Rawdon could move to support it, forcing its surrender. Fort Granby and Orangeburg fell to the Patriots in short order, cutting the line of communications from Charleston to the interior of the Carolinas. Lord Rawdon had to retreat to Monck's Corner close to Charleston. This allowed Greene to turn his attention to the two remaining British strongholds in the backcountry: Augusta and Ninety-Six.

Elijah Clarke, Andrew Pickens, and Henry Lee were dispatched to deal with Augusta, where Fort Cornwallis was garrisoned with five hundred King's Carolina Rangers under Loyalist commander Thomas Brown. Patriot militias began to arrive in the area in mid-April, but the main force arrived on May 21 and began preparing their lines for a siege. Greene arrived at Ninety-Six with his troops the next day.

Having used a tower successfully at Fort Watson, Lee had one constructed that could fire a cannon into Fort Cornwallis. When it was operational, Brown sallied outside the fort to attack the Patriots but was pushed back. For several days, the cannon caused considerable damage inside the fortifications. Having initially refused Patriot requests for surrender, Brown capitulated on June 5. Austin Dabney was shot through the thigh, breaking his leg and requiring months of convalescence. John Busby was present with the South Carolina militia. Thomas Lively, who had survived Valley Forge and lost an eye at Monmouth, only to reenlist and later be wounded in the leg at the fall of Charleston, served during the siege of Augusta in the Continental line under Lee in the Fifth Virginia.

THE SIEGE OF NINETY-SIX (MAY 22–JUNE 19, 1781)

Sixty miles to the north, deep in the South Carolina backcountry, stood Ninety-Six, a fort crucial to the British to communicate and supply their Cherokee allies (the name itself notes how many miles it was from a main Cherokee town). Accordingly, it was heavily fortified and well garrisoned and would prove a formidable challenge for Greene despite outnumbering the British and Loyalist troops two to one. The town was fortified and additionally protected by a heavily defended star fort (remains of which are preserved as a state park today). The action at Ninety-Six was the longest field siege of the Revolutionary War.

The Continental troops assailed the fort from the air, on land, and underground. Colonel Thaddeus Kosciusko, the Continental army's chief engineer, with his orderly Agrippa Hull, directed the construction of the siege works. As a thirty-foot tower was built for riflemen to fire into the fort, parallel entrenchments were dug closer by the day to increase the effectiveness of the Patriot artillery, and a mine was excavated to go underneath the fort's defenses, where explosives would be detonated to create a breach that Greene's soldiers could pour through. But after nearly four weeks of siege at Ninety-Six, word arrived that British reinforcements under Lord Rawdon were headed to the fort from Charleston and Moncks Corner. Greene had to either take the fort before the reinforcements arrived or withdraw to prevent getting trapped between the fort and the arriving force. He decided to launch a frontal assault on the fort with a team of fifty men on June 18. They hoped this dangerous "forlorn hope" attack would make it through the defenses and enter the fort, keeping the defenders occupied while reserve troops could exploit the breach. However, this didn't happen. The attack lasted only forty-five minutes, and thirty of the fifty Patriot attackers were casualties.

Thomas Carney, a Black Patriot veteran from the Seventh Maryland, demonstrated extraordinary bravery during the siege when his company commander, Captain Perry Benson, was severely wounded. Carney, who was described as at least six feet tall with incredible strength, picked Benson up and carried him out of harm's way where his injuries could be treated. This act of heroism forged a lifelong friendship between the two men. Carney's brother-in-law, Adam Adams of the First Maryland, participated in the siege, as did Lazarus Harman, David Wilson, and Boston Medlar of the Maryland Continental line. Evans Archer, Isaac Brown, John Key, John Pipsico, and Luke Valentine were part of Virginia units at Ninety-Six, as were Malachi Nickens, Aaron Spellman, and Joel Taburn from North Carolina. Returning to action at Ninety-Six was Andrew Ferguson, who had a metal plate placed in his head as a result of his injuries at Guilford Court House.

Green ordered the siege of Ninety-Six abandoned on June 20. Yet again, however, he lost the tactical battle but won the strategic position. Under pressure everywhere from Patriot forces, the British had evacuated several garrisons and the heavily defended fortifications at Camden, Augusta, and Georgetown (abandoned on June 5 during the siege). Now so far from reinforcements and supplies, holding a fort so far into the interior was no longer feasible. Lord Rawdon burned the town and the fort at

Ninety-Six on July 8, leaving almost the entire Carolina backcountry in Patriot control.

As the summer of 1781 progressed, Francis Marion's troops continued to conduct raids and fight skirmishes on an almost daily basis, such as at Biggin Church, Wadboo Bridge, and Parker's Ferry. Riding with Marion were brothers George and James Kersey, rifleman Harden Denham, Jasper Browngaurd, John Rawls, Jacob Perkins, Jeremiah Bunch, and famed drummer Jim Capers. Two former Black Patriot POWs who were taken at Charleston but escaped captivity, Spencer Bolton and Adam Ivey, were able to join up with Marion's column and participate in these summer raids.

CORNWALLIS RETREATS TO VIRGINIA

After the Siege of Ninety-Six, Greene and his army regrouped in the High Hills of Santee, where the soldiers could escape the summer heat of South Carolina. Sitting in Wilmington, North Carolina, Cornwallis had already made the fateful decision to abandon the Carolinas for Virginia, believing that subduing the largest and richest state in the Americas would break Patriot resistance. From there, he could also receive reinforcements and supplies from New York City in a timely manner. Arriving in Virginia on May 10 (as the Patriots in South Carolina were preparing their sieges of Augusta and Ninety-Six), Cornwallis took command of all forces in the state, meeting in Petersburg with traitor Benedict Arnold, who had been conducting raids up the James River and ordered the burning of Richmond. The British campaign in Virginia during the summer of 1781 was intended to inflict as much damage as possible on the state's economy. Shadowing the British movements was an army largely composed of Virginia militiamen under the leadership of the Marquis de Lafayette and General Anthony Wayne. The two armies clashed on July 6 near Jamestown at the Battle of Green Springs, where Lafayette's army was nearly destroyed. Two Black Patriots known to have been at the battle are Jacob Gowen and James Mealey. On August 1, Cornwallis went to Yorktown, anticipating troops and supplies from New York City to continue the campaign of destruction. Lafayette relayed this news to General Washington.

In South Carolina, Greene's encampment in the High Hills of Santee was being watched by a British column under Colonel Alexander Stewart, who had taken over operations following the departure of Lord Rawdon to England due to illness. Stewart moved his column to Eutaw Springs, closer to Charleston. Greene followed a week later with his army, now composed of Continental regiments from Virginia, Maryland, Delaware, and North Carolina, as well as North and South Carolina militias. What followed was one of the bloodiest battles and fiercest fighting of the entire southern campaign.

BATTLE OF EUTAW SPRINGS (SEPTEMBER 8, 1781)

Elements of both armies ran into each other in the early morning of September 8 near Eutaw Springs. By mid-morning, both sides had lined up for battle, the British troops abandoning their breakfast to quickly form. The Americans had the upper hand, pushing back the British line composed largely of Loyalist troops until Stewart deployed his reserves, pushing the Americans back. It was at that point that Greene unleashed his Continental regulars, forcing the British line back to their main defenses. Believing victory in hand, some of Greene's troops stopped to plunder the British camp. This broke up the American momentum just as the condensed British line launched a hard counterattack, battering the looters and retaking the British camp. As casualties mounted, Greene ordered his troops back to their positions held earlier in the morning, leaving Stewart in command of the field.

The battle had lasted four hours, but the casualties on both sides were staggering. One Black Patriot, Elijah Bass of the Tenth North Carolina, was killed in action. Among the American wounded was the famous drummer Jim Capers serving with Francis Marion's troops. He later reported that he received four wounds at Eutaw Springs: one to the head, two sword wounds to the face, and a musket ball that passed through his left side and killed the drummer behind him. Isaac Hammond of the Second North Carolina had wounds to his thigh and underneath his arm. William Lomack, who had been taken prisoner at Charleston, later escaping and rejoining the army, was wounded twice. Andrew Pebbles of Henry Lee's Virginia Light Infantry was wounded three times: He lost his left thumb, received a wound to his shoulder, and took a bayonet to his belly. James Scott of the Third North Carolina was wounded in the leg. Robert Owls of the First Virginia had been wounded on the head at the Battle of Hanging Rock, and at Eutaw Springs had been shot through the leg, breaking the bone. In applying for a pension in 1818, he stated that his leg wound had never properly healed and caused great pain. John Key, in the same regiment as Owls, later reported a severe unspecified wound in the battle, as did James Scott of the Third North Carolina.

At least three dozen Black Patriots served in the battle, including James Nickens. Earlier in the war he had served three years in the sea service then enlisted in the army, serving in a regiment of artillery. Israel Pearce saw his company captain killed in the battle. Many Black Patriots who had served throughout the southern campaign—fighting at Camden, Kings Mountain, Cowpens, Guilford Court House, Hobkirk Hill, and the sieges at Augusta and Ninety-Six—were also present at Eutaw Springs, which proved to be the last major engagement of the war in the Carolinas. British casualties in the battle fell hard on the Loyalist units under Colonel Stewart. Loyalist support had been the cornerstone of Henry Clinton's southern campaign strategy, but British losses and victories had come at a considerably high cost. After Eutaw Springs, Stewart retreated to the safety of Charleston. The contributions and continued sacrifices of Patriot militias and Continental regulars during 1781 had broken the British hold in the South, which now largely consisted of only the occupied coastal cities of Savannah, Charleston, Wilmington, and…Yorktown.

Painting by William Rainey, "Battle of Cowpens," depicting a decisive moment in the battle when Col. William Washington was dueling with British Lt. Col. Banastre Tarleton, and was saved by his Black Patriot waiter, William Collin or Collins. Several Continental officers at the battle later recorded the incident. The original painting hangs in the South Carolina State House. (Image: Wikimedia Commons)

Monument at the First Presbyterian Church of Yorktown, Yorktown Heights, New York, commemorating the Black Patriots of the First Rhode Island Regiment who were killed in the Loyalist raid on their position at Pines Bridge on May 13, 1781. Four Black Patriots—Cato Bannister, Africa Burke, Jack Minthorn, and Jeremiah Greene—were killed in the fighting, and two others—Nathaniel Weeks and Prince Childs—were mortally wounded. (Image: Patrick S. Poole)

Tablet erected on the walls of Fort Griswold in Groton, Connecticut, commemorating Jordan Freeman's killing of British Major William Montgomery, who was leading an attack on the fort on September 6, 1781. Freeman and another Black Patriot, Lambo Latham, were both killed in action during the attack. (Image: Patrick S. Poole)

James Forten enlisted at age fourteen on a Patriot privateer during the Revolutionary War. The ship was captured by the British, and he survived imprisonment on the notorious HMS *Jersey* prison ship. After the war, he took up sail-making and became one of the most successful businessmen in Philadelphia. He was also one of the most prominent abolitionists of his time, funding many abolition efforts. A daguerreotype believed to be Forten was taken by Robert Cornelius circa 1840. His death was national news, and he is interred in Eden Cemetery, Collingsdale, Pennsylvania. (Images: Middlebury College Museum of Art; Patrick S. Poole)

CHAPTER 10

1781–1783: END GAME

WITH NEARLY 250 YEARS of hindsight, Washington's decision to leave New York to trap Cornwallis at Yorktown in Virginia seems obvious. At the time, however, it was anything but. Nor was it his first option. The commander in chief's primary plan was to take advantage of the presence of Rochambeau and his French troops to lay siege to New York City. The French commander counseled against such an attack. In the five years of British occupation of New York, stout defenses had been built, making the city nearly impregnable. In order to be successful in a siege, Washington would have to defeat the greatest strength of the British Empire: their navy. That would require the French Navy, which was known to be in the West Indies, but when and where they would arrive on American shores was unknown. Lafayette's message to Washington of the whereabouts of Cornwallis and his army provided a second option. When news arrived that the French fleet under Admiral de Grasse would be sailing from the West Indies to Virginia with an additional three thousand troops, the die was cast. Within five days, Washington and light infantry units from Massachusetts, Connecticut, New York, New Jersey, Pennsylvania, and the Rhode Island Regiment were on the move south.

One of Rochambeau's aides, Baron Ludwig von Closen, described Washington's army, which was camped at White Plains at the time:

> I had a chance to see the American Army, man for man. It was really painful to see these brave men, almost naked, with only some trousers and little linen jackets, most of them without

> stockings, but, would you believe it, very cheerful and healthy in appearance. A quarter of them are Negroes, merry, confident and sturdy…I admire the American troops tremendously! It is incredible that soldiers composed of men of every age, even children of fifteen, of whites and blacks, unpaid and rather poorly fed, can march so fast and withstand fire so steadfastly.[1]

In the meantime, Virginia militias were trying to hold off raids and foraging parties. James Cropper commanded a militia company from Accomack County on the opposite side of Chesapeake Bay from Yorktown. An attack on Henry's Point was met by a counterattack by Cropper's militia on barges. An account of the event published by the Virginia Historical Society more than a century later relates an act of heroism by one Black Patriot at Henry's Point who formed a lifelong friendship:

> Among the attacks of the enemy from the barges was one near Henry's Point, where they landed from their boats, and were met by the militia, under Cropper. During the fight the militia retreat, leaving Cropper and a Negro named George Latchom, who were in advance of the rest, engaged actively with the invaders. These two kept up firing, until the foe were within a few rods of them, when they were compelled to fall back. Cropper had to retreat through a sunken, boggy marsh, in which he stuck fast up to the waist in soft mud, the enemy at the time being so close as to prepare to bayonet him. At this critical juncture, the faithful colored man fired and killed the foremost man, and seized hold of Cropper and dragged him by main strength out of the mud, and taking him back carried him safely to dry land. This required great strength upon his part, Cropper weighing in the neighborhood of two hundred pounds. Latchom was at the time a slave, and was purchased and set free by Colonel

> Cropper, who befriended him in every way he could, as an evidence of his gratitude, till Latchom's death.[2]

This incident, among many others involving Black Patriots during the Revolutionary War, demonstrates how martial brotherhood could transcend the boundaries of race, class, and slavery of the times.

BLACK PATRIOTS AT SEA

One other arena of the war where the erosion of social and legal barriers can be seen is in the service of thousands of Black Patriots who took to sea on privateers and in the state and Continental navies during the war. While facing the dangers of the ocean in addition to combat, capture, disease, and death, these "Black Jacks" found some measure of equality and the opportunity for advancement. Some sources indicate that by the end of the war up to one quarter of the navy were Black Patriots.

When Captain John Paul Jones put to sea in 1777, among his crew were two of his former—now freed—slaves, Cato Calite and Scipio Africanus, as were two other Black Patriots identified only as Prince and Charles. Ten members of the Nickens family served on ships of the Virginia State Navy, with Hezekiah Nickens taken prisoner of war during his service and dying in captivity. James Forten served as a powder boy on the *Royal Lewis* commanded by Stephen Decatur Sr., who counted twenty Black Patriots on his crew and was captured by the British and held captive on the notorious prison ship *Jersey*, anchored in Wallabout Bay off New York City. According to records compiled by the Daughters of the American Revolution, more than two dozen Black Patriot prisoners of war were held on the ship during the war. Later released, Forten witnessed the Black Patriots of the Rhode Island Regiment march through Philadelphia on his fifteenth birthday as they headed toward Yorktown.

He became a wealthy Philadelphia businessman making sails after the war, and was active in the abolitionist movement. Another captive held on the *Jersey* was Black Patriot sailor Jesse Caples from Connecticut, imprisoned there April–June 1781. John de Baptist, born in St. Kitts, was one of twenty-three Black Patriots who served on the *Dragon*, which fought in at least twenty engagements. Timothy and Williams Laws were brothers who both went to sea and died in the service late in the war. Private John Martin escaped from slavery, served as a marine on the USS *Reprisal*, and perished along with all but one of its crew when it foundered in a gale in October 1777.

One of the most decisive naval engagements of the entire war took place on September 5, two weeks before the American and French troops under Washington and Rochambeau arrived near Yorktown. The "Battle of the Capes" was fought for control of the entrance to Chesapeake Bay. The British needed control to reinforce and supply Cornwallis at Yorktown; the Allied forces needed control to prevent that from happening. The naval battle was largely fought between the French and British fleets, but American ships participated. One of those was the schooner *Patriot* of the Virginia State Navy, piloted by Caesar Tarrant. It had been ordered to defend the James River and Chesapeake Bay and was engaged off the Virginia Capes. Tarrant was reported to have "behaved gallantly" during the action. After the battle, the French fleet controlled access to Chesapeake Bay. Historian Luther Porter Jackson records that the Patriot crew also included Plato, Cuffee, David Baker, Jack Knight, and "Captain" Starlins (another pilot). The whole crew was later taken prisoner by the British and paroled following the battle at Yorktown. The freedom of Caesar Tarrant was purchased by the Virginia State Legislature in 1786.

Black Patriots were engaged in skirmishes around Yorktown as both sides prepared for the siege. One of those engagements occurred on September 28, as American and British troops fought over Pidgeon Hill, the farm of Virginia Governor Thomas Nelson, overlooking Yorktown.

Black Patriot Matthew Williams, who had been wounded in the knee at Guilford Court House, was part of the force that took possession of the property from the retreating British. Colonel Alexander Scammell of New Hampshire was mortally wounded two days later. At the time of his death he commanded a light infantry regiment partly composed of Black Patriots from the Rhode Island Regiment, many of whom had traveled south with the army and served at Yorktown.

By the time the Allied troops arrived in Williamsburg, about thirteen miles north of Yorktown, General Lafayette already had two secret weapons deployed against the British. Saul Mathews was the slave of American Brigadier General Thomas Mathers and served in the militia of Colonel Josiah Parker. Parker deployed him as a spy in the British camp of Cornwallis in Portsmouth leading up to Yorktown. Pretending to avail himself of the British offers of freedom for slaves defecting to their camp, Mathews was able to convey information on the intended movements of Cornwallis and his army to Colonel Parker and ultimately to Lafayette.

BLACK PATRIOT SPIES IN THE BRITISH CAMP

James Armistead had ingratiated himself to Benedict Arnold's camp while he was still in Virginia, much like Pompey Lamb at Stony Point, by bringing produce for sale to the British camp. James's owner was William Armistead, who served as commissary of military supplies under Lafayette. Later brought into Cornwallis's headquarters after Arnold's recall back north, he not only gathered intelligence but passed messages from other Patriot spies in the British camp back to Lafayette. Some of this information was sent directly to the commander in chief, including the news of Cornwallis establishing a base in Yorktown. Remarkably, Armistead convinced the British that he could spy on the American camp. As a double agent, he provided the British with useless or misleading information, while providing vital intelligence on British plans to Lafayette and Washington. The spying conducted by both Saul Mathews and James Armistead proved to be critical components of the Allied campaign at Yorktown.

Washington arrived in Williamsburg on September 14, and twelve days later most of the Allied forces coming from the North had congregated there. Many soldiers from the northern army had been drawn from their existing units to form light infantry regiments comprised of battle-hardened veterans. Some even served with French units, including some Black Patriots. Men from the Rhode Island Regiment—now under the command of Colonel Jeremiah Olney, who replaced their previous commander, Colonel Christopher Greene, killed earlier that year at Pines Bridge—were also present and participated in the siege. Black Patriots from New Hampshire, Massachusetts, and Connecticut were present as well. Jethro Freeman of the Second Connecticut had fought at White Plains during the New York campaign in 1776, serving until the end of the war. His discharge was signed by General Henry Knox. John Cook had fought with the Second New Hampshire at Fort Ticonderoga and Saratoga, then tended to his sick comrades at Valley Forge. Pomp Peters was with his Massachusetts regiment at the Battle of Monmouth and served at Yorktown in a light infantry unit under General Benjamin Lincoln, who had surrendered Charleston the year before and was later exchanged by the British. Fortune Freeman had been a slave when he enlisted in 1776 and had been selected from the Fourth Massachusetts to serve in Colonel Scammell's light infantry, which had marched with Washington to Yorktown. Hamet Achmet had served as a drummer at Germantown and Monmouth, wintered at Valley Forge, assaulted Stony Point with "Mad" Anthony Wayne, and continued his service at Yorktown. Obed Coffin of the First Massachusetts had served at Saratoga and Fort Montgomery and was in the American siege lines facing a trapped Cornwallis.

Black Patriots who had served in Maryland, Virginia, and North Carolina regiments during the Philadelphia campaign in 1777, wintered at Valley Forge, and fought in the sweltering heat at Monmouth had marched south to attempt to turn back the British army's southern campaign. Adam Adams of the First Maryland had fought in his regiment's battles at Brandywine, Germantown, and Monmouth, then in the South at Camden, Guilford Court House, and Yorktown. George Buley had enlisted with the Fourth Maryland in March 1781 and was now at Yorktown. After the battle, he would guard Cornwallis and his army as prisoners at Fredericksburg. Samuel Stewart had enlisted in 1778 for two years in the Fourth Virginia and been marched to Valley Forge, fought at Monmouth, and was discharged at the end of his term of service. But he was called up to serve in the Virginia militia for the siege of Yorktown. Samuel Overton of the Tenth North Carolina received two wounds at Germantown and was taken prisoner at Charleston. Released before the siege, he would return to his regiment to see some of the same British soldiers that had taken him captive, now themselves made prisoners of war.

SIEGE OF YORKTOWN (SEPTEMBER 28–OCTOBER 19, 1781)

On September 28, Washington and Rochambeau moved out of Williamsburg with their joint army to begin the siege at Yorktown. Absalom Ailstock of the Virginia militia later recounted his arrival:

> [M]arched below Williamsburg...where the Brigade camped until Washington's troops came on from the north, in the rear of which, this brigade fell and marched on to York... The battle was commenced on Sunday morning, by the French at the Poplar Redoubt, and the next day, the regiment to which this applicant belonged, was transferred to this redoubt, for the purpose of changing it into a gun battery. This applicant states that

> he was occupied during the siege in digging entrenchments, and making sand baskets and fascines for the entrenchments and batteries.[3]

Most of the American soldiers were involved in building the entrenchments to move their artillery closer to the British lines and Yorktown.

Some Black Patriots were engaged across the York River from Yorktown where they had surrounded a British detachment at Gloucester. One of the primary reasons that Cornwallis had chosen to make his base at Yorktown was that the heights of Gloucester commanded the river at one of its narrowest points. Banastre Tarleton had attempted to break through the American lines on October 3, but was driven back to his defenses. With the French and American fleet in control of Chesapeake Bay following the Battle of the Capes, the surrounded detachment at Gloucester was now as vulnerable as the rest of Cornwallis's army half a mile across the river in Yorktown. Among the Black Patriots laying siege to the Gloucester detachment were William Guy, Charles Riley, James McCoy, and Thomas Brandom—all from the Virginia state militia.

The siege progressed rapidly. By October 6, the allies had begun digging the first parallel toward the British lines. Three days later it was complete, with artillery batteries in place. General Washington fired the first gun that morning. Allied guns were able to fire 1,700 rounds into Yorktown each day. On October 11, a second parallel closer to the British lines was begun. Two redoubts manned by some of Cornwallis's best troops were in position to fire into the new parallel and had to be subdued to get closer to Yorktown for the siege artillery to have its full effect.

The attack on British Redoubts 9 and 10 occurred on the night of October 14. In an operation under the command of Lafayette, the French attacked the larger Redoubt 9, while Alexander Hamilton led the assault on Redoubt 10. All of the troops charged across the three-hundred-yard expanse with their bayonets fixed but muskets unloaded to prevent an accidental discharge that might prematurely warn the British of their attack. Hamilton's force made quick work of Redoubt 10 as John Laurens, the outspoken advocate of Black Patriot recruiting, led a force to attack the redoubt from behind. The French faced stiffer resistance at Redoubt 9, but had it in control within thirty minutes.

Black Patriots took part in this action that accelerated the allied victory. Tim Jones of the Third Virginia was wounded in the attack with a musket ball to his leg, which required amputation. He was serving as a replacement for his owner who had enlisted while drunk and promptly sent his slave in his place. Comfort Eddy of the Rhode Island Regiment was also wounded in action. James Robinson later recounted how he had to fight three enemy soldiers at once in the attack on the redoubt, killing them all and reportedly receiving a French military medal from Lafayette for his heroism. Cash Africa of Litchfield, Connecticut, had enlisted with several other Black Patriots early in the war, reenlisted in 1777, and survived the winter at Valley Forge. Nearly four years later, he was part of the taking of Redoubt 10.

The attack and seizure of Redoubts 9 and 10 now allowed artillery to be fired directly into Yorktown. This forced Cornwallis to attempt to evacuate the remains of his army to Gloucester on the evening of October 16, but the mission had to be abandoned when a storm blew many of their boats out of control, necessitating their return to Yorktown.

The next day, October 17, Cornwallis sent a messenger with a flag of truce to request a parlay to negotiate a ceasefire. Washington ordered the cannons to continue firing until Cornwallis had submitted to the terms he requested. Unfortunately, London Slocum of the Rhode Island Regiment was killed by British fire that same day before the ceasefire went into effect. Bristol Rhodes, another Black Patriot of the Rhode Island Regiment, lost two limbs to artillery fire during the siege. Captain Jeremiah Collins later testified that he found William Anderson of the Sixth Maryland near death with a severe thigh wound but was able to get him to a surgeon to save his life. While two-thirds of the allied casualties at Yorktown were French troops, Americans incurred casualties too. After the conclusion of the siege, Baron von Closen described the scene around Yorktown, writing of the allied dead, "There were graves badly covered, with the limbs of white men and negroes sticking out of them."

The surrender of Cornwallis and his army finally came on October 19, 1781. British requests to surrender under honors and for their troops to be paroled and allowed to go back to England were rejected. The Continentals who surrendered at Charleston the year before were denied the same terms, and a number of Patriots who were taken as prisoners of war at that time died in captivity; most had been held in deplorable conditions. The British emerged from Yorktown marching double file in a line that stretched longer than a mile. Cornwallis refused to surrender in person, feigning illness and sending a subordinate, General Charles O'Hara, in his place. The British troops marched to the surrender field and stacked their weapons, and their forces across the York River at Gloucester surrendered the same day. In addition to eight thousand muskets, the British lost two hundred artillery pieces and two thousand swords. The prisoners of war were held at Winchester, Virginia; Frederick, Maryland; and Lancaster, Pennsylvania; until they were exchanged. Cornwallis was exchanged for Henry Laurens, the former Continental Congress president and father of John Laurens, who had been captured at sea and held prisoner by the British in the Tower of London. After his release, Laurens joined the American peace commissioners in Paris.

The allied victory at Yorktown did not end the Revolutionary War, but it set in motion the events that led to it. The British had lost one-third of all their forces in America, but still held New York City, Charleston, and Savannah. The French army under Rochambeau remained in winter quarters at Yorktown. Washington ordered the Continental forces under his command to march back to the North and rejoin the remainder of the northern army that continued to hold Henry Clinton at bay in New York, while the southern army under General Nathanael Greene tried to contain the British forces occupying Charleston and Savannah. Immediately after the British surrender at Yorktown, Washington dispatched one of his aides-de-camp, Tench Tilghman, to notify the Continental Congress of the victory. He arrived in Philadelphia on October 22. The news of Yorktown reached London just over a month later. British Prime Minister Lord North resigned in March 1782 after losing a no-confidence vote in Parliament.

THE MISFORTUNES OF THE BLACK REGIMENT

The Rhode Island Regiment, including the former elements of the Black Regiment, also headed back north to winter quarters in Philadelphia. Notwithstanding the attack at Pines Bridge in May 1781, where the regiment saw their colonel and major killed, along with several of the regiment killed and wounded, the Rhode Island Regiment and their Black Patriots suffered its greatest tragedy following their participation in the victory at Yorktown. As historian Dan Popek records, the regiment was struck with sickness from their travels south, as were many other units from the northern army that had traveled with Washington to Yorktown. Recent recruits who had not been inoculated were particularly susceptible to smallpox that may have been carried by their French allies. As the regiment sailed north up Chesapeake Bay, soldiers began succumbing to disease. Popek records that in November 1781, ten enlisted soldiers of the Rhode Island Regiment died. This included Black Patriots James Niles Jr., Prince Rodman, and Prince Power. Bristol Arnold, who had been wounded at Pines Bridge and did not make the journey to Yorktown, died on November 29 at West Point. The regiment landed at Head of Elk, Maryland, and marched north to Philadelphia. In December 1781, another forty-three soldiers from the regiment died. Most of those deaths were Black Patriots, despite their numbers being a minority of the integrated regiment. From their departure from Yorktown, during their winter quarters in Philadelphia, until June 1782, one officer and 115 enlisted men from the Rhode Island Regiment died. More than 40 percent of Black Patriots in the regiment died during these seven months, as well as 20 percent of White soldiers. Unfortunately, this was not the last tragedy suffered by the brave Black Patriots of the Rhode Island Regiment.

Even prior to their arrival in Yorktown they lost one of their number, but not to sickness. One of the regiment's Black Patriots, Anthony Griffith, was traveling south with the regiment and encamped in Head of Elk, Maryland. According to Dan Popek, one Luke Griffith appeared at the local courthouse, claiming that Anthony Griffith was a slave of his who had escaped slavery in August 1777. He enlisted in the Second Rhode Island Regiment of the Continental army at Valley Forge in February 1778 and had served the four years since. Despite his years of service in the cause of freedom, General Benjamin Lincoln ordered him discharged and returned to slavery under his previous owner.

Another Black Patriot in the Rhode Island Regiment befell misfortune on their victorious return from Yorktown. While encamped in Head of Elk in December 1781, Fortune Stoddard was assaulted by a mob that attacked the soldiers in their lodgings. Stoddard had enlisted in the regiment at the end of 1780. The fight ebbed but escalated again when an officer arrived to enquire about the disturbance. His men eventually forced the soldiers out of the building with their arms and bayonets. Several leaders of that mob reappeared the next day and assaulted a White soldier, at which point Stoddard fired his musket, wounding one of the men, who died later that day. As Popek observes in his review of the incident, "The symbolism of this scene cannot be denied: a colored soldier, a veteran of the trenches of Yorktown, fired his weapon to defend his white brother in arms."

Stoddard was tried by a civilian court, acquitted of murder but convicted of manslaughter. He was branded on his thumb and required to pay court costs. Unable to pay those costs, the court threatened to sell Stoddard into slavery to pay the fines. The matter dragged out for a number of months. The regiment's commander, Lieutenant Colonel Jeremiah Olney, wrote to General Washington in letter dated August 4, 1782, interceding on his soldier's behalf:

> I beg leave to lay before Your Excellency the case of Fortune Stoddard, a Negro Soldier of my regiment, who is now in the State of Maryland in Civil Custody in the County of Cecil, for killing one James Cunningham, who with some others bred a riot in the soldiers' quarter on the 21st December 1781. This includes a copy of the inquest taken at Elk before John Neide Esq., one of the coroners for Cecil County, and the enclosed letter from Patrick Hamilton Esq., sheriff of said county (to Lt. Shearman who was on duty at Elk when this misfortune happened) will give your Excellency every information I am possessed of. Respecting this unhappy affair it appears from the sheriff's letter the soldier had his trial in June last, and was acquitted of murder but found guilty of manslaughter, and that from the laws of the State he will be sold to pay the cost of prosecution, etc. Except some person appears to settle the charges... that have accrued in the prosecution of a criminal case, that being alone incumbent on the State where the fact was committed, it appears to me very cruel, the soldier should be sold to pay charges, as he was in a line of his duty defending himself and quarters against the insults of the rioters—I confess myself at a loss to know the necessary measures to be pursued for recovering the soldier again into service. I therefore must resort to your Excellency and desire your interference in the matter.

The fines imposed on Fortune Stoddard were eventually paid by the Continental Congress, and though he continued to be imprisoned until the close of the war, he was released and eventually returned to Rhode Island.

A LOVE LETTER FROM THE FIELD

As the war continued to drag on, soldiers tried to maintain some attachment to the lives and loved ones they left behind at home. This is seen in a unique document held by the National Archives in the pension application of one Black Patriot widow. Among the items Judith Lines (Lynde) had included in her application was a letter sent by her husband, John, from the extensive Continental camp at Fishkill, New York, dated November 11, 1781. The couple had recently wed, being married by Esquire John Watrous, and Judith was living in Colchester, Connecticut, with her three children from her first marriage (her previous husband had died in 1777). She came from a committed Patriot family, with three brothers (Jeruel, Reuben, and Shubael) and a half-brother (Samuel) all serving in Continental and state services. Her brother Shubael had died in the service on December 9, 1777. John had been drafted into the Connecticut state militia in August 1777 to support the northern army under General Horatio Gates at Saratoga. His regiment was engaged in both Saratoga battles at Freeman's Farm and Bemis Heights, and he was discharged shortly after the surrender of Burgoyne's army. Judith's half-brother Samuel served in the same company, and may have at some point introduced his comrade to his sister. Susan Nevins, a researcher that has written on the life of John and Judith, observes that in John's later enlistments he served with a number of other Black Patriots from Connecticut, including Cuff Liberty, Peter Freeman, Benjamin Black, Nero Cross, Pomp Edore, Jack Arabas, Lebbeus Quy, and Backus Fox.

From Fishkill, John writes Judith of his love and solicits news from home:

> November the 11, 1781
> I take this opportunity to send to you my dear and loving wife to let you known that I am well and hoping these lines may find you and the children well. I am…[illegible] I should be very glad to hear from you my deer [sic] and loving wife. I can't but think it hard that I haven't had one letter since I left from home and this is the fifth letter I sent. I have seen my father, and my mother is dead and one of my brothers. Mother died three years ago and brother died two years ago. I have two brothers living and all my sisters. Father is very much pleased of you and he intends to come and see you this fall or the first of winter. It is about six weeks since I've seen my father. He gives his kind compliments to you and so does all my brothers and sisters. They are at the north river about sixteen miles from Fishkill. O my dear and loving wife…[illegible] the love the kind love that I have for you. I have gone a…[illegible] for your sake and could not help it, God bless your deep love. …[illegible] and his wife is well. …[illegible] was in camp last week and he say they was all well. I belong to Colonel Sherman's regiment, Captain Rice's Company. We lay at Fishkill now. I should be very glad if you would take some time and send me a letter how you have lived this summer and whether the house is done and whether you killed that cow or whether you have not another. I want to know all these thing very much. I intend to come home this winter if I can but don't know if I can. God bless your dear soul, if I could see you myself then I could talk with you my dear wife as I like. I have seen hard times of late. I fear…[illegible] I have lived a-11-day

> with bread only. I have the...[illegible] a good deal bad, so I remain your loving husband until death.
>
> John Lines

This letter, written by Lines's own hand, and the letter of Thomas Nichols to his former master, mentioned earlier, are the only two known existing letters written by Black Patriots serving in the field during the Revolutionary War. Judith kept this treasured letter for more than fifty years before attaching it to her widow's pension affidavit in 1837, nearly a decade after John's death, explaining why it had faded in places. She noted that it was written and signed in his own hand, attesting to his literacy. When he fell ill the following summer of 1782, he sent for her. She attested to staying with him in camp for three or four months and catching smallpox herself. He was discharged at West Point on November 15, 1783, his discharge signed by Major General Henry Knox. After the war, one of Judith's sisters, Hulda, married Thaddeus Jacklin, another Black Patriot, as did her sister Elizabeth, who married Philip Phillips in 1789.

MONK ESTILL AND THE ATTACK OF FORT BOONESBOROUGH

The allied victory at Yorktown did little to stop attacks along the frontier. Daniel Boone had established Fort Boonesborough in modern-day Kentucky in 1775, one of the first non-native settlements west of the Appalachian Mountains. Slaves had been brought with the settlers as laborers. In the first attack on Boonesborough in March 1775, a Black slave, Sam, was killed in the fight. An attempted siege by Shawnee in the spring of 1778 was also repelled with the help of their slaves. One of the settlers during this time was Captain James Estill, who left

Boonesborough in 1780 with his brother, Colonel Samuel Estill, to establish their own settlement, Fort Estill and Estill's Station, for travelers along the Wilderness Road.

In March 1782, a messenger arrived at Fort Estill requesting assistance after signs of a Wyandot war party were spotted. The British had flooded the frontier with weapons and money for native tribes to attack frontier settlements, prompting bloody clashes in Kentucky throughout the year. Captain Estill set off with forty men to help track down the war party. The next day, Estill's Station was attacked. A teenage girl, Jennie Glass, was killed and scalped in the attack, and Estill's slave, Monk, was taken captive. He convinced the Wyandot warriors that the nearby fort was fully defended, when in fact most of the men were away with Captain Estill, prompting the war party to flee the area and saving the fort's defenseless inhabitants. Word reached the tracking party of the attack, and Captain Estill set off in pursuit of the Wyandots. They met at Little Mountain Creek on March 22, near modern-day Mount Sterling. In a close-quarters battle between the two parties, Monk was able to make his escape from his native captors. Fighting was at times hand to hand, and Captain Estill was one of the last men killed. The survivors of both parties broke off the attack, having suffered severe casualties. James Berry was severely wounded with a shot through his thigh, and he was carried the twenty-five miles back to Fort Estill on Monk's back. Deadly attacks in Kentucky continued at Strode's Station, Bryan's Station, and Blue Licks.

Monk was freed by the Estill family shortly after the return of the survivors, no doubt in reward for his deceiving the Wyandot attackers and his grueling assistance to the wounded James Berry. The first known Black freeman in Kentucky, he became known for tanning hides and making gunpowder after discovering a source of saltpeter in nearby Peyton Cave. Later a Baptist minister, he fathered an astounding thirty children. Other Black Patriots who had served in the Continental army would move to

Kentucky after the war, including Daniel Goff, who survived the ordeal of Valley Forge and fought at Monmouth, and Joseph Sidebottom, who crossed the Delaware with Washington for the critical Patriot victory at Trenton in December 1776. During that battle, Sidebottom rendered aid to a Virginia officer wounded in the fight, James Monroe, who later became the fifth President of the United States.

FIGHTING ALONG THE OHIO

Abraham Moore, a freeman living in Western Pennsylvania, did several militia tours in 1781–1782, fighting British-backed tribes on the frontier along the Ohio River, serving as a substitute for Augustus Moore. Marching into the Ohio country under General Daniel Brodhead in June 1781, they fought a battle at the major Shawnee town of Wakatomika, during which Moore was shot through the arm. The militia returned to Pennsylvania and was discharged the following month, only to be called up again that fall, when they marched through the wilderness to the Muskingum River, crossed the Ohio, and fought and defeated another band of Indians. They returned in late October 1781, when they may have been greeted by the news of the victory at Yorktown. Moore participated in another expedition in the spring of 1782 after native raids had killed settlers and burned settlements. He served his final tour in a scouting expedition in spring 1783 and was discharged. Several years after the war he moved to Steubenville, on the Ohio side of the river, applied for a pension there in 1833, and died in 1837 in the land he had helped to pacify during the war. He is buried in the Union Cemetery in Steubenville in a grave bearing a military marker recording his Revolutionary War service.

SKIRMISHING IN SOUTH CAROLINA

Notwithstanding the allied victory at Yorktown, the war had continued in the South, where American troops under Nathanael Greene had to deal with British foraging parties, Loyalist militias, and British-backed Creek and Cherokee raids. Among the Black Patriots confronting this threat was John Redman of Virginia, who had marched south from Virginia with the First Continental Light Dragoons to support Greene's army shortly after the Battle of Guilford Court House. Redman was with his unit in the Carolinas at the time of the surrender of Cornwallis at Yorktown. They were subsequently attached to General Anthony Wayne to maintain American control in Georgia and to keep the British garrison at Savannah in place. It was during this duty on the night of June 23, 1782, that a band of Creek warriors under Chief Emistisiguo and a detachment of British soldiers launched a surprise attack on Wayne's camp near Savannah. The Americans were initially driven out of their camp but rallied and defeated the attackers. Emistisiguo was killed during the attack. This is the only battle in which Redman claimed to have participated in his pension affidavit. Weeks later, the British evacuated Savannah for Charleston on July 11, and Wayne's troops took control of the city. John Redman served until the end of the war. His fifth great-grandson is Harvard scholar Henry Louis Gates Jr.

With the recapture of Savannah, Redman's unit was sent to assist the efforts to repel British foraging raids near Charleston. John Laurens, one of the most vocal advocates of Black Patriot enlistment and emancipation, was killed in a skirmish with one of these foraging parties at Combahee Ferry on August 28, 1782. Andrew Pebbles, who had fought at Monmouth and Guilford Court House and been seriously wounded at Eutaw Springs, reported witnessing the death of Colonel Laurens.

THE BRITISH EVACUATE CHARLESTON (DECEMBER 14, 1782)

British ships arrived in Charleston Harbor in September 1782 to evacuate the troops, but it would take months to complete preparations. Meanwhile, British foraging raids continued. On November 14, Colonel Thaddeus Kosciuszko attempted an attack on a British woodcutting party at Dills Bluff on James Island, but was heavily outnumbered and outgunned. Several American officers were killed, and a slave, William Smith, was wounded and taken prisoner during the skirmish. Smith died in British captivity. These are considered the last combat casualties in the southern theater of the war. The British evacuated Charleston exactly a month later on December 14, 1782. Weeks later word arrived that the British government had acknowledged American independence. The war began to wind down but was not entirely finished as the peace commissioners in Paris continued negotiations.

Even as it seemed that the war was close to an end, issues related to the status of Black Patriots continued to arise. A series of letters held by the Library of Congress documents the controversy over Richard Hobby, a soldier in the Third Massachusetts. A slave of Jonathan Hobby of Concord, he had enlisted in 1781. In February 1783, his owner appeared in camp at West Point demanding the discharge and return of his slave, whom he claimed had enlisted without his permission. A court of inquiry appointed to investigate the matter issued its opinion on February 3: Their presumption was that the muster master had enlisted Richard properly according to the rules of Massachusetts, and he therefore had to serve out his three-year term. Any remedy sought by Jonathan Hobby needed to be addressed by the State of Massachusetts, not the Continental army. Hobby wrote directly to General Washington on February 7, pleading that any possible remedy would be near impossible to obtain from the state and asking for his intervention in the matter. He was perhaps aware of the several freedom lawsuits working their way through the state court that were expected to go against slaveholders (in fact, they did). That same day, the court of inquiry reaffirmed its decision, and David Humphreys, an aide for General Washington, wrote to Hobby informing him that the commander in chief stood behind the ruling and declined to intervene. Richard Hobby left West Point empty-handed, and within a few months the Massachusetts State Supreme Court effectively ended any legal basis for slavery in the state. After his term of service ended, Richard Hobby was a free man.

THE LAST MISSION OF THE BLACK REGIMENT

The very next day on February 8, 1783, nearly a hundred miles north, the Rhode Island Regiment set off on a military operation under Colonel Marinus Willett. The regiment had suffered considerable deaths on their return from Yorktown and in the following months. Stationed for the winter in Saratoga, they aimed to march a hundred miles up the Mohawk River in an attempt to seize the British-held Fort Oswego on Lake Ontario, which continued to be a base of operations and supply for British-allied tribes and Loyalist attacks in upstate New York. Marching in the snow, they were led by native guides. Instead of being led to Fort Oswego, they ended up lost in a swamp some miles away. With the prospect of losing the element of surprise, the column reversed course and began a march to Fort Stanwix before they could be discovered. Food proved scarce on the return march, and frostbite was widespread. Toney Phillips, a Black Patriot on the mission, died of injuries a few days after their return. Others were left behind and captured by the British, such as Prime Watson, who became a prisoner of war for the second time, having previously been captured at Pines Bridge in May 1781. Historian Dan Popek estimates that the number of Black Patriots serving after the Fort Oswego mission was reduced to less than 20 percent of the regiment. A number of mission participants noted their frozen toes and feet, including one of the most veteran Black Patriot members of the regiment, Guy Watson.

A PEACE TREATY AND DISBANDING THE ARMY

Just over a month after the ill-fated Fort Oswego mission, General George Washington reported to his army that a peace treaty had been drawn up in Paris. All nations involved in the conflict still needed to ratify the treaty, but by summer 1783 entire regiments were being furloughed, effectively discharged. At the main Continental army camp, many of the discharges were personally signed by Washington, becoming treasured possessions for many soldiers.

Many Black Patriots that had served for years, including a few who began their service responding to the Lexington Alarm, were finally seeing the war come to an end. Cato Howe had enlisted after the battles at Lexington and Concord, fought at Bunker Hill, and continued to serve until the end of the war. Julius Cezar of New York had seen his fair share of both defeat and victory, fighting at Long Island, Trenton, Brandywine, Stony Point, and Yorktown. Adam Adams of the First Maryland had begun his service fighting under Washington at Brandywine, Germantown, and Monmouth, and then was sent south to fight at Camden, Guilford Court House, and Yorktown. He was discharged on November 11, 1783. Oliver Cromwell of New Jersey had crossed the icy Delaware with Washington for the victory at Trenton, fighting at Brandywine, Monmouth, and Yorktown. Nathan Fry had enlisted in Virginia in 1775 and served until after the victory at Yorktown. Winsor Fry was one of the first Black Patriots to enlist in the First Rhode Island in 1776—two years before the formation of the Black Regiment. Fighting against overwhelming odds at Red Bank, he survived the winter at Valley Forge to fight with the regiment's detachment at Monmouth. In all, he earned ten battle stars during his service but narrowly avoided execution after a court martial—spared with the personal assent of the commander in chief—to serve until the end of the war, earning an honorable discharge. John Reed began his military service with the militia in 1776, enlisted with the First New Hampshire, and was noted for nursing his sick comrades at Valley Forge. He and his regiment were among the last soldiers discharged from the Continental army in January 1784.

These Black Patriots had fought and bled for American independence. They endured unimaginable hardships to ensure the survival of the Patriot cause. Sometimes without food and regularly without pay, fighting sickness and disease more frequently than the enemy, they and the thousands of other Black Patriots serving in the Revolutionary War were present for every battle and major (and most minor) skirmishes over eight years of combat. With the British evacuation of New York City and the final ratification of the Treaty of Paris by the Continental Congress on January 14, 1784, the war was finally ended. Regardless of whether they were officers or enlisted, White or Black, slave or free, all soldiers returned to a country fundamentally changed, facing uncertainty about what the independence they had fought for would entail.

The remnants of Redoubt No. 10 at Yorktown, Virginia. Black Patriots from Rhode Island helped seize the redoubt under the command of Lt. Col. Alexander Hamilton on the night of October 14, 1781. The British surrendered three days later. (Image: Patrick S. Poole)

Monk Estill

A drawing of Monk Estill, one of the heroes of the attack on Estill's Station, Kentucky, in March 1782. After the battle, he carried a wounded colleague twenty miles to safety. A free man after the war, he manufactured gunpowder and was a respected member of the Kentucky frontier. The drawing appeared in Z.F. Smith's book *The History of Kentucky* (1895). (Image: Internet Archive)

Discharge for Brister (also identified as Bristol) Baker of New Haven, signed by George Washington, which first appeared in William Cooper Nell's book *The Colored Patriots of the American Revolution* (1855). Enlisting in the Sixth Connecticut in April 1777 for the duration of the war, Baker served in Capt. Joseph Mansfield's company. The regiment was involved in several raids on Long Island and skirmishes with the British near New York City. The Sixth Connecticut participated in the Patriot victory at Stony Point and defended West Point after Benedict Arnold's treason. The regiment was reorganized in early 1781, and Baker completed his service in the Second Connecticut. He received the Badge of Merit for his six years of service. (Image: Internet Archive)

By His Excellency
GEORGE WASHINGTON, Esq;
General and Commander in Chief of the Forces of the United States of America.

THESE are to CERTIFY that the Bearer hereof Brister Baker Soldier in the Second Connecticut Regiment, having faithfully ferved the United States from April 9th 1777 to June 8th 1783 and being inlifted for the War only, is hereby Discharged from the American Army.

GIVEN at Head-Quarters the 8th June 1783

G Washington

By His Excellency's Command,
J Trumbull Jun Secy

REGISTERED in the Books of the Regiment,
Adjutant,

THE above Baker has been honored with the BADGE of MERIT for Six Years faithful Service.

Head-Quarters, June 8th 1783.

THE within CERTIFICATE fhall not avail the Bearer as a Difcharge, until the Ratification of the definitive Treaty of Peace; previous to which Time, and until Proclamation thereof fhall be made, He is to be confidered as being on Furlough.

GEORGE WASHINGTON.

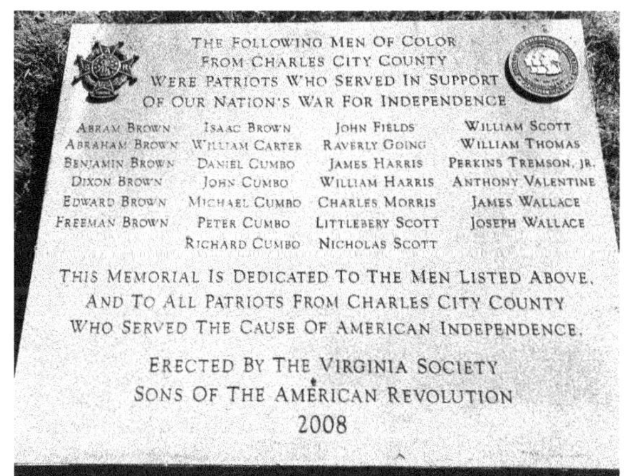

Monument erected in honor of the Black Patriots from Charles City County, Virginia. One soldier identified, Michael Cumbo, enlisted in the Sixth Virginia in September 1777 and died in the Continental service a year later. (Image: Patrick S. Poole)

CHAPTER 11
UNFINISHED BUSINESS

PRINCE ESTABROOK WAS a slave who served in Captain John Parker's company of minutemen and was wounded in the shoulder at Lexington Green in the very first shots of the Revolutionary War. Two months later he served in Cambridge at the time of the Battle of Bunker Hill. Alice M. Hinkle's prizewinning biography of Estabrook documents his continued service on duty at Fort Ticonderoga. After the surrender of the British army under General Burgoyne at Saratoga in October 1777, he served in Cambridge again, likely guarding the British prisoners. Now nearing forty years old, he was called up again in 1780 and reenlisted in 1781 for three years. His regiment was among the last to be discharged in 1784. Receiving his freedom after the war, he continued to live in Lexington with his former owner, Benjamin Estabrook, and later in Ashby, Massachusetts, with Benjamin's son, Nathan. Prince may have been married at some point, but there are no indications he had any children. When he died sometime around 1830, he was buried in the pauper's section of the Ashby town cemetery. His grave was finally marked a century later, his military headstone requested in 1929 by Henry Estabrook of the local Sons of the American Revolution chapter. A monument erected by the Alice M. Hinkle Memorial Fund for his service as the first Black Patriot of the Revolutionary War was placed in front of the Buckman Tavern in 2008 directly across the street from Lexington Green. The Lexington Historical Society holds the only known artifact from his life: a psalm book he once found on the road, which he later sold to Rufus Meriam.

Prince Estabrook's life was otherwise unremarkable, and yet he was a participant in one of the most important events in modern history. In the battles and events that led to American independence, the participation of Black Patriots was significant. At the moments where the likelihood of victory seemed distant, they were there to keep the hopes of American independence alive. Their participation, contributions, and sacrifice to achieve the final victory should be recognized as equal to any other.

But Black Patriots' role in achieving American independence was the beginning, not the end, of their story. There were now more questions than answers about their role and status in this new country they helped bring forth. Primary among them was how the continued existence of slavery in America could be compatible with the fundamental ideals of the American Revolution. For many Black Patriots, this was not an academic question but an existential one.

The Vermont Republic had explicitly outlawed slavery in its 1777 constitution, and a number of Black Patriots and their families from other states ended up settling there after the war. Vermont entered the Union in March 1791. The state constitution of Massachusetts had declared that all men were born free and equal. Elizabeth Freeman challenged her continued enslavement with the help of lawyer Theodore Sedgewick (later Speaker of the US House of Representatives), and a jury agreed with her lawsuit, thereby freeing her and awarding her damages. Sedgewick also employed returning Black Patriot veteran Agrippa Hull. All three are buried in the same cemetery in Stockbridge, Massachusetts. Quock Walker sued for his freedom, ultimately argued before the Massachusetts Supreme Court in 1783. Chief Justice William Cushing ruled:

> I think the idea of slavery is inconsistent without conduct and Constitution, and there can be no such thing as perpetual servitude of a rational creature unless his liberty is forfeited by criminal conduct or given up by personal consent or contract.

The decision in the Quock Walker case effectively ended any legal basis for slavery in Massachusetts, which had enlisted more Black Patriots during war than any other state. Those Black Patriots from the state returning after the end of the war, regardless of status, would be freemen. By the time of the 1790 Census, there were no longer any slaves counted in the state.

A NEW BATTLE FOR FREEDOM

Tragically, that was not the experience in other states. Some Black Patriots returning home from the war found themselves in a new battle for freedom. Jack Arabus served six years fighting for his country as a substitute for the son of his owner, Thomas Ivers, on the promise of his freedom after his service was over. But on his return to Connecticut, Ivers reneged on the deal. Arabus fled but was caught by Ivers, who had him jailed in New Haven. Arabus sued, claiming false imprisonment, and the judge agreed, "upon the ground that he was a free man, absolutely manumitted from his master by enlisting and serving in the army." Sadly, this standard was not applied statewide. Jason Yawpon of Lebanon, Connecticut, served in the state brigade with the permission of his owner and was wounded in the service. But as he had never been freed, after his service he returned to slavery and reportedly died a slave. Titus Kent of the Third Connecticut also appears to have died in slavery, and after his death the children of his former owner applied as his heirs at law for a land warrant based on his service.

In chapter 7 the story of Samuel Sutphen is recounted, including his service in the New Jersey militia at the battles of Long Island, Princeton, Monmouth, and Newtown. He had been sold at the beginning of the war to serve as the substitute for his new owner, with the promise of being manumitted from slavery after his service was over, only to be sold again when he raised the issue of freedom after his service. Despite the protests of Samuel's former commanders urging for his freedom, he wasn't released from slavery until 1805. William Cooper Nell tells the story of another New Jersey Black Patriot, Samuel Charlton, who was enlisted by his owner as a teamster for the Continental army. His served at Monmouth and other battles only to be returned to slavery, continuing as a slave until the death of his owner. The *Forgotten Patriots* research conducted by the Daughters of the American Revolution records that the muster roles of the Delaware Regiment bears an entry for George Laha, noting that he was "discharged February 14, 1782, being a slave for life and claimed." It's unknown if this Black Patriot was ever freed.

Ned Griffin of North Carolina was sent as a replacement by his owner who had deserted from his militia service just prior to the Battle of Guilford Court House. Fighting in his place with the promise of freedom when he completed his owner's term, he was denied his freedom and returned to slavery. Griffin appealed to the North Carolina legislature for his freedom with the written support of his former colonel. The General Assembly approved his petition, declaring:

> Be it therefore enacted by the General Assembly of the State of North Carolina, and it is hereby enacted by the authority of the same, that the said Ned Griffin, late the property of William Kitchin, shall forever hereafter be, in every respect, declared to be a free man, and he shall be and is hereafter enfranchised and forever delivered of the yoke of slavery. Any law, usage or custom to the contrary thereof in any ways notwithstanding.

With his freedom that had been unjustly denied by his cowardly former owner now secured, the legislature added a monetary payment for him and 640 acres of land granted in thanks for his service.

Ned Streeter had also served as a substitute for his owner in the Virginia militia, being wounded in combat by a musket ball to his leg that left him crippled. But he remained a slave upon his return home. The death of his owner in 1792 didn't see him freed, either, as the widow remarried and her new husband claimed ownership of Streeter. It was only when he sued in 1814—more than thirty years after his discharge—that he finally receive his freedom. At trial, the jury awarded him damages for the time he was held in slavery, beginning from the time he left the militia until the death of his owner, and an even greater amount of damages for being illegally held for sixteen subsequent years.

The re-enslavement of Black Patriots after their service appears to be the exception rather than the rule. Hundreds, if not thousands, received their freedom after their Revolutionary War service. Some states moved quickly to address these situations. Just weeks after the official end of the war, the Virginia legislature passed a law on November 10, 1783, granting freedom to any slave who had served as a substitute. It was on the basis of this law that Ned Streeter was able to obtain his freedom and receive payment for the years he was illegally held in slavery after the war.

Other situations had to be dealt with individually. James Armistead and Saul Mathews had served as Patriot spies, providing critical information during the Yorktown campaign. But neither had enlisted in the army. Both men successfully petitioned the legislature for their freedom, Armistead assisted by a handwritten letter provided by Lafayette before he returned to France attesting to his service to the cause. After he received his manumission, he changed his name to James Lafayette. Census records indicate that he later became a slave owner himself.

Other Black Patriots had to deal with the reality that while they were free men, their families were still in slavery. Isham Carter had served in the South Carolina artillery, fought at Stono Ferry and the siege of Savannah, and was taken as a prisoner of war at the fall of Charleston. But when applying for his pension more than forty years later, he testified that his wife and children were still slaves. Philip Savoy joined the famed First Maryland in 1778, fought for the Patriot victory at Monmouth, and was later taken prisoner at Elizabethtown. After his release, he was present for the siege at Yorktown and the surrender of Cornwallis and his army, being discharged two years later in November 1783. But in 1818 his wife and children were also still held in slavery.

Former commanders made efforts to ensure that Black Patriots who served with them were able to keep their freedom. One example is a certificate written by General Henry Knox dated January 9, 1784, for Romeo Smith, who had enlisted in the Seventh Massachusetts as a slave with the promise of freedom. After the war, that freedom seemed uncertain, prompting Knox to write:

> This is to certify that the bearer hereof Romeo Smith is a free man, and has served three years in the Army of the United States of America. Any person attempting to circumvent or trepan him as a slave will incur the severest penalty of the Law and the indignation of Heaven.

The original certificate signed by Knox is in the collection of the Gilder Lehrman Institute of American History.

Colonel Jeremiah Olney, who took command of the Rhode Island Regiment after Christopher Greene was killed by Loyalist raiders at Pines Bridge, intervened on behalf of at least one of his soldiers after the war. John Burroughs had been purchased from his owner in 1778 by the State of Rhode Island and was given his freedom conditioned upon his enlistment in the newly reformed First Rhode Island, known as the Black Regiment. But after his discharge at the end of the war, Burroughs was claimed again by his former owner and returned to slavery. Olney appealed to the Providence Abolition Society to act on Burroughs's case.

They did and eventually secured his freedom after filing a lawsuit on the veteran's behalf.

Colonel Olney also submitted affidavits for his former Black Regiment soldiers who applied for pensions. Examining more than seven hundred pensions and land warrants of Black Patriot veterans (identified in Appendix 1), former officers submitting affidavits on behalf of their Black Patriot colleagues was a common affair, which was reciprocated on a few occasions by Black Patriots providing affidavits in support of their former officers. In one case, Lewis Hinton testified to the service of his former lieutenant, Stafford Lightburn, on behalf of his heirs who had applied for a land warrant. The commissioner investigating the case noted that the documentary evidence to Lightburn's time in the Virginia State Navy was missing, and the testimony of Hinton and other witnesses compelled him to approve the claim.

PENSION POLITICS

Pensions proved to be an important lifeline for many Black Patriots in their later years. During the war, the Continental Congress had provided for pensions of widows and orphans of soldiers who had died in the service and for soldiers who had lost limbs or become invalid to a degree that they couldn't work. One such pension was received by Prince Vaughan of the Rhode Island Black Regiment for toes lost to frostbite during the failed Oswego expedition in 1783. But it wasn't until 1818 that Congress passed a comprehensive pension act for veterans of past wars. To qualify, the soldier had to have served at least nine months and be in "reduced circumstances." Congress anticipated two thousand applications, but was overwhelmed with ten times as many requests, which threatened to bankrupt the government. Two years later, all those receiving pensions had to resubmit and meet a means test. Those who didn't meet the requirements or did not provide a list of possessions and income were struck from the rolls. In 1832, with many surviving Revolutionary War veterans entering their seventies and eighties, a comprehensive pension act was passed, providing pensions for all those who had served six months or more, regardless of their property or income.

These pension applications provide considerable detail about the military service and post-war life of many Black Patriots. They provide researchers with much of what we know about the battles they were present for, the injuries they received, and the life and hardships they experienced while still in the field. The records accompanying their applications also give an indication of the obstacles and issues that these veterans faced in receiving their pensions. Decades after their service, time had eroded many memories of people and places. Providing evidence in support of their claims in many cases proved difficult. A discharge certificate could easily have been lost after fifty years, especially when soldiers had no idea they would be needed decades later for their pensions. As the war began to wind down, many units were furloughed without being given discharges. American independence meant that many veterans and their families moved away from where they had enlisted, making it difficult to locate former comrades and officers. Federal and state military records were incomplete and lost. A fire at the War Department in 1800 destroyed much of what the federal government had from the Revolutionary War period, and what remained was likely lost in the burning of Washington DC by the British in 1814. These were just a few of the obstacles that pension applicants faced.

During the war, Jehu Grant had fled a Loyalist owner in Rhode Island in 1777 and joined up with the army in Connecticut. He served in several roles, including as a teamster and a waiter. On discovery of his location and enlistment, his owner appealed to have him returned after he had already served nine or ten months. He was later sold to another owner, then later yet allowed to buy his freedom. At the time he applied for a pension, he was eighty years old and blind. His application was rejected since he was still considered a slave at the time of his service and hadn't served in a military role, even though White veterans who had served in the same capacity qualified for pensions. He appealed the decision, and in his second declaration he provides a subtle sarcastic rebuke:

> I was then grown to Manhood in the full Vigour and Strength of life, and heard much about the Cruel and arbitrary things done by the British. Their ships lay within a few miles of my Master's house which stood near the shore and I was confident that my Master traded with them, and I suffered much from the fear that I should be sent aboard a ship of war, this I disliked. *But when I saw liberty poles & the people all engaged for the support of freedom, I could not but like & be pleased with such things. (God forgive me if I sinned in feeling)* [emphasis added] And living on the borders of Rhode Island where whole companies of coloured people enlisted, it added to my fears and dread of being sold to the British. These considerations induced me to enlist in the American Army where I served faithful about 10 months.

Jehu Grant's admission to being seduced by the language of liberty wasn't enough to overturn the rejection. He died several years later on December 25, 1840, having never received a pension.

Peter Nash had served for several years in a Connecticut coast guard company commanded by his owner. Yet when his widow applied for a pension her request was denied, notwithstanding affidavits from men who had served with him, because he was also a slave at the time of his service. Caesar Spragues had enlisted in the Fourth Massachusetts in June 1777 and had his left foot shot off by a cannonball during the Battle of Monmouth a year later. He began receiving a disability pension in April

1794 for his injury but was subsequently removed from the rolls when it was discovered that he had deserted from the Invalid Corps in 1780. Julius Cezar enlisted in a New York regiment shortly after the beginning of the war, serving at the battles of Long Island, Trenton, Brandywine, Stony Point, and Yorktown. Despite his service for almost the entire duration of the war, his pension application was denied because he had been assigned as a waiter to one of the officers and was deemed not to have been in the military corps. William Anderson, another Black Patriot, had been presumed dead from wounds when found on the battlefield outside Yorktown, but an officer testified that he had found him alive and took him to the hospital. Even though War Department examiners believed that Anderson had served as he and his witnesses claimed, they couldn't find the corresponding records for his service and his application and appeals were denied five times.

Primes, known in pension records as Record Primes as he had no known surname, was a free man who had enlisted in 1777 in North Carolina. During his service he had been taken prisoner at the fall of Charleston, was paroled but violated his parole by rejoining Patriot forces, was captured again at Gum Swamp and freed by General Francis Marion. He was wounded in the head at Gates's defeat at Camden, served at the Patriot victories at Kings Mountain and Cowpens, then was at Guilford Court House and Eutaw Springs. When he applied for a pension while living in Tennessee in 1846, it was returned by the War Department asking for additional evidence of his service from the state of North Carolina. He died without receiving his pension.

Bristol (Budd) Sampson had enlisted in the Second Connecticut in 1777 and served in the battles at Saratoga, White Marsh, and Monmouth and the capture of Stony Point. He was later detailed to a light infantry company drawn from several regiments and served until the end of the war. In December 1820, Sampson, now blind, applied for a pension and was supported by statements from several other veterans who knew him and believed his account but had not served with him. It was returned with a demand for more proof of his service. Now living in Pennsylvania, he walked two hundred miles to Connecticut, led by a string held by his young son, eventually locating a former officer from his regiment, Stephen Betts, who provided him with an affidavit attesting to his service. It appears the War Department accepted this new evidence, only to suspend payments when a document was found claiming that Sampson had deserted. Undeterred, he and his son set off again on foot for Connecticut, obtaining yet another affidavit from Betts attesting that Sampson had indeed served until the end of the war. By his own admission, Sampson and his son had walked more than seven hundred miles in the two trips to obtain the necessary documents. That satisfied the pension office, and his pension was reinstated and paid arrears from the date of his first application.

Black Patriots applying for pensions sometimes received assistance from some surprising sources. Cuff Leonard served five years in several Massachusetts regiments. He received a discharge at the end of his service in June 1783, but as was the case with many veterans, his discharge was either lost or destroyed. However, Cuff Leonard was able to provide a suitable replacement to accompany his pension application, namely, a handwritten certificate of service from his former commander, Colonel John Brooks, who was not only alive but at the time was the sitting governor of Massachusetts. Among the many tasks demanding the time of the state's chief executive, Governor Brooks took the time to provide the certificate to a Black Patriot veteran comrade, as he did in other cases for soldiers who had served under his command.

Robert Wood had enlisted early in the war in the Third Virginia, fighting at Monmouth and Yorktown. After finishing his term of service, he reenlisted in the Virginia state artillery and served until the end of the war under Colonel Thomas Marshall. When he applied for his pension in 1818, his former commander had died. But he was able to obtain a handwritten certificate attesting to his service from his late colonel's son,

John Marshall, the sitting Chief Justice of the Supreme Court, the former Secretary of State under President John Adams, and a former officer in the Virginia Continental line. This was not the only pension case where Chief Justice Marshall assisted a Black Patriot. Nathan Fry of Henrico County, Virginia, had enlisted in 1775 and served as a drummer fighting the Creek in Georgia. After returning from Savannah, he enlisted in the Continental army and endured the winter at Valley Forge. Seeing action at Monmouth and Stony Point, Fry became the batman to Baron Von Steuben, who commanded a brigade under Lafayette in Virginia and was present for the surrender of Cornwallis at Yorktown. Residing in Richmond after the war, he was able to obtain the assistance of Chief Justice Marshall, who took the testimony of his veteran comrade and wrote it down for submission to the Pension Bureau.

Manuel Goodenough, also known as Manuel Soto, was a Black Patriot veteran originally from Portugal or Spain. He enlisted as an eight-month man at the beginning of the war in John Glover's Marblehead marine infantry regiment. At the beginning of 1776, he reenlisted in the regiment and served until the end of the war. During the siege of Boston, Glover's Marbleheaders ran into conflict with Dan Morgan's Virginians, who reacted to the regiment's inclusion of minorities, which reflected Marblehead's integrated mariner community. The Marbleheaders justly earned reputation began when they saved Washington's entire army, rowing them to safety across the Hudson River at night following the disaster on Long Island. Shortly after, they were praised for their performance at Kip's Bay, where they fought against a British landing on Manhattan Island. At the end of 1776, they secured their fame in American military history by rowing Washington's army across the frozen Delaware River for the surprise Patriot victories at Trenton and Princeton. Dr. Elisha Story of Marblehead served as the Glover Regiment's surgeon, and when Manuel Goodenough applied for a pension in 1820, he was able to submit an affidavit in support of his application, attesting to his service and indigence, from Dr. Story's son, Associate Justice of the Supreme Court Joseph Story—one of the paragons of early American jurisprudence.

Black Patriots sometimes received the support of their communities to obtain their pensions. Benjamin Simmons, who had served as Benjamin Black during the war, enlisted in Connecticut in May 1777 and served in a light infantry regiment, the Sixth Connecticut. He likely was involved in the regiment's actions at Sag Harbor and Stony Point. He obtained a pension in 1818, and his supporting affidavits are highly complimentary, praising his honesty, reputation, and moral character, as well as the "reputable manner" in which he had raised his family. Benjamin died in January 1838, and when his wife applied for a widow's pension, attached was a letter signed by several neighbors, who attested to knowing the couple for more than fifty years. A separate letter described how one neighbor had lent them money to pay a clergyman for their wedding.

William Jones of Fredericksburg served three years in the Virginia State Navy successively on the *Protector*, *Tartar*, and *Tempest*. During his service he had been wounded during a well-known action off Cape Charles with HMS *Lord Howe*. Jones appealed to the Virginia General Assembly in 1824 for aid due to indigence and infirmity, which was supported by two Fredericksburg physicians. Unsuccessful in his first attempt, his second appeal included a memorial from more than two dozen citizens, including the town mayor, attesting to his labor and industry in the decades of his residence there and declaring him to be a veteran worthy of the state's support. The appeal of his fellow townsmen may have made a difference, as he was granted an annual pension the following year.

When applying for pensions, a number of Black Patriots were able to submit their discharges signed by the commander in chief and other Revolutionary War luminaries. John Lines, Jethro Jones, Philip Phillips, and Prince Tyler all provided discharges signed by General Henry Knox, later Secretary of War under President Washington. Charles Charity was discharged on July 6, 1783, at Winchester Barracks, Virginia, by General Peter Muhlenberg. George Knox served three months in the New Hampshire militia at Fort Ticonderoga beginning in late 1776. At the end of his term, he reenlisted in the First New Hampshire, serving from March 1777 to May 1781, possibly seeing action at Trenton, Princeton, and the Sullivan expedition. After the war, he and his wife became indentured servants. Once their contract was completed, they moved to Thetford, Vermont, where they spent the rest of their lives. Applying for a pension in 1820, Charity was able to submit his 1781 discharge signed by his former commander, Colonel Alexander Scammell, who had been killed in action shortly after that, during the Yorktown campaign.

As the Continental army awaited the ratification of the Treaty of Paris to end the war, many regiments stationed near Washington's Newburgh, New York, headquarters were furloughed, with General Washington personally signing many of the discharges. A number of Black Patriots submitted their discharges signed by Washington to support their pension applications, including Oliver Cromwell, Arthur Clark, Nero Cross, Prince Danforth, Fortune Freeman, Philo Phillips, Pelatiah McGoldsmith, and others. As Judith Van Buskirk notes, a newspaper interview of one-hundred-year-old Oliver Cromwell reported that the Black Patriot still wept at the memory of having to surrender his discharge, signed by the commander in chief, to obtain his pension. A letter held by the National Archive from Agrippa Hull's attorney to the Pension Bureau requests the return of his discharge. It appears the discharge may in fact have been returned, as it is not part of Hull's pension file.

In his book *The Colored Patriots of the American Revolution* (1855), William C. Nell includes a related episode from Honorable Calvin Goddard, who assisted eighteen Black Patriot veterans from his area in obtaining their pensions.

> I cannot refrain from mentioning one aged black man, Primus Babcock, who proudly presented me an honorable discharge from the service during the war, dated at the close of it, wholly in the handwriting of George Washington. Nor can I forget the expressions of his feelings, when informed, after his discharge had been sent to the War Department, that it could not be returned. At his request it was written for, as he seemed inclined to spurn the pension and reclaim the discharge.

Primus Babcock had been one of the slaves whose freedom was purchased by the State of Rhode Island in exchange for their military service in the Black Regiment in 1778. His pension file includes the unfortunate reason why the War Department held onto the discharge. Babcock had sent it to his congressman to obtain the pension, but the Pension Bureau subsequently reported that it had been used by some unknown party to obtain a land warrant in his name. When it was asked for, Goddard was informed that they were holding onto it to avoid it being used further for fraudulent purposes.

Nell's book also featured a copy of the discharge of Bristol Baker of the Second Connecticut, also signed by Washington. Baker had served in the Connecticut line from April 1777 until June 1783, earning a Badge of Merit for six years' service in the Continental army. He had also been part of Captain David Humphrey's all-Black company. His discharge, which was held by a private party in Boston, was recently sold by Sotheby's. The discharge of Cash Pallentine, another Black Patriot, is held in the collection of the American Revolution Institute in Philadelphia. He too was awarded the Badge of Merit for six years' service, having wintered at Valley Forge, fought in the sweltering heat at Monmouth, and helped guard the Hudson River Valley. Another document held by the institute bears Pallentine's mark recording payment for his service in the Connecticut line prior to January 1, 1781.

In the absence of a discharge, veterans had to rely on each other to prove their service. Black Patriots were quick to provide affidavits for one another. Daniel Strother had two other Black Patriots attesting to his service, who were also living in Knox County, Indiana. Peter McAnelly testified to knowing Strother at Yorktown, and Andrew Ferguson recalled his fellow veterans during General Greene's campaign in the Carolinas in 1781. Strother reciprocated by providing affidavits for both McAnelly and Ferguson. Adam Adams was able to testify on behalf of his fellow Maryland Black Patriot Frederick Hall. Prince Hull had fought at Bunker Hill and served until after the surrender of Burgoyne at Saratoga, attested to by Devonshire Freeman of the same regiment. James Bass solicited his White colleague James Mosely to file an affidavit for his pension application. William Hughes had two Black Patriots who attested to his service, Cummy Simon and Peter Galloway. Pomp McCuff reminisced about playing ball with Prince Williams (Starkweather) on the parade grounds while stationed together at Frogg's Neck, New York, and gave additional affidavits for two White comrades, Captain Andrew Fitch and Benjamin Farnum.

The pension application of Major John Brent of Virginia provides the only known details of one Black Patriot, identified only as Henry, who was a wagoner that Brent places at the battles of Brandywine, Germantown, Camden, and Guilford Court House. He was close enough to the action at Camden that he was forced to flee on one of his horses. These pension applications are the only source of detailed service information for many Black Patriots, and thankfully much of it is their firsthand testimony. These pension applications also provide a glimpse of their life after their service. Since the number of Black Patriots who applied for pensions is a fraction of the thousands known to have served, personal and service details for many are sadly forever lost.

BUILDING A NEW WORLD

Given the sheer number of Black Patriots who served during the Revolutionary War, numbering in the thousands, it's impossible to characterize the experience of the entire group after the end of the war. Having secured American independence, an unknown world awaited them. Those who died shortly after the war, such as Pomp Edore, never even had an opportunity to experience this new world that they made possible. While some flourished, many were frustrated by the political, legal, and cultural remnants of the old world that stood against their hopes to pursue happiness as they saw fit.

Primus Hall was one of those who tried to improve his community. He served at the siege of Boston, the battles of Long Island, Harlem Heights, White Plains, Princeton, Bemis Heights (the second major engagement of the Saratoga campaign), and the Sullivan expedition to Rhode Island. He later worked for the quartermaster department and witnessed the surrender of Cornwallis at Yorktown, afterward returning home to Massachusetts. Working with his father, Prince Hall, who founded the first all-Black Masonic Lodge, they both signed an appeal to the state legislature in February 1788 calling for an end to the slave trade after three freemen were kidnapped from the city and taken to the Caribbean to be sold as slaves. Within weeks, the legislature passed a law ending the slave trade in the state and establishing protections against any further such kidnappings. Frustrated at the lack of a public school for the Black children in Boston, Hall and other community leaders established the African School, which first held classes in his home. He continued to work for abolition and educational opportunities in his community and nationally until his death on March 22, 1842.

The threat of kidnappings was not isolated, as one of the most famed Black Patriots tragically experienced. Jude Hall of New Hampshire fled from slavery and enlisted in May 1775, just weeks after Lexington and

Concord. His regiment was in the heat of the Battle at Bunker Hill, and Hall narrowly escaped death in action when he was thrown by the force of a cannonball landing nearby. He served at Fort Ticonderoga, was in the battles of Trenton, Hubbardton, and Saratoga, and earned the moniker "Old Rock" for his valor fighting in the one-hundred-degree heat at Monmouth. His service continued until after the end of the war. Jude Hall was among the longest-serving veterans of the conflict. Returning to New Hampshire, only two years later he was "warned out" by the town of Exeter. It was years before he was able to collect on back pay and bounties due from his military service. A series of incidents led to three of Jude Hall's freeborn sons being seized and enslaved: James was taken from the family home over a four dollar debt and sold into slavery; Aaron, a sailor, was swindled and put back to sea to cover a debt, never to be heard from again; and William also went to sea and was sold into slavery when he arrived in the West Indies. It was only after Hall's death in 1827 that the family heard from William, who had escaped from his captors and was living in England. Hall is buried in the Winter Street Cemetery in Exeter, near the grave of fellow Black Patriot veteran Tobias Cutler. Cutler and another Black Patriot, London Dailey, organized a society to benefit and support the free Black community in Exeter that began to grow after the war.

Building communities after the war was important for many formerly enslaved veterans as they tasted freedom and could own property for the first time. Relationships built during the war became the basis for a number of free Black communities established by Black Patriots in the early years of peacetime America. Peterborough, near modern-day Warren, Maine, was one such community, founded by Amos Peters and his wife, Sarah. Both had been enslaved before the war, with Amos receiving his freedom following his military service and Sarah having sued for her freedom after the Massachusetts Supreme Court effectively ended slavery (Maine was still part of Massachusetts at the time). The community grew into the thousands before the Civil War and had its own school district and churches.

Four Black Patriot veterans were the basis for the Parting Ways settlement outside of Plymouth, Massachusetts. Plato Turner was the first to purchase property there during the war. He had fought in Canada, Valcour Island, and Saratoga, and bought the land in 1779 prior to reenlisting until the end of the war. Several dozen Black Patriots from Plymouth County had enlisted during the war, including Cato Howe and Quamony Quash. Cato Howe had fought at Bunker Hill, and both men served together in the Second Massachusetts at Valley Forge and afterward. Prince Godwin received his freedom following the war. The four veterans are buried together at the settlement cemetery, their individual graves marked only by field stones. An interpretive sign for the settlement and the four Black Patriots who lived and died there was erected in 2012.

Another such community is well-known as a result of being mentioned in one of the classic works of American literature. Brister Freeman and Charlestown Edes were among the former slaves from Concord, Massachusetts, who settled around Walden Pond—later made famous in Henry David Thoreau's 1854 book *Walden*. Brister and Charlestown had met during their military service and later purchased property near the pond. Brister had been left money in the will of his former owner, John Cuming. Another Black Patriot living nearby was Caesar Robbins, whose former home in Concord has recently been relocated across the street from the Old North Bridge, where "the shot heard round the world" was fired, and is now a museum. Jube Savage, who was among the heroes at Hubbardton covering the Continental army's retreat from Fort Ticonderoga in the summer of 1777, also later moved to the area. The families around Walden Pond tried to scrape together a living from the rough boulder-strewn earth of the area. Thoreau in his book mentions the apple trees planted by Brister Freeman, and misattributes a quote to his tombstone (it was actually from the tombstone of Scipio Brister, another

Black Patriot from the area). A recent book, *Black Walden* by Elise Lemire, helpfully documents the personalities, trials, and tribulations of the souls who lived and died around the Black community of Walden Pond.

The Dennis Farm Charitable Land Trust in Susquehanna County, Pennsylvania, preserves the legacy of two Black Patriots, Prince Perkins and Bristol Budd Sampson, who had served together in the Fourth Connecticut, wintered at Valley Forge together, and eventually intermarried their families. The farm was established by Perkins in 1793 with money he had obtained from his military service. Sampson later married Perkins's daughter, Phebe, and settled on the farm. The farm was a stop on the Underground Railroad, and it remains in family hands more than two hundred years later. Both Prince Perkins and Bristol Budd Sampson are buried in the family cemetery on the farm, as are Black Patriot veterans from the War of 1812 and the Civil War.

ESTABLISHING A BLACK AMERICAN MILITARY TRADITION

It is important to note that the military legacy of Black Patriots doesn't conclude with the end of the Revolutionary War. Henry Cato of New Jersey, who had fought at Long Island, White Plains, Trenton, Princeton, Monmouth, and Yorktown, later served in 1791 in the Indian Wars under Colonel Zebulon Pike and General "Mad Anthony" Wayne, including the Battle of Fallen Timbers. Moses Sash was arrested in January 1787 for his role in the anti-tax Shays' Rebellion in Massachusetts but was never tried, and later received a pension for his Revolutionary War service. Other Black Patriot veterans who participated in Shays' Rebellion included Tobias Green, Peter Green, and Aaron Carter. Peter Hartless had served in the Virginia militia prior to the Yorktown campaign and moved to Pennsylvania following the war. There, he was called again for militia duty in 1794 to put down the Whiskey Rebellion, again fighting under his commander in chief—this time as President George Washington. William Flora, the hero of the Battle of Great Bridge, later sailed with famed Captain Stephen Decatur in the War of 1812 (Decatur's father had also employed Black Patriots on his ship during the revolution). George Latchom, who had saved his commanding officer from being gunned down by the British in the "Battle of the Barges" prior to Yorktown, may have also served in the War of 1812.

James Forten had been inspired as a fifteen year old watching Black Patriots of the Rhode Island Regiment marching through Philadelphia on their way to Yorktown (a scene depicted in Don Troiani's painting *Brave Men as Ever Fought*). As a ten-year-old boy, he had previously witnessed the first reading of the Declaration of Independence in July 1776. While volunteering on the privateer *Royal Louis*, the ship was captured by the British and Forten was imprisoned on the notorious Jersey prison hulk in New York harbor. Exchanged after seven months, he had to walk home to Philadelphia. After the war, he went to sea and spent a year working in an English shipyard. Returning home, he apprenticed to a sailmaker, eventually buying the company and becoming one of the wealthiest businessmen in Philadelphia. When the War of 1812 brought conflict back to America's shores, Forten and other leaders of the Black community raised a volunteer regiment to defend the city. He was also an outspoken abolitionist, founding the American Anti-Slavery Society and financially backing William Lloyd Garrison's prominent abolitionist paper *The Liberator*.

James Robinson had been enlisted in a Maryland light infantry regiment commanded by his owner, Francis De Shields, with the promise that he would be freed after his service. Fighting at Brandywine and several other engagements, he was part of the force that took Redoubt 10 at Yorktown, reportedly killing three British soldiers and being recognized by the Marquis de Lafayette after the battle. Denied his freedom, the heirs of his owner sold him in New Orleans to a new owner. It was there in

1814 when he was conscripted along with other slaves by Colonel Andrew Jackson to fight in the famed Battle of New Orleans, Robinson's second war service. Despite being twice wounded in action, he did not obtain his promised freedom. He was eventually manumitted in the 1830s and became a Baptist pastor. His life story was the subject of book published in 1858 under the name James Roberts, recounting his life in slavery and his wartime experiences in the Revolutionary War and the War of 1812. He lived to see the end of the Civil War, where his son, Private Wesley Robinson Sr., served in the First Michigan Colored Infantry and fought in eleven battles. James Robinson died in March 1868 and is buried in Elmwood Cemetery in Detroit, Michigan. His grave finally received a military marker in 2019.

The Black Patriots of the American Revolution established a military legacy that they handed down to their descendants. Benjamin Lyndes, the son of John and Judith, died from wounds he received at the Battle of Chippewa during the War of 1812. Chester Phillips, the grandson of Jeruel Phillips, was serving in the Twenty-Ninth Connecticut Volunteers in the Civil War when he was killed in action at age eighteen on September 23, 1864, at Petersburg, Virginia. He is buried in the Poplar Grove National Cemetery near the battlefield, but a memorial erected in his memory stands beside that of his Revolutionary War veteran grandfather at Center Cemetery in New Milford, Connecticut. Lemuel Freeman, great-grandson of Asher Freeman, wrote to the governor of Rhode Island in August 1862 after the outbreak of the Civil War, asking if the state would be enlisting colored soldiers as it had in the Revolutionary War. A year later he was serving in the Fifty-Eighth Massachusetts, which was not a colored regiment, even being promoted to sergeant over White troops. He was wounded in action at the siege of Petersburg and died of his wounds in a military hospital in Washington DC on July 1, 1864. His remains are possibly buried among the unknowns at Arlington National Cemetery.

A number of descendants of Revolutionary War Black Patriots enlisted in the famed Fifty-Fourth Massachusetts, the first all-Black regiment of the Civil War. Asher Freeman had two other great-grandsons, Warren F. Freeman and William Henry Freeman, who served in the unit. Richard Gundeway had three great-grandsons in the Fifty-Fourth. Jude Hall's grandson, Aaron Hall, was in Company D of the regiment, and Moses Hall was enlisted in the Third US Colored Troops. James Haskell, grandson of Anthony Clark, served in the same company with Aaron Hall, and First Sergeant Alexander Freeman Hemenway of Company F was the grandson of Bunker Hill veteran Jeffrey Hemenway. Plato Turner, one of the Black Patriot veterans who founded the Parting Ways settlement in Plymouth County, Massachusetts, had his great-grandson Cornelius Weeden serve as a corporal in Company C of the Fifty-Fourth Massachusetts.

After serving four years in the Seventh Maryland, fighting at Monmouth, Camden, Cowpens, Guilford Court House, and Eutaw Springs, Bazaleel Norman moved to Marietta, Ohio, after the war. The city was founded by former Revolutionary War officers who had formed the Ohio Company. Three of Norman's descendants died during the Civil War: Henry L. Norman served in the West Virginia Cavalry, died in captivity in the notorious Confederate prison at Andersonville, and is buried in the national cemetery there; Azariah Norman died of wounds during the war and may be buried as an unknown in Arlington National Cemetery; and Corporal Horace Norman died on April 24, 1864, and is buried at Hampton National Cemetery. Bazaleel Norman's great-great-grandson Henry A. Norman graduated from flight school on December 7, 1943, as one of the famed Tuskegee Airmen. He served in both World War II and Korea, and retired from the air force as a major. Bazaleel Norman is also the great-great-grandfather of actress Rebecca Hall.

FIGHTING FOR THE FREEDOM OF OTHERS

Another Black Patriot who moved to Ohio was Richard Stanhope, the one-time slave of George Washington. He had been willed to the future commander in chief by his father, and Stanhope followed Washington into the field as his valet, being wounded at Long Island and Stony Point. He returned to Mount Vernon after the war and was freed after the death of Martha Washington. Settling in Ohio and purchasing land, he became a farmer and a Baptist preacher, serving as a pastor of Kings Creek Baptist Church near Urbana, Ohio, which is still in operation more than two hundred years later. Married three times, he fathered a reported twenty-eight children. Several of his children were active in the Underground Railroad, and his sons Levi and David Stanhope (Stanup) were arrested in March 1853 for inciting a riot as a diversion for other conductors to move a group of escaped slaves out of the area. Richard Stanhope is just one of a handful of Revolutionary War soldiers who lived long enough to have their picture taken, dying at the age of 114 on September 20, 1862.

Several other Black Patriots and their families were also active in the Underground Railroad, including Cesar Beman of Middletown, Connecticut, and Abraham Talbot in Kennebec County, Maine. John Jack of Portsmouth, New Hampshire, was a forty-seven-year-old slave when he enlisted in 1780, but it is for his actions years later, as the protector of one of George Washington's escaped slaves, that he is remembered. Ona Judge was the body slave of Martha Washington when the First Couple lived in Philadelphia. Fleeing from the president's house on May 21, 1796, she later recounted, "Whilst they were packing for Virginia, I was packing to go, I didn't know where; for I knew that if I went back to Virginia, I should never get my liberty." Judge found her way to Greenland, New Hampshire, and it was there that George Washington sent his nephew, Burwell Basset, to locate her and bring her back to Virginia. The former president was likely unaware that she was being sheltered by one of his former soldiers. All attempts to recover Ona Judge were unsuccessful, and she lived out her days in the area, dying in 1848 after living most of her life as a wanted escaped slave. She, her husband, and her children are buried in a small overgrown cemetery with John Jack and his family.

Following three years' service in the Fifth and Third Virginia, John Chavis became one of the more professionally accomplished Black Patriots in his post-war life. Having received some Latin classical education training and making a living by tutoring, he came to the notice of Presbyterian church authorities, who arranged in 1792 for him to study at the College of New Jersey, today Princeton University, with the college president, Reverend John Witherspoon, who had lobbied the college trustees to approve funds for Chavis's studies. Witherspoon was the preeminent statesman of New Jersey. He signed the Declaration of Independence as a member of the Continental Congress and was the only clergy member to do so. He had also recruited for the Continental army from among his students. One of Witherspoon's former students was James Madison, one of the primary architects of the US Constitution. After two years of study at Princeton, Chavis completed his education at Liberty Hall Academy in Lexington, Virginia, which changed its name in 1796 during his studies to Washington Academy (modern-day Washington and Lee University). Chavis was the first Black graduate of the school, and one of the residence halls at the university now bears his name.

Chavis was licensed to preach as a missionary to the freemen and slaves in the community by the Lexington Presbytery in 1800, and he regularly preached to White congregations. An announcement in the *Raleigh Minerva* in 1808 advertised his school based on a classical curriculum to the small Raleigh community. He instructed White students during the day and Black students at night. It was in his role as educator that he gained considerable influence, teaching future governors, congressmen, diplomats, judges, attorneys, and pastors from North Carolina.

He was a close mentor to his former student, US Senator Willie Person Mangum, and twenty years of their correspondence is held by the Library of Congress. His school in Raleigh prospered, and its reputation for quality education spread, expanding his education enterprise to the five surrounding counties.

An item in the April 22, 1830, edition of the *Raleigh Register* reports on a visit by the newspaper editor reviewing the school's success firsthand:

> On Friday last, we attended an examination of the free children of color, attached to the school conducted by John Chavis, also colored, but a regularly educated Presbyterian minister, and we have seldom received more gratification from any exhibition of a similar character. To witness a well-regulated school, composed of this class of persons—to see them setting an example both in behavior and scholarship, which their white superiors might take pride in imitating, was a cheering spectacle to a philanthropist. The exercises throughout, evinced a degree of attention and assiduous care on the part of the instructor, highly creditable, and of attainment on the part of his scholars almost incredible. We were also much pleased with the sensible address which closed the examination.

Events took an unfortunate turn for Chavis in the wake of Nat Turner's slave rebellion in August 1831, as legislatures in the South imposed harsh measures targeting Black citizens that became the basis for discriminatory laws and policies that would continue for more than another century. Nat Turner was a free man and an educated preacher (much like John Chavis), and the slave revolt he inspired became the deadliest in American history. The following year the North Carolina legislature banned preaching by Black ministers. In 1835, they stripped the voting rights of all free Black citizens, including John Chavis, a Revolutionary War veteran. His military service became part of the pushback during the legislative debate, when it was claimed by the bill's supporters that no free Black man had even taken the Oath of Association in the early years of the Revolutionary War. The *Fayetteville Weekly Observer* reported on October 27, 1835:

> It was stated, as a fact, in the late debate on this subject, that when the Act passed during the Revolutionary War, calling upon all men to take the Oath of Allegiance, no free colored man had ever taken that oath. Since that debate took place, an old colored man, a resident of this county, named John Chavis, who is, he was informed, a licensed preacher in the Presbyterian Church, and well known not only in this country, but in several of the neighboring counties, had handed to him a Certificate of his having taken the Oath of Allegiance, dated Dec. 20, 1778, and signed, James Anderson, Mecklenburg, Va.

In fact, as Luther Porter Jackson documented during World War II, approximately half of the existing Black freemen of Virginia enlisted at some point during the war, and even more who were drafted slaves or serving as substitutes. Freemen were also found in all of North Carolina's regiments, fighting in both the northern and southern theaters of the war, some wounded and dying in the biggest battles of the war on land and sea, and others dying of sickness and disease, including during the brutal winter at Valley Forge.

Now disenfranchised, his schools suffered as the frailties of old age began to take hold. The Presbyterian church voted to provide support for John Chavis and his family as his health continued to decline. He died in June 1838, and his influence continues with some of his works still in publication. A recent biography of his life and work was published by one of his descendants, Helen Chavis Othow, who also founded the John Chavis Historical Society. In 1988, the society located what they believe to be the grave of John Chavis in the abandoned farm cemetery of the former plantation of his pupil and friend, Senator Willie Mangum.

Many Black Patriots from the Black Regiment struggled after the war. Dick Rhodes, one of the most experienced veterans of the group, had been at Fort Mercer, survived the winter at Valley Forge, and been wounded at the Battle of Monmouth. Born in Africa, he obtained his freedom by enlisting in the regiment. When he applied for a pension in 1820, he declared that the real property he owned was less than what he had mortgaged. A surgeon certified that he was disabled in the arm from the wound he received in the war and couldn't work. Dick Rhodes froze to death in Pawtuxet in January 1821, and his obituary published just a week later declared:

> This man rendered signal services during our Revolutionary War. He distinguished himself when Cornwallis was taken, and was one of the few brave followers of General Barton, who succeeded in taking Prescott from the midst of the enemy on Rhode Island.

His wife was able to collect his pension until her death twenty years later. The grave of Dick Rhodes was only recently discovered, and the site is currently being surveyed and documented.

Guy Watson was a battle-hardened veteran from Rhode Island. His first enlistment on February 19, 1777, was likely as a substitute while still a slave and a year prior to the passage of the Slave Enlistment Act by the Rhode Island legislature and the formation of the Black Regiment. He is named among those men chosen to participate in the successful nighttime raid to capture British General Richard Prescott, who commanded British forces occupying Newport, on July 10, 1777. He is also among the fifty to seventy-five Black Patriots of both Rhode Island regiments who served during the valiant defense of Fort Mercer and Fort Mifflin. He was likely at the Battle of Rhode Island in 1778 and in the area for the disastrous Loyalist raid at Pines Bridge, New York, that claimed the life of the regiment's colonel, major, and several Black Patriots in May 1781. He would have witnessed the surrender of Cornwallis at Yorktown and survived the sickness that claimed the lives of dozens of the Rhode Island Regiment in the months that followed. State records indicate that he lost "three joints from the toes of the right foot" as a result of frostbite during the Oswego expedition and was discharged from the army at Albany with the rest of the Rhode Island line on June 15, 1783. Due to his war injuries, he was awarded a disability pension of four dollars a month in February 1786. He and thirteen other Rhode Island Black Patriots, with the assistance of an attorney, were finally able to settle with the War Department in 1794 for their back pay owed from their service. Watson received $342. Years later he applied for and received a federal pension.

Guy Watson did not live in obscurity as many of his Black Regiment comrades but became one of the leaders of his community. He was elected chief marshal, a position that served as a mediator of the racial dividing line in South Kingstown. Black Patriots in other towns and states served in similar positions, sometimes identified as "governor" or "king." Watson was apparently respected by all and was celebrated in the annual Fourth of July festivities in Providence, where he was reported to appear "in full regimental costume, singing songs, and telling tales of his old campaign."[1] A notice published following the event in 1831 identifies three members of the Black Regiment present: Guy Watson, Benoni Bates, and Reuben Roberts. It also noted the steep decline of the number of living Revolutionary War veterans participating: from seventy-six the year before to fifty-three. Later that year Watson became somewhat of a local sensation when he was depicted in a play authored by S. S. Southworth entitled *Capture of Prescott, or the Heroism of Barton.* The review noted both White and Black attendees (the latter seated upstairs in the gallery) and the enthusiastic reception given to one Mr. McGuire, a Black actor playing the role of Guy Watson. When Watson died in 1837, his funeral was attended by members of the community of all races. One attendee wrote that the burial occurred on land owned by J. B. Dockray near Kingstown, very likely the Dockray slave cemetery identified as Rhode Island Historical Cemetery South Kingstown #A33.

For some Black Patriots, including Barzillai Lew, David Lamson, and Simon Deering, the Revolutionary War was their second conflict in the service. Same too for Ishmael Titus, who was with George Washington at Braddock's defeat during the French and Indian War, where he was a teamster hauling supplies for the British column. When he died in 1855 at nearly 110 years of age, he was identified as the last survivor of the colonial-era battle. He entered the American Revolution as a slave and substitute for his owner in 1779 for one year, and then reenlisted on his own volition. By his own account, he and his unit narrowly missed Gates's defeat at Camden, arriving after the American retreat had already begun. Two months later he was part of the decisive Patriot victory at Kings Mountain, and a monument there dedicated to some of the Black Patriots who participated in the battle bears his name. He also served at Guilford Court House and Deep River. He was subsequently taken prisoner by Loyalists and held in St. Augustine.

After the war and now a freeman, Titus moved north to New York, living in several cities along the Hudson River and then Bennington, Vermont, eventually settling just over the border in the White Oaks community in the Berkshires northeast of Williamston, Massachusetts, on the other side of the Hoosic River. There were few Black families living in the area when he arrived with his family in 1817, but one reason they may have moved there was his marriage in 1812 to Lucy Rogers, who was from the area. The position of White Oaks near the border of New York may have drawn some refugees escaping slavery there, where the institution was still legal (New York would outlaw slavery in 1827), to the community. One of the few Black families in White Oaks at the time was that of another Black Patriot veteran, Cato Dunsett. Enlisting in May 1777 in the Second Massachusetts, he fought at Bemis Heights in the second Battle of Saratoga and later at Monmouth after surviving the winter at Valley Forge. Both men applied for pensions from Williamston in 1818 shortly after the passage of the first pension act. The pension for Dunsett was approved, but Titus saw his rejected for lack of documentation, a common problem for veterans decades after their discharge. Titus was also hampered by now living seven hundred miles from his former home, where soldiers he had served with could have provided supporting affidavits. Denied a pension, Titus was on the town's poor rolls by 1840. He died on January 27, 1855, the same year the story of his service appeared in William Nell's *The Colored Patriots of the American Revolution*. A marker memorializing his military service can be found on the Charlotte Liberty Walk in front of the Harvey R. Gantt Center for African-American Arts and Culture, representing the thousands of Black Patriots who also served. But the Revolutionary War memorial in Williamston, where Ishmael Titus spent the last thirty-eight years of his life, does not bear his name. Recent efforts at Williams College, located in Williamstown, have encouraged research of the Black community in White Oaks, and a class at the school has established a project focused on the life and service of Ishmael Titus, especially trying to locate and appropriately mark his grave.

Thomas Carney of the Western Shore of Maryland not only fought in the critical southern campaign of 1780–1781 but began his military service in the militia responding to an alarm caused by General Howe's occupation of Philadelphia in 1777. His unit arrived to participate in the battles of Germantown and White Marsh, and prior to the Battle at Monmouth he enlisted in the Fifth Maryland and afterward marched south with his regiment to confront the threat posed by Cornwallis and his army. He continued to serve two years after the victory at Yorktown until he was discharged in November 1783.

Following Carney's death on June 30, 1828, the Maryland newspaper *Easton Star* published the following obituary:

> Died near this village on the 30th ult. *Thomas Carney,* a colored man, at the advanced age of 74. At the commencement of the revolution, Tom enlisted as a soldier under Col. Peter Adams, and was soon afterwards marched to the north, and was in the memorable battle of Germantown. In this action the Maryland troops bore a conspicuous part, but the Americans were compelled to yield to a superior force. Soon after this, Washington retired to Valley Forge, and took up his winter quarters. The sufferings of the army during that severe winter are well known to every American. With the true spirit of patriotism, Tom bore his share of privation and suffering. When the Maryland and Delaware lines were ordered south, Tom marched with his brave regiment, and shared in that quarter with his companions the hardships, misfortunes, and glories of war. At the battle of Guilford Court House he bore a conspicuous part as a soldier, and has often persisted that when the Maryland troops came to the charge he bayoneted seven of the enemy. At Camden, Hobkirk's Hill, and Ninety-Six, he bore his part, and was always with his brave regiment under [John Eager] Howard, among the first to charge. At Ninety-Six his captain (the late Major Gen. [Perry] Benson) received a dangerous wound, but regardless of nothing but opposing the enemy, he forgot his commander until ordered to take him to the surgeon. Though Benson was considerably above the common size, he carried him on his shoulders some distance to the place at which the surgeon was stationed; but, like a true soldier, held on to his musket that had so often protected him in the hour of danger. At length, overcome by excessive fatigue and heat, as he laid

> the almost lifeless body of Benson at the feet of the surgeon he fainted. After he came to himself he determined to join his regiment again, but to his great mortification was peremptorily ordered by the commanding officer to remain, and protect his captain, which he did with care and tenderness. For this kindness and attention, Benson never forgot him, and, whenever he came to this country, invariably paid his first visit to Tom, and while reviewing the militia, would always have him mounted on a horse at his side.
>
> As the infirmities of age advanced, he began to feel the necessity of pecuniary aid, and at the instance of General [William] Potter of this county, who was then a member of our state legislature, he was granted a pension without a dissenting voice, and shortly afterwards received one from the United States, which enabled him to live in comfort the rest of his life. He was better than six feet high and well made in proportion, and in early life was a man of great physical powers. Few men of his color ever conducted themselves with more propriety, and whenever met by those who knew him, he was sure to receive a cordial greeting.

Such would be as fine an epitaph for any soldier of that war, but that it was written and published for a Black Patriot with no high military office, civil title, and little property to his name makes it all the more remarkable.

While there is much available for the modern historian to explore on the topic of the Black Patriots (my research files reached thirty-thousand-plus pages in two years' time), there is much more from their life and service to be learned and discovered. In the course of researching and writing this book, innumerable dead ends and mysteries were encountered.

One of those unsolved mysteries involves a Black Patriot from Springfield, Massachusetts, by the name of Archelaus Fletcher. His military service began in March 1776, and during his one-year term he served in the disastrous Canada campaign. Subsequently discharged, he was called up in response to the Saratoga alarm, serving three months until the surrender of Burgoyne and his army. There is very little information about him until he reappears in Ontario County, New York, years later. Archelaus and his son James appeared at the county courthouse in April 1812, asking a judge to document and affirm their status as freemen (slavery still being legal in New York at the time). The county judge gave them a certificate of freedom:

> State of New York Ontario County. I do hereby certify that Archelaus Fletcher, late of West Springfield in the State of Massachusetts now a resident of Canandaigua in the county of Ontario from the testimony of Moses Bissel, and his own affidavit, appears to be free according to the laws of this State that the said Archelaus is a tall black man, about six feet and an half high, fifty four years of age, last October, and that he was born in the town of West Springfield in the State of Massachusetts, and that he was born free. As witness my hand at Canandaigua, this 25th day of April 1812, one of the Judges of the court of Common Pleas in and for the county of Ontario in the State of New York.
>
> Moses Atwater

The document was recorded by the court and is available on the county's website today. That such a certificate would be necessary says something about the times and circumstances that Black Patriot veterans regularly experienced and how foreign it is to us today.

Archelaus Fletcher applied for and received a federal pension in 1818. A notation in the 1837 pension roll records his death, but that is clearly in error as his name and payments made to him by the federal government are recorded the following year and afterward. He, his wife Matilda, and four of their children appear in the 1850 Census in Naples, Ontario County, New York. In the 1860 Census, Archelaus is living with his two sons and a daughter in Italy, Yates County, New York. Two of his sons, Martin Van Buren and Charles, enlisted during the Civil War in the Twenty-Sixth US Colored Troops, and both of them died in the service. Martin Van Buren Fletcher died on August 18, 1864, and his brother Charles Fletcher died several months later on November 7, 1864. Both are buried at the Beaufort National Cemetery in South Carolina.

At some point, Archelaus became a ward at the county poor home. Remarkably, that is where a reporter for the *Rochester Express* found him in late 1875 or early 1876—more than a decade after the conclusion of the Civil War. What is remarkable is that if this story is correct, Archelaus Fletcher would be the last known living Revolutionary War veteran. Daniel Bakeman of Freedom, New York, died on April 5, 1869, and is generally considered the last living Revolutionary War pensioner. The article states:

> Fletcher can read and write, is temperate, eye sight good, and does light work about the county house. He does not remember ever seeing Washington, but says he drank some of the tea that was "spilled" in Boston Harbor. Fletcher has been married twice, and says he has been the father of twenty-five children—twenty-four boys and one girl. His wives and several children died many years ago; but he has no knowledge of the whereabouts of the other children, if any are yet alive… His statements are believed to be truthful by those who know him. Prof. Noel T. Clark, principal of the Canandaigua academy, knows Fletcher, and has no doubt of his being the full age he claims—113

> years. His health is good, and he bids fair to live many years yet. Preparation has been made to take him to Philadelphia next Fourth of July.

Sadly, he didn't make it to the centennial Independence Day celebrations, dying just two weeks before the celebrations on June 18, 1876. He was buried in the County Home Cemetery in Canandaigua, New York.

There are still many facts that need to be confirmed, as dates and spellings don't always match in this case, such as references to Fletcher as Archelaus, Arkless, and even Richard—a testament to the problems of different spellings and missing documents that can plague any investigation into our country's earliest decades. But if the last living Revolutionary War soldier was a Black Patriot, that is an important and fascinating detail to add to our American history as a permanent reminder of the pervasive presence of thousands of Black Patriots in securing American independence. A handful of historians and researchers have done yeoman's work trying to tell the stories of these American heroes, yet there are considerably more stories to discover and tell.

The service, sufferings, and sacrifices of the Black Patriots of the American Revolution to secure a better future for themselves and for future generations demand the attention they justly deserve.

New-Haven County adjourned Superior Court, A. D. 1784.

Jack Arabas *verſ.* Thomas Ivers.

THE caſe was—Jack was a ſlave to Ivers, and enliſted into the continental army with his maſter's conſent—ſerved during the war, and was diſcharged. Ivers claimed him as his ſervant; Jack fled from him *to the* caſtward, Ivers purſued him, and took him and brought him to New-Haven on his return *to* New-York, where he belonged, and for ſafe-keeping while he ſtayed at New-Haven, he got the gaoler to commit Jack to priſon; and upon Jack's application to the court, complaining of his being unlawfully and unjuſtly holden in priſon, the court iſſued a habeas corpus, to bring Jack before the court; alſo ordering the gaoler to certify wherefore he held Jack in priſon; which being done, Ivers was cited before the court; and upon a ſummary hearing, Jack was diſcharged from his impriſonment, upon the ground that he was a freeman, abſolutely manumitted from his maſter by enliſting and ſerving in the army as aforeſaid.

Contemporary court reporting on the case of Jack Arabus, a slave who enlisted in the Connecticut Line with the promise of his freedom. Having served his term, an attempt was made to re-enslave him, prompting his escape. When captured, he was imprisoned in the jail in New Haven. Arabus appealed to the courts, who heard his case and ordered him freed. This case was recently cited by the US Supreme Court. (Image: Internet Archive)

Daguerreotype of Agrippa Hull, dated March 18, 1844. Hull fought at Saratoga and became the orderly and close friend of Polish engineer Col. Thaddeus Kosciuszko. The two men worked together to establish the defenses at West Point and later participated in the Southern Campaign. They reunited in 1797 on Kosciuszko's return to America. Hull married an escaped slave in 1785 and became a significant landowner in Western Massachusetts. He is buried at the Stockbridge Cemetery in Stockbridge, Massachusetts. (Images: Stockbridge Library Museum and Archives; Patrick S. Poole)

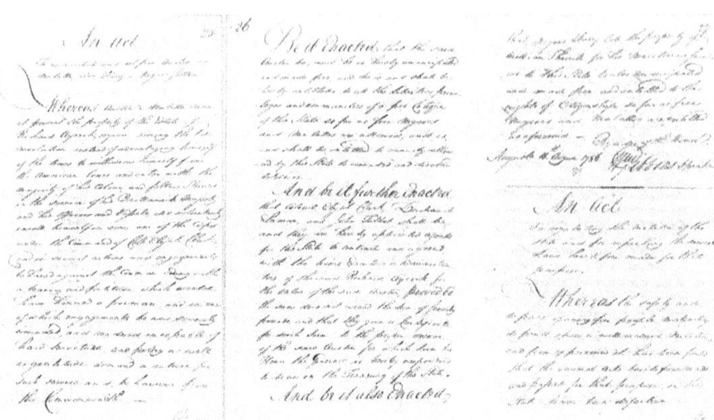

An act of the Georgia General Assembly manumitting Austin Dabney from slavery for his service during the Revolutionary War. He had been badly wounded at the siege of Augusta. The act was approved on August 14, 1786. The legislature subsequently approved a land grant for Dabney's support in 1821. (Image: Georgia State Archives)

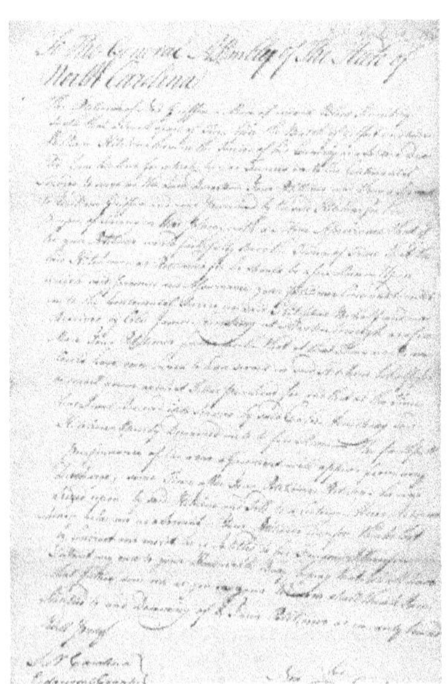

Shortly before the Battle of Guilford Courthouse, William Kitchen had deserted the field and sent his slave, Edward "Ned" Griffin as a substitute. Following Griffin's discharge in 1782, he was re-enslaved by Kitchen. After the conclusion of the war, Griffin petitioned the North Carolina legislature for his freedom on April 4, 1784, which was approved, securing his release from slavery on May 15, 1784. (Image: State Archives of North Carolina)

This is to Certify that the Bearer by the Name of James Has done Essential Services to me While I Had the Honour to Command in this State. His Intelligences from the Enemy's Camp were Industriously Collected and More faithfully delivered. He perfectly Acquitted Himself with Some Important Commissions I Gave him and Appears to me Entitled to Every Reward his Situation Can Admit of. Done Under My Hand, Richmond November 21st 1784.
Lafayette

Portrait of James Armistead Lafayette after the painting by John B. Martin (ca. 1824), with a reproduction of the letter given to him by the Marquis de Lafayette certifying his Continental service in support of his legislative appeal for his freedom. (Image: Library of Congress)

The tombstones of Tobias Cutler and Jude Hall in the Winter Street Cemetery, Exeter, New Hampshire. Cutler was a slave who received his freedom after enlisting in the Second New Hampshire in 1779, serving until the end of the war. He became a prominent leader in helping the free Black community in Exeter. Jude Hall enlisted on May 10, 1775, and fought at Bunker Hill. He was one of the most battle-hardened Black Patriot veterans in the Continental Army, serving until the end of the war. Sadly, three of his adult male children were illicitly abducted and enslaved, never to be heard from again. Three of his grandchildren served in the US Colored Troops during the Civil War. (Images: Patrick S. Poole)

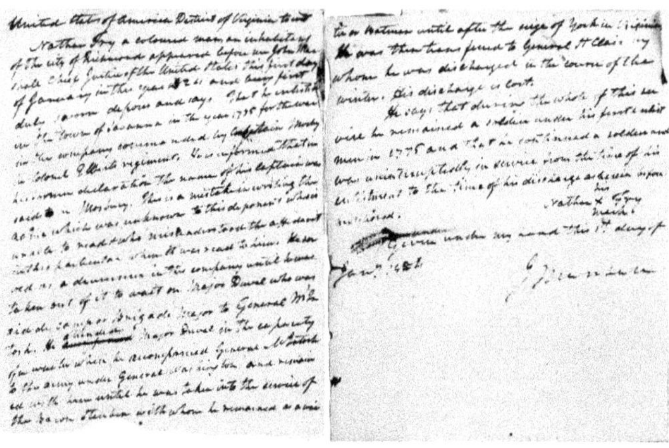

Deposition of Nathan Fry taken in Richmond, Virginia, by sitting US Chief Justice of the Supreme Court John Marshall in January 1821. Fry was a Black Patriot who enlisted in 1775 in Savannah, Georgia, and served nearly the entire war. Most of his service was spent in the military family of General Baron von Steuben. Chief Justice Marshall, a Revolutionary War veteran himself, took Fry's deposition in aid of his successful pension application. (Image: National Archives)

Affidavit of Joseph Story, Associate Justice of the US Supreme Court, in support of the pension application of Manuel Soto, a Black Patriot who had served in the famed Marblehead Regiment with Story's father. (Image: National Archives)

The graves of Timothy Cesar, Jeff Liberty, and Philemon Freeman, all of whom were in a Connecticut all-Black Patriot company commanded by Captain David Humphrey, one of Washington's aides-de-camp. Timothy Cesar is buried at Grove Street Cemetery in New Haven; Jeff Liberty at Old Judea Cemetery in Washington; and Philemon Freeman lies in the Old North Burying Grounds in Middlefield, all in Connecticut. (Images: Patrick S. Poole)

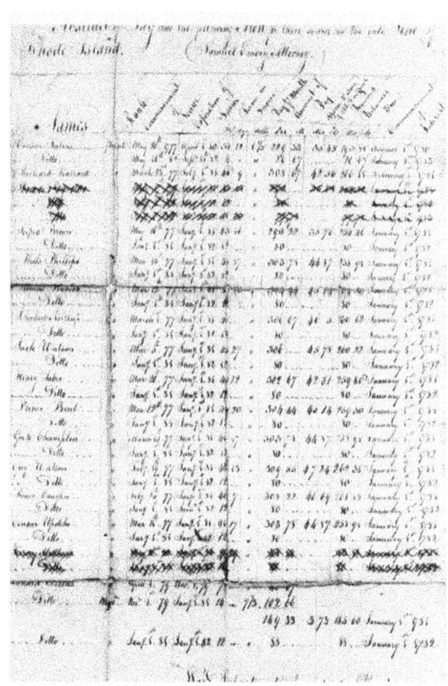

An accounting from the War Department showing the back wages due to Black Patriot members of the Rhode Island Line who had enlisted in 1777—one year before the formation of the all-Black First Rhode Island Regiment. All of these men would have likely served at the Battles of Red Bank, Monmouth, Rhode Island, Yorktown, and the failed Oswego Expedition. They did not receive their back wages until June 1794, and only with the assistance of an attorney. (Image: National Archives)

CONCLUSION

WHEN I BEGAN THIS PROJECT more than three years ago, there was no way to tell where it would take me. My working supposition was that anywhere that I wanted to look for Black Patriots in the American Revolution, I was likely to find them. When I saw their presence by the dozens at Bunker Hill, not even two months into the conflict, I assumed their participation in the quest for American independence would have grown. That hypothesis proved true beyond expectation. What I discovered is that from the first shots at Lexington Green to the last skirmishes preceding the British evacuation at the end of the war, they were there. Thanks to the noble efforts of scholars, historians, and researchers in recent decades, and the online availability of service records and pension files, the ever-present contributions of Black Patriots to the founding of America can be firmly documented. This book is an attempt to aid in that documentation.

In the last weeks of writing this book I was in New England documenting the graves of several dozen Black Patriots. Of the thousands who served in the Revolutionary War, most lie in unknown or unmarked graves. Many of the early African-American burial grounds have been lost to time, and the graves of brave and faithful Patriots forever lost with them. Frequently these graves would be marked with little more than field stones with the initials of the decedent's name roughly carved on them. Vandalism sometimes aids in their disappearance where neglect and development have yet to take hold. Some recent efforts have seen government military markers installed where the graves are known but have gone unmarked. Notwithstanding those efforts, less than two hundred graves of Black Patriots were able to be identified and documented for this work (the results of which can be found in Appendix 7).

There is a parallel here to the history of Black Patriots. For many there is little more to speak of their service than notations on muster rolls and marks on voided payment vouchers. As for the stories of their experiences in the fight for American independence or their lives after the war, with precious few exceptions, that history is lost to us. That makes preserving what history we do have available all the more imperative.

The epitaphs on two Black Patriot graves I visited one day on that trip stood out. The first was that of Pomp Lovejoy of Andover, Massachusetts. His gravestone in the South Church Cemetery is only one of two in the churchyard marking former slaves. Though at the time of burial his grave was located in the potter's field (the cemetery has since has grown around it), his is a tall hand-carved slate stone still in good condition after two centuries. His epitaph reads:

> Born in Boston, a slave
> Died in Andover a freeman.
> Much respected as a sensible
> Amiable and upright man.

A flag holder for Revolutionary War veterans also marks his grave as a testament to his service. He was one of 329 members of the Andover militia that responded to the Lexington Alarm. Marching with Pomp Lovejoy was Salem Poor, later one of the heroes of Bunker Hill. Both men had purchased their freedom years before. They arrived in Lexington after the bloody arrival of the British and joined in the running battle with other responding militia units chasing the redcoats back to Boston on the Battle Road. Pomp Lovejoy was paid for one and a half days for his militia service. Existing town records don't record any further service, but when the call came and his town needed him, he was there to aid in the defense of his community. A pond in Andover near his former property is named for him.

Sharper Freeman rests in Laurel Hill Cemetery in Reading, Massachusetts. He enlisted in 1780, serving his term in Massachusetts and New Jersey, and reenlisted in 1782 for three years in the Seventh Massachusetts, serving until the end of the war. He settled in Reading and became a farmer. His epitaph records the dramatic transitions he experienced in life: "Kidnapped in Africa when about 16 years of age and enslaved. He was a soldier in our army of the Revolution for which he received his freedom and a pension. He died January 1, 1822 aged about 80 years."

This implies that Sharper was a slave when he first enlisted in the army and likely a freeman when he reenlisted. While his first term of service may have been involuntary, he thought enough of the fight for independence to increase his commitment to the cause; he wasn't just serving for his personal interest of obtaining his freedom but fighting for the possibility of independence and freedom and what they might hold for all Americans.

What strikes me about the epitaphs for both Pomp Lovejoy and Sharper Freeman is they document that in their lives personally, but also for their communities as a whole, the revolution had changed things. Both men had witnessed the end of slavery in Massachusetts which had previously oppressed them. Recall that the language in the state constitution that would be used to abolish slavery was approved in 1780 when the outcome of the war was still uncertain. Within a few decades, slavery had been abolished in half of the new states. What course would America have taken if the remaining states had also willingly abandoned that terrible scourge?

It wasn't until this manuscript had been sent off to the editors that I was involved in a conversation that illuminated why this book is needed and why continued research on this subject demanded. My partner, Kara, and I were in a meeting with a young professional woman when Kara told her about the book project and its forthcoming publication. She told us she was of both Black and Cherokee background and had many questions about what I had discovered about the Black Patriots, which I was glad to share. At the end of our meeting she asked me why I thought the story of the Black Patriots was important. Admittedly I was taken back and unprepared for such a direct question, but it got to the heart of why I had spent several years of my life researching and writing on the subject. After a few seconds thought, I replied, "I think it's important for you to know that you belong here. Your ancestors were part of the founding of this country, and you are as much an inheritor of America as anyone else." I believe that's true, and I'm grateful to have been put on the spot to sum it up concisely.

In our day, we have many narratives thrown at us to divide us. If you want to be aggrieved at the state of our country, there is no shortage of outrages to draw from to alienate us from one another. But stories that unite and inspire seem harder to come by. If by telling the story of the Black Patriots and their role in the War of Independence someone might feel less alienated from their country and our shared history as we all continue to move along in this great ongoing American political experiment, then I will feel my efforts here to be fully worthwhile. For all those who have occasion to read this book, I hope you experience some degree of the feelings of unity and inspiration intended by my efforts.

APPENDIX 1

BLACK PATRIOT PENSIONS AND BOUNTY LAND WARRANTS

S = Soldier
W = Widow
R = Rejected
DIS = Disability
BLWt = Bounty Land Warrant
VAS = Virginia State
SC = South Carolina State

Name	Number
Cato Abbott	S32625
Benajah Abro	S38104
Hamet Achmet	S38107
Adam Adams	S34623
Peter Adams	W15152
Thomas Addams	W13615
Cash Africa	BLWt5375
Absalom Ailstock	S6475
Charles Ailstock	VAS1056
James Ailstock	VAS1056
William Ailstock	VAS1060
Prince Ames	S23439
William Anderson	R203
Jack Anthony	BLWt297
James Anthony	S38494
Evans Archer	S41415
James Arcules	S32658
John Artis	S41416
Gad Asher	S17244
Cuff Ashport (Mitchell)	W27332
London (Lyon) Atis	W23468
Ceasar Augustus, Jr.	BLWt5363
Caesar Babcock	R339
Primus Babcock	S37698
Caesar Bagden	BLWt5465
Caesar Bailey (Dickinson)	R371
Prince Bailey (Dunsick)	W17230
Henry Bakeman	R400
Jacob Banks	S8056
John Banks	W5763
William Barber	S6572
Caesar Barnes	BLWt2102
Charles Barnett	S8048
Scipio Bartlett	R4010
Simon (Simeon) Barton	BLWt2976
James Bass	S1745
Benoni Bates	S38515
Sampson Battis (Moore)	S13961
Shadrach Battles	S37713
Shadrach Battles	VAS1821
Lodowick Beach	R706
Samuel Bell	S6598
Cesar Beman (Beamont)	S39190
Brister (Bristol) Bennett	W24654
Abel Benson	W23574
Prince Bent	S38541
Solomon Bibbie (Bibby)	S6644
John Biddie	S10374
Peter Biddy (Biddie)	SC AA 480
Silas Bingham	S2076
Reuben Bird	S37776
Cato Black	W17313
Jacob Black	S9281
Martin Black	S41441
Jacob Blake	S34654
Elisha Boon	S35196

Lewis Boon	S6683
Willis Boon	S41455
Cato Boose	S15342
Peter Boston	W3650
Spencer Boulton (Bolton)	R995
Charles Bowles	S44640
Abraham Bowman	W396
Giels Bowry	VAS2587
James Bowser	BLWt2001
Jeffrey Brace (Stiles)	S41461
Thomas Brandom (Brandon)	W4643
Sampson Bray	S28659
Joshua Brewington	S8091
Aaron Brister	W17341
John Brister	W20772
Benjamin D. Brooker (Cain)	S34080
John Brooks	S6732
Francis Brown	S45610
Isaac Brown	S39214
James Brown	S3066
Joseph Brown	W1543
Joshua Brown	S21661
Samson Brown	DIS
Scipio Brown	S38584
Bristol Budd (Sampson)	W25304
George Buley	W27576
Jeremiah Bunch	S17867
Francis Bundy	S37799
Silas Burdoo	S21099
George Burk (Burke)	S32152
Fortune Burnix	BLWt3796
Seymour (Semo) Burr	W23726
John Busby	SC1
Samuel Bush	S36450
John Butler	S41463
Nace Butler	R1549
Darius (Deras) Cady	BLWt3900
Levi Caesar (Caezer)	S39269
Medford Caldwell	S39277
Thomas Camel	R1609
Sharp Camp	S37821
Jim Capers	R1669
Thomas Carney	S35203
Aaron Carter	W22726
Isham Carter	S39293
James Carter	S9162
John Carter	R1749
Moses Carter	S41470
Joseph Case	S41472
William Case & John Case	BLWt1826
William Casey (Kersey)	W29906.5
Henry Cato	R1815
James Causey	VAS1078
Julius Cezar	R1822
Cuff Chambers (Blanchard)	W23810
Edward Chambers	S34684
York Champlin	S34689
Caesar Chapman	BLWt5565
Edward Carter Chappel	W20850
Charles Charity	S39317
John Chavis	VAS1907
Lazarus Chavis	S9316
Anthony Chavers (Chavors)	R1889.5
Isaac Chavos	VAS1742
Corydon Chesley	S45635
Wentworth Cheswell	W24831
Anthony Clark	W9388
Arthur Clark	BLWt892
Beriah Clark (Clarke)	S34209
Caesar Clark (Negro)	S37871
William Clarke	W6687
Primus Coburn	S34703
John Cockran	S39353
Obed Coffin	W14569
Salem Colby	S38619
Tobias Cole	S40849
Daniel Coleman	No number
Edward Coleman	R2160
Francis Coley	S3197
Jeffrey Coley (Cooley)	W4160
John Collins	W6736
Mason Colllins	S39355

Abraham (Abram) Cook	S5019	Prince Du plex	W16963
John Cook	S45694	Domine Earl	S16776
James Cooper	S39362	James Easton	DIS
Cato (Cader) Copeland	W17665	William Ebet (Ebit)	W8204
William Couch (Freeman)	R2358	Anthony (Tony) Edor	W7073
Richard Cozzens	W9817	John Ellis	S32223
Jeremiah Crocker	S12619	John Epps	S8423
Oliver Cromwell	S34613	Thomas Evans	VAS1084
Prince Crosley	W24833	James Fergus	W25573
Sawney Crosley (York)	S36862	Andrew Ferguson (Furgason)	S32243
Nero Cross	S39370	David Ferguson	S35925
Gustavus Croston	S39379	John Ferrell	S6836
Cato Cuff	S36487	John Ferrit	S34845
Samson (Sampson) Cuff	S34516	Thomas Fisher	W21121
William Cuff (Coff)	S39347	Cato Fisk	W14719
Charles Cuffey (Cuffee)	W9402	Archelaus Fletcher	S44822
Elisha Curtis	BLWt3869	William Flora (Florey)	VAS3604
Tobias Cutler (Cuttler)	S45710	Richard Fortune (Putnam)	S37933
Austin Dabney	GA14	Cato Foster	BLWt4118/W7305
London Dailey	W5260	Peter Foster	W14745/R3691
Prince Danford	S43472	Bacchus (Bachus) Fox	BLWt5764
Dolphin Dart	S36496	Robert Fox	BLWt2177
Solomon Davids	S38651	John Foy	S29802
Edmond Davis	W3393	Jacob Francis	W459
Cato Dawes (Daws)	BLWt99	Jacob Francis (SC)	R2160
George Day	VAS1082	Andrew Frank	S21207
David Denham	W27540	Joshua Frank	S37945
Hardin (Heardin) Denham	S30985	William Frank (Franck)	BLWt3127
Elias Dewey	R2912	Andrew Frashur (Frazier)	S13079
Francis DeWitt	R2919	George Freeborn	BLWt1402
Scipio DeWolf	W2562	Cato Freedom	S44849
George Dias	S42161	Dick Freedom	BLWt590
James Diner (Dinah)	S37891	Ned Freedom	S37946
Earl Doming	S16776	Prince Freedom	S39549
Henry Dorton	S5362	Andrew Freeman	S34884
James Due	S34771	Artillo Freeman	S44853
Joshua Dunbar	W19198	Asher Freeman	S34890
Samuel Dunbar	S15106	Call Freeman	S36513
Frank Duncan (Dunkins)	S34773	Caser (Caser) Freeman	S43567
Cato Dunsett (Gray)	W14659	Charles Freeman	S38711
Prince Dunsick (Bailey)	W17230	Chatham Freeman	S36524

Cuff Freeman	W19298
Cuff Freeman	S36522
Devonshire Freeman	S36519
Doss Freeman	W14760
Edmund Freeman (Freedom)	S18825
Fortune Freeman	S43572
Francis Freeman	S35951
Jack (John) Freeman	S34889
Jethro Freeman	S36520
John Freeman	S36517
Juba Freeman	BLWt5785
Peter Freeman	S36516
Peter Freeman (2nd)	S36521
Philemon (Philo) Freeman	S36523
Plymouth Freeman	S44852
Primus (Primas) Freeman	BLWt5802
Prince Freeman	S39549
Providence Freeman	W739
Samson (Sampson) Freeman	S17419
Sharper Freeman	S34891
Nathan Fry	S39545
Winsor Fry	S38709
Titus Fuller	W21501
Sharper Gardner	BLWt619
Thomas Gardner	W7500
Anthony Garnes (Garner)	S38723
John George	W13248
Prince George	S43594
Peter Gibbs	BLWt5869
Charles Gibson (Gipson)	S41575
Joel Gibson	S35968
John Gibson	S3395
Thomas Gibson	S8560
Wilbourne Gibson	R4000
Anthony Gilman	S32729
Israel Glines	W1851
Caesar Glover	S32738
Caesar Godfrey	S32739
David Goens	S3406
Abraham Goff	S39596
Daniel Goff	S15586
Samuel Goff	VAS3719
Zachariah Goff	W2730
Edward Going	S6899
Sherard Going	W7545
William Goings	W930
Levy Goins	R3865
Manuel Goodenough (Soto)	S32761
Prosper Gorton	S38741
Frederick Gowen (Going)	R4167
Jacob Gowen	S32273
Zephaniah Gowen	R4165
Charles Gowens	S31072
Simeon Grandison	S32776
Jehu Grant	R4197
Cato R. Greene	S38753
Cuff (Cuffe) Green (Greene)	S38758
Jack Green	S43631
Joseph Green	W27415
Prince Green	S38754
Robert Greene	S33268
Cato Greene	S38753
Gideon Griffin	W8877
Morgan Griffin	S18844
Cato Griger	W2731
William Guy	W17969
David Hall	S1823
Frederick Hall	R7569
Jude Hall	W23238
London Hall	BLWt3234
Primus Hall (Trask)	W751
Isaac Hammond	W7654
Prince Hammond	BLWt3237
John Hammonds	S8654
George Harman	BLWt1361
Lazarus Harman	S34911
Edward Harmon	S36000
Drury Harris	SC2077
Edward Harris	R4649
James Harris	S38006
James Harris	W11223
Jesse Harris	W1277

John Harris S37997
Sherwood Harris W3984
Pharo Hart S34392
Peter Hartless S5470
Willliam Hartless S5498
Charles Haskell S38817
James Haskins W19732
Job Hathaway BLWt1931
James Hawkins S37991
Joseph Hawley W19686
Nero Hawley S20784
Levi Hazard S44397
London Hazard S17463
Peter Hazard BLWt3235
Sampson (Samson) Hazard BLWt3236
Thomas Hazard S29213
Jeffrey Hemenway (Hemingway) W19757
Holiday Hethcock (Hathcock) R4812
John Hathcock VAS1821
Prince Hazeltine S33282
Ephraim Hearn S38020
James Heathcock S2613
Monday Hecktor W13441
Micajah Hicks W7738
Henry Hill S41639
Primus (Ebenezer) Hill S43677
Richard Hill S39687
Prince Hinkley W14906
Lewis Hinton S10831
Major Hitchens S36017
Benjamin Holly W8941
Jacob (Jesse) Holly W21388
Titus Homer (Hosmer) S38834
Charles Hood S41659
William Hood W25781
Edward Hopps (Jeremy) W10111
Prince Hotchkiss BLWt5909
Cato Howe W2354
Robert Howel VAS1620
David Howland (Spencer) W22290
Fortune Howland S32861
Agrippa Hull W760
Prince Hull S36596
Benoni Hunt S44954
Elisha Hunt S13486
Hardy Hunt VAS1822
James Huzzey W18091
Adam Ivey R5507
Ebenezer Jacklin S32891
Abednego Jackson S10909
William Jackson W7877
Primus Jacobs S41688/W21446
Zachariah Jacobs W5304
Jamaica James S44984
Jeremiah James W467
Allen Jeffers S1770
Berry (Benjamin) Jeffers W10145
Drewy (Drurie) Jeffrey S7067
John Jeffreys, Sr. S8754
John Jeffreys (Jeffers), Jr. W26158
Prince Jenks (Jencks) BLWt3253
Peter Jennings S4436
Bristol Johnson W20207
Joseph Johnson R5626
Peter Johnson S36643
Shubel (Shubal) Johnson BLWt6018
Prince Johonnot S18057
Burwell Jones R6750
Fowler Jones R5701
Francis Jones S36653
Hardy Jones S41699
James Jones S41701
Jeremiah Jones S32924
Jethro Jones S32921
Tim Jones S18063
William Jones VAS1325
Calvin Jotham S35476
Luther Jotham W9911
Alexander Judd BLWt6029
George Kearsey R5801
Zack Kelsey S44478

George Kendall	R5859	Nicholas Manuel	R6887
Cato Kent (Negro)	S34392/W26169	Absalom Martin	S41800
Titus Kent	BLWt1665	Jesse Martin	R6949
George Kersey	R5801	Thomas Martin	S18964
James Kersey	S8788	Patrick Mason	S41810
John Key	W10163	Thomas Mason	R6993
David King	W20347	Peter McAnelly	S16467
Moses Knight (Sharper)	W10182	George McCoy	VAS416
George Knox	S40904	Pomp McCuff	S36084
Lamon Land	W20401	Malcolm McFee	R6709
Prime Lane (Coffin)	S44499	Pelatiah McGoldsmith	S36114
Job Lathrop	W10256	Bennett McKey	S38197
Benjamin Lattimore	S13683	James McKoy	S5750
Richard Leet	S38908	Prince McLellan	S37228
Cuff Leonard	S32982	James Mealey	S9408
Barzillai Lew	W20461	Boston Medlar	S38212
Ambrose Lewis	S36041	Peter Middletown	S36140
Morgan Lewis	S41766	Titus Minor	S36133
Peter Lewis	W17463	Isham Mitchell	W18510
Cuff Liberty	BLWt6110	Oliver Mitchell	W1632
James Liberty	BLWt6125	Peter Mix	BLWt6214
Pomp Liberty	BLWt1761	Jeremiah Moho	BLWt1991
Sharp Liberty	R7266	Ambrose Month	W7477
Prince Light	S44511	Caesar Morey	S38951
Prince Limas	BLWt3293	William Morgan	S9034
John Lines	W26775	Abraham Moore	S2855
Thomas Lively	S38144	Simeon Moore	S41960
Valentine Locus	W20497	Phillip Morris	S28815
William Lomack	S41783	Anthony Morrison	VAS761
Paul (Peter) Long	S44516	Cyphax Moseley	BLWt6146
Dick Loomis	BLWt6088	George Mozingo	S5783
William Loughry	W8263	Pero Mowrey (Mowry)	S38952
Robin Loyd	R6501	Milan Murphy	S33146
Peter Maguira (McGuire)	R6830	Mark Murray (Murry)	R7522
Pomp Magus	S33059	Mark Murray (Murril)	R7523
Thomas Mahorney	S38166	Robert Mursh (Marsh)	W8416
Wilmore Mail	S38171	Peter Nash	R7558
Ironmonger Major	VAS5474	Luke Nickelson	S37270
Dan Mallory	W25678	Richard Nicken	S5830
Moses Manley (Manly)	S41796	Hezekiah Nickens	VAS1120
Christopher Manuel	S7182	James Nickens	S38262

Malachi Nickens	S41925	Mingo Pollock	W17469
Robert Niles	S5828	David Pone	S7330
Bazabeel Norman	W5429	Jabez Pottage	S36241
Ichabod Northup	W20279	David Potter	S22445
Ichabod Nye	S9444	Richard Potter	R8380
Isaac Odell	W21863	Fortunatus Prescott	W22013
Emanuel Olvis (Alvis)	VAS339	Record (John) Primes	R8486
Joseph Otis	S27276	Job Primus	W10256
Jonathan Overton	S8915	Ammy Prince	S17027
Samuel Overton	S41928	Cato Prince	S33514
Robert Owls (Owl)	S36713	Philip Prince	S35580
Charles Pane (Paine)	S33418	Timothy Prince	S41079
Elisha Parker	S11211	Gideon Quash	R8539
Adam Pearce (Pierce)	S34468	Quamony Quash	R18097
Israel Pearce	S3660	Libbeus Quy	S36249
Abraham Peavy	W10880	Kenaz Ralls	S18561
Andrew Pebbles	S38297	Jack Rand	S41092
Edward Pellom	S36216	Jack Randall	S35593
Isaac Perkins	S41953	Robert Randall	S45165
Jacob Perkins	R8105	Joseph Ranger	S7352
Nimrod Perkins	S5904	Ezra Rathbun (Rathborne)	S40314
Galloway Peters	W18736	Thomas Ray	W13843
Jesse Peters	R8146	Warwick (Warrick) Ray	S35602
Peter Peters	S36210	Eber Raymond	S36250
Pomp Peters	S45062	John Redman	W5691
Robinson Peters	S11232	Richard Redman	S38327
Samuel Peterson	W26880	William Redman	R8645
Drury Pettiford	S41854	Abram Read	S7364
George Pettiford	W9223	Amariah Read	R8627
Philip Pettiford	S41952	Amos Read	R8628
William Pettiford	S41948	Benjamin Reed	S41976
Richard Pettigrew	S46639	Pomp Reeves	W12762
Jeruel Phillips	W17440	Sampson Reynolds (Raynolds)	S21442
Philip Phillips	W5532	Thomas Reynolds	W17524
Philo Phillips	S39013	Primus Rhodes	BLWt3457
Reuben Phillips (Philips)	W15214	Richard (Dick) Rhodes	W22060
Samuel Phillips	W21965	Samuel Rhodes	R8732
Stephen Phillips	R37	Benjamin Richardson	W4061
Francis Pierce (Pearce)	R8235	Charles Riley	R8824
John Pipsico	S36230	Job Ripley	W1487
Asher Pollock	BLWt3410	Cuff Roberts	S33586

Esek Roberts	W2351
Reuben Roberts	S39834
Richard Roberts	S38339
Amos Robinson	S36265
Benjamin Robinson	S41996
Cato Robinson	BLWt6406
Prince Robinson	R8894
Mingo Rodman	BLWt1687
Philip Rodman	S39835
Charles Roe	S7416
John Roe	S39045
Sharp Rogers	BLWt6384
John Rolls (Rawls)	S39056
Marlin Roorback	R6978
Peter Rouse	S23880
Jack Rowland (Freeman)	S17058
Peleg Runnels	W15295
George Russel	S39059
Samuel Russell (Rusel)	W26423
Brittain Saltonstall (Salterson)	BLWt3520
Edward Sands	W16148
Ceasar Sankee	S41124
Moses Sash	S36291
Philip Savoy	S35057
Prince Sayward	S27467
David Scott	S9473
Drury Scott	S35644
Exum Scott	W5994
Isham Scott	S42004
James Scott	S39064
John Scott	S46522
Shadrach Shavers	S38368
Samuel Shelly	S36306
Caesar Shelton	S19764
Lewis Shepherd	W24944
Pomp Sherburne	W17297
Ahimaaz Sherwin	S40424
John Sidebottom	W8775
Joseph Sidebottom	W8727
Benjamin Simmons (Black)	W24974
Cummy (Cumney) Simon	S36315
Simeon Simons (Simonds)	R9587
Jesse Sip	S36316
Cuff Slade	S33684
Primus Slocum (Slocumb)	S39844
Cuff (Cuffee) Smith	S36321
Caesar Smith	W19380
Lewis Smith	S6112
Thomas Smith	S21985
William Smothers	S38375
Edward Sorrel	W26493
James Sorrell	VAS1145
Thomas Sorrell (Sonell)	S6137
Aaron Spelman	S42023
Asa Spelmore (Spelman)	S42022
Thomas Spencer	W22285
Richard Spinner	S6140
Caesar Spragues	DIS
Richard Stanhope (Stanup)	R10049
Sallady Stanley	R10057
Prince Starkweather (William)	R10076
Robin Starr	S36810
Cato Stedman	BLWt6434
Thomas Steward	W4594
William Steward	S4890
Barney Stewart	S1727
Dempsey Stewart	W3734
Jordan (Jurdon) Stewart	R10160
Samuel Stewart	W7220
William Stewart (Steward)	R10173
Charles Stourman	R10240
Ned Streater	S7645
Barzillai Streeter	W16076
Daniel Strother	R10275
Joseph Sudwick	BLWt2312
Samuel Sutphen	R10321
Allen Swett	W16
Cicero Swett	S43189
Henry Tabor	W1331
Burrell Tabourn	S7694
Joel Taburn (Taborn)	S42037

William Taburn (Tabour)	W18115
Abraham Talbot	W22368
Drury (Drewry) Tann	S19484
Quom Tanner	S42445
Oxford Tash	W16155
Prince Taylor	S42463
Jacob Teague	S41235
Gamaliel Terry	W16755
Buckner Thomas	S41248
William Thomas	S38435
Cuff Tindy	S33804
Ishmael Titus	R10623
Job Tobias	BLWt1927
Arthur Toney	W4835
John Toney	W9859
William Tracy	S35362
Cato Treadwell	S35358
Plato Turner	S33832
George Tyler	S41276
Primus Tyng	R10795
Shadrach Underwood	S33849
Caeser Updike	S39871
James Updike	S22028
Daniel Valentine	R10820
Peter Valentine	R10820a
Luke Valentine	S6299
Plato Van Dorn (Vandorum)	BLWt3543
John Van Huff	S42575
Prince Vaughan	S42603
Benjamin Viers	S6313
Jeremiah Virginia	S19141
Drury Walden	R11014
Zebulon Wallis	R11083
Caesar Wallace	S43250
James Wallace	S7834
Joseph Wallace	R11068
London Wallace	W18290
Cato Wallingford	BLWt109
William Wanton	S22035
Solomon Washburn	W14108
Guy Watson	S39874
Jack Watson	S36366
Sipeo Watson	W18240
Thomas Watson	W22505
Aaron Weaver	VAS1140
John Weaver	S42061
Amintus Weeden	R11276
James Weeks	S33269
Cuff Wells	W18103
John Wheeler	W14148
Charles Whetmore	S11739
Sawney Whistler	VAS1162
Archelaus White	S43299
Cuff Whittemore	S33896
Arthur Wiggins	S7952
Benjamin Wilkins	R11545
Peter Willard	S34548
Daniel Williams	W11569
Hector Williams	BLWt6621
Henry Williams	W3638
Isaac Williams	R11577
Mathew Williams	S6414
Stacy Williams	S40688
David Wilson (Willson)	S35119
Javin Wilson	S35738
Zachariah Winn	S18286
John Womble	S42083
Jesse (Jessey) Wood	S7962
Robert Wood	S39909
Samuel Wood	S33945
Cornelius Woodmore	BLWt7957
Dan Woodman (Martin)	S44103
Asahel Wood	S33947
Pompey Woodward	W4867
Congo Zado	BLWt6721
Bristo Zibarre (Bibbere)	R11986

APPENDIX 2

BLACK PATRIOTS AT BUNKER HILL

MUCH OF THE RESEARCH on the Black Patriots who fought at Bunker Hill was conducted and documented by George Quintal Jr. in his study published by the National Park Service, *Patriots of Color: African Americans and Native Americans at Battle Road and Bunker Hill*. This present lists incorporates that research, adding some additional names that have been found and clarifying where those Black Patriots may have fought on the field that day.

REDOUBT

Phillip Abbot (KIA)
Capt. Benjamin Ames,
Col. James Frye

Caesar Bailey
Capt. Oliver Parker,
Col. William Prescott

Caesar Bason (KIA)
Capt. Abijah Wyman,
Col. William Prescott

Cuff Chambers
Capt. Charles Furbush,
Col. Ebenezer Bridge

London Citizen
Capt. Charles Furbush,
Col. Ebenezer Bridge

Sampson Coburn
Capt. Oliver Parker,
Col. William Prescott

Smith Coburn
Capt. Oliver Parker,
Col. William Prescott

Titus Coburn
Capt. Oliver Parker,
Col. William Prescott

Robert (Robin) Currier
Capt. John Currier,
Col. James Frye

Jacob Danforth
Capt. Reuben Dow,
Col. William Prescott

James Fiske
Capt. Oliver Parker,
Col. William Prescott

Cato Freeman (Liberty)
Capt. Benjamin Farnum,
Col. James Frye

Caesar Frye
Capt. Benjamin Farnum,
Col. James Frye

Scipio Gray
Capt. John Currier,
Col. James Frye

Pero Hall
Capt. Jonathan Evans,
Col. James Frye

Cuff Hays
Capt. Oliver Parker,
Col. William Prescott

Prince Hull
Capt. Oliver Parker,
Col. William Prescott

Prince Johonnot (WIA)
Capt. John Davis,
Col. James Frye

Barzillai Lew
Capt. John Ford,
Col. Ebenezer Bridge

Peter Oliver
Capt. Abijah Wyman,
Col. William Prescott

Chester Parker
Capt. Oliver Parker,
Col. William Prescott

Salem Poor
Capt. Benjamin Ames,
Col. James Frye

Caesar Porter
Capt. Charles Furbush,
Col. Ebenezer Bridge

Peter Poor (KIA)
Capt. Reuben Dow,
Col. William Prescott

Job Potamia
Capt. Benjamin Locke,
Col. Thomas Gardner

Titus Potamia
Capt. Ebenezer Bancroft,
Col. Ebenezer Bridge

Silas Royal
Capt. Jonas Richardson,
Col. James Frye

Marcus Shed
Capt. Charles Furbush,
Col. Ebenezer Bridge

Cato Tufts
Capt. Oliver Parker,
Col. William Prescott

Caesar Wetherbee
Capt. Oliver Parker,
Col. William Prescott

Cuff Whittemore (WIA)
Capt. Benjamin Locke,
Col. Thomas Gardner

Cato Wood
Capt. Edward Blake,
Col. Jonathan Brewer

Cuff Wood
Capt. Edward Blake,
Col. Jonathan Brewer

BREASTWORK

Tony Andrews
Capt. William Smith,
Col. John Nixon

Blaney Gerusha
Capt. Thomas Drury,
Col. John Nixon

Cato Hart
Capt. Thomas Drury,
Col. John Nixon

Jeffrey Hemenway
Capt. Thomas Drury,
Col. John Nixon

Caesar Quawco
Capt. Joseph Butler,
Col. John Nixon
Peter Salem
Capt. Thomas Drury,
Col. John Nixon
Cato Smith
Capt. William Smith,
Col. John Nixon
Archelaus White
Capt. Jeremiah Gilman,
Col. John Nixon
"Robin"
Capt. Jeremiah Gilman,
Col. John Nixon
"Scippio"
Capt. Jeremiah Gilman,
Col. John Nixon

DIAGONAL

James Arcules
Capt. Benjamin Bullard,
Col. Jonathan Brewer
James Huzzey
Capt. Moses Harvey,
Col. Jonathan Brewer
Charleston Lines (Lyndes)
Capt. Edward Blake,
Col. Jonathan Brewer
Cuff Nimrod
Capt. Thaddeus Russell,
Col. Jonathan Brewer
Jacob Speen
Capt. Thaddeus Russell,
Col. Jonathan Brewer

RAIL FENCE

Peter Brown
Capt. Ezra Towne,
Col. James Reed
Ezra Fuller
Capt. Ezra Towne,
Col. James Reed
Asaba Grosvenor
Capt. Jedediah Waterman,
Col. Israel Putnum
Jude Hall
Capt. Jacob Hinds,
Col. James Reed
Peter Kent
Capt. Hezekiah Hutchins,
Col. James Reed
Eden London
Capt. James Burt,
Col. Asa Whitcomb
Aaron Oliver
Capt. Ezra Towne,
Col. James Reed
Anthony Shaswell
Capt. Jonathan Davis,
Col. Asa Whitcomb
Nathan Weston
Capt. Ezra Towne,
Col. James Reed

OTHERS

Joseph Anthony
Capt. Luke Drury,
Col. Jonathan Ward
Mark Anthony
Capt. Jacob Gerrish,
Col. Moses Little
Peter Ayres
Capt. Andrew Haskell,
Col. Asa Whitcomb
Isaiah Barjonah
Capt. Benjamin Locke,
Col. Thomas Gardner
Pompey Blackman
Capt. John Baker,
Col. Samuel Gerrish

Jack Briant
Capt. Samuel Sprague,
Col. Samuel Gerrish
Micah Bumbo
Capt. Abijah Child,
Col. Thomas Gardner
Fortune Burnee
Capt. Luke Drury,
Col. Jonathan Ward
Prince Buxton
Lt. Daniel Galusha,
Col. Benjamin Woodbridge
John Chowen
Capt. Benjamin Hastings,
Col. Asa Whitcomb
Joseph Demas
Capt. Timothy Barnard,
Col. Moses Little
Thomas Dority
Capt. James Mellen,
Col. Jonathan Ward
Cato Fair
Capt. James Mellen,
Col. Jonathan Ward
Cato Green
Capt. Samuel Sprague,
Col. Samuel Gerrish
Jack Green
Capt. Samuel Sprague,
Col. Samuel Gerrish
Pomp Green
Capt. Samuel Sprague,
Col. Samuel Gerrish
Caesar Hammon
Capt. James Mellen,
Col. Jonathan Ward
Titus Hayward (Tuttle)
Capt. Abel Wilder,
Col. Ephraim Doolittle
Charles Jarvis
Capt. Benjamin Perkins,
Col. Moses Little
Plato Lambert
Capt. James Mellen,
Col. Jonathan Ward
Cornelius Lenox
Capt. John Wood,
Col. Samuel Gerrish
Peter Mitchell
Capt. John Baker,
Col. Samuel Gerrish
Cato Newell
Capt. Joseph Chadwick,
Col. Richard Gridley
Boston Osborn
Capt. Nathaniel Wade,
Col. Moses Little
Caesar Prutt
Capt. Reuben Dickinson,
Col. Benj. Woodbridge
Scipio Shaw
Capt. John King,
Col. Benjamin Woodbridge
Nathaniel Small
Capt. Barnabas Dodge,
Col. Samuel Gerrish
Prince Sutton
Capt. John Wood,
Col. Samuel Gerrish
Caesar Wallace
Unit unknown
Asahel Wood
Capt. Reuben Dickinson,
Col. Benj. Woodbridge
Eber Wood (Allis)
Capt. Reuben Dickinson,
Col. Benj. Woodbridge

APPENDIX 3

BLACK PATRIOTS AT SARATOGA

*Militia regiment +Died in Service

MASSACHUSETTS

"Cato"
Capt. Daniel Sackett,
Col. Ruggles Woodbridge

"Georges"
Capt. Samuel King,
Col. Thomas Marshall

Philemon (Phillip) Allen
Capt. Joshua Brown,
Col. Timothy Bigelow

Daniel Alvord
Capt. Oliver Lyman,
*Col. Ezra May**

James Anthony
Capt. Reuben Slayton,
Col. William Shepard

Joseph Anthony
Capt. John Blanchard,
Col. James Wesson

James Arcules
Capt. Moses Knapp,
Col. William Shepard

Prince Bailey
Capt. Seth Drew,
Col. John Bailey

+Isaac Barbadoes
Capt. Edward Munro,
Col. Timothy Bigelow

James Barrett
Capt. Edward Munro,
Col. Timothy Bigelow

Scipio Bartlett
Capt. Samuel Page,
Col. Benjamin Tupper

Brister Bennet
Capt. Isaac Warren,
Col. John Bailey

+Richard Black
Capt. Daniel Wheelwright,
Col. Benjamin Tupper

Pompey Blackman
Capt. Edmund Munro,
Col. Timothy Bigelow

Caesar Blake
Capt. Judah Alden,
Col. John Bailey

+Junior Boston
Capt. Silas Clark,
Col. Benjamin Tupper

Zachariah Bray
Capt. James Bancroft,
Col. Michael Jackson

Anthony Briffin
Capt. Amasa Soper,
Col. Thomas Marshall

Prince Brown
Capt. Samuel Carr,
Col. James Wesson

Prince Brown (2)
Capt. Elijah Deming,
*Col. John Ashley**

Sampson Brown
(WIA, cannonball to the hip)
Capt. Joseph Hodgkins,
Col. Timothy Bigelow
Eli Burdoo
Capt. Samuel Farrar,
*Col. Jonathan Reed**
Fortune Burnix (Fortin Barnix)
Capt. Amos Cogswell,
Col. James Wesson
John Chowen
Capt. Moses Brewer,
Col. Samuel Brewer
+Titus Coburn
Capt. Joshua Brown,
Col. Timothy Bigelow
Obed Coffin
Capt. Robert Miller,
Col. Joseph Vose
Caesar Cogswell
Capt. Benjamin Farnum,
Col. Benjamin Tupper
William Davison
Capt. Joseph Balch,
Col. Thomas Craft
Cato Dawes
Capt. William Gates,
Col. Timothy Bigelow
Peter Dego
Capt. John Chadwick,
Col. Samuel Brewer
Cuff Dole
Capt. Benjamin Adams,
*Col. Samuel Johnson**
Prince Douglass
(Killed in action, Sept. 19, 1777)
Capt. Isaac Warren,
Col. John Bailey
Fortune Ellery
Capt. Peter Page,
Col. Edward Wigglesworth
Archelaus Fletcher
Capt. John Morgan,
Col. Ruggles Woodbridge
Fortune Fogg
Capt. Isaac Warren,
Col. John Bailey
Cato Fortunatus
Capt. John Howard,
Col. Samuel Brewer
Cato Foster
Capt. Benjamin Farnum,
Col. Benjamin Tupper
Jupiter Free
Capt. Edward Munro,
Col. Timothy Bigelow
Asher Freeman
Capt. Nathaniel Winslow,
Col. Charles Marshall
Brister Freeman (Cuming)
Capt. John Buttrick,
*Col. Jonathan Reed**
Cato Freeman (Stedman)
Capt. Reuben Slayton,
Col. William Shepard
Cato Freeman
Capt. Moses Brewer,
Col. Samuel Brewer
Doss Freeman
Capt. James Bancroft,
Col. Michael Jackson
Fortune Freeman
Capt. Abraham Childs,
Col. James Wesson
Cato Frye
Capt. John Wiley,
Col. Michael Jackson
Thomas Gibbs
Capt. Moses Harvey,
Col. Ruggles Woodbridge

Tobias Gilmore
Capt. James Cooper,
Col. Samuel Brewer
Cato Gray
Capt. Hugh Maxwell,
Col. John Bailey
Joseph Green
Capt. Ephraim Burr,
Col. John Bailey
Primus Hall (Trask)
Capt. Samuel Flint,
*Col. Samuel Johnson**
+Prince Hall
Capt. Jacob Allen,
Col. John Bailey
Cato Hart
Capt. Robert Allen,
Col. Ichabod Alden
Jeffrey Hartwell (Jesse Freeman)
Capt. Edward Framer,
Col. Jonathan Reed
John Harvey
Capt. Stephen Buckland,
Col. Ebenezer Stevens
Job Hathaway
Col. William Shepard
+Titus Hayward
Capt. Edmund Munro,
Col. Timothy Bigelow
+David Hill
Capt. John Burnham,
Col. Michael Jackson
Richard Hill
Capt. Benjamin Brown,
Col. Michael Jackson
Samuel Hill
Capt. Benjamin Gardner,
Col. Rufus Putnam
Cato Howe
Capt. George Dunham,
Col. John Bailey

+Cato Hubbel
Capt. Jeremiah Miller,
Col. Joseph Vose
Agrippa Hull
Capt. John Chadwick,
Col. Samuel Brewer
Amos Hull
Capt. Joshua Benson,
Col. Rufus Putnam
Fleet Hull
Capt. William Moore,
Col. William Shepard
Thomas Hull
Capt. Reuben Slayton,
Col. William Shepard
Harvard Humphrey
Capt. Roswell Downing,
*Col. John Ashley**
+Cato Inches
Capt. Nathaniel Winslow,
Col. Charles Marshall
Pomp Jackson
Capt. Belcher Hancock,
Col. Joseph Vose
Robert Jackson
Capt. Richard Mayberry,
Col. Timothy Bigelow
Primus Jacobs
Capt. Samuel Page,
Col. Timothy Bigelow
Jamaica James
Capt. Daniel Lunt,
Col. Benjamin Tupper
Charles Jarvis
Capt. Moses Greenleaf,
Col. Benjamin Tupper
Benjamin Jones
Capt. Joseph Wadsworth,
Col. Gamaliel Bradford

Jethro Jones
Capt. Adam Martin,
Col. Timothy Bigelow
James Knox
Capt. Samuel Carr,
Col. James Wesson
David Lamson
Capt. Joseph Fuller,
*Col. Samuel Bullard**
Cuff Leonard
Capt. James Cooper,
Col. Gamaliel Bradford
Job Lewis
Capt. Samuel King,
Col. Thomas Marshall
+Charleston Lines
Capt. Robert Allen,
Col. Ichabod Allen
Eden London
Capt. William Warner,
Col. Thomas Marshall
John Lope
Capt. Jacob Allen,
Col. John Bailey
Pomp Magus
Capt. Joseph Fuller,
*Col. Samuel Bullard**
Drover Minor
Capt. John Russell,
Col. Gamaliel Bradford
Cambridge Moore
Capt. Stephen Russell,
*Col. Samuel Bullard**
Caesar Morey
Capt. Moses Knapp,
Col. William Shepard
+Ezra Negro
Capt. John Lamont,
Col. Gamaliel Bradford
Mark Negro
Capt. John Chadwick,
Col. Samuel Brewer
Peter Nelson
Capt. Samuel Farrar,
*Col. Jonathan Reed**
+Daniel Newport
Capt. John Chadwick,
Col. Samuel Brewer
Luke Nickelson
Capt. John Reed,
Col. Ichabod Alden
Britton Nichols
Capt. Theophilus Wilder,
*Col. Benjamin Gill**
Peter Oliver
Capt. Edmund Munro,
Col. Timothy Bigelow
Daniel Page
Capt. John Blanchard,
Col. James Wesson
Caesar Perry
Capt. James Cooper,
Col. Gamaliel Bradford
+John Peters
Capt. Amasa Soper,
Col. Thomas Marshall
Salem Poor
Capt. Nathan. Alexander,
Col. Ed. Wigglesworth
Brister Pratt
Capt. Ephraim Cleaveland,
Col. Michael Jackson
Caesar Prescott
Capt. George Minott,
*Col. Samuel Bullard**
John (Jack) Rand
Capt. Elijah Danforth,
Col. Thomas Nixon

Job Ripley
Capt. Abraham Watson,
Col. John Greaton
York Ruggles
Capt. Moses Ashley,
Col. Joseph Vose
Peter Salem
Capt. John Holden,
Col. Thomas Nixon
Moses Sash
Capt. Joseph Warner,
Col. Ruggles Woodbridge
Cato Shattuck
Capt. Paul Ellis,
Col. Timothy Bigelow
Scipio Shaw
Capt. Samuel Flint,
*Col. Samuel Johnson**
Lewis Shepherd
Capt. Silas Clark,
Col. Benjamin Tupper
+Nathaniel Small
Capt. Abraham Childs,
Col. James Wesson
Peter Smith
Capt. James Donnell,
Col. Samuel Brewer
William Smith
Capt. Noah Allen,
Col. Edward Wigglesworth
William Smith (2)
Capt. John Burnam,
Col. Michael Jackson
Sipio Solomon
Capt. Jacob Alden,
Col. Joseph Vose
Cato Stedman
Capt. Reuben Slayton,
Col. William Shepard
Zubal Stone
Capt. Peter Page,
Col. Edward Wigglesworth
Prince Sutton
Capt. Edward Munro,
Col. Timothy Bigelow
Oxford Tash
Capt. Moses Greenleaf,
Col. Benjamin Tupper
Caesar Thompson
Capt. Reuben Slayton,
Col. William Shepard
+Cuff Tilden
Capt. Seth Drew,
Col. John Bailey
Cuffey Townsend
Capt. Christ. Marshall,
Col. Thomas Marshall
Jethro Townsend
Capt. Moses Greenleaf,
Col. Timothy Bigelow
Jack Toy
Capt. Abraham Foster,
Col. Samuel Bullard
Ishmael Turner
Capt. Joshua Benson,
Col. Rufus Putnam
Thomas Turner
Capt. John Reed,
Col. Ichabod Alden
John Van Huff
Capt. Jeremiah Miller,
Col. Joseph Vose
Jeptha Ward
Capt. John Williams,
Col. Rufus Putnam
Charles Watts
Capt. Christ. Marshall,
Col. Thomas Marshall

John Webb
Capt. Job Whipple,
Col. Rufus Putnam
John Wheeler
Capt. John Reed,
Col. Ichabod Alden
+Abijah White
Capt. Caleb Keep,
Col. William Shepard
Peter Willard
Capt. Job Whipple,
Col. Rufus Putnam
Cuff Whittemore (POW)
Capt. Isaac Pope,
Col. William Shepard
+Thomas Williams
Capt. William Moore,
Col. William Shepard

NEW HAMPSHIRE
Peter Abbott
Capt. William Hawkins,
Col. Alexander Scammel
Cato Baker
Capt. John Drew,
Col. George Reid
Caesar Barnes
Capt. Amos Morrill,
Col. Joseph Cilley
Peter Blanchard
Capt. Peter Kimball,
*Col. Thomas Stickney**
Charles Bowles
Capt. Jeremiah Post,
*Col. David Hobart**
Peter Brewer
(Killed in action, Oct. 7, 1777)
Capt. Amos Morill,
Col. Joseph Cilley
Jesse Brown
Capt. Kimball Carleton,
*Col. Moses Nichols**
Wentworth Cheswell
*Col. John Langdon**
Primas Coffin
Capt. James Norris,
Col. George Reid
Tobias Cole
Capt. James Libby,
*Col. Stephen Evans**
John Cook
Capt. Frederic Bell,
Col. George Reid
Thomas Dunkin
Capt. John House,
Col. Joseph Cilley
Cato Fisk
Capt. William Rowell,
Col. George Reid
Jockey Fogg
Capt. Michael McClary,
Col. Alexander Scammel
Benjamin Fox
Capt. Mark Wiggins,
Col. Pierce Long
Oliver French
Capt. James Norris,
Col. George Reid
+Ezra Fuller
Capt. Isaac Frye,
Col. Alexander Scammel
Anthony Gilman
Capt. Nathaniel Hutchins,
Col. Joseph Cilley
Thomas Griffin
Capt. Daniel Runnels,
*Col. Moses Nichols**
Jude Hall
Capt. Elijah Clayes,
Col. George Reid

Pero Hall
Capt. John Noyes,
*Col. Samuel Johnson**
George Hayes
Capt. Daniel McDuffee,
*Col. Steven Evans**
Jesse Knott
Capt. Jason Wait,
Col. Joseph Cilley
George Knox
Capt. John House,
Col. Joseph Cilley
Paul Long (Jeness)
Capt. Isaac Frye,
Col. Alexander Scammel
+Cato Marcy
Capt. Jason Wait,
Col. Joseph Cilley
Dan Martin
Capt. William Rowell,
Col. George Reid
+Sidon Martin
Capt. Michael McClary,
Col. Alexander Scammel
Jonathan Miller
Capt. Isaac Frye,
Col. Alexander Scammel
Robert Miller
Capt. John House,
Col. Joseph Cilley
Fortune Moore
Capt. Michael McClary,
Col. Alexander Scammel
Cato Moulton
Capt. Isaac Frye,
Col. Alexander Scammel
Prince Negro (Thompson)
Capt. Ebenezer Frye,
Col. Joseph Cilley
William Nelly (Nelle)
Capt. Amos Morrill,
Col. Joseph Cilley
Derrick Oxford
Capt. John House,
Col. Joseph Cilley
+Pomp Peter
Capt. Michael McClary,
Col. Alexander Scammel
John Reed
Capt. Ebenezer Frye,
Col. Joseph Cilley
Reuben Roberts
Capt. Nathaniel Hutchins,
Col. Joseph Cilley
Prince Robinson (Light)
Capt. Zebulon Gilman,
*Col. Nicholas Gilman**
Cato Rogers
Capt. Elisha Shapleigh,
*Col. Joseph Storrs**
Isaac Tatten
Capt. Oliver Ashley,
*Col. Benjamin Bellows**
Caesar Wallace
Capt. Caleb Robinson,
Col. George Reid
Cato Wallingford
Capt. James Carr,
Col. George Reid
Gloster Watson
Capt. John Ward,
Col. George Reid
Samuel Wier
Capt. William Scott,
Col. Joseph Cilley
Prince Whipple
*Gen. William Whipple**
Archelaus White
Capt. Jesse Page,
*Col. Abraham Drake**

Pomp White
Capt. Nicholas Rawling,
*Col. Abraham Drake**
Samuel White
Capt. Nicholas Rawling,
*Col. Abraham Drake**
Dan Woodman
Capt. William Rowells,
Col. George Reid

NEW YORK
Marlin Brown (Roorback)
Capt. Barent Ten Eyck,
Col. Philip Van Cortlandt
Cornelius Woodmore
Capt. Charles Graham,
Col. Philip Van Cortlandt

CONNECTICUT
Bristol Budd
Capt. Stephen Betts,
Col. Samuel Webb
Prince Hull (WIA)
Capt. Jon. Wadsworth,
*Col. Thaddeus Cook**
John Lines
Capt. Nathaniel Wales,
*Col. Jonathan Latimer**
Samuel Phillips
Capt. Nathaniel Wales,
*Col. Jonathan Latimer**

APPENDIX 4

BLACK PATRIOTS WHO DIED AT VALLEY FORGE

Lonnon Rhode
15th Massachusetts
Died: December 9, 1777

Titus Hayward
15th Massachusetts
Died: December 14, 1777

"Jethro" from Guilford, CT
7th Connecticut
Died: December 25, 1777

Joseph Anthony
9th Massachusetts
Died: December 26, 1777

Jackson Hull
3rd North Carolina
Died: January 1778

James Going
10th Virginia
Died: January 1, 1778

Prince Free
1st Connecticut
Died: January 6, 1778

Thomas Pinn
1st Virginia State Regiment
Died: January 11, 1778

John Day
2nd North Carolina
Died: January 14, 1778

Cuff Tilden
2nd Massachusetts
Died: January 18, 1778

Cesar Cole
1st Rhode Island
Died: January 23, 1778

Richard Black
15th Massachusetts
Died: February 1, 1778

Brutus Johnston
10th North Carolina
Died: February 15, 1778

Josiah Munroe
4th Connecticut
Died: February 19, 1778

Pomp Free
1st Connecticut
Died: February 26, 1777

Peter Pomp
3rd New Hampshire
Died: March 15, 1778

Joseph Usurp
8th Connecticut
Died: March 22, 1778

John Peters
10th Massachusetts
Died: April 1778

George Frances
10th Virginia
Died: April 3, 1778

Prince Freeman
7th Connecticut
Died: April 5, 1778

Pomp Moss
8th Connecticut
Died: April 10, 1778

Titus Coburn
15th Massachusetts
Died: April 18, 1778

Titus Prescot
3rd Connecticut
Died: April 20, 1778

Prince Williams
1st Connecticut
Died: April 21, 1778

David Pomp
1st Connecticut
Died: April 28, 1778

Thomas Cezar
Spencer's Cont. Regiment
Died: April 30, 1778

John Pompey
1st Connecticut
Died: May 1, 1778

James Edwards
1st Rhode Island
Died: May 1, 1778

Prince Lipett
2nd Rhode Island
Died: May 1, 1778

Isham Reed
15th Virginia
Died: May 6, 1778

Tobias Pendall
1st Connecticut
Died: May 10, 1778

Richard Pomp
2nd Rhode Island
Died: May 13, 1778

Sylvanus Ames
1st Rhode Island
Died: May 15, 1778

John Goff
15th Virginia
Died: May 16, 1778

Jack Allen
1st Rhode Island
Died: May 18, 1778

Abraham Issacks
1st Rhode Island
Died: May 19, 1778

Cato Marcy
1st New Hampshire
Died: May 27, 1778

Francis Tiffts
1st Rhode Island
Died: June 1, 1778

Peter Bristol
1st Rhode Island
Died: June 6, 1778

Pomp Cuffwer
10th Massachusetts
Died: June 14, 1778

Primus Emanuel
8th Massachusetts
Died: June 11, 1778

Prince Jackson
1st Rhode Island
Died: June 11, 1778

William Archer
1st Rhode Island
Died: June 12, 1778

Amos Stedman
1st Rhode Island
Died: June 13, 1778

Pomp Cuffwer
10th Massachusetts
Died: June 14, 1778

Edward Negro
5th Connecticut
Died: June 15, 1778

Ezra Fuller
3rd New Hampshire
Died: July 14, 1778

Sipeo Solomon
2nd Massachusetts
Died: June 24, 1778

Caesar Stewart
4th Connecticut
Died: July 31, 1778

David Burnett
5th North Carolina
Died: Unknown

Jeffery Garnes
7th North Carolina
Died: Unknown

Kitchen Roberts
3rd North Carolina
Died: Unknown

"Robben"
7th Connecticut
Died: Unknown

"Frederick" (drummer)
2nd North Carolina
Died: Unknown

APPENDIX 5

BLACK PATRIOTS AT THE BATTLE OF MONMOUTH (1778)

THE FIRST ATTEMPT to compile a list of Black Patriots is found in Richard S. Walling's *Men of Color at the Battle of Monmouth, June 28, 1778* (1994). This present list significantly expands upon that work, yet only accounts for approximately half of the seven hundred Black Patriots who were identified in the brigades at Monmouth two months after the battle in the "Return of Negroes" compiled by Alexander Scammell at White Plains in August 1778. Therefore, this list is by no means complete.

NEW HAMPSHIRE

Peter Abbott
Capt. Zachariah Beal,
Col. Alexander Scammelll

Cato Baker
Capt. John Drew,
Col. George Reid

Caesar Barnes (Ceasor Burns)
Capt. Amos Morrill,
Col. Joseph Cilley

Caesar Black
Capt. Caleb Robinson,
Col. George Reid

Charles Bowles
Capt. Amos Emerson,
Col. Joseph Cilley

Scipio Brown
Capt. Amos Emerson,
Col. Joseph Cilley

Corydon Chesley
Capt. John Drew,
Col. George Reid

Cezar Clough
Capt. Caleb Robinson,
Col. George Reid

Primas Coffin
Capt. James Norris,
Col. George Reid

John Diamond
Capt. Caleb Robinson,
Col. George Reid

Cato Fisk
Capt. William Rowell,
Col. George Reid

Jockey Fogg
Capt. Michael McClary,
Col. Alexander Scammell

Anthony Gilman
Capt. Nathaniel Hutchins,
Col. Joseph Cilley
Jude Hall
Capt. Elijah Clayes,
Col. George Reid
Silvanus Hastings
Capt. Isaac Farwell,
Col. Joseph Cilley
Zach Kelsey
Capt. John Drew,
Col. George Reid
Thomas Kimble
Capt. William Scott,
Col. Joseph Cilley
George Knox
Capt. John House,
Col. Joseph Cilley
Jesse Knott
Capt. Jason Wait,
Col. Joseph Cilley
Dan Martin
Capt. William Rowell,
Col. George Reid
Jonathan Miller
Capt. Isaac Frye,
Col. Alexander Scammell
Robert Miller
Capt. John House,
Col. Joseph Cilley
Fortune Moore
Capt. Michael McClary,
Col. Alexander Scammell
Cato Moulton
Capt. Isaac Frye,
Col. Alexander Scammell
John Reed
Capt. Ebenezer Frye,
Col. Joseph Cilley
Reuben Roberts
Capt. Nathaniel Hutchins,
Col. Joseph Cilley
Prince Thompson
Capt. Ebenezer Frye,
Col. Joseph Cilley
Caesar Wallace
Capt. Caleb Robinson,
Col. George Reid
Cato Wallingford
Capt. James Carr,
Col. George Reid
Gloster Watson
Capt. John Drew,
Col. George Reid
Dan Woodman (Martin)
Capt. William Rowell,
Col. George Reid

MASSACHUSETTS

James Anthony
Capt. Reuben Slayton,
Col. William Shepard
James Arcules
Capt. Moses Knapp,
Col. William Shepard
Prince Bailey
Capt. Seth Drew,
Col. John Bailey
Scipio Bartlett
Capt. Samuel Page,
Col. Benjamin Tupper
Fortune Black
Capt. Daniel Lyman,
Col. Michael Jackson
Pompey Blackman
Capt. Edmund Munro,
Col. Timothy Bigelow
Brister/Bristol Bennett
Capt. Isaac Warren,
Col. John Bailey

+Caesar Boston
Capt. Reuben Slayton,
Col. William Shepard
+Junior Boston
Capt. Samuel Thomas,
Col. Benjamin Tupper
Comfort Chaffee
Capt. Jonathan Brown,
Lt. Col. William Smith
Peter Dego
Capt. John Chadwick,
Col. Samuel Brewer
Zerubbabel Eager
Capt. Daniel Barnes,
Col. Timothy Bigelow
Fortune Fogg
Capt. Isaac Warren,
Col. John Bailey
Doss Freeman
Capt. James Bancroft,
Col. Michael Jackson
Fortune Freeman
Capt. Abraham Childs,
Col. James Wesson
Tobias Gilmore
Capt. James Cooper,
Col. Samuel Brewer
Richard Hill
Capt. Benjamin Brown,
Col. Michael Jackson
Agrippa Hull
Capt. John Chadwick,
Col. Samuel Brewer
Pomp Jackson
Capt. Robert Davis,
Col. Joseph Vose
Jabez Jolly
Capt. John Russell,
Col. Gamaliel Bradford
Job Lewis
Capt. Samuel King,
Col. Thomas Marshall
Plato McClellan
Capt. Paul Ellis,
Col. Timothy Bigelow
Drover Minor
Capt. John Russell,
Col. Gamaliel Bradford
Jeremiah Moho
Capt. Isaac Pope,
Col. William Shepard
Pomp Peters
Capt. Josiah Smith,
Col. Thomas Marshall
Boston Phillips
Capt. William Gates,
Col. Timothy Bigelow
Salem Poor
Capt. Nathaniel Alexander,
Col. Edward Wigglesworth
Jabez Price
Capt. Nathaniel Cushing,
Col. Joseph Vose
Peter Salem
Capt. Thomas Barnes,
Col. Thomas Nixon
Cato Shattuck
Capt. Paul Ellis,
Col. Timothy Bigelow
+Nathaniel Small
(Died August 13, 1778; of wounds?)
Capt. Abraham Childs,
Col. James Wesson
Prince Sutton
Capt. Edmund Munro,
Col. Timothy Bigelow
Oxford Tash
Capt. Moses Greenleaf,
Col. Benjamin Tupper

Cato Wood
Capt. Amasa Soper,
Col. Thomas Marshall

CONNECTICUT

Benajah Abro (WIA)
Capt. Lemuel Clift,
Col. John Durkee

Cash Affrica
Capt. Eli Catlin,
Col. Philip Bradley

Bristol Baker
Capt. Joseph Mansfield,
Col. Return J. Meigs

Caesar Black
Capt. Josiah Childs,
Col. Philip Bradley

John Brister
Capt. Abner Prior,
Col. Philip Bradley

Bristol Budd (Sampson)
Capt. Stephen Betts,
Lt. Col. Isaac Sherman

Samuel Bush
Capt. Stephen Betts,
Lt. Col. Isaac Sherman

Edward Carter
Capt. Andrew Fitch,
Col. John Durkee

Esau Carter
Capt. Andrew Fitch,
Col. John Durkee

Bristol Caesar
Capt. Samuel Comstock,
Col. Joseph Hait

+Jack Congo
Capt. Eli Catlin,
Col. Philip Bradley

Prince Crosley
Capt. Ebenezer Hills,
Col. Heman Swift

Nero Cross
Capt. Elijah Humphrey,
Col. Return J. Meigs

Cato Cuff
Capt. Samuel Hait,
Col. Philip Bradley

Lemuel Cumber
Capt. Phineas Beardsley,
Col. Heman Swift

Caesar Edwards
Capt. James Beebee,
Col. Charles Webb

Dick Fortune
Capt. John McGreigier,
Col. John Durkee

Backus Fox
Capt. Andrew Fitch,
Col. John Durkee

Coll Freeman
Capt. Phineas Beardsley,
Col. Heman Swift

Cuff Freeman
Capt. Phineas Beardsley,
Col. Heman Swift

Silas Glasgow
Capt. Theophilus Monson,
Col. Joseph Hait

London Goodluck
Capt. Samuel Sanford,
Col. Joseph Hait

Jack Green
Capt. Josiah Child,
Col. Philip Bradley

Pharo Hart
Capt. Joseph Wright,
Col. Philip Bradley

Nero Hawley
Capt. James Beebee,
Col. Charles Webb

Prince Hodgkiss
Capt. Nehemiah Rice,
Col. Joseph Hait
Prime Hubbell
Capt. Phineas Beardsley,
Col. Heman Swift
Job Hull
Capt. Nehemiah Rice,
Col. Joseph Hait
Ebenezer Jacklin
Capt. Ezekiel Sanford,
Col. Philip Bradley
Caesar Jowler
(Died of wounds, August 7, 1778)
Capt. Sylvanus Brown,
Col. Joseph Hait
James Liberty
Capt. Samuel Mattocks,
Col. Joseph Hait
Peter Meranda
Capt. Samuel Sanford,
Col. Joseph Hait
Caesar Negro (Clark)
Capt. Beriah Bill,
Col. John Durkee
Ned Negro
Capt. Abner Prior,
Col. Philip Bradley
Plymouth Negro
Capt. Abner Prior,
Col. Philip Bradley
Prince Negro
Capt. Jonathan Parker,
Col. Isaac Sherman
Cuff Niger
Capt. Stephen Hall,
Col. Hemen Swift
Lemuel Pete
Capt. Ebenezer Hills,
Col. Heman Swift
Samuel Phillips
Capt. Ebenezer Hills,
Col. Heman Swift
Samuel Pompey
Capt. Christopher Darrow,
Maj. David Sill
Jabez Pottage (POW)
Capt. Thomas Converse,
Col. Heman Swift
Ebor Raymond
Capt. John McGreigier,
Col. John Durkee
Pomp Raymond
Capt. John McGreigier,
Col. John Durkee
+Thomas Sacket
Capt. Stephen Hall,
Col. Heman Swift
Caesar Negro (Shelton)
Capt. Beriah Bill,
Col. John Durkee
Prince Simbo
Capt. Ebenezer Hills,
Col. Heman Swift
Cesar Sipeo
Capt. John Harmon,
Col. John Durkee
Robin Starr
Capt. Theodore Woodbridge,
Col. Heman Swift
Ceasar Stewart
Capt. John McGreigier,
Col. John Durkee
Mingo Treat
Capt. Ebenezer Hills,
Col. Heman Swift
Sip Watson
Capt. Christopher Ely,
Maj. David Sill

Cuff Wright
Capt. John Harmon,
Col. John Durkee

VIRGINIA

Shadrack Battles
Capt. Clough Shelton,
Col. John Green

Sylvester Beverly
Capt. John Nichols,
*Col. George Gibson**

Thomas Camel
Capt. Wilson,
Col. John Nevill

Anthony Chavers
Unit information unknown

William Clarke
Capt. Thomas Willis,
Col. John Cropper

Daniel Cumbo
Capt. William Cunningham,
Col. Richard Parker

Thomas Evans
Capt. Henry Dudley,
*Col. Gregory Smith**

Daniel Goff
Capt. Thomas Willis,
Col. John Cropper

John Harris
Capt. Thomas Willis,
Col. John Cropper

Henry Hill
Capt. Reuben Lipscomb,
Lt. Col. William Heth

Thomas Lively
Capt. William Fowler,
Lt. Col. William Heth

Thomas Mahorney
Capt. Henry Garnett,
*Col. Gregory Smith**

Drury Pettiford
Capt. Henry Dudley,
*Col. Gregory Smith**

John Roe
Capt. Francis Taylor,
Col. Christian Febiger

Samuel Stewart
Capt. John Steed,
Col. John Nevill

William Thomas
Capt. John Anderson,
Col. Josiah Parker

Daniel Williams
Capt. George Rice,
Col. John Cropper

William Lee
Gen. George Washington

NORTH CAROLINA

Martin Black
Capt. Clement Hall,
Col. John Patten

Anthony Garnes
Capt. Lemuel Eli,
Col. James Hogon

Isaac Perkins
Capt. Clement Hall,
Col. John Patten

Benjamin Reed
Capt. Thomas Donoho,
Col. Hardy Murfree

William Stewart
Capt. Robert Fenns,
Col. John Patten

PENNSYLVANIA

Levi Burns
Capt. William Mackey,
Col. Richard Humpton

James Campbell
Capt. Joseph Erwin,
Col. Richard Butler
James Caruthers
Capt. Isaac Seeley,
Col. Francis Johnson
Josiah Crane
Capt. Samuel Moore,
Col. David Geier
James Hamilton
Capt. William Butler,
Col. Thomas Craig
Ned Hector
Capt. Francis Proctor,
Col. Thomas Proctor
Richard Lewis
Capt. George Jenkins,
Col. Henry Becker
John Nagel
Capt. Joseph Erwin,
Col. Richard Butler
William Price
Capt. Alexander Parker,
Col. David Geier
Peter Rice
Capt. John Murray,
Col. Henry Bicker
George Roberts
Capt. Henry Miller,
Col. Henry Bicker
Stacey Williams
Capt. Jacob Humphrey,
Col. Robert McGaw

NEW JERSEY

James Array
Capt. Henry Luse,
Col. Israel Shreve
John Caesor
Capt. William Bond,
Col. Ephraim Martin
Jonathan Cato
Capt. William Bond,
Col. Ephraim Martin
Oliver Cromwell
Capt. Nathaniel Bowman,
Col. Israel Shreve
Negro Cuff
Capt. Thomas Paterson,
Col. Elias Dayton
William Cuffey
Capt. Jonathan Phillips,
Col. Israel Shreve
Thomas Martin
Capt. Jonathan Forman,
Col. Ephraim Martin
Sambo Negro
Capt. John Anderson,
Col. Ephraim Martin
Adam Pierce
Capt. John Cumming,
Col. Israel Shreve
Amos Tomson
Capt. John Hollingshead,
Col. Israel Shreve

MARYLAND

Adam Adams
Capt. Henry Gaither,
Col. John Stone
William Balontino
Col. Thomas Price
Nace Butler
Col. Thomas Price
Thomas Carney
Capt. John Hawkins,
Col. William Richardson
Francis Freeman
Lt. John Hardman,
Col. Thomas Price

Boston Medlar
Capt. Daniel Stull,
Col. John Gunby
Bazabeel Norman
Capt. Richard Anderson,
Col. John Gunby
Christopher Poynos
Col. Thomas Price
James Price
Capt. James Jones,
Col. John Gunby

RHODE ISLAND

Anthony Ann
Edward Antony
Benedict Aaron
Hampton Barton
Ebenezer Caesar
James Carpenter
John Charles
Prince Childs
Tobey Coyes
James Dailey
Abraham Demus
Benjamin Frank
William Frank
Winsor Fry
Frank Gould
James Greene
Robert Greene
Anthony Griffin
Charles Hansley
Gideon Harry
Henry Hazzard
Pharo Hazzard
Robin Howland
Cuff Peckham
Jehu Pomp
Richard Potter
Thomas Reynolds
Richard Rhodes
George Rogers
Moses Rogers
George Sambo
Thomas Smith
Josiah Sole
Thomas Spencer
London Thompson
George Thomkins
Derrick Vanzover
Cato Varnum
Solomon Wanton
Pomp Watson
Primus Watson
Prince Watson
Jesse Willis
Capt. Thomas Arnold,
Col. Christopher Greene

DELAWARE

Edward Harmon
Capt. Robert Kirkwood,
Col. David Hall

NEW YORK

William Condo
Capt. Joseph McCracken,
Col. Goose Van Schaick

APPENDIX 6

BLACK PATRIOTS IN SOUTHERN CAMPAIGN

PORT ROYAL
(FEB 2, 1779)
Jim Capers

KETTLE CREEK
(FEB 14, 1779)
Austin Dabney
"Old Dick" Pickens

BRIER CREEK
(MARCH 3, 1779)
Isham Carter
Francis Coley
James Fergus
Zacharia Jacobs
Berry Jeffers
Nicholas Manuel
William Taburn
Drury Walden

STONO FERRY
(JUNE 20, 1779)
Thomas Bibby
Isham Carter
Joseph Case
Lazarus Chavis
Edward Harris
Lemerick Farr
Gideon Griffin
Hardy Jones
Ed Harris
William Lomack
Jesse Martin
Elisha Parker
Charles Roe (WIA – lost an eye)
John Tann

SIEGE OF SAVANNAH
(SEPT 19–OCT 16, 1779)
Shadrack Battles
Randal Bowers (died 10.10.1779)
Jim Capers
Isham Carter
Lazarus Chavis
Drury Harris
Edward Harris
Gideon Griffin
Drury Harris (WIA)
Edward Harris
Allan Jeffers
Moses Knight
Andrew Marshall
Israel Pearce
David Scott
John Womble
Henri Christoph
Monsier de Bordeaux

CHARLESTON
(MARCH 29–MAY 12, 1780)
Martin Black (POW, escaped)
Spencer Bolton (POW, escaped)
Jasper Browngaurd (POW)
Thomas Buckner (POW)

William Burnett (POW)
John Campbell
Isham Carter (POW)
John Edward Carter (POW/MIA)
Edward Chambers
Negro Charles (POW)
Cato Copeland (POW)
Edmond Davis (POW)
Bacchus Elliot
William Foster
Simon Fralix
John Freeman (died a POW)
Anthony Garnes (POW, escaped)
Abraham Goff
Gideon Griffin
Edward Harris
Ephraim Hearn (POW for 9mos, taken to NY escaped)
Micajah Hicks
Elisha Hunt (WIA - lost arm)
Adam Ivey (POW, paroled after 10mos, joined Gen. Marion)
Allan Jeffers
Berry Jeffers
Osbourne Jeffers (KIA)
Hardy Jones (POW)
William Kersey (POW)
Thomas Lively (WIA)
William Lomack (POW)
Nicholas Manuel
Bennett McCoy/McKey
Caleb Overton
Samuel Overton (WIA twice)
Israel Pearce (POW)
Isaac Perkins (POW)
Record Primes (POW)
Caesar Santee
Andrew Smith
Joel Taburn
Isham Valentine
John Weaver
Negro Wexford
Arthur Wiggins
Matthew Wiggins
"Capt" William Williams
John Womble (paroled until the end of war)
"Frances"
"Peter" (POW)

MONCKS CORNER (APRIL 4, 1780)

Edward Coleman
Gideon Griffin
Edward Harris

WAXHAWS/BUFORD'S DEFEAT (MAY 29, 1780)

William Clark
Asher Crockett/James Anderson
James Cooper
George McCoy (WIA, petitioned VA for leg wounds)
Robert Owls (WIA - head wound)

RAMSEUR'S MILL (JUNE 20, 1780)

John Chavis (WIA)

HUCK'S DEFEAT/BRATTONVILLE (JULY 11, 1780)

Watt Bratton

HANGING ROCK (AUG 6, 1780)

James Anderson
Asher Crockett
Ed Harris
"Henry"
Robert Owls
Israel Pearce

CEDAR SPRINGS
(AUG 8, 1780)
Benjamin Scott Mayes

MUSGROVE MILL
(AUG 18, 1780)
Lemerick Farr

CAMDEN
(AUG 16, 1780)
Adam Adams
Solomon Bibbie
Reuben Bird
Willis Boon
Thomas Carney
Isom Carter (POW)
James Carter (WIA)
Guinea Cato
Asher Crockett
Edmond Davis (POW)
Andrew Ferguson
Fortune Freeman
Francis Freeman
John Hammonds
Edward Harman
Edward Harris
James Harris
Adam Ivey (POW)
Tim Jones (POW)
George Kendall
Ambrose Lewis (WIA, POW)
Phillip Maroney
Thomas Mason
Ambrose Month
Bazaleel Norman
Record Primes (WIA)
Ed Sorrell
Lucas Valentine (WIA)
David Wilson

KINGS MOUNTAIN
(OCT 7, 1780)
Esais Bowman
John Broddy
Andrew Ferguson
Benjamin Mayes
Record Primes
Joseph Sidebottom
Ishmael Titus

FISHDAM FORD
(NOV 10, 1780)
"Moses" (WIA)

BLACKSTOCKS
(NOV 20, 1780)
Edward Coleman
Lemerick Farr
"Soldier Tom"

COWPENS
(JAN 17, 1781)
James Anderson/Asher Crockett
John Biddie
Julius Cesar
"Collins"
Lemirick Farr
Andrew Ferguson
Fortune Freeman
Francis Freeman
Gideon Griffin
Morgan Griffin
John Hammonds
Edward Harris
Micajah Hicks
Agrippa Hull
Thomas Jordan
Bazaleel Norman
Andrew Peleg
Dick Pickens
Record Primes

Daniel Strother
William Taburn
David Wilson

COWAN'S FORD (FEB 1, 1781)
William Taburn

TARRANT'S TAVERN (FEB 1, 1781)
William Taburn

GUILFORD COURT HOUSE (MARCH 15, 1781)
Adam Adams
Sylvester Beverly
Jacob Blake
Willis Boon
Cyfax Brown
Isaac Brown
Francis Coley
Thomas Carney
William Cuff
Edward Coleman (WIA)
Andrew Ferguson (WIA)
Simon Fralix
Negro George
John Gibson
Edward Going
William Going
Ned Griffin
John Hammonds
Lazarus Harman
Edward Harris
Nathaniel Harrison
Micajah Hicks
Henry Hill
Major Hitchens
Agrippa Hull
Zacharia Jacobs (WIA leg, hospitalized)
Tim Jones (POW)
George Kendall
Moses Knight
William Lomack
Robin Loyd
Thomas Mason
Ambrose Month
Bazaleel Norman
Andrew Pebbles
Richard Pendergrass
Jesse Peters
John Pipsico
Record Primes
Matthew Williams
David Wilson

HOBKIRK HILL (APRIL 25, 1781)
Jacob Blake
William Goings
Lazarus Harman (WIA)
Henry Hill
Major Hitchens
Jesse Peters
John Pipsico
David Wilson

SIEGE OF AUGUSTA (MAY 22–JUNE 5, 1781)
John Busby
Austin Dabney (WIA)
Thomas Lively

NINETY-SIX (MAY 22–JUNE 19, 1781)
Evans Archer
Jacob Blake
Isaac Brown
John Busby
Thomas Carney
Andrew Ferguson

Lazarus Harman
Agrippa Hull
Malachi Nickens
John Pipsico
Aaron Spellman
Joel Taburn
Luke Valentine
David Wilson

GREEN SPRINGS (JULY 6, 1781)

James Mealey

BIGGIN CHURCH (JULY 16, 1781)

Jim Capers
Old Sandy

WADBOO BRIDGE (JULY 17, 1781)

Jeremiah Bunch

BEATTIE'S BRIDGE (AUG 4, 1781)

John Hammonds

PARKER'S FERRY (AUG 1781)

Adam Ivey

EUTAW SPRINGS (SEPT 8, 1781)

Evans Archer
Elijah Bass (KIA)
Prince Bent
Solomon Bibby
Jacob Blake
Isaac Brown
William Burnett
Jim Capers (WIA—four wounds)
Thomas Carney
Drury Chavis
William Cuff
Andrew Ferguson
Freeman Fortune
Gideon Griffin
John Hammonds
Isaac Hammonds
Edward Harris
Micajah Hicks
Henry Hill
Charles Hood
Agrippa Hull
James Jeremiah
William Lomack (WIA twice)
Bazaleel Norman
Robert Owls (WIA—leg broken by musket ball)
Andrew Pebbles (WIA three times)
Jesse Peters
John Pipsico
Record Primes
Joel Taburn
David Wilson

BATTLE OF THE CAPES (SEPT 5, 1781)

Caesar Tarrant
Pluto, slave of Robert Boughs

PIDGEON HILL (SEPT 28, 1781)

Matthew Williams

GLOUCESTER

William Guy
Charles Riley

YORKTOWN (SEPT 29–OCT 19, 1781)

Adam Adams
Hamet Achmet

Cash Affrica
Absalom Ailstock
William Anderson (WIA)
James Armistead Lafayette
Charles Barnett
Prince Bent
Sylvester Beverly
Scipio Brown
George Buley
James Carter
Julius Cesar
Edward Chambers
Anthony Chavis
Obed Coffin
Edward Coleman
John Cook
Oliver Cromwell
Abraham Curtillo
Tobias Cutler
Comfort Eddy (WIA)
William Flora
Simon Fralix
Fortune Freeman
Jethro Freeman
Nathan Fry
Sherard Going
Robert/Prince Green
Primas Hall
Agrippa Hull
Tim Jones (WIA—lost leg)
George Kendall
Thomas Lively
William Matthews
James Mealey
Jonathan Overton
Pomp Peters
Record Primes
John Randall
Bristol Rhodes (WIA)
James Robinson
John Roe
Philip Savoy
Cuff Slade
London Slocum (KIA)
Daniel Williams
Daniel Sharp
Sampson Cozzens
Joshua Dick
Bristol Olney
Peter Harris
Samuel Niles
James Niles

COMBAHEE FERRY (AUG 27, 1782)

Andrew Pebbles

MARION RIDERS

Spencer Bolton
Jasper Browngaurd
Jim Capers
Adam Ivey (joined at Parker's Ferry, Aug 1781)
George Kersey
James Kersey
John Rawls

APPENDIX 7

BLACK PATRIOTS BURIALS

(u) = Unmarked
(c) = Cenotaph

"Pomp" (u)
KIA July 5, 1779
West Haven Green Cemetery
West Haven, Connecticut

William Anderson
February 2, 1841
Ashland Cemetery
Ashland, Ohio

Cuff Ashport
August 31, 1827
First Cemetery
Bridgewater, Massachusetts

Crispus Attucks
KIA Boston Massacre March 5, 1770
Granary Burying Ground
Boston, Massachusetts

London Atus
July 7, 1843
Court Street Cemetery
Machias, Maine

Henry Bakeman
February 6, 1835
South Onondaga Cemetery
South Onondaga, New York

John D. Baptist
September 3, 1804
Falmouth Union Cemetery
Falmouth, Virginia

Caesar Barnes
June 24, 1803
East Smithfield Cemetery
East Smithfield, Pennsylvania

Sampson Battis
October 23, 1847
Canterbury Village Cemetery
Canterbury, New Hampshire

Abel Benson
September 16, 1843
Church Hill Cemetery
Framingham, Massachussets

Ephraim Blackman
March 18, 1833
Streetsville Memorial Cemetery
Mississauga, Ontario, Canada

James Bowes
1800
Eastern Cemetery
Portland, Maine

Rev. Charles Bowles
March 16, 1843
Constable Cemetery
Constable, New York

Jeffrey Brace
April 20, 1827
Brace Family Cemetery
Georgia, Vermont

Sippio Brister
November 1, 1820
Lincoln Cemetery
Lincoln, Massachusetts

John Broddy
1859
John Broddy Cemetery
Saltville, Virginia

Joseph Brown
1834
Old Burial Hill Cemetery
Marblehead, Massachusetts

Silas Burdoo
January 23, 1837
Baileys Mill Cemetery
Reading, Vermont

Samuel Bush
November 24, 1826
Putnam Cemetery
Greenwich, Connecticut

Cyrus Bustill (u)
1806
Eden Cemetery
Collingdale, Pennsylvania

Jim Capers (c)
April 1, 1853
Bethlehem Missionary Baptist Church
Orion, Alabama

Isaac Carter, Sr.
1811
George Family Cemetery
North Harlowe, North Carolina

Joshua Carter
1820
George Family Cemetery
North Harlowe, North Carolina

Timothy Cesar
March 27, 1822
Grove Street Cemetery
New Haven, Connecticut

Cuff Chambers
June 18, 1818
Knapp Cemetery
Leeds, Maine

Wentworth Cheswell
March 8, 1817
Cheswell Family Graveyard
Newmarket, New Hampshire

Anthony Clark
January 8, 1856
Pine Grove Cemetery
Warner, New Hampshire

William Clark (c)
1827
Grandview Cemetery
Chillicothe, Ohio

Titus Coburn (c)
May 5, 1821
South Church Cemetery
Andover, Massachusetts

Jeremiah Crocker
June 14, 1836
Old Cemetery
Henniker, New Hampshire

Oliver Cromwell (u)
January 27, 1853
Burlington Methodist and Baptist Cemetery
Burlington, New Jersey

Nero Cross
September 1830
Brookfield Cemetery
Brookfield, Vermont

Paul Cuffe
September 9, 1817
Friends-Central Cemetery
Westport, Massachusetts

Prince Cutler (u)
UNK
Old Burying Ground
Arlington, Massachusetts

Tobias Cutler
September 12, 1834
Winter Street Burial Ground
Exeter, New Hampshire

Joseph Cutt
January 15, 1782
Adams Cemetery
Wilbraham, Massachusetts

Austin Dabney
1830
Harris Cemetery
Zebulon, Georgia

Daddy Jack
UNK
Heard Cemetery
Elberton, Georgia

William Dailey (c)
1850
Grandview Cemetery
Chillicothe, Ohio

Prince Danforth (Danford)
1836
Presbyterian Burial Ground
Little Britain, New York

Cuffee Dole
August 17, 1816
Union Cemetery
Georgetown, Massachusetts

Caesar Drake
February 7, 1806
Scotch Plains Baptist Church Cemetery
Scotch Plains, New Jersey

Joshua Dunbar
April 26, 1826
Dunbar Family Cemetery
Seneca, New York

Prince Estabrook
1830
Ashby First Parish Burial Ground
Ashby, Massachusetts

Andrew Ferguson
October 1, 1855
Rose Hill Cemetery
Bloomington, Indiana

Archelaus Fletcher, Sr.
April 29, 1781
Meeting House Hill Cemetery
West Springfield, Massachusetts

Archelaus Fletcher, Jr.
June 18, 1876
County Home Cemetery
Canadaigua, New York

Ozias Fletcher
December 20,, 1823
Silver Street Cemetery
Granville, Massachusetts

James Forten, Sr.
March 4, 1842
Eden Cemetery
Collingdale, Pennsylvania

Jacob Francis
July 26, 1836
Flemington Baptist Churchyard
Flemington, New Jersey

Andrew Frazier
June 2, 1846
Rhinebeck Cemetery
Rhinebeck, New York

Scipio Freeman
April 20, 1820
Allin Burial Ground
Barrington, Rhode Island

Asher Freeman
February 3, 1820
Hanover Center Cemetery
Hanover, Massachusetts

Azariah Freeman
August 4, 1828
Olde Mansfield Center Cemetery
Mansfield, Connecticut

Cato Freeman
January 29, 1828
Zoar Cemetery
Newtown, Connecticut

"Col" Cato Freeman
May 19, 1828
Butternut Valley Cemetery
Burlington, New York

Cato Freeman
August 9, 1853
Second Burying Ground
North Andover, Massachusetts

Charles Freeman
May 1842
North Burial Ground
Providence, Rhode Island

Chatham Freeman
February 13, 1834
Broad Street Cemetery
Meriden, Connecticut

Peter Freeman
1807
Shawsheen Cemetery
Bedford, Massachusetts

Philemon Freeman
May 18, 1820
Old North Burying Ground
Middlefield, Connecticut

Sharper Freeman
January 4, 1833
Laurel Hill Cemetery
Reading, Massachusetts

Neptune Frost
UNK
Old Burying Ground
Cambridge, Massachusetts

Winsor Fry
February 1, 1823
Winsor Fry Lot
East Greenwich, Rhode Island

Cesar Frye (u)
September 1811
Old North Parish Burying Ground
North Andover, Massachusetts

Adam Gardner
UNK
Walnut Street Cemetery
Brookline, Massachusetts

Toby Gilmore
April 19, 1812
Hall and Dean Cemetery
Raynham, Massachusetts

Prince Goodwin
November 1821
Partying Ways Cemetery
Plymouth, Massachusetts

Brister Gould
August 18, 1823
Gould Family Burial Ground
Abington, Massachusetts

Peter Green
1836
Brick School Cemetery
Colrain, Massachusetts

Prince Green
UNK
Common Burying Ground
Newport, Rhode Island

Richard Gunderway
May 17, 1820
Center Cemetery
Pembroke, Massachusetts

Jude Hall
August 22, 1827
Winter Street Burial Ground
Exeter, New Hampshire

Primus Trask Hall
March 22, 1842
Mount Hope Cemetery
Boston, Massachusetts

Prince Hall
December 4, 1807
Copp's Hill Burying Ground
Boston, Massachusetts

Jesse Hartwell
July 20, 1816
Hamblett Cemetery
Lowell, Massachusetts

Charles Haskell
December 17, 1833
North Burial Ground
Providence, Rhode Island

Nero Hawley
January 30, 1817
Riverside Cemetery
Trumbull, Connecticut

Rev. Lemuel Haynes
September 28, 1833
Lee-Oatman Cemetery
South Granville, New York

Edward "Ned" Hector (u)
January 3, 1834
Jonathan Roberts Burial Ground
King of Prussia, Pennsylvania

Jeffrey Hemenway (Hemingway)
August 15, 1819
Hope Cemetery
Worcester, Massachusetts

Francis Heuston
June 1, 1858
Heuston Cemetery
Brunswick, Maine

Henry Hill (c)
1833
Grandview Cemetery
Chillicothe, Ohio

Cato Howe
February 29, 1824
Parting Ways Cemetery
Plymouth, Massachusetts

Agrippa Hull
May 21, 1848
Stockbridge Cemetery
Stockbridge, Massachusetts

Prince Hull (u)
November 23, 1821
Ancient Burying Ground
Hartford, Connecticut

Sipp Ives (u)
KIA August 17, 1777
Old Bennington Cemetery
Bennington, Vermont

John Jack
October 19, 1817
Staines-Jack Cemetery
Greenland, New Hampshire

John Jacklin
August 4, 1825
East Cemetery
Manchester, Connecticut

Peter Jennings (c)
January 22, 1842
Old City Cemetery
Murfreesboro, Tennessee

Caesar Jones (u)
UNK
Old Burying Ground
Bedford, Massachusetts

Calvin Jotham
March 1841
Talbot Cemetery
China, Maine

Luther Jotham
June 22, 1832
Talbot Cemetery
China, Maine

Pompey King
April 8, 1844
Oak Grove Cemetery
Delaware, Ohio

George Knox
July 28, 1825
Knox Cemetery
Thetford, Vermont

Job Lathrop
September 22, 1829
Westminster Cemetery
Canterbury, Connecticut

William "Billy" Lee
1810
Mount Vernon Estate
Mount Vernon, Virginia

Barzillai Lew
January 18, 1822
Old Burying Ground
Lowell, Massachusetts

Job Lewis
1820
Dry Pond Cemetery
Stoughton, Massachusetts

Jeff Liberty
May 24, 1797
Old Judea Cemetery
Washington, Connecticut

Eden London
March 1810
Old Centre Burial Ground
Winchedon, Massachusetts

Pomp Lovejoy
February 3, 1826
South Church Cemetery
Andover, Massachusetts

John and Judith Lynde (Lines)
July 13, 1828
Brookfield Cemetery
Brookfield, Vermont

Mammy Kate
UNK
Heard Cemetery
Elberton, Georgia

Ben Scott Mayes (u)
March 10, 1820
Zion Presbyterian Church Cemetery
Zion, Tennessee

Plato McClellan
UNK
Eastern Cemetery
Portland, Maine

Prince McLellan
July 19, 1829
Eastern Cemetery
Gorham, Maine

Cato Mead
April 25, 1846
Montrose Cemetery
Montrose, Iowa

George Middleton (u)
April 6, 1815
Copp's Hill Burying Ground
Boston, Massachusetts

Caesar Mirick
Unknown
Adams Cemetery
Wilbraham, Massachusetts

Abraham Moore
1837
Union Cemetery
Steubenville, Ohio

Cambridge Moore
UNK
Old Burying Ground
Bedford, Massachusetts

Luke Nickerson
May 4, 1829
Growstown Cemetery
Brunswick, Maine

Bazabeel Norman (c)
July 17, 1830
Mound Cemetery
Marietta, Ohio

Jonathan Overton
1853
Providence Burial Ground
Edenton, North Carolina

Derrick Oxford
UNK
Coryville Cemetery
Plainfield, New Hampshire

George Perkins
November 27, 1840
Sharon Cemetery
Mount Hamill, Iowa

George Perkins
1790
George Family Cemetery
North Harlowe, North Carolina

Isaac Perkins
May 23, 1830
George Family Cemetery
North Harlowe, North Carolina

Amos Peters
December 25, 1830
Peterborough Cemetery
Warren, Maine

John Jacob Peterson
1850
Bethel Cemetery
Croton-on-Hudson, New York

Jeruel Phillips
December 16, 1829
Center Cemetery
New Milford, Connecticut

Samuel Phillips
November 1, 1815
Center Cemetery
New Milford, Connecticut

Dick Pointer
1827
African Cemetery
Lewisburg, West Virginia

Peter Pomp (c)
March 15, 1778
McClary Cemetery
Epsom, New Hampshire

David Potter
May 13, 1846
Chippenhook Cemetery
Clarendon, Vermont

Caesar Prescott
UNK
Old Burying Ground
Bedford, Massachusetts

Gershom Prince
KIA July 3, 1778
Battle of Wyoming Burial Ground
Wyoming, Pennsylvania

Quamony Quash
April 18, 1833
Parting Ways Cemetery
Plymouth, Massachusetts

Ebenezer Raymont (u)
June 1780
Fishkill Supply Depot Burial Ground
Fishkill, NY

Thomas Reynolds
April 14, 1845
Brick Church Cemetery
Sodus Center, New York

Richard Rhodes
January 24, 1821
Richard Rhodes Lot
Warwick, Rhode Island

Prince Richards
February 17, 1833
Jennings Hill Cemetery
Bridgewater, Massachusetts

James Robinson
March 27, 1868
Elmwood Cemtery
Detroit, Michigan

Silas Royal (u)
May 3, 1826
Varnum Cemetery
Dracut, Massachusetts

Peter Salem
August 16, 1816
Church Hill Cemetery
Framingham, Massachusetts

John Scott
December 17, 1847
Maineville Cemetery
Maineville, Ohio

Cato Shattuck
UNK
Eastern Cemetery
Portland, Maine

Lewis Shepherd
December 22, 1833
Eastern Cemetery
Portland, Maine

Moses Sherwood
February 17, 1837
Sparta Cemetery
Ossining, New York

Richard Stanhope
September 20, 1862
Johnson Cemetery
Crayon, Ohio

Cato Stedman (u)
UNK
Old Burying Ground
Cambridge, Massachusetts

Prince Thompson
1847
Paxton Center Cemetery
Paxton, Massachusetts

Hannah Archer Till
December 13, 1826
Eden Cemetery
Collingdale, Pennsylvania

Cuff Trot
April 1813
Second Parish Burial Ground
Burlington, Massachusetts

Plato Turner
July 11, 1819
Parting Ways Cemetery
Plymouth, Massachusetts

Henry Van Meter
February 12, 1871
Bangor City Cemetery
Bangor, Maine

Guy Watson (u)
1837
Dockray Family Slave Lot
South Kingstown, Rhode Island

Slave Watt
December 1837
Brattonville Slave Cemetery
Brattonville, South Carolina

Nathan Weston
Oct 1832
Mount Vernon Cemetery
Augusta, Maine

Caesar Wheaton (c)
February 20, 1780
North Burial Ground
Providence, Rhode Island

Prince Whipple
November 23, 1796
North Cemetery
Portsmouth, New Hampshire

Peter Willard
August 24, 1817
West Milbury Cemetery
Millbury, Massachusetts

Benjamin Williams
1839
Clemens Cemetery
Long, Ohio

Pompey Woodward
January 13, 1843
Four Corners Cemetery
Sullivan, New Hampshire

SOURCES

BOOKS

Babits, Lawrence E. *A Devil of a Whipping: The Battle of Cowpens.* Chapel Hill: University of North Carolina Press, 1998.

Beach, E. Merrill. *From Valley Forge to Freedom: A Story of a Black Patriot.* Chester, CT: Pequot Press, 1975.

Bolster, Jeffery. *Black Jacks: African American Seamen in the Age of Sail.* Cambridge, MA: Harvard University Press, 1977.

Borkow, Richard. *George Washington's Westchester Gamble: The Encampment on the Hudson and the Trapping of Cornwallis.* Charleston, SC: The History Press, 2011.

Brown, Barbara W., and James M. Rose. *Black Roots in Southeastern Connecticut, 1650-1990.* Detroit, MI: Gale Research, 1980.

Carvalho, Joseph III. *Black Families in Hampden County, Massachusetts, 1650-1865.* n.p., 338p.

Brown, Roscoe Conkling. *Ebony Patriots: Participation of Blacks in the Battles of the American Revolution in the New York City Area, 1776-1779.* New York: New York City Bicentennial Corp. Historical Committee, Sub-Committee on Black Contributions, 1976.

Cox, Clinton. *Come All You Brave Soldiers: Blacks in the Revolutionary War.* Scholastic Press, 1999.

Crow, Jeffrey J. *The Black Experience in Revolutionary North Carolina.* Raleigh, NC: North Carolina Dept. of Cultural Resources, Division of Archives and History, 1996.

Crowder, Jack Darrell. *African Americans and American Indians in the Revolutionary War.* Jefferson, NC: McFarland & Company, 2019.

von Daacke, Kirt. *Freedom Has a Face: Race, Identity, and Community in Jefferson's Virginia.* Charlottesville, VA: University of Virginia Press, 2012.

Diaz, Briana L., Eric Grundset, Hollis L. Gentry, and Jean D. Strahan. *Forgotten Patriots: African American and American Indian Patriots in the Revolutionary War, a Guide to Service, Sources, and Studies.* Washington D.C.: National Society of the Daughters of the American Revolution, 2008.

Diaz, Briana L., Hollis L. Gentry, and Eric Grundset. *Forgotten Patriots: African American and American Indian Patriots in the Revolutionary War, a Guide to Service, Sources, and Studies – Supplement 2008-2011.* Washington D.C.: National Society of the Daughters of the American Revolution, 2008.

Dughan, George C. *Revolution on the Hudson: New York City and the Hudson River Valley in the American War of Independence.* New York: W.W. Norton, 2017.

Dunkerly, Robert M. *Eutaw Springs: The Final Battle of the American Revolution's Southern Campaign.* Columbia, SC: University of South Carolina Press, 2017.

Fowler, William M., Jr. *American Crisis: George Washington and the Dangerous Two Years after Yorktown, 1781-1783.* New York: Walker, 2011.

Geake, Robert A. *From Slaves to Soldiers: The 1st Rhode Island Regiment in the American Revolution.* Yardley, PA: Westholme, 2016.

Glickstein, Dan. *After Yorktown: The Final Struggle for American Independence.* Yardley, PA: Westholme, 2014.

Greene, Jerome A. *The Guns of Independence: The Siege of Yorktown, 1781.* New York: Savas Beatie, 2005.

Greene, Robert Ewell. *Black Courage, 1775-1783: Documentation of Black Participation in the American Revolution.* Washington DC: National Society of the Daughters of the American Revolution, 1984.

Greenwalt, Phillip S. *The Winter That Won the War: The Winter Encampment at Valley Forge, 1777-1778.* El Dorado Hill, CA: Savas Beatie, 2021.

Groom, Theodore. *Remembering Gad Asher.* Totoket Historical Society, 2013.

Harris, Michael. *Brandywine: A Military History of the Battle That Lost Philadelphia but Saved America.* El Dorado Hills, CA: Savas Beatie, 2014.

Hazelgrove, William. *Henry Knox's Noble Train: The Story of a Boston Bookseller's Heroic Expedition That Saved the American Revolution.* Lanham, MD: Prometheus, 2020.

Hinkle, Alice M. *Prince Estabrook: Slave and Soldier.* Lexington, MA: Pleasant Mountain Press, 2001.

Jackson, Luther Porter. *Virginia Negro Soldiers and Seamen in the Revolutionary War.* Norfolk, VA: Guide Quality Press, 1944.

Kaplan, Sidney. *The Black Presence in the Era of the American Revolution, 1770-1800.* New York: New York Graphic Society, 1973.

Knoblock, Glenn. *"Strong and Brave Fellows": New Hampshire's Black Soldiers and Sailors of the American Revolution, 1775-1784.* Jefferson, NC: McFarland & Co., 2003.

Langguth, A.J. *Patriots: The Men Who Started the American Revolution.* New York: Simon & Shuster, 1988.

Lemire, Elise. *Black Walden: Slavery and Its Aftermath in Concord, Massachusetts.* Philadelphia, PA: University of Pennsylvania Press, 2009.

Lucas, Marion B. *A History of Blacks in Kentucky: From Slavery to Segregation, 1760-1891.* Lexington, KY: University Press of Kentucky, 2003.

Massachusetts, Office of the Secretary of State. *Massachusetts Soldiers and Sailors of the Revolutionary War: A Compilation from the Archives.* 17 vols. Boston, MA: Wright and Porter, 1896-1908.

McCullough, David. *1776.* New York: Simon & Shuster, 2005.

Moore, George H. *Historical Notes of the Employment of Negroes by the American Army of the Revolution.* New York: Charles T. Evans, 1862.

Moore, George H. *Notes on the History of Slavery in Massachusetts.* New York: D. Appleton, 1866.

Moss, Bobby G., and Michael C. Scoggins. *African-American Patriots in the Southern Campaign of the American Revolution.* Blacksburg, VA: Scotia-Hibernia Press, 2004.

Newman, Debra. *List of Black Servicemen Compiled From the War Department Collection of Revolutionary War Records.* Washington D.C.: National Archives and Records Service, 1974.

Nell, William Cooper. *Colored Patriots of the American Revolution.* Columbia, SC: CreateSpace, 2020.

O'Donnell, Patrick K. *The Indispensibles: The Diverse Soldier-Mariners Who Shaped the Country, Formed the Navy, and Rowed Washington Across the Delaware.* New York: Atlantic Monthly, 2021.

O'Donnell, Patrick K. *Washington's Immortals: The Untold Story of an Elite Regiment Who Changed the Course of the Revolution.* New York: Atlantic Monthly, 2016.

Philbrick, Nathaniel. *In the Hurricane's Eye: The Genius of George Washington and the Victory at Yorktown.* New York: Viking, 2018.

Pingeon, Frances D. *Blacks in the Revolutionary Era.* Trenton, NJ: New Jersey Historical Commission, 1975.

Popek, Daniel M. *They "…fought bravely, but were unfortunate": The True Story of Rhode Island's "Black Regiment" and the Failure of Segregation in Rhode Island's Continental Line, 1777-1783.* Bloomington, IN: AuthorHouse, 2015.

Price, George R. *The Eastons: Five Generations of Human Rights Activism, 1748-1935.* No publisher listed, 2020.

Quarles, Benjamin. *The Negro in the American Revolution.* Chapel Hill, NC: University of North Carolina Press, 1961.

Quintal, George Jr. *Patriots of Color, "A Peculiar Beauty and Merit": African Americans and Native Americans at Battle Road and Bunker Hill.* Boston, MA: Division of Cultural Resources, Boston National Historical Park, 2004.

Rees, John U. *'They Were Good Soldiers': African-Americans Serving in the Continental Army, 1775-1783.* Warwick, UK: Helion & Co., 2019.

Ryan, D. Michael. *Concord and the Dawn of Revolution: The Hidden Truths.* Charleston, SC: History Press, 2007.

Smith, Stephen R. *Record of Service of Connecticut Men: Vol 1. War of the Revolution.* Hartford, CT: Case, Lockwood & Brainard, 1889.

Sutton, Karen E. *The Nickens Family: Non-Slave African American Patriots.* Baltimore, MD: K.E. Sutton, 1994.

Thorenz, Matt. *Substitutes, Servants and Soldiers: The Black Presence at New Windsor Cantonment in the Continental Army.* Fishkill, NY: Mount Beacon Press, 2022.

Walters, Kerry. *Revolutionary War: Essential Library of the American Revolution.* New York: Sterling, 2007.

Weintraub, Stanley. *General Washington's Christmas Farewell: A Mount Vernon Homecoming, 1783.* New York: Free Press, 2003.

Whittemore, Janet Wethy. *The Black Soldiers of New Hampshire, 1775-1783.* No publisher listed, no publication date.

Zwonitzer, Mark. *The Statesman and the Storyteller: John Hay, Mark Twain, and the Rise of American Imperialism.* Chapel Hill, NC: Algonquin Books, 2016.

ARTICLES

Allen Lambert, David, "Salem Poor (1743/44–1802): A Forgotten Hero of Bunker Hill Rediscovered," *New England Ancestors* 8:4 (Fall 2007), pp. 40–41.

Anders, Philip M., "James Forten: A Man—and a Patriot—Before His Time," *SAR Magazine* (Spring 2014), pp. 22–23.

Arnold, Paul T., "Negro Soldiers in the United States Army," *Magazine of History* 10:2 (Aug. 1909), pp. 61–70; 10:3 (Sept. 1909), pp. 123–129; 10: 4 (Oct. 1909), pp. 185–193; 10:5 (Nov. 1909), pp. 247–255; 11:3 (March 1910), pp. 119–125.

Becton, Joseph W., "African Soldiers of the Rhode Island Regiment at the Battle of Fort Mercer, October 22, 1777," *Bulletin of the Gloucester County Historical Society* 24:4 (June 1994), pp. 24–29.

Beeching, Barbara J. , "African Americans and Native Americans in Hartford, 1636–1800: Antecedents of Hartford's Nineteenth Century Black Community," *Hartford Studies Collection: Papers by Students and Faculty* 7 (1993).

Belton, Bill, "Prince Whipple, Soldier of the American Revolution," *Negro History Bulletin* 26:6 (Oct. 1973), pp. 126–127.

"Blacks at Fort Ticonderoga," *Fort Ticonderoga Research Notes* (2008).

"Blacks in Massachusetts and the Shays' Rebellion," *Contributions in Black Studies* 8 (1986).

Blanck, Emily, "The Legal Emancipation of Leander and Caesar: Manumission and the Law in Revolutionary South Carolina and Massachusetts," *Slavery & Abolition* 28:2 (August 2007), pp. 235–254.

Bly, Antonio T., "Wheatley's ON THE AFFRAY IN KING STREET," *Explicator* 56:4 (Summer 1998), pp. 177–180.

Bogin, Ruth, "'Liberty Further Extended': A 1776 Antislavery Manuscript of Lemuel Haynes," *William and Mary Quarterly, 3rd Series*, 40 (Jan. 1983), pp. 85–105.

Bowman, Larry, "Virginia's Use of Blacks in the French and Indian War," *Western Pennsylvania History* 53 (Jan. 1970), pp. 57–63.

Brown, Wallace, "Negroes and the American Revolution," *History Today* 12 (March 1962), pp. 556–563.

Bustill Smith, Anna, "The Bustill Family," *Journal of Negro History* 10:4 (Oct. 1925), pp. 638–644. [Cyrus Bustill]

Buxbaum, Melvin H., "Cyrus Bustill Addresses the Blacks of Philadelphia," *William and Mary Quarterly* 29:1 pp. 99–108.

Cahill, Barry, "The Black Loyalist Myth in Atlantic Canada," *Acadiensis* 29:1 (Autumn 1999), pp. 76–87.

Calderhead, William L., "Thomas Carney: Unsung Soldier of the American Revolution," *Maryland Historical Magazine* 84 (Winter 1989), pp. 319–325.

Carvalho III, Joseph, "Uncovering the Stories of Black Families in Springfield and Hampden County, Massachusetts: 1650–1864," *Historical Journal of Massachusetts* 40:1/2 (Summer 2012), pp. 59–93.

Charles City County Historical Society, "More Blacks in Blue – Charles City Country's Free Black Revolutionary War Soldiers," *Charles City Country Historical Society Newsletter* 6 (March 1996), pp. 10–14.

Cody, Col. Michael A., "Black Patriots of the Revolution," *Army* (February 1998), pp. 46–52.

Collins, Elizabeth M., "Black Soldiers in the Revolutionary War," *Soldiers Live* (March 4, 2013)

Conkright, Bessie Taul, "Estill's Defeat or the Battle of Little Mountain, March 22, 1782," *Register of Kentucky State Historical Society* 22:66 (September 1924), pp. 311–322. [Monk Estill]

Cregeau, Damien, "Historically Speaking: 'Doctor Cuffee' Saunders, Free Man of Connecticut," *Norwich Times* (February 23, 2022).

Dalton, Bill, "Salem Poor's Heroism and Disappointing Life," *Andover Townsman* (Feb. 7, 2013).

Davis, Damani, "The Rejection of Elizabeth Mason: The Case of a 'Free Colored' Revolutionary Widow," *Genealogy Notes* 43:2 (Summer 2011).

Davis, Thomas J., "Emancipation Rhetoric, Natural Rights, and Revolutionary New England: A Note on Four Black Petitions in Massachusetts, 1773–1777," *New England Quarterly* 62:2 (June 1989), pp. 248–263.

Dean, Abbey, "Illuminating Hannah Till," *American Spirit* (Jan.–Feb. 2020), pp. 12–13.

Dishman, Robert B., "'Natives of Africa, Now Forcibly Detained,' The Slave Petitioners of Revolutionary Portsmouth," *Historical New Hampshire* 61 (Spring 2007), pp. 7–27.

Dishman, Robert B., "Breaking the Bonds: The Role of New Hampshire's Courts in Freeing those Wrongly Enslaved, 1640s–1740s," *Historical New Hampshire* (Fall 2005), pp. 79–91.

Dixon, David T., "Freedom Earned, Equality Denied: Evolving Race Relations in Exeter and Vicinity, 1776–1876," *Historical New Hampshire* 61:1 (Spring 2007), pp. 28–47.

Dole, Samuel T., "Windham's Colored Patriot," *Collections of the Maine Historical Society Third Series, Vol. 1* (1904), pp. 316–321. [Lonnon Rhode]

Erkkila, Betty, "Phillis Wheatley on the Streets of Revolutionary Boston and in the Atlantic World," *Early American Literature* 56:2 (pp. 351–372

Evans Logan, Gwendolyn, "The Slave in Connecticut during the American Revolution," *Connecticut Historical Society Bulletin* 30:3 (July 1965), pp 73–80.

Farley, M. Foster, "The South Carolina Negro in the American Revolution," *South Carolina Historical Magazine* 79:2 (Apr. 1978), pp. 75–86.

Fisher, J.B., "Who Was Crispus Attucks?" *American Historical Record 1* (1872), pp. 531–533.

Fitzhugh Millar, John, "The Black Privateersman," *Newport History: Bulletin of the Newport Historical Society* 54:2 (Spring 1981), pp. 51–57.

Fogelberg, John E., "Slavery Did Exist in Early Burlington," *Daily Times and Chronicle* (October 16, 1979). [Cuff Trot]

Francis, Jacob, "An Important Revolutionary Record of a Negro Solider," *Journal of Negro History* 17:3 (July 1932), pp. 379–381.

Frey, Sylvia R., "Between Slavery and Freedom: Virginia Blacks in the American Revolution," *Journal of Southern History* 49:3 (Aug. 1983), pp. 375–398.

Goodstein, Anita S., "Black History on the Nashville Frontier, 1780–1810," *Tennessee Historical Quarterly* 38:4 (Winter 1979), pp. 401–420.

Greene, Lorenzo J., "Some Observations on the Black Regiment of Rhode Island in the American Revolution," *Journal of Negro History* 37 (Jan. 1952), pp. 142–172.

Greene, Lorenzo J., "The Negro in the Armed Forces of the United States, 1619–1783," *Negro History Bulletin* (March 1951), pp. 123–127, 138.

Hadaway, William S., "Negroes in the Revolutionary War," *Westchester County Historical Society Quarterly Bulletin* 6 (1930), pp. 8–12.

Hamilton, Abbe, "Jube Savage and Titus Wilson were Black Revolutionary War Soldiers with ties to the Monadnock Region," *Monadnock Ledger–Transcript* (February 17, 2021).

Hartgrove, W.B., "The Negro Soldier in the American Revolution," *Journal of Negro History* 1:2 (Apr. 1916), pp. 100–131.

Hartz, Louis, "Otis and the Anti–Slavery Doctrine," *New England Quarterly* 12:4 (December 1939), pp. 745–747.

Haulman, Daniel, "The American Revolution and the Beginning of the End of Slavery in America," *SAR Magazine* (Fall 2020), pp. 18–20.

Henry Lyons, Elizabeth, "A Soldier of the Revolution," *DAR Magazine* 51:5 (Nov. 1917), pp. 280–283. [James Armistead Lafayette]

Hinton, P.M. and Marker, Jr., John L., South Carolina Free Men of Color in the American Revolution (Sept. 2020)

Hitchings, Robert, "Billy Flora: Patriot Hero of the Revolutionary War Battle of Great Bridge," *Virginian–Pilot* (Feb. 17, 2017).

Holland, Jacqueline, "Pompey Lamb, Revolutionary War Hero," *South of the Mountains* 28:1 (Jan.–Mar. 1984), pp. 3–7.

Hudgins, Bill, "'Lest We Forget': DAR's Forgotten Patriots Project Lifts Ancestors from Obscurity," *American Spirit* (July–Aug. 2021), pp. 31–32. [Sampson Moore Battis]

Jeffway, Bill, "To the Manor Born: The Extraordinary Journey of Dutchess County's African American Revolutionary War Veteran Andrew Frazier," *History Speaks* (Feb. 2017), 6p.

Kaplan, Sidney, "A Negro Veteran in Shays' Rebellion," *Journal of Negro History* 33:2 (April 1948), pp. 123–129. [Moses Sash]

Knight, Edgar, "Notes on John Chavis," *North Carolina Historical Review* 7:3 (July 1930), pp. 326–345.

"Letters of George Washington Bearing on the Negro," *Journal of Negro History* 2:4 (October 1917), pp. 411–422.

Leubsdorf, Ben, "234 Years Later, N.H. Legislature Might Answer Slaves' Plea for Freedom," *Concord Monitor* (February 28, 2013).

Lewis, Noah, "Being Edward Hector – The Life and Times of a Black Revolutionary War Hero," *Bulletin of the Historical Society of Montgomery County* 36:4 (2013), pp. 19–33.

Lewis, Noah, "Ned Hector – Revolutionary War Hero," *Past Masters News* 13:3 (Summer 2011), pp. 1–4.

MacGunnigle, Bruce, "'Ichabod Northup, "Soldier of the Revolution," and His Descendants'," *Rhode Island Roots* 43:3 (Sept. 2008), pp. 113–142.

MacMaster, Richard K., "Arthur Lee's 'Address on Slavery': An Aspect of Virginia's Struggle to End the Slave Trade, 1765–1774," *Virginia Magazine of History and Biography* 130:2 (April 1972), pp. 141–157.

Maslowski, Pete, "National Policy toward the Use of Black Troops in the Revolution," *South Carolina Historical Magazine* 73:1 (January 1972), pp. 1–17.

McBurney, Christian, "Amazing Letter Discovered from a Black Soldier of the First Rhode Island Regiment – Containing a Shocking Request," *Small State, Big History* (http://smallstatebighistory.com).

Mills, Borden H., "Troop Units at the Battle of Saratoga," *New York History: Quarterly Journal of the New York State Historical Association* 9:2 (April 1928), pp. 136–158.

Nevins, Susan, "For Colored People [they] had a great many friends': The Phillips–Lynde Family of Windham, Connecticut, and Brookfield, Vermont," *Vermont History* 88:1 (Winter–Spring 2020), pp. 1–34. [John Lynde/Lines]

Nunnery, Jackie, "In Plain Sight: The Story of James Armistead," *House & Home Magazine* (August 12, 2019).

Overton, Julie M., "Abraham Moore of Pennsylvania and Ohio: Revolutionary War Pension Application – 2–2855," *Journal of the Afro–American Historical and Genealogical Society* 8:4 (Winter 1987), p. 156.

Owens, Carole, "Agrippa Hull – Soldier, Farmer, Philosopher," *The Berkshire Edge* (Feb. 17, 2015).

Padeni, Scott, "The Role of Blacks in New York's Campaigns of the Seven Years' War," *Bulletin of the Fort Ticonderoga Museum* 16 (1999), pp. 153–169.

Paine, Silas H., "Soldiers of the Champlain Valley," *Proceedings of the New York State Historical Association* 17 (1919), pp. 300–428.

Palmer, Alex, "The Revolutionary War Patriot Who Carried This Gunpowder Horn was Fighting for Freedom—Just Not His Own," *Smithsonian Magazine* (June 22, 2016). [Prince Simbo]

Perreault, Denise, "Unraveling the Life of Scituate's Mystery Soldier," *The Valley Breeze* (Sept. 4, 2013). [Prosper Gorten]

Phillips, David E., "Negroes in the American Revolution," *Journal of American History* 5:1 (1911), pp. 143–146.

Pierce, R. Andrew, "Sharper Michael, Born a Slave, First Islander Killed in the Revolution," *Dukes County Intelligencer* 46:4 (May 2005), pp. 147–152.

Pitts, Jonathan M., "Twice Denied the Freedom He'd Fought For, a Black Revolutionary War Hero from Maryland is Honored at Last," *Baltimore Sun* (June 21, 2019). [James Robinson]

Porter Jackson, Luther, "Virginia Negro Soldiers and Seamen in the American Revolution," *Journal of Negro History* 27:3 (July 1942), pp. 247–287.

Pressley Montes, Sue Anne, "Post–Revolutionary Recognition: Slave Honored as 'African American Patriot' at Capitol," *Washington Post* (December 16, 2006). [Oscar Marion]

Price, George R. and Brewer Stewart, James, "The Roberts Case, the Easton Family, and the Dynmics of the Abolitionist Movement in Massachusetts, 1776–1870," *Massachusetts Historical Review* 4 (2002), pp. 89–115. [James Easton]

Prouty, Alan, "Private Asher Freeman of the Continental Army," *North River Packet* (Winter 2022), p. 3, 5.

Pybus, Cassandra, "Jefferson's Faulty Math: The Question of Slave Defections in the American Revolution," *William and Mary Quarterly* 62:2 (April 2005), pp. 243–264.

Quarles, Benjamin, "The Colonial Militia and Negro Manpower," *Mississippi Valley Historical Review* 45:4 (March 1959), pp. 643–652.

Quinlan, Maurice J., "George Knox, a Black Soldier in the American Revolution," *Dartmouth College Library Bulletin* 20 (April 1980), pp. 54–62.

Ranlet, Philip, "The British, Slaves, and Smallpox in Revolutionary Virginia," *Journal of Negro History* 84:3 (Summer 1999), pp. 217–226.

Reed, Elodie, "Integrating History: The Black Men Who Fought for American Liberty," *Bennington Banner* (January 31, 2019).

Rees, John U., "'Left in the Field for Dead…': African American Continental Soldiers at the Battle of Monmouth," Academia.edu (March 8, 2020), 14p. [Benajah Abro]

Rees, John U., "Nineteenth Century Remembrances of Black Revolutionary Veterans," Academia.edu (n.d.), 21p. [Hannah Till, Thomas Carney, Edward Hector, Jacob Francis, and Oliver Cromwell]

Renick, Sharelle, "Fort Donnally," *West Virginia Daily News* (March 3, 1969). [Dick Pointer]

Rider, Sidney S., "The Black Regiment of the Revolution," *Rhode Island Historical Tracts* 10 (1880), pp. 1–50.

Rimkunas, Barbara, "Exeter's Black Revolutionary Veterans," *Exeter News–Letter* (Jan. 18, 2018).

Rockingham Gilmer, George, "Austin Dabney," in *Sketches of the First Settlers of Upper Georgia, of the Cherokees, and the Author* (New York, NY: D. Appleton & Co., 1855), pp. 213–215.

Saillant, John, "Lemuel Haynes and the Revolutionary Origins of Black Theology, 1776–1801," *Religion and American Culture* 2:1 (Winter 1992), pp. 79–102.

Salmon, John S., "'A Mission of the Most Secret and Important Kind': James Lafayette and American Espionage in 1781," *Virginia Cavalcade* 31:2 (1981), pp. 78–85.

Schleicher, William and Winter, Susan, "Patriot and Slave: The Samuel Sutphen Story," *New Jersey Heritage Magazine* 1:1 (Winter 2002), pp. 30–42.

Scott, Travis, "This Black Abolitionist Fought in the Revolutionary War with George Washington," *The Federalist* [Primus Hall]

Selig, Robert A., "The Revolution's Black Soldiers: They Fought for Both Sides in Their Quest for Freedom," *Colonial Williamsburg* 19:4 (Summer 1997), pp. 14–22.

Sellick, Gary, "'Undistinguished Destruction': The Effects of Smallpox on British Emancipation Policy in the Revolutionary War," *Journal of American Studies* 51:3 (2017), pp. 865–885.

Sesay, Jr., Chernoh M., "The Revolutionary Black Roots of Slavery's Abolition in Massachusetts," *New England Quarterly* 87:1 (March 2014), pp. 99–131.

Sloan, Eugene, "Peter Jennings," *Rutherford County Historical Society Publication* No. 10 (1978), 19p.

Smith, Nicola, "Research Assembles a Portrait of a Man Brought to Valley as a Slave," *Valley News* (May 11, 2018). [Derrick Oxford]

Staples, Rev. Carlton A., "The Existence and the Extinction of Slavery in Massachusetts," *Proceedings of the Lexington Historical Society* 4 (1912), pp. 48–60.

Sutton, Karen E., "African American Soldiers and Sailors of the American Revolution from Northumberland County," *Bulletin of the Northumberland County Historical Society*, 34 (1997), pp. 74–80.

Taylor, David A., "Black Soldiers Played an Undeniable but Largely Unheralded Role in Founding the United States," *Smithsonian Magazine* (Feb. 24, 2021).

"The Elusive Peter Hunter," *American Revolution Institute* (July 8, 2020) americanrevolutioninstitute.org.

Trauner, Scott, "Wallingford African Americans Fought for Freedom," *Wallingford Voice* (February 16, 2003).

Varnum, John M., "The Story of Silas Royal," *The Varnums of Dracut (in Massachusetts): A History* (Boston: David Clapp & Son, 1907), pp. 218–223.

Weiselberg, Erick, "Revolutionary Westchester: John "Jack" Peterson," *Rivertowns News* (Aug. 27, 2020).

Weltner, Linda, "Black Joe: A Mythical, Musical, and Unforgettable Man on Gingerbread Hill," *Marblehead Magazine* 1:2 (Summer 1980).

"William Jones, of Fredericksburg: Gentleman of Color and Revolutionary Patriot," *Sons of the American Revolution in the State of Virginia Semi–Annual Magazine* 5:1 (Jan.–June 1927), pp. 62–66.

Williams–Myers, A.J., "Out of the Shadows: African Descendants – Revolutionary Combatants in the Hudson River Valley; A Preliminary Historical Sketch," *Afro–Americans in New York Life and History* 31:1 (January 2007), pp. 91–111.

Williams–Myers, A.J., "Out of the Shadows: African Descendants – Revolutionary Combatants in the Hudson River Valley; A Preliminary

Historical Sketch," *Afro–Americans in New York Life and History* 31:1 (January 2007), pp. 91–111.

Wise, Barton Haxall, "Memoir of General John Cropper," *Collections of the Virginia Historical Society* N.S. 11 (1892), pp. 273ff. [George Latchom]

Woodson, Carter G., "An Important Revolutionary Record of a Negro Soldier," *Journal of Negro History* 17:4 (Oct. 1932), pp. 379–381. [Jacob Francis]

Woodson, Carter G., "Three Fighters for Freedom," *Journal of Negro History* 28:1 (Jan. 1943), pp. 51–72. [Felix Cuff]

Zilversmit, Arthur, "Quok Walker, Mumbet, and the Abolition of Slavery in Massachusetts," *William and Mary Quarterly* 25:4 (October 1968), pp. 614–624.

DATABASES

Ailes, Jane. *The Patriots of Color Database.* https://www.archives.com.

Graves, Will, and C. Leon Harris. *Southern Campaigns Revolutionary War Pension Statements & Rosters.* http://www.revwarapps.org.

Heinegg, Paul. *Free African Americans in the Revolution: Virginia, North Carolina, South Carolina, Maryland, and Delaware.* http://www.freeafricanamericans.com.

Hinton, P.M., and John L. Marker, Jr. *South Carolina Freemen of Color in the American Revolution.* https://www.southcarolina250.com/wp-content/uploads/A-A-Soldiers-List-9.1.2020.pdf.

Valley Forge Park Alliance. *Valley Forge Muster Roll.* http://valleyforgemusterroll.org.

DISSERTATIONS AND THESES

Bettasso, Antoinette Dorothy. "'In Justice and the Public Good': John Laurens and the Fight for the Continental Black Battalion." Master's thesis, Kansas State University, 2019. https://krex.k-state.edu/handle/2097/41766.

Bilal, Kolby. "Black Pilots, Patriots, and Pirates: African-American Participation in the Virginia State and British Navies During the Revolutionary War in Virginia." Master's thesis, College of William and Mary, 2000. https://scholarworks.wm.edu/etd/1539626268/.

Freeman, W. Trevor. "North Carolina's Black Patriots of the American Revolution." Master's thesis, East Carolina State University, 2020. https://thescholarship.ecu.edu/handle/10342/8572.

Green, Shirley L. "Freeborn Men of Color: The Franck Brothers in Revolutionary North America, 1755-1820." PhD diss., Bowling Green State University, 2011. https://scholarworks.bgsu.edu/hist_diss/18/.

McMahon, Kate E. "'A Sufficient Number': The Historic African American Community of Peterborough in Warren, Maine." Master's thesis, University of Southern Maine, 2013. https://digitalcommons.usm.maine.edu/etd/2/.

Schmidt, Ashley K. "Black Revolutionaries: African-American Revolutionary War Pensions in the Early Republic, 1780-1850." PhD diss., Tulane University, 2018. https://digitallibrary.tulane.edu/islandora/object/tulane%3A79045.

Sutton, Karen E. "The Nickens Nine: Free African Americans in Lancaster and Northumberland Counties, Virginia, During the American Revolution." PhD diss., Morgan State University, 2021. https://www.proquest.com/openview/7506f6d0185938ae27a4cf3f3e91ca2e/1?pq-origsite=gscholar&cbl=18750&diss=y.

Watson, Lt. Col. Larry. "Blacks in the Integrated Army of the American Revolution." U.S. Army War College Strategy Research Project, 1999. https://apps.dtic.mil/sti/tr/pdf/ADA364524.pdf.

JOURNAL OF THE AMERICAN REVOLUTION

Boutin, Cameron. "The 1st Rhode Island Regiment and Revolutionary America's Lost Opportunity." January 17, 2018. https://allthingsliberty.com/2018/01/1st-rhode-island-regiment-revolutionary-americas-lost-opportunity/.

McBurney, Christian. "The Discovery of an Important Letter from a Soldier of the 1st Rhode Island Regiment." April 14, 2021. https://allthingsliberty.com/2021/04/the-discovery-of-an-important-letter-from-a-soldier-in-the-1st-rhode-island-regiment/.

Rees, John. "Nineteenth-Century Remembrances of Black Revolutionary Veterans: Hannah Till, George Washington's Cook." February 2, 2021. https://allthingsliberty.com/2021/02/nineteenth-century-remembrances-of-black-revolutionary-veterans-tannah-hill-george-washingtons-cook/.

Rees, John. "Nineteenth-Century Remembrances of Black Revolutionary Veterans: Jacob Francis, Massachusetts Continental and New Jersey Militia." February 11, 2021. https://allthingsliberty.com/2021/02/nineteenth-century-remembrances-of-black-revolutionary-veterans-jacob-francis-massachusetts-continental-and-new-jersey-militia/.

Rees, John. "'She Had Gone to the Army… to Her Husband': Judith Lines' Unremarked Life." April 20, 2021. https://allthingsliberty.com/2021/04/she-had-gone-to-the-army-to-her-husband-judith-liness-unremarked-life/.

REVOLUTIONARY WAR JOURNAL

Schenawolf, Harry. "African American Dragoon in the American Revolution: John Redman." June 2, 2020. https://revolutionarywarjournal.com/african-american-dragoon-in-the-american-revolution-john-redman/.

Schenawolf, Harry. "African Americans in the American Revolution: James Forten – Privateer, Businessman, Inventor, and Leading Abolitionist." February 17, 2023. https://revolutionarywarjournal.com/african-americans-in-the-american-revolution-james-forten-privateer-businessman-inventor-and-leading-abolitionist/.

Schenawolf, Harry. "Austin Dabney, Black Artilleryman's Astonishing Bravery in the American Revolution." March 15, 2018. https://revolutionarywarjournal.com/austin-dabney-african-american-artilleryman-slave-in-the-revolutionary-war-georgia-honored-him-for-his-bravery-and-fortitude-his-life-fact-fiction/.

Schenawolf, Harry. "Benjamin Scott Mayes: African American Soldier Hanged Three Times by the British." August 3, 2013. https://revolutionarywarjournal.com/benjamin-scott-mayes/.

Schenawolf, Harry. "Boyrereau Brinch: Black Continental Soldier's Breathtaking Battle with British Dragoons." November 11, 2018. https://revolutionarywarjournal.com/boyrereau-brinch-african-american-continental-soldiers-hand-to-hand-combat-and-daring-escape-from-british-dragoons/.

Schenawolf, Harry. "George Latchom: Black Soldier's Remarkable Strength and Courage in the American Revolution." October 18, 2018. https://revolutionarywarjournal.com/african-american-george-latchom-in-the-american-revolutionary-war-courage-and-incredible-strength-gains-his-freedom/.

Schenawolf, Harry. "Jack 'Prince' Sisson – Black Soldier in the Revolutionary War and the Capture of British Brigadier General Richard

Prescott." March 28, 2013. https://revolutionarywarjournal.com/jack-prince-sisson/.

NATIONAL PARK SERVICE

"Cato Smith: Enlisted and Enslaved?" National Park Service. https://www.nps.gov/people/cato-smith-enlisted-and-enslaved.htm.

"Patriot Minorities at the Battle of Cowpens." National Park Service. https://www.nps.gov/cowp/learn/historyculture/patriot-minorities-at-the-battle-of-cowpens.htm.

"Patriots of Color at Valley Forge." National Park Service. https://www.nps.gov/vafo/learn/historyculture/patriotsofcoloratvalleyforge.htm.

Hannigan, John. "Enslavement and Enlistment." National Park Service. https://www.nps.gov/articles/000/john-hannigan-patriots-of-color-paper-3.htm.

Hannigan, John. "Independence or Freedom." National Park Service. https://www.nps.gov/articles/000/john-hannigan-patriots-of-color-paper-5.htm.

Hannigan, John. "Patriots of Color in Massachusetts." National Park Service. https://www.nps.gov/articles/000/john-hannigan-patriots-of-color-paper-1.htm.

Hannigan, John. "Patriots of Color Service on April 19, 1775." National Park Service. https://www.nps.gov/articles/000/john-hannigan-patriots-of-color-paper-4.htm.

Oswald, Anjelica. "Seeking Fortune: The Revolutionary Path(s) of Fortune Freeman and Fortune Conant." National Park Service. https://www.nps.gov/articles/000/fortune-freeman-conant.htm.

Oswald, Anjelica, and Danielle Rose. "Primus Hall: A Revolutionary Life of Service." National Park Service. https://www.nps.gov/articles/000/primus-hall-story-map.htm.

Rose, Danielle. "Luther Jotham: A Journey for Country and Community." National Park Service. https://www.nps.gov/articles/000/luther-jotham-story-map.htm.

AMERICAN BATTLEFIELD TRUST

"African Americans and the War for Independence." American Battlefield Trust. https://www.battlefields.org/learn/articles/african-americans-and-war-independence.

"African American Service during the Revolution." American Battlefield Trust. https://www.battlefields.org/learn/articles/african-american-service-during-revolution.

Zeller, Bob. "Black Valor at Princeton." N.D. American Battlefield Trust. https://www.battlefields.org/learn/articles/black-valor-princeton.

Zielinski, Adam. "Fighting for Freedom: African Americans Choose Sides During the Revolutionary War." November 30, 2020. American Battlefield Trust. https://www.battlefields.org/learn/articles/fighting-freedom-african-americans-during-american-revolution.

ENDNOTES

CHAPTER 1

1 William C. Nell, *The Colored Patriots of the American Revolution* (Boston: R.F. Wallcut, 1855), p. 6.

2 William Bradford, *History of Plymouth Plantation*, 1620-1647, vol. 2 (Boston: Massachusetts Historical Society, 1912), p. 363.

3 Nell, p. 12.

4 Martin Luther King, Jr., *Why We Can't Wait* (United Kingdom: Penguin Publishing Group, 2000), p. ix.

5 Phyllis Wheatley, *The Poems of Phyllis Wheatley: with Letters and a Memoir* (Mineola, NY: Dover Publications, 2012), pp. 3-4.

6 James Otis, *The Rights of the British Colonies Asserted and Proved* (Boston: Edes and Gill, 1764), p. 29.

7 Mary Caroline Crawford, *Romantic Days in Old Boston; the Story of the City and of its People during the Nineteenth Century* (Boston: Little, Brown and Co., 1912), p. 85.

8 George Henry Moore, *Historical Notes on the Employment of Negroes in the American Revolution* (New York, Charles T. Evans, 1862), p. 4.

9 Herbert Aptheker, ed., *A Documentary History of the Negro People in the United States, vol. 1* (New York: Citadel Press, 1951), pp. 6-7.

10 George Tolman, *John Jack, the Slave, and Daniel Bliss, the Tory; Read before the Concord Antiquarian Society* (Concord, Mass.: Concord Antiquarian Society, 1902), p. 4.

CHAPTER 2

1 United States Congress, *Reports and Documents, vol. 14* (Washington D.C.: United States Government Printing Office, 1959), p. 37.

2 Ibid.

3 Ibid, p. 41.

4 Ruth Bogin, *"'The Battle of Lexington': A Patriotic Ballad by Lemuel Haynes," William and Mary Quarterly* 42:4, pp. 501-502.

5 Ethan Allan, *A Narrative of Col. Ethan Allan's Captivity* (Burlington, VT: Charles Goodrich, 1846), pp. 14-15.

6 Wilson Waters, *History of Chelmsford, Massachusetts* (Salem, MA: Higgison Book Co., 1987), pp. 231-232.

7 Edwin R. Hodgman, *History of the Town of Westford, in the County of Middlesex, Massachusetts, 1659-1883* (Lowell, Mass.: Westford Town History Association, 1883), p. 113.

8 Roland D. Sawyer, *The History of Kensington, New Hampshire: 1663 to 1945* (Farmington, ME: Knowlton & McCleary, 1946), pp. 200-201.

9 J.H. Temple, *History of Framingham, Massachusetts* (Framingham, Mass.: Town of Framingham, 1887), p. 325.

10 Joseph T. Wilson, *The Black Phalanx: African American soldiers in the War of Independence, the War of 1812, and the Civil War* (Hartford, CT: American Pub. Co., 1870), p. 37.

11 George Quintal, Jr., *Patriots of Color 'A Peculiar Beauty and Merit': African Americans and Native Americans at Battle Road & Bunker Hill* (Boston, MA: Boston National Historical Park), p. 36.

12 Massachusetts Office of the Secretary of State, *Proceedings of the Provincial Congresses*, 1774-1775 vol. 2, p. 762.

13 Instructions for the officers of several regiments of the Massachusetts-Bay forces, who are immediately to go upon the recruiting service ... Given at the headquarters at Cambridge, this

10th day of July 1775. Horatio Gates, adjutant-general. (Watertown, MA)

14 John E. Goodrich, *Rolls of the Soldiers in the Revolutionary War, 1775 to 1783* (Rutland, VT: Tuttle Co., 1904), p. 832.

15 Letter to John Adams from William Heath, 23 October 1775.

16 Letter to John Adams from John Thomas, 24 October 1775.

17 General Orders, 12 November 1775.

18 William Maxwell (ed.), *The Virginia Historical Register and Literary Companion for the Year 1853, vol. 6 no. 1* (Richmond, McFarland & Fergusson, 1853) pg. 5.

CHAPTER 3

1 Alexander Graydon, *Memoirs of A Life, Chiefly Passes in Pennsylvania* (Harrisburg, PA: John Wyeth, 1811), p. 131.

2 John C. Dann (ed.), *The Revolution Remembered: Eyewitness Accounts of the War for Independence* (Chicago: University of Chicago Press, 1998), pp. 408-409.

3 Arthur Gilman, *The Cambridge of 1776: Wherein is set forth an Account of the Town* (Cambridge, MA: Lockwood, Brooks, & Co., 1875), p. 59.

4 Letter from Abigail Adams to John Adams, 16 - 18 March 1776.

CHAPTER 4

1 Sergeant R——, *"Battle of Princeton," Pennsylvania Magazine of History and Biography, vol. 20* (1896), pp. 515–16.

2 National Archives Pension Application of Peter Jennings (S4436).

3 Reprinted by *Newark Daily Advertiser* (August 5, 1839).

4 William L. Stone, *Letters of Brunswick and Hessian Officers during the American Revolution* (Albany, NY: Joel Munsell's Sons, 1891), p. 142.

CHAPTER 5

1 National Archives Pension Application of Benjamin Latimore (S13683).

2 Ibid.

3 Ibid.

4 Instructions to Colonel Christopher Greene, 8 October 1777.

5 To George Washington from Colonel Christopher Greene, 14 October 1777.

CHAPTER 6

1 James Thacher, *A Military Journal During the American Revolutionary War, From 1775 to 1783* (Boston, MA: Richardson & Lord, 1823), p. 153.

2 To George Washington from Brigadier General James Mitchell Varnum, 2 January 1778.

3 To George Washington from Nicholas Cooke, 23 February 1778.

4 National Archives Pension Application of Benajah Abro (S38104)

CHAPTER 7

1 From Alexander Hamilton to John Jay, 14 March 1779.

2 Ibid.

3 From Henry Laurens to George Washington, 16 March 1779.

4 National Archives Pension Application of Henry Dorten (S5362)

5 National Archives Pension Application of Francis DeWitt (R2919)

6 National Archives Pension Application of Samuel Sutphen (R10321).

7 Ibid.

8 South Carolina Audited Accounts No. 3356A.

CHAPTER 9

1 National Archives Pension Application of Anthony Gilman (S32729).

2 John Marshall, The Life of George Washington vol. 3 (New York: Wm. H. Wise & Co., 1925), pp. 307-308.

3 National Archives Pension Application of William Taburn (W18115).

CHAPTER 10

1 Evelyn M. Acomb, ed., *The Revolutionary Journal of Baron Ludwig von Closen*, 1780–1783 (Chapel Hill, N.C., 1958), p. 89.

2 Robert A. Brock (ed.), *Proceedings of the Virginia Historical Society vol. 11* (1892), pp. 296-297.

3 National Archives Pension Application of Absalom Ailstock (S6475).

CHAPTER 11

1 Sidney S. Rider, "An Historical Inquiry Concerning the Attempt to Raise a Regiment of Slaves by Rhode Island during the War of the Revolution," Rhode Island Historical Tracts No. 10 (1880), p. 62.

ABOUT THE AUTHOR

PATRICK S. POOLE is a recognized public policy expert, with more than a quarter century's experience working in Washington D.C. and many state capitals. A life-long student of history, he is a graduate of The Ohio State University. He makes his home in central Ohio with his partner, Kara, and their dog, Huckleberry, except when they're traveling the country visiting friends and family, or touring battlefields and old graveyards.

www.ingramcontent.com/pod-product-compliance
Lightning Source LLC
Chambersburg PA
CBHW021132090426
42740CB00008B/756

* 9 7 8 1 6 3 3 3 7 8 5 1 3 *